D0857361

Scripting Reading Motions

Scripting Reading Motions

The Codex and the Computer as Self-Reflexive Machines

Manuel Portela

The MIT Press
Cambridge, Massachusetts
London, England

MIT Press books may be purchased at special quantity discounts for business or sales promotional use. For information, please email special_sales@mitpress.mit.edu or write to Special Sales Department, The MIT Press, 55 Hayward Street, Cambridge, MA 02142.

This book was set in Stone Sans and Stone Serif by Toppan Best-set Premedia Limited, Hong Kong. Printed and bound in the United States of America.

Library of Congress Cataloging-in-Publication Data

Portela, Manuel, 1964–
Scripting reading motions : the codex and the computer as self-reflexive machines / Manuel Portela.
  pages cm
ISBN 978-0-262-01946-0 (hardcover : alk. paper)
1. Reading, Psychology of. 2. Books—Format. 3. Electronic publications—Design. 4. Hypertext literature. 5. Literature and technology. 6. Information visualization. 7. Books and reading. I. Title.
BF456.R2P75   2013
028—dc23
2013000048

10 9 8 7 6 5 4 3 2 1

Contents

Acknowledgments

I do not know exactly when or why the argument for this book began to form in my mind. The origin for this project remains difficult to locate in any precise way, but in October 2009, I had written the title and a first draft of the contents. *Scripting Reading Motions* is an unforeseen synthesis of my work as artist, researcher, translator, and teacher fascinated by language, reading, and writing. The work I had done on the material and social history of literature in the 1990s deepened my interest in processes of cultural and technological mediation. Starting in 2003, I began teaching several courses that sought to place cultural and literary practices within the expanding field of new media studies, with a particular focus on digital editing and digital literature. My teaching and research activities increasingly linked to my artistic interest in aesthetic investigations of material forms, embodied perceptions, and signifying processes.

This cluster of technocultural questions has engaged many brilliant artists, writers, thinkers, and researchers over the past decade. I am indebted to all of them for helping me to think through the question of medium reflexivity in relation to reading acts. I am especially grateful to all the artists whose works contain the formal instantiations of reflexivity that I have tried to analyze in detail. It was only by playing with their textual objects that I have been able to think about what it means to feel myself reading. My indebtedness to their embodied ideas is apparent on every page of this book. I acknowledge, in particular, their generous permission to use images from their work.

My students, with whom I have explored many of the works I analyze in this book, have made invaluable contributions. Advanced Studies in the Materialities of Literature, the doctoral program started at the University of Coimbra in 2010, has provided a fresh intellectual environment for testing many insights and speculations for this book. I mention, in particular, my colleagues Osvaldo Manuel Silvestre and Fernando Matos Oliveira, whose scholarly work and public interventions have remained a source of inspiration for me for more than a decade. I extend my gratitude to the anonymous reviewers for MIT Press whose comments and suggestions helped me revise the manuscript. Doug Sery, the first to see this project, has been a committed and supportive editor. I thank Katie Helke Dokshina and the MIT Press editors and designers for their expert steering of the editorial and production process.

Parts of this book have appeared in different versions as conference papers and journal articles between 2006 and 2012. I acknowledge their first presentation or publication as follows. Chapter 2 includes revised and extended versions of two papers: "Codex Codes: The Syntax, Semantics, and Pragmatics of Bookscapes," an unpublished paper, was originally presented at the conference Art, Fact, and Artifact: The Book in Time and Place (organized by the College Book Art Association and the Iowa Center for the Book, University of Iowa, January 8–10, 2009), and "Embodying Bookness: Reading as Material Act" was presented at the conference WordImageTextObject (organized by the College Book Art Association, and held at Indiana University, Bloomington, January 13–16 2011). This latter paper was published in the *Journal of Artists' Books*, no. 30 (Fall 2011): 7–13. Chapter 3 includes revised and extended versions of "Flash Script Poex: Digital Recoding of the Experimental Poem," originally published in Portuguese in *Cibertextualidades* 3 (2009): 43–57, and of "Concrete and Digital Poetics," originally published in *Leonardo Electronic Almanac* 14, no. 5–6 (2006, online). Chapter 4 includes revised versions of the following articles: "Between Code and Motion: Generative and Kinetic Poetry in French, Portuguese, and Spanish," published in *Romance Notes*, 51 (2011): 305–333, and "Autoauthor, Autotext, Autoreader: The Poem as Self-Assembled Database," published in *Writing Technologies* 4 (2012, online). Chapter 5 includes a revised and extended version of "The Letter, the Language, and the Book," a paper originally presented at the conference Le pied de la lettre: créativité et littérature potentielle (organized by the Department of Translation, University of Vigo, and the Center for Humanistic Studies, University of Minho, held at the Museo Verbum-Casa das Palabras, Vigo, Spain, April 22–24, 2009). This paper was published under the title "The Book as Computer: A Numerical and Topological Analysis of *Only Revolutions*," in *Openings: Studies in Book Art* 1 (2012, online). Chapter 6 includes a revised version of "The Battle of Poetry against Itself: On Jim Andrews's Digital Poetry," originally presented at the conference From Sea to Sea: Canadian Literature and Culture in Lisbon (organized by the Center for Anglistic Studies at the University of Lisbon, November 18–20, 2009). It was later published in *Revista Anglo Saxonica,* ser. 3, no. 2 (2011): 183–200. The second text rewritten for this chapter is "Scripting Writing and Reading in Jim Andrews's Digital Poems," an unpublished paper originally presented at the conference Humanities + Digital: Visual Interpretations Conference: Aesthetics, Methods, and Critiques of Information Visualization in the Humanities, Arts, and Social Sciences (organized by Hyperstudio MIT, Cambridge, MA, May 19–22, 2010). I am grateful to the organizers of these conferences and the editors of these journals.

A significant part of the research for writing this book was sponsored by the Fundação para a Ciência e a Tecnologia (FCT, Foundation for Science and Technology). I received this support through the Center for Portuguese Literature at the University of Coimbra, a research center coordinated by José Augusto Cardoso Bernardes, and through research grants for specific projects. These include an FCT-funded postdoctoral fellowship, which allowed me to spend the 2008 spring semester as a visiting scholar at the Institute for Advanced Technology in the Humanities at the University of Virginia. Equally important has been the FCT-funded research work I undertook for the project *Po-Ex: A Digital Archive of Portuguese Experimental Literature* (2010–2013), coordinated by Rui Torres. Without the research and academic context outlined here, this book would not exist.

It Reads, It Writes: An Introduction

Will I ever be able to say, "Today it writes," just like "Today it rains," "Today it is windy"? Only when it will come natural to me to use the verb 'write' in the impersonal form will I be able to hope that through me is expressed something less limited than the personality of an individual.

And for the verb "to read"? Will we be able to say, "Today it reads" as we say "Today it rains"? If you think about it, reading is a necessarily individual act, far more than writing. If we assume that writing manages to go beyond the limitations of the author, it will continue to have a meaning only when it is read by a single person and passes through his mental circuits. Only the ability to be read by a given individual proves that what is written shares in the power of writing, a power based on something that goes beyond the individual. The universe will express itself as long as somebody will be able to say, "I read, therefore *it* writes."

This is the special bliss that I see appear in the reader's face, and which is denied me.

—Italo Calvino, *If on a Winter's Night a Traveller*

Calvino's narrator seems to suggest that it is the bliss of reading that makes writing write. Like the impersonal writing act that has freed the writing self from the personal self, the reading self becomes an "I" through whose mental circuits writing passes. The fundamental productivity of writing and reading as correlative practices derives from their dependence on the combinatorial enhancement of linguistic codes once they become externalized as a series of abstract differential marks. Writing and reading release the subject from individuality and open up self and universe to the articulation of codes. As a neurophysiological activity, reading implies a complex bodily engagement with the materiality of signs and inscriptional spaces. This relation has been creatively explored as a source for awareness of the performativity of the reading act in its multiple physical, emotional, and conceptual resonances. In those works, the "it writes" of writing may be said to parallel the "it reads" of reading, thus offering a glimpse into the proliferation of meaning contained in the codes.

I.1   First Scene of Reading

What if the reading of writing could script itself back into writing? Into a writing of reading? A reading reading itself? The conversion of writing into reading and of reading into writing depends on the iterability of inscriptions and the recursivity of codes. This endless semiotic iteration induces a sensation of vertigo as I watch an automatic text generator produce new texts. A short poem is turned into a syntactic matrix for permutating lists of lexical items according to their grammatical classes. The room is dark, and the light from the computer monitor lights my face as I drag and click the mouse, experimenting with other textual states. What kind of presence am I being given in the text through this mode of inputing and activating programmed instructions? What kind of reading intervention am I performing? How am I made aware of my act of reading? Of its function in producing my textual experience?

Poemas no meio do caminho (Poems in the middle of the road) (2008), a programmed work by Rui Torres, is based on the virtualization of the texts used as textual matrixes (figure I.1). Each of the eight textual matrixes is associated with lists of words that can occur in the same syntactical positions. With each click, the reader activates the random replacement of one word by another that is part of the poem's database. Substitutions in the paradigmatic or vertical axis originate new associations in the syntagmatic or horizontal axis of the text. Through this basic combinatorial principle, the generative productivity of the textual engine text makes visible the generative structure of language itself. This property is one of the fundamentals of linguistic and poetic creativity, since it enables us to produce new utterances, resignifying its elements as an effect of the concurrent processes of replacement and reassociation. Metaphorical motions of semantic intersection, transfer, and creation result from new copresences produced by this generative mechanism.

The formalization of the syntactic and lexical description of languages allowed this process to become programmable through automatic text generation. Textual engines emulate the poetic function of carving the sayable out of the possibility of saying contained in language. In this case, the factorial permutation of each sequence contains a very large number of combinatorial possibilities for each of the eight texts (999999500523517 + 999999649572661 + 213347198 + 999999293069498 + 999999490684422

Figure I.1
Rui Torres, *Poemas no meio do caminho* (Poems in the middle of the road) (2008).
Screen captures. © Rui Torres. Reprinted with permission.

e quebram-se os ovos - espalham-se

Figure I.1
(continued)

+ 999999732519308 + 999999843470197 + 46968862498 possible poems).
Each instance created by the intervention of a reader is one less possibility
in this virtual potentiality. While playing randomly with the lexical database, each reader can also record a specific instantiation of his or her
combinatorial reading and post it on a blog. This new recorded textual
instance is a variation whose closeness to or distance from the textual
matrix will depend on the number of substitutions made at each syntactic
position and on the semantic relationship between the items of the actual
poem and original template.

The virtual hypermedia environment allows me to experience in a
sensory and spatialized mode the verbivocovisual dimension of this language text by integrating the textual engine into a set of four three-dimensional panoramas, accompanied by voice files (reading a random set of
predefined possible poems) and music. Text becomes a navigable space.
The four panoramas, which can be traversed in all axes (x, y, z) and in 360
degrees, consist of images made of the lexical lists used in the work and
whose color patterns suggest different atmospheric effects. Immersed in
this visual semiotic three-dimensional space, the reader sees lines of text
forming above, below, or near the horizon line. Those lines gradually disappear to the left of the screen, following the automatic rotation of the
panorama in retrograde direction. While reading the line of text in the

foreground, on which substitutions can be activated by clicks, the reader is listening to recorded readings of other possible combinations, including variants of the textual matrix that are not present on the screen at that moment. Visual text and sound text are unsynchronized and only partially identical. The multimodality of the work (verbal text, visual text, animation, voice, music) contributes to the experience of the poem as an emergent possibility in the generative flow of language.

Giving readers the possibility of intervening in that flow and codetermining an instantiation of the textual program, *Poemas no meio do caminho* allows meaning to be experienced as an effect of semiosis, that is, the constant replacement of one signifier by another. The formal identity of a textual instantiation appears less as the result of an absolute need for a unique form and more like an open exploration of possible forms resulting from the programmed algorithm and from random and intentional interventions of readers. The poem reveals itself as a throw of the dice of language, giving rise to dynamic combinatorial poems that stand in the way of the reader. Using as templates fragments of actually produced texts, it returns the semiotic and hermeneutic potential of those fragments to the associative turbulence of language through automatic reactivation of new chains of words. Following the reading instructions, the reader now sees himself or herself in the way of the poem, forced to confront the movement of form and meaning that his or her intervention triggers in the dynamics of the poem's program: *"história sem coração sonha e nega—em ti olhos se desviam"* (heartless story dreams and denies—in you eyes are turned away).

I.2   Second Scene of Reading

What if the reading of writing could script itself back into writing? Into a writing of reading? A reading reading itself? My second scene of reading takes place in *Through Light and the Alphabet* (1986), by Johanna Drucker (figure I.2). As I leaf through this book, my hands and eyes move forward and back trying to make sense of its multiple and interconnected typographic lines and graphic spaces. They seem to diverge and converge at the same time, at once splitting and superimposing layers of language. Codex syntax, verbal syntax, and typographic syntax are interactively articulated. Each turning of the leaf opens onto an incrementally reconstellated graphic field with parallel reading areas that partially overlap and intersect. The running lines of continuous type are interrupted by changes in font size, font style, font face, and position on the page. The resulting

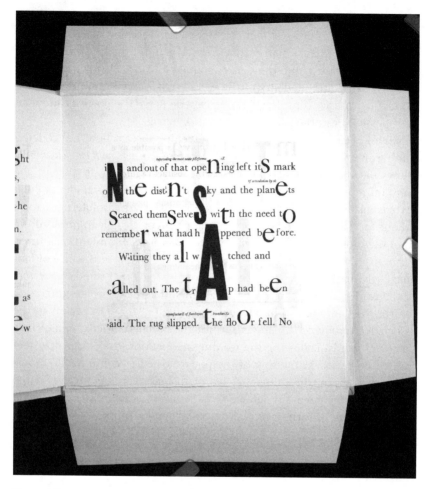

Figure I.2
Johanna Drucker, *Through Light and the Alphabet* (1986), pp. 15, 16, and 17. ©
Johanna Drucker. Reprinted with permission.

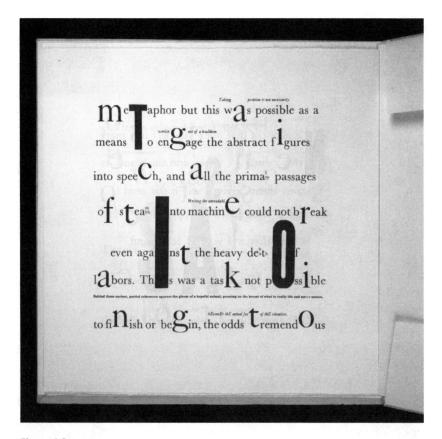

Figure I.2
(continued)

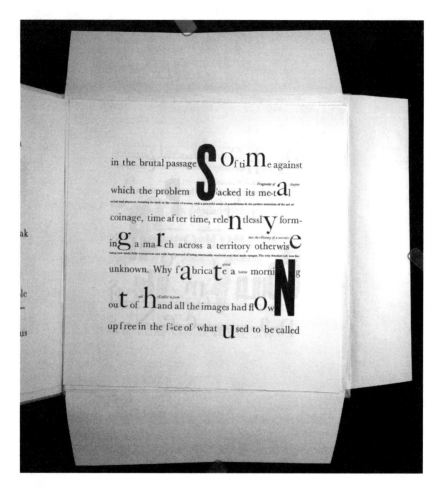

Figure I.2
(continued)

topographic patterning of each individual page and opening creates a tension between the simultaneous presence of the visuality of language and typography, on the one hand, and the sequentiality of the syntactic articulation of discourse and codex, on the other.

Page layout explores printed written signs as both typograms and topograms. Signs are typogrammatic because of the interpretational clues or values they provide within a given system of differences (face versus face, size versus size, uppercase versus lowercase, italics versus normal, bold versus normal). They are also topogrammatic, because as notational marks, their position on the page will contain particular interpretational clues as to sequence, hierarchy, relevance, intensity, and other aspects. With these two concepts of typogram and topogram, we can think about specific layers of meaning in typography as a semiotic system. Verbal meaning will also fluctuate according to inflections created by typographic design, from letter units to page setting. Visual narratives and poems are inflected by the additional reverberation of typography and topography on the discursive and linguistic codes.

As an inscriptional space, *Through Light and the Alphabet* has topographed its typography in ways that require exploratory and recursive feedbacks among the actions of turning the pages, seeing the patterns, and reading the signs. Reading takes place at least at four levels: a continuous line defines the underlying type-page pattern, to which are added two interlinear interrupted lines in small type, one of which is set in italics and the other in bold; both the continuous main line and the interlinear fragmented italic line are intermittently connected by shared letters that have been typeset in larger sizes. In addition, within the continuous line of type, smaller type inserted into certain letter sequences will split those sequences into two different word forms. In turn, the scattered large-font letters can also be connected to each other to form another reading path overlaid on the other three. The number of interlinear and intralinear connections increases as we turn the pages, making the syntactic articulation of bound leaves another material element in its enactment of meaning.

Through Light and the Alphabet becomes a literary experiment devised for reading explorations of letter-word-sentence associations as a function of typographic and bibliographic codes. Through a dialectics of accretion, interruption, and transformation, the motion of reading is forced to engage with its own recursivity. Readers have to constantly interrupt the left-right and top-bottom movement and direct their eyes back at particular areas of the page in order to take in other simultaneous and concurrent textual fragments. Like an interpolated phrase within a larger syntactic unit of discourse, a new reading motion is performed within a previously scanned and interpreted space. Ambiguity and undecidability of language are expressed by means of typographic layout and codex structure as the play of language is experienced through the recursivity of reading.

On page 16, for instance, the textual body layer reads: "metaphor but this was possible as a means to engage the abstract figures into speech, and all the primal/primary passages of steam/stealth into machine could not break even against the heavy debt/death of labors. This was a task not possible to finish or begin, the odds tremendous." One of the interrupted interlinear layers reads: "Taking a position is not necessarily working out of a tradition. Writing the unreadable becomes the actual fact of the situation." The large-size fonts embedded in the main textual body read, "magic after taking to." The sans serif headline type, which bridges across two or three lines, creates an extra level of presence of single-letter type, resisting incorporation into words. They stand as signifiers that do not translate into signifieds, transfixed in their written and printed condition at the border between the semiotic and the semantic. With these simultaneous and overlapping reading trajectories, the field of reading becomes a series of interlayered and constellated possibilities that cannot be resolved into a single line of discourse.

Textual layers are spread out across the page and the entire codex, and they become materially connected with the self-descriptive import of the work's discourse. The syntax of page openings and page turnings participates in the syntactic articulation of letters within words and of words within sentences. Semantic associations that contribute to the proliferation of meaning are a function of the combined effects of verbal proximity created by linguistic syntax, topographic proximity created by the printing layout, and codex proximity created by pages and openings. Interferences among those three levels produce an experience of the potentiality of language when actuated by the materiality of typography and codex and the motions of reading.

I.3   Reading the Writing of Reading

A self-conscious play with the dynamics of writing and reading can be found in both codex-based explorations and electronic literature. This study examines the expressive use of book forms and programmable media for insights about the semiotic and interpretative actions through which readers produce meaning as they interact with codes. The interventions contained in this book are concerned with embodied acts of reading that have been formally scripted through material programs. I analyze the features that sustain loops between the semiotic processing of codes and the retroactive motions of reading that become scripted in the textual fields. It is not a question of finding a model for intermedial readings of multimodal interactive codex and computer works, but rather of using their self-reflexive layers or functions as probes into the relations between material programs and reading performances. In the selected works, the performative production of meaning through the articulation of codes is thematized and simulated through material interventions that call for an embodied awareness of the performance.

Chapter 1 offers a general introduction to the book, explaining its critical approach and outlining its argument. Besides providing a theoretical context for this study of self-referential enactments of reading, it also contains a brief introduction to the use of books and computers as expressive media in literature. Bookness and digitality are foregrounded by a performance of reading that has been formally scripted in bibliographic layout and computer code. These scripts attempt to choreograph the formal and physiological dimension of interacting with signs in ways that help us understand how seeing and reading establish a signifying space dependent on material programs. When engaging with the signifying field of the work, readers experience how their own haptic actions and eye movements coinstantiate the object that they have to read. A self-reflexive function in these works explicitly enacts the actions of reading as constitutive of their textual fields. By means of self-conscious interactions with the material codes of codex and computer, those reading acts become scripted in the literary artifact. A series of instructive examples explains how the works' material programs explore this reading reflexiveness.

Chapter 2 discusses the specifics of self-referential operations in bibliographic codes. Artists' books expose and explore the structures and conventions that turn the material book into a signifying device. They show how textuality is not only a verbal and visual phenomenon, but also a function of a particular bibliographic operation or code. Bibliographic codes as reading devices are examined through an analysis of the relations of narrative, bookness, and typography in artists' books by Johanna Drucker. In these works, certain kinds of imaginary spaces depend on codex codes, and reading is called on to perform those codicological marks. As part of the general argument of this book, typographic and bibliographic marks are described as choreographic notations for reading movements. Bibliographic scripts are highlighted through the perspective provided by representations of those operations and codes in the repository *Artists' Books Online*. Combining digital facsimile representation with extensive editorial description of the works, *Artists' Books Online* has created a critical space for mapping the feedback among bibliographical structures, verbal codes, and visual codes.

Chapter 3 looks at the digital remediation of print literary artifacts that contain simulations and enactments of reading. The use of print texts as storyboards and scripts for kinetic, generative, and interactive texts has shown the continuity between constellated print works and digital animation. The rewriting and transcoding of constellated and permutational print works in digital media are examined as material reflections, intersemiotic translations, and acts of remediated metareading. This differential dynamics of print literacy and screen literacy is analyzed in works by Augusto de Campos and also in digital re-creations of experimental poems contained in Po.Ex: A Digital Archive of Portuguese Experimental Literature. While digital re-creations redefine the source texts by adding the programming layer intrinsic to computational media, they also reveal the complex linguistic and graphical coding of the printed page as a reading machine. Digital transformations, visualizations, and interactions provide new insights into a concrete poetics centered on the materiality of reading, and also about the dynamics of reading across media.

Chapter 4 examines how constellated words, animation of verbal text, and automatic text generation have been used to enact the act of reading as a motion of association and substitution of various kinds of signs. The motion of writing on the screen becomes a self-conscious engagement with the movements of reading and with specific properties of digital materiality as they are bodily and cognitively actuated by reading actions. The scripting of reading as writing in motion explores semiosis in both graphic and electronic codes. The substitution and association of signs in the chain of signifiers can be modeled through screen layout, interactive animation, and algorithmic text generation. Writing-in-motion becomes a metarepresentation of the productivity of signifiers and the performativity of reading. Two kinds of programmable works are given particular attention: generative and kinetic texts. These works emulate reading as a mode of seeing that links proprioceptive motions and sense perceptions to conceptual processing. Motions from sign to sign function as both paratextual notations and algorithmic tropes for referring readers back to their own seeing and reading actions. Through analysis of computer-assisted multimodal retroactive works, this chapter discusses the role of code and motion in simulating the play of signifiers through reading interventions.

Chapter 5 contains an extended analysis of the topological and mathematical structure of *Only Revolutions: The Democracy of Two Set Out and Chronologically Arranged* (2006), by Mark Danielewski. This novel-poem establishes a relationship between its bibliographic coding (its graphical and material form as a book made of letters, pages, and openings with a specific typographic design), its linguistic coding (its phonetic, syntactic, semantic, and pragmatic form), and its narrative coding (its form as story). *Only Revolutions* uses the Möbius strip and the circle, in their multiple material and symbolic manifestations, including letter and number shapes, as the organizing principle of this triple universe of signs. Circularity and mirror symmetry function simultaneously as the structure of the book, of language, and of narrative. This chapter describes the book's numerical and topological form as a mechanism for creating feedback loops between those structures and also as an extreme remediation of computer codes in bibliographic form. The work's algorithms are analyzed with the help of tables and diagrams that offer a visualization of its bibliographic, linguistic, and narrative program. Through this ensemble of algorithms, the book becomes a machine for generating readings and scripting those readings in its material and phenomenological space.

Chapter 6 argues for the critical relevance of interactive kinetic poetry and dynamic programming for understanding the emergent nature of meaning as a function of reading performances and a tool for visualizing interpretation. Interactive dynamic scripts enact the temporality of writing and the temporality of reading in medium-specific forms and genres that call attention to the way their machine and human processing happens. The cinematic enactment of time in the combined motions of computer-executed code and human-activated kinetic display is analyzed in digital poems by Jim Andrews. In his playable kinetic works, mouse clicking and mouse dragging are brought into the work's signifying field and become part of the algorithmic tropes programmed into the text. His scripts are described as models for both digital reflexivity and reading interactions. Self-awareness of the spatial, procedural, encyclopedic, and participatory nature of the medium becomes explicit through coordination of eye and hand motions in the performance of textual events. By framing readers' actions as a material part of the sign field of the work, the performance of the computer and the performance of the reader become codependent and intertwined as an entangled field. Through dynamic programming, his works visualize and sonify this entanglement between inscriptional forms and reading acts. The expressive use of code in his works offers a poetics of seeing and reading for the digital medium in which its specific affordances and its programmability are engaged through self-reflexive interactions.

Chapter 7 brings together the various reflections on the enactment and representation of reading acts as kinetic and cognitive interactions between situated selves and material signs. The aesthetic and expressive use of codex and computer codes is a powerful simulator of the semiotic, interpretative, and affective operations embodied in reading processes. Motions of reading in codex and computer works offer a model for the textual field as a turbulent and unstable entanglement between signs and readers. Through investigation of those motions, this book identifies a number of material programs that are crucial for a poetics of reading. Whether in print or in programmable media, seeing and reading establish a signifying space maintained by an embodied interaction between an ensemble of signs and material interventions on a network of inscriptions. Analysis of self-reflexive functions related to reading acts opens up an account of their particular performativity across different media.

1 The Codex and the Computer as Self-Reflexive Machines

1.1 Seeing Reading

In *Interior with a Young Girl (Girl Reading)* (1905–1906), by Henri Matisse, color has been expressively emancipated from drawing and from any straightforward mimetic and perspectival correspondence to the objects depicted (figure 1.1). It is as if colors had been freed even from the grid of lines that sustain the distorted perspective of space. The composition suggests the flickering transience of a living perception of natural light coming into the interior to animate space, objects, and human subject. The changing frequencies of visible light in their interaction with the human eye foreground the subjective experience of perceiving the world. Lines have been substituted by patches of color that are independent of the local color of objects and spaces. Even the three-dimensionality of successive planes seems to blend under the power of colors that pull them toward the surface of the canvas. Color patches respond to heightened perceptions of the optical processing of light and color as autonomous elements of perception. Color is treated as an expressive quality of biological perception and subjective emotion. The thingness of objects dissolves in the sensations of color as a dynamic correlation between the changing incidence and variable intensity of light and its subjective apprehension. The young girl reading, the fruit bowl, the table, and the whole room become expressions of the joyful presence of the materiality of light as sensed and perceived color.

As a representation of reading, Matisse's painting seems to capture the reader's immersion in the virtual imaginary space created by the book. The sitter's eyes are fully absorbed in the processing of the page, and her arms lean against the bookstand on the table. Her head rests on her left hand, while her right hand is placed on the book, a reminder of the ergonomics of moving across the page and turning over the leaves of the codex. The

Figure 1.1
Henri Matisse, *Interior with a Young Girl (Girl Reading)*, 1906. Oil on canvas, 28 5/8 × 23 1/2″ (72.7 × 59.7 cm). Fractional gift of a private collector. Acc. n.: 79.1991. Digital image © 2012, The Museum of Modern Art, New York/Scala, Florence.

act of reading is shown as an embodied system constituted by eyes, hands, head, body, codex, and the processing of signs. The girl's temporary unawareness of the space around her is transmitted by showing her eyelids completely engaged in the reading and is underlined by the sitter's unawareness of being depicted. Matisse is trying to simulate the perceptual thingness of human subject, objects, and space as apprehended through sensations of color. The young reader, as an object among objects, becomes just another element in the still life nexus of the painting in its attempt to make the vibrancy of color stand for a surrogate of living sensations.

The reading girl's absorbed and unself-conscious posture, a consequence of the deep immersion in the space of reading, is heightened in this depiction of every object in the scene as a pure effect of color sensations. Although this painting is concerned with the problems of object representation as a projection of subjective apprehension—in which color is expressively and experimentally treated as independent of formal outlines—the theme of the reader, and particularly of the young girl or the young woman reading, has had a continuing presence in the history of painting. The concentration and quiet required for the activity have perhaps made it suitable for sitters and painters alike, as testified by the many depictions of readers, from the Renaissance reader of sacred books to the bourgeois reader of novels or newspapers in the eighteenth and nineteenth centuries.[1] Representation of reading within a moral, religious, and educational framework was gradually replaced by a more detached attention to the actual physical and affective nature of the act. In these paintings, reading is also being objectified as an ergonomic behavior that links human body and a device in a particular space.

Painters have represented reading as a deep immersion in the virtual world maintained by the symbolic power of signs. Fully absorbed by the surface of the page, readers' senses seem to be suspended from their immediate surroundings as head posture, eyes, arms, and hands converge intently on the signs. Friedrich Kittler (1990, 1999) has suggested that this hallucination of meaning depends on writing and reading practices capable of producing a sensuous apprehension of the world through the evocative power of words. Writing and reading techniques converged in the luscious nineteenth-century literary re-creation of the sensuous phonovisual apprehension of the real. This intense intimacy of the individual reading act is an important modern *topos* for painters and photographers, but the specifics of the interaction between reader and writing have remained opaque, mysterious, and difficult to depict. Viewers can sometimes see the effect of reading on the reader's face in the form of a particular moral or emotional state, but the process and the medium cannot be accessed. Reading, one of the technologies through which self-production takes place, appears as just another attribute of the modern self.

In *Read for Us* (2010), an installation by John Cayley and Daniel Howe, we find a new kind of representation of reading in which readers are made perceptually aware of reading processes (figure 1.2).[2] Human readers are invited to see automatic readers traversing a textual field. In this instance, the textual field is constituted by a digital edition of Adam Smith's *The Wealth of Nations*. The software reader goes through the text phrase by phrase, and, with the use of a search engine, matches those textual phrases to occurrences in online sources other than Smith's text. It is as if that particular discursive structure had become disseminated across the Internet database of English language. Reading marks itself in a socialized text whose authorial signature has been algorithmically distributed and reattributed to numerous sources.

This reading agent, called the Perceptual Reader, presents the line of the text being read (up to six words at a time) in constant movement at the center of the screen. The moving line of reading is given a typographic neighborhood—a certain number of adjacent characters to the right, left, below, and above the reading focus. The concept of typographic neighborhood is inspired by reading studies that show that we tend to see thirty to forty characters around the focal point of our attention. The reading machine works as a model of optical and motor processing in the field of signs but also as a reminder of the social networks of language that make meaning happen. The physical, cognitive, and social dimensions of the process of reading are algorithmically simulated in a way that invites readers to see their own act of reading in action.

Reading has been a major object of study for several disciplines, including cognitive and educational psychology, linguistics, literary theory, and cultural history. The body of relevant research is too large to be mentioned here, but a few examples give a sense of the complexities related to the visual, social, and cultural semiotics of reading. As a neurophysiological activity, reading has been studied through functional magnetic resonance imaging and other imaging techniques, such as eye tracking (Knowles et al. 2012; Roberts et al. 2013). Experiments have been devised to account for many aspects of the visual processing of signs, including eye movement control in reading (Rayner 2009), the influence of adjacent words in determining the visual parameters of eye movement (Pynte and Kennedy 2006), the processing of graphemes as perceptual reading units in alphabetic writing systems (Rey, Ziegler, and Jacobs 2000), morphological

Figure 1.2
John Cayley and Daniel Howe, *Read for Us* (2010; mixed media installation, custom software). Installed for the Faculty Triennial Exhibition, David Winton Bell Gallery, Brown University, December 4, 2010 –February 12, 2011. Photo © Danny Cannizzaro. Reproduced with permission.

Figure 1.2
(continued)

decomposition in the visual processing of complex words (Longtin and Meunier 2005), effects of perceptual learning in the recognition of words (Nazir et al. 2004), and adaptive eye movements in word processing (Liu and Reichle 2010), among other subjects. Reading has also been studied in terms of the neural mechanisms involved in the recognition of visual and phonological forms (Turkeltaulb et al. 2003; Harm and Seidenberg 2004) and also in evolutionary terms (Dehaene 2009).

Some of the works examined in this book contain perceptual experiments designed to increase readers' awareness of their own visual and cognitive processing of foreground-background relations as readable and semantic forms. These works engage reading at its most embodied level as the feeling of reading, in which its perceptual component is primed. In several print texts I examine, relations between seeing and reading are designed to give readers an optical awareness of their own cognitive performance. Interactive scripts in digital works are used to produce reflexive perceptual effects. There also instances in which this reading awareness has been transcoded from print to digital and from digital to print. Translations of this cognitive reflexivity across media, through a remediated poetics of reading, provide further possibilities for analysis.

The pace of current changes in reading devices has prompted new research on the relations between text technologies and ways of reading. Digital reading practices have received critical attention from a variety of disciplinary perspectives (for an extended annotated bibliography, see Koolen et al. 2011). For instance, researchers have contrasted the discontinuous and fragmented reading mode of the Web with the continuous reading mode of paper-based long-form texts (Hillesund 2010). They have also examined particular reading practices, such as types of marginal annotations in academic contexts, for improving the functional design of interfaces for manipulating electronic text in the act of reading (Blustein, Rowe, and Graff 2011). The actual physical handling of codex and digital forms has also received significant comparative attention, bringing together fruitful insights developed within the fields of book design and human–computer interaction. Gary Frost (2004, 2005, 2006, 2007) has written eloquently on the haptic nature of codex reading, and Johanna Drucker (2008a, 2009a, 2010, 2011) has thought about the functional affordances of e-space and electronic interfaces beyond the mere emulation of codex spaces.

N. Katherine Hayles (2010, 2012) has recently argued for a reconceptualization of current reading practices that takes into account the ways in which hyper- and machine reading are placing the act of reading for pattern and the act of reading for meaning in new relationships. As we will see in the following chapters, this synergy between context-free and context-dependent production of meaning is at the core of self-reflexive generative works. Jason Nelson's works, for instance, cannot be engaged without a reading performance that goes beyond the conventional reading-for-meaning mode or the conventional distinctions among reading, watching, and playing. Textual instruments and playable texts place readers in a perceptual relation with language and multimodal forms, in which reading and seeing interact in new ways.

Johanna Drucker (2011) has described online reading in terms of the changing temporalities and spatialities created by the combined effects of multimodal communication and the constant reframing of point of view. Web page reading mobilizes conflicting strategies, which imply a shifting back and forth between practices associated with reading print text and practices associated with reading signages in public spaces. A constant reframing of textual objects requires that readers resituate themselves in temporal and spatial contexts. Multiple modalities and multiple framings are intrinsic to the informative-intensive environments of online textuality, and they have become embodied in various types of interface and in specific reading practices (Gendolla and Schäfer 2007). A number of digital artists have looked at cognitive and cultural aspects of digital literacy, highlighting the conventions and constraints contained in computer-mediated textual environments, platforms, and programs. Scripts and coded functions are dysfunctionalized in various ways and are used as critical tools for examining software culture, including particular programs, interfaces, digital genres, and digital reading practices in general (Ryan 2008, 2010; Stefans 2011).

Retroactive effects of screen structures and Web environments on print structures can be seen in several print books produced during the past twenty years. The design of these works implies a composite reading mode in which reading protocols of the screen have been assimilated by the printed page. In these works, changes in layout and other typographic and codex features, including the syntactic articulation of pages and of printed areas within the pages, show the ongoing dynamics between printed book and new media forms. Significant examples include N. Katherine Hayles's *Writing Machines* (2002), in which the print design is formally linked to the Web supplement of the work as a self-explanatory instance of the concepts of technotextuality and intermediation developed in the printed book; Mark Z. Danielewski's intricate use of typographic features and page design in both *House of Leaves* (2000) and *Only Revolutions* (2006); Steve Tomasula's *VAS: An Opera in Flatland* (2002); and Jonathan

Safran Foer's *Tree of Codes* (2010)—instances of the reification of the materiality of the book in a digital context that has been theorized as "bookishness" (Pressman 2009; Liu 2009) and "media divergence" (Wurth et al. 2013).

Material features of printed books have also provided haptic and parodic metaphors for digital works. In Erik Loyer's *Hollowbound Book* (2002), the hollow space between quires and spine (which allows a 180-degree arc around the binding axis) is visually translated into interactive animations that suggest the spinning of arguments in the free openings of leaves. In *Grafik Dynamo* (2005), by Kate Armstrong and Michael Tippett, comic book and graphic novel are transcreated through a randomized collage of predefined text with images collected from the Internet (Tabbi 2010). In *Zero Whack* (2010), by David Jhave Johnston, book titles and plot lines (which were zero counts on Google searches made on December 15, 2010), along with authors' names, publishing house names, blurbs, book cover photographs, and bar codes, are randomly permutated. The originality of discourse as the quintessential basis for individual authorship, materialized in the cover codes of a printed codex, is given a mechanic, formulaic, and nonsensical expression. The idea of the book as the necessary unity between a certain unit of discourse and a discrete bound codex is dissolved in a parody of its presentation as a commodified, machinic, and ultimately arbitrary unity between discourse and material object.

Sections 1.2 and 1.3 of this chapter look at works that foreground the presence of eye and hand movements as constitutive of textual fields, and sections 1.4, 1.5, and 1.6 look at works that foreground bibliographic or computer codes as particular kinds of signifiers. Taken together, these sections explain what is meant by the expressive use of codex forms and programmable media, laying the ground for the more detailed analyses in the following chapters. Material representations and simulations of reading motions are embodied and enacted through expressive uses of formal devices in codices and computers. These formal operations contain insights about the semiotic, cognitive, and affective modes of meaning production through acts of reading. The interactions between reading body and embodied codes are reflexively choreographed, through inscription and language, in ways that illuminate the performativity of cognition and interpretation.

1.2 Moving Eyes

Eye movements, which are conditioned by the physiology of the eye, have been conceptualized by experimental psychologists in terms of two basic components: saccades (the movement from object to object) and fixations (the period when eyes remain still and acquire new information from the visual field). New information is acquired during fixation, but cognitive processing takes place in most situations also during saccades. Saccade latency (the time needed to initiate an eye movement) has been calculated as about 175 to 200 milliseconds. The saccade duration (the time it takes to move the eyes) is a function of the distance moved. A 2-degree reading saccade has been calculated as about 30 milliseconds. A 5-degree scene perception saccade takes about 40 to 50 milliseconds. The metric used for saccade size in reading continuous text is the number of letters: for readers of alphabetic writing systems, the average saccade length is seven to nine letter spaces. In reading, eye movements have been described as follows:

> Eye movements are necessary because of the anatomy of the retina and limitations due to acuity outside of the fovea. In reading, for example, the line of text that the reader is looking at can be divided into three regions: the foveal region (2 degrees in the center of vision), the parafoveal region (extending from the foveal region to about 5 degrees on either side of fixation), and the peripheral region (everything beyond the parafoveal region). Although acuity is very good in the fovea, it is not nearly so good in the parafovea, and it is even poorer in the periphery. Hence, viewers move their eyes so as to place the fovea on that part of the stimulus they want to see clearly. (Rayner 2009, 1459)

Perception of written words and other visual forms as both linguistic and iconic objects is a characteristic mode of operation of visual and kinetic poetry. Suggestion of motion on the page and awareness of eye movements as they scan for written marks on the page call our attention to reading as cognitive processing. Aesthetic experimentation with eye movements in reading explores the perception of visual forms in ways that make readers aware of the interactions between visual and cognitive processes and oculomotor control. It is as if texts were triggering and tracking eye movements during these complex processing tasks in order to give readers awareness of reading as an embodied motion in which the symbolic is embedded in the physical. In such cases, we may say that formal operations have been applied to signs and marks in order to engage readers with saccades and fixations that work against conventional reading codes.[3]

One of my hypotheses is that self-reflexive operations in codex and computer works often play with readers' awareness of eye movements during reading. In this way, they foreground the cognitive processing that takes place through the act of reading as a perceptual interaction with various layers of material signs. Readers are made aware not just of the inscriptional materiality of alphabetic or multimodal forms, but also of their own way of acquiring and constructing them as perceived forms. Printed page and electronic screen become exploratory reading fields designed for a perceptual experiment with the dynamic nature of textual forms. Reading is defamiliarized by means of constellations, fragmentations, aggregations, superpositions, combinations of verbal and pictorial signs, and other verbivocovisual techniques. Surfaces of inscription offer themselves as sites for complex visual searches and perceptual queries. These self-conscious movements show the signifying productivity of reading as a function of the signifying dynamics of the visual and tactile field created by material forms actuated by reading events. Reading is experienced as embodied cognition in which meaning is a probabilistic distribution resulting from moment-to-moment interactions with material codes.

Experimental visual works that combine text with other visual stimuli can draw readers' attention to their eye movements across the text's visual field. The process of visual search is primed as readers have to match an alphabetic order of writing, which they already master, with visual codes that have to be inferred, deciphered, or constructed during the act of reading. By means of a series of fixations and saccades that traverse the textual field, this second-level code in visual texts is gradually perceived and interpreted. The automatic movement of reading a familiar form of writing becomes denaturalized through an instance-specific spatialization of characters and words. A constellated layout, for instance, makes readers aware of various possible connecting paths, hierarchies, or the background and foreground relations of textual elements.

The tentative path they choose for making those forms readable gradually shows itself before readers' eyes in a way that makes viewers experience the constructed nature of the acts of seeing and reading. This perception of the reading self is also a perception of codes that enable a signifying process, as if readers had to learn how to read each time they read. Fixations are longer than usual, saccades are shorter, and more regressions are needed. All of these recursive and divergent movements on the textual surface create a feedback loop between recognizing the forms and looking for a metacode that articulates them as signifiers in the new composition. Readers can see themselves reading as a consequence of defamiliarization caused by this explicit presence of codes in the surface of the work itself. Reading is consciously split between semiotic deciphering of signals and semantic chains of interpretation.

Visual texts by Augusto de Campos play out this formal tension between seeing and reading, with fixations and saccades that respond to the complexity of the visual array. Letters are ambiguously placed in conflicting perceptual frames as if they were gestalt exercises for apprehending forms and recognizing patterns. Reading is enacted as a material and perceptual activity, from oculomotor level to high-level lexical and semantic processes. Awareness of eye movement and form recognition are an integral part of the cognitive mechanism that produces readability out of black and white fields on the page. To a degree seldom matched by other visual poets, his works are experimental objects that investigate the complexities of reading from the physiological to the conceptual levels. Since many of de Campos's texts require readers to enact what the text says, one of their layers of meaning becomes attached to the very action of reading the text.

As self-descriptions of decoding acts, they sustain a semiotic feedback between the inscribed marks and the marks as produced by reading, that is, they disclose the specific nature of a reading act as a particular kind of speech act. This heightened experiencing of reading is also an underlying reference in the text's semantics, which refers back to the processing of signals. Because readers are constrained to do what the text says, reading always expresses itself as a self-conscious and self-productive act: part of the meaning of the text becomes attached to the activity of reading the text. In his poetics of reading, the poem becomes a cognitive experiment in the apprehension of forms, from the sense of sight to high-level semantic and emotional processing of signs.

This double presence of reading can be illustrated in two of de Campos's poems. "Tudo está dito" (All is said) (1974) and "Código" (Code) (1973). In "Tudo está dito," white letters on black form a pattern that suggests a labyrinth or some sort of geometric abstract structure depending on whether white or black spaces are foregrounded (figure 1.3). Because some of the white areas of the angular and squared shapes of letters interconnect without clearly defined borders in black, the eye cannot easily make out all the letters in the text. Many of them have to be reclaimed from the white space by brain-imposed border lines, and it is through this processing that their shapes become readable. This tension between visible and readable is augmented because readers have to perceive letter-defining spaces using the eye-brain mechanisms for focusing and refocusing in order to recognize patterns. At the same time, readers have three other patterns to disentangle: they have to construct word boundaries that will enable them to join letters, they have to discern a two-column structure as the visual layout of text, and they have to build larger syntactical units that aggregate words according to rhythmic and semantic clusters. In other words, the layout stages major processes for transforming visual forms into readable

Figure 1.3
Augusto de Campos, "Tudo está dito" (All is said) (1974). © Augusto de Campos.
Reproduced with permission.

forms (i.e., letter and word recognition and articulation of line and column spaces).

Colin Ware (2008) describes the visual search process in terms of three loops: a move and scan loop, which describes a sequence of fixations toward the target; an eye movement control loop, the planning and execution of eye moments biasing the target; and a pattern-testing loop, which tests the pattern to see if it is the search target. All of these loops have been explicitly targeted in "Tudo está dito," a sort of optical test for visual processing of the materiality of writing. The entire mechanics of reading as evidence of distributed cognition is made experientially present in this work: the eye movements that direct the visual search for distinctive features, the visual processing of features in specialized areas of the brain, and the high-level recognition of writing patterns and verbal language.

The defamiliarization created by the ambiguity between abstract drawing and letter form and between border and inside or outside area requires readers to experience reading as a perceptual activity that depends on pattern-finding motions. The eyes scan the textual surface trying to resolve the figure and background conflicts into individual letter shapes. Eye movements also zoom in and out attempting to form words out of letters and sentences out of words. There is a persistent tension between the overall black and white pattern and the embedded writings that gradually emerge from this pattern.

This visual processing of letters, words, and sentences is by itself a major element in the semantic processing of the text because visual semantic layers echo verbal semantic layers, and vice versa. Once the text is deciphered it reads, "Tudo está dito tudo está visto nada é perdido" (All is said all is seen nothing is lost) in the first column and "nada é perfeito eis o imprevisto tudo é infinito" (nothing is perfect here the unforeseen all is infinite) in the second column. The text plays with the modern desire of saying new things and, at the same time, the recognition of the impossibility of not repeating what has been said before. Unpredictability and infinity, on the one hand, and imperfectibility and repeatability, on the other, describe the creative tension between artistic legacy and the inexhaustible expressive use of codes.

"Código" functions in a similar way, but with black letters on a white surface (figure 1.4). The lines that make up the letters also form a visual pattern suggestive of a circular labyrinth. This labyrinth or abstract structure is the product of a series of four concentric circles with four straight lines of different lengths within the inner circular lines. As eyes search for letter forms, they gradually realize that the word *código* has been written

Figure 1.4
Augusto de Campos, "Código" (Code) (1973). © Augusto de Campos. Reproduced with permission.

as if letters had been nested within each other based on their geometric similarity: *C* is the outer circle, followed by *O*, and then by the two half-circles of *G* and *D*, at each side of *I*, which becomes the central axis of the pattern, and with the second letter *O* placed as the innermost circle. The layout of the word is the code required for reading the word: the direction of reading has been recodified in a way that allows both left-to-right and right-to-left movements. Letters contain and mirror each other in their circular placement, whose geometry also suggests a three-dimensional spiraling vortex. A slight dizziness induced by these optical effects is a physical reminder of the vertigo inherent in the tremendous productivity of signifiers.

The entire system of differences of our Latin alphabet emerges from an extremely limited number of variations on a minimal set of distinctive features. This visual pattern suggests both the labyrinth of signification and the vortex of the code. It also contains an emulation of binary code in the fact that each element is a slight variation on the same underlying circular pattern—an image of the differential structure of language, writing, and other digital semiotic systems. Its extreme formalism recalls the theorization of information theory. This text is both a code and an instance of the code designed to briefly unmake and remake reading. As code and instance of code, *código* is a graphical reminder or metonymy of the several codes required for generating meaning out of inscriptional signs—verbal language and alphabetic inscription but also social and cultural patterns structured in discourse. Through this perceptual mode of production of signifying forms, readers see meaning as a code-dependent function, and they experience the concrete poem as an exercise in perception and cognition. The signifier is a material instantiation of the signified in this self-reflexive loop that makes the word *code* an instance of the code that determines the layout of its letters.

In effect, concrete poetry can be examined as a visual and cognitive exploration of reading, that is, as a poetics of codes, patterns, and signs, and of interpretability as a function of semiotic mechanisms and embodied perceptions. Legibility and illegibility are the result of internal tensions between the material differences suggested by textual transformations and the relation of these formal operations to the limits of the reading codes available for producing sense. These transformed codes work by converting visual features into readable traces and making visual properties interpretable within the semantic layers provided by verbal forms. The reinvention of reading called for by concrete poetics responds to the reinvention of writing that is taking place through graphical processes of intermediation, fragmentation, spatialization, and visualization of language. Ana Hatherly's experiments with handwriting also place viewers within this continuum between legibility and illegibility (figure 1.5). Her abstract expressionist use of the string of writing contains at once a calligraphic gestural and emotional presence of the writing act and a challenging reading encounter with the opacity of signifiers as material vortexes for emergent meanings.

Her visual texts establish a relationship between seeing and reading that is both archeological and personal, in the sense that they take us back to the origins of writing in human culture but also in individual psyche. A trace drawn becomes a readable sign without ever losing the presence of the writing hand and the visual code that generates the legible. In her calligraphic texts, the presence of the line of writing and its graphical layout makes the layer of meaning, contained in the fragments of words and phrases repeated on the surface of the page, interact with the visual configuration they assume as drawings made of writing. A signifying line of calligraphic gesture dissolves, partially or totally, the presence of recognizable letters. These visual texts are not mere statements about the identity between *ikon* and *logos*. Above all, they are creative exercises to enable the productivity of personal acts of reading as coinstantiators of the readability of their objects. Through their mode of expressing the physical and emotional mechanisms of writing, the opacity of writing traces becomes readable as a perceptual and affective encounter with form.

The unpredictability of a visuality that emerges from the repetition of sentences, phrases, words, and letters, calligraphically inscribed by hand on paper, emphasizes the power of the graphical instantiation of text. This

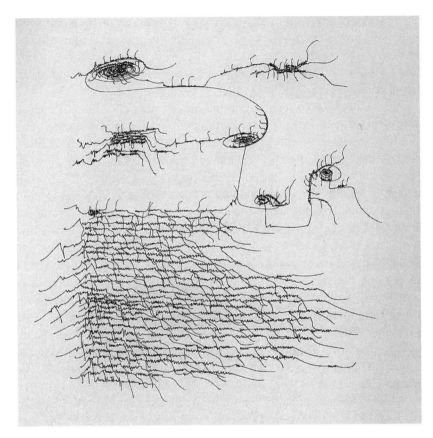

Figure 1.5
Ana Hatherly, "Carta cheia de esperança" (Letter full of hope), in *A Reinvenção da Leitura*, 1975 (original drawing: india ink on paper). © Ana Hatherly. Reproduced with permission.

materialization is sustained by the tension between the macrovisuality of the layout of the lines of writing and microlegibility of the verbal fragments contained in those lines. The movement of the hand gets registered in the movement of lines and letters, their contractions and extensions, their interruptions and overlaps, and their waves and spirals—in short, in the motor and emotional gesture that determines the form of each particular writing trail. The tension between seeing and reading becomes inscribed in the original calligraphic act, which requires the recognition of differences capable of making signs of writing appear within the continuum of black lines. These in turn are likely to be integrated into visual patterns in other scales of perception, giving rise to a movement of back and forth between legible and visible. Ana Hatherly's reinvention of reading implies both a way of reading that redefines the relationship between visibility and legibility and the full assumption of the creative productivity of the act of reading.

A series of two-color paintings of acrylic on paper (35 × 35 centimeters) by Valencian performance artist Bartolomé Ferrando (also published as a box of postcards, 10.5 × 18.5 centimeters) contains another powerful reflection on the entangled and codependent nature of writing and reading. All the paintings are made of a single-color background, either in black or in a slightly shaded white tone. Painted over each colored square, a column of center-aligned words is made to cohere into a sentence. These words are uniformly written in one color for each of the squares. The patterns of the letter/background colors are golden/white, golden/black, black/white, white/black, red/white, red/black, and green/black. Each square has ten to eleven and twelve to thirteen lines. Letters of words in consecutive lines partially overlap. At the points where letters touch and move across each other, the superimposition suggests links and knots in a thread. At these junctures, letters become perceptually ambiguous as either letter shapes that we recognize in terms of their abstract differences or iconographic lines that dissolve into a mimetic representation of an entangled line (figure 1.6).

This perceptual ambiguity communicates itself to the entire text, which exists in a tension between the semantics of the words and their abstract material shape. A sensorial apprehension of the materiality of writing as a thread of shapes is emphasized by the fact that these written colored lines are not flat. Their relief suggests an embossed engraving or the luminous surface of neon lights because of the shining quality of the silvery and golden paint, which is also reminiscent of medieval illuminations. The visual effect thus produces the illusion of a three-dimensional calligraphy, particularly when one attempts to disentangle the superimpositions and decipher letters and words. Because their planes of inscription become perceptually confused, letters and words seem to reassemble in a three-dimensional space that emerges at a certain distance from the actual acrylic background surface. When looking at the postcards that reproduce the works, readers tend to move the card away or toward themselves as if looking for the right angle and point of focus for disentangling the superimpositions that enable them to make sense of the various layers of paint. This tension in depth is stressed by the tension between linking letters in order to form words—the works use a print script in which letters

Figure 1.6
Bartolomé Ferrando, *escrituras superpuestas* (2002): "Escribes con tus ojos sobre la sombra que se desliza y huye" (You write with your eyes on the shadow that glides and flees). © Bartolomé Ferrando. Reproduced with permission.

are individualized—and separating lines for letter, word, and sentence recognition.

Readers are expected to disentangle letters and words that overlap, that is, to disimpose them and recover their usual forms. In order to distinguish letters and words, perception shifts back and forth between their painted materiality and their verbal materiality. By this simple perceptual exercise, attention is immediately directed to the act of reading at its multiple levels: reading as deciphering traces, reading as recognition of signs, reading as vocalization of a graphical notation (vocal interpretation), and reading as a series of embedded semantic and hermeneutical operations (conceptual interpretation). The extraordinary complexity of writing thus becomes the theme of this series of works. What is writing? Is it just a code of a second order, that is, a code for the linguistic code? What other possibilities of meaning does writing contain? Since it is also a minimalist code for phonetic notation (which tells, for example, how to separate and associate signs, how to emphasize, how to pause), what is the role of the performer? Why is it that writing seems to contain a specific order of representation that exceeds human speech and human voice? How are all of these levels articulated in written notation? How do we perform them?

All of the visual texts in the series "superimposed writings" are also self-descriptive. They contain at least one word or a group of words that, in a literal or metaphorical way, can be taken as a reference to the surface they are inscribed in, or to the ink they are inscribed with, or to particular acts of writing and reading in their relation with body movements or bodily functions. The powerful aesthetic function of this self-referential rhetoric comes from the fact that it is used to increase the semantic ambiguity of each poetic sentence. Self-description thus becomes a way of pointing to the semantic instability of language as a condition for poetic possibilities and a field for new descriptions of the experience of the world. Two of Bartolomé Ferrando's autopalimpsests read: "el sonido incrustado en si mismo alberga absorto su propio nacimiento" (encrusted in itself the absorbed sound houses its own birth) and "escribe y camina sobre su propia pagina hueca escritura sin voz" (write and walk over its own hollow page voiceless writing) (figure 1.7). The "encrusted in itself" and "its own hollow page" are references to the inscription of sound and writing on the page. While the first visual text seems to point to writing as notation for sound, the second text suggests that writing, in its materiality, exceeds any strictly representational function. This tension between representing something (writing as notation) and being (writing as trace) is at the core of Bartolomé Ferrando's *Escrituras superpuestas*. In their intermedia nature, that is, as forms in which visual and linguistic meaning are inseparable, they make us look again into the specific entanglements between writing and reading operations.

Many of the phrases and sentences are metaphorical descriptions whose reference and semantics remains ambiguous. In most of them, two or more layers of meaning are played against each other. In "Sangre aérea arterias incoloras sobre un libro de páginas de luz" (Aerial blood colorless arteries upon a book of pages made of light), for example, the paradoxical material immateriality of meaning is paralleled in the antitheses related to the body and the book. This doubling and layering of meanings echoes the doubling

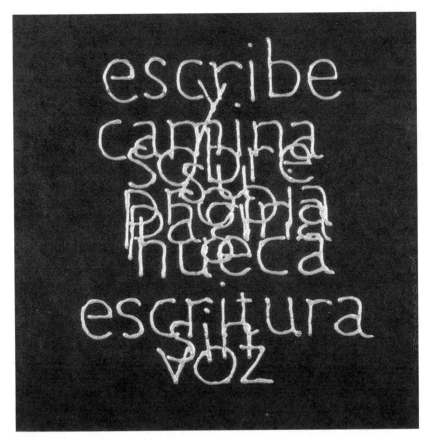

Figure 1.7
Bartolomé Ferrando, *Escrituras superpuestas* (2002): "Escribe y camina sobre su propia
pagina hueca escritura sin voz" (Writes and walks over its own hollow page voiceless
writing). © Bartolomé Ferrando. Reproduced with permission.

and layering of the painted strings of writing. Metaphorical motions from
one layer to the next emulate the visual reading motions that try to keep
perceptually distinct those entanglements created by the superimpositions
in the script, as readers focus and refocus their eyes in order to distinguish
a letter or word on the front layer from a letter or word at the back.

In "Lo que tu piensas roza los huecos de sus palabras hechas viento"
(What you think tears the hollows of its words turned into wind), thought
is cut out in the wind of words as negative space of their sound. Most
sentences reflect on the material and formal nature of language by talking
about relations between voice and speech, sound and meaning, and reading

and writing, all of which are imaged as the embodied forms of the human body (blood, arteries, body, eyes, breath), sound waves in the air (air, wind, music, sound), and written signs on the page (page, book, letter, word, script). The superimposition is thus also the superimposition of writing on sound—the presence of the trace that carves signs out of material differences into the hollowness of form.

These acts of writing are being used as metaphorical representations of the sounds of language. Bartolomé Ferrando is attempting to describe the sound waves of human speech in terms of their inscription on the medium of air. The hollowness of spoken signs echoes the hollowness of written signs as marks that emerge through ripples of material differences in a physical medium. How is the act of reading made present in the work? Reading is made perceptually present in the gestalt effects with the apprehension of form. When layers of paint recede into the same flat plane, writing becomes an entangled thread. When they separate into three-dimensional shapes that seem to hover over the colored background, writing reappears again as signs. Through this double imaging, meaning is not allowed to break completely free from its material instantiation, which is underlined because each text contains metaphors that can refer to textual properties and to acts of reading as visual-vocal decipherment and semantic interpretation of those properties. "Superimposed writings" reiterate a looping interaction each time readers encounter a new sequence of words: they are forced to see themselves reading. Being caught in the entanglements of the script, they perceive themselves perceiving, as if the work mirrored the dynamic interaction that makes it readable. This formal operation intensifies the duration of textual time as readers struggle to decipher its visual and semantic layers. Words have to be experienced in their sound and visual materiality.

This series of works may be said to have been conceived as a series of oculomotor exercises. The slight strain readers feel as they focus and refocus their eyes on the superimposed lines of writing makes them aware of the tiny saccadic movements caused by attention shifts from target to target. Awareness of the material and cognitive processing of the optical and semiotic properties of the letters becomes an integral part of the meaning of work. The act of reading is experienced through this techno-textual device that points to the processing of its material differences as a productive aspect of the signifying process. Because all texts in the series contain a self-referential layer, each verbal description about writing, language, sound, and voice becomes performatively connected to the actual reading of the text. As self-descriptive written forms are disentangled to become readable, the very act of reading them is perceived as a self-conscious neurophysiological and conceptual intervention in the material field of writing.

1.3 Reading Hands

Twentieth-century experimental literary practices have been driven by a desire of animating written signs as symbolic tokens of the presence of life in writing. This kinetic desire has led to an intense exploration of the visuality of writing and the development of intermedia forms, which were also encouraged by the new expressive possibilities opened up by optical and sound media. Kineticism became a material trope across different media, including the constellated poem; the futurist "parole in liberta," with its program for freeing words from the constraints of conventional syntax and linear typesetting; the Dadaist newspaper collages; the red-and-black typographic expressiveness of the Russian avant-garde; the experiments of abstract filmmakers with visual music and painting in motion; the automatic collages of surrealist writers; the phonetic and lettrist fragmentation of words; the self-referential verbivocovisuality of concrete aesthetics; and, more recently, the digital programming of letter movements on pixel screens. From the suggestion of motion on the page to the actual cinematic motion of written signs on screens, animation has been a major expressive and rhetorical feature of modernist and postmodernist intermedia forms.

One particular kind of animation has been obtained by treating the book as a tactile three-dimensional projector that animates writing and other graphical forms through the movements of its movable parts. The motion of book parts is translated into the semiotic and semantic layers of the work as hands perform the particular reading choreography embodied in the work's binding and folding axes. The use of folds and cut-out forms is one way of inscribing writing in the three-dimensional space of the book and giving mobility to printed signs. A number of artists' books—works that explore reflexiveness between bibliographic structure and their visual and linguistic content —make use of this feature as a way of contributing to the tactility of the book form. The use of folded structures in conjunction with words and letters points to the action of handling folios, gatherings, and openings as an element in the reading process. Hand movements are shown as part of the process of embodying reading in a given material form. The motions of the various parts of the book respond to the motions of hands opening and closing folios and folds. This folding and unfolding of spaces within codex-based structures is used in *Poemobiles* (1974), by Julio Plaza and Augusto de Campos, as a way of suggesting the mobility of signifiers. Pop-up structures serve to fragment or associate letters and words. A doubling and layering of meaning is obtained through the separation and aggregation of bibliographic and verbal units, whose material form becomes variable in response to the spatial changes actualized by the mobility of the paper structures.

The result is a dynamic textual configuration in which signifiers gain an oscillating form created by the motions of paper responding to the motions of hands. Thus, mechanical spaces, established by this swinging back and forth of various folded surfaces, sustain intersecting signifying planes (figure 1.8). In this way, the multidimensionality of codex space and the productivity of reading transactions are experienced through a correlation between hand and eye movements. Changes in the angles between left- and right-hand pages as they rotate around the axis of the spine reveal two different word sequences, nested on each other, as if one of them was concealed within the other. This mechanical motion of the

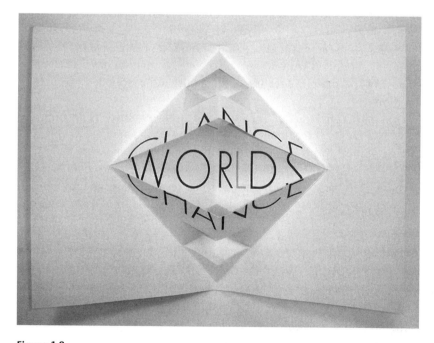

Figure 1.8
Augusto de Campos and Julio Plaza, *Poemobiles* (2010): "chance worlds." © Augusto de Campos and Julio Plaza. Reproduced with permission.

folds transmits its kinetic effect to the verbal signifiers, suggesting the possibility of coexistence and reversibility between two simultaneous textual states. The semantic mobility of the poem is a function of the semiotic mobility of the words, which in turn results from the mechanical mobility of the codex. In the particular dynamics of *Poemobiles*, the three-dimensional tactile properties of the folded folio are translated into the motion of letters and words. Codex visuality is also a function of codex tactility and of the particular ergonomy that links book, hands, and eyes during the motions of reading. All of them work together to produce a kinetic experience of the signifying chains of language embodied in reading artifacts.

In this work, color is also used to further juxtapose, embed, and interweave various textual elements, creating a graphical equivalent of the combinatorial structures sustained by cutting and folding strips of paper (figures 1.9 and 1.10). The poemobiles *abre* and *open* establish a pattern of three colors that is in correlation with the folds, which also serves to break or blend words and parts of words. Word division, color division, and fold

Figure 1.9
Augusto de Campos and Julio Plaza, *Poemobiles* (2010): "abre." © Augusto de Campos and Julio Plaza. Reproduced with permission.

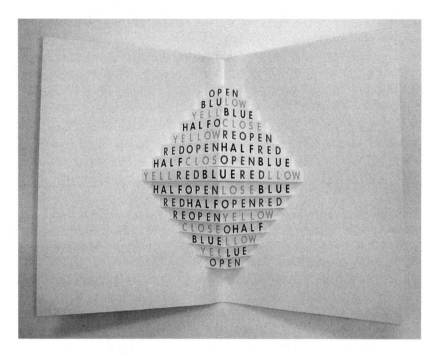

Figure 1.10
Augusto de Campos and Julio Plaza, *Poemobiles* (2010): "open." © Augusto de
Campos and Julio Plaza. Reproduced with permission.

division are placed in a three-partite tension, and these internal microlevel
patterns function within an overall left-right and top-bottom color, layout,
and folding macrolevel symmetry. When considered as an interlinguistic
pair that matches Portuguese and English, *abre* and *open* offer a three-
dimensional image of translation as the product of dynamic symmetries
and asymmetries between languages. The tensions that sustain their visual
and haptic space are mirrored in the interlinguistic equivalences created
by the need to observe the numerical pattern of letters in each line (4 + 6
+ 8 + 10 + 12 + 14 + 16 + 18 + 16 + 14 + 12 + 10 + 8 + 6 + 4).

The intersection of folds, letters, colors, and languages creates a performative space for multiple reading motions. The dynamic relation between
word division and word intersection is achieved by opening and closing
folds, strips, and pages. In the case of *abre/open*, it is also materialized by
the uncoincidence between fold separations and color separations. In this
visual text, the signifying dynamics of the three-dimensionality of the
codex in its relation to writing signs has a verbal correlative in the dynam-

ics between the two languages. The visual and haptic movements within graphical and codicological space become an analog of the force fields between languages. Association of characters and words in the in-between space created by folds and colors contains new words or half-words. These in turn have been transferred across the linguistic gap in ways that evidence linguistic differences and asymmetries.

Open and *close* are self-descriptive words for the manipulation of this folded book. They also refer to the general process of semiosis that opens up the material signifiers to the substitution and equivalence loops between visual, linguistic, and tactile layers of the work. Augusto de Campos's visual untranslations explore the possibility of intersemiotic transfer of semantic layers between verbal, graphical, and codex codes. Layers of verbal meaning are transferred to graphical signifiers and codex structures. Words are graphically and haptically opened and closed to reveal other words within or beneath or above themselves. The relation between source text and translation is mediated by a visual and bibliographical layout that takes on its own particular semantic value when the Portuguese and English versions are compared. The depth of the book is a material surrogate for the depth of meaning, the ambiguities within and across words, and the radical differences between languages.

Hand motions and the sense of touch are also integral parts of human–computer physical interactions. The participatory affordance of the digital medium is largely predicated on haptic feedbacks on programmed algorithms mediated by physical and graphical interfaces. Dragging and clicking the mouse, pressing keys, and touching screens, as modalities of interaction, can be invested with reflexive functions that address the movements of reading. The processing and displaying of signifiers by the machine is experienced as the result of data inputs created by moment-to-moment interactions. Play with the mouse and with touch screen can be used to show the haptic presence of the hand in defining its reading space, which is codependent on a spatially and temporally situated motion that activates a textual program. Caught in the recursive loop between computer processing of codes and human processing of textual events, the hand is able to feel itself reading.

Human and machine processing of signs through haptic and audio interfaces that sustain a system of interactions is the theme of a recent work by Serge Bouchardon: *Touch: Six Scenes on the Paradox of Screen Touching* (2009) (figure 1.11). This work is structured into five parts associated with each of the five fingers: "Move" (thumb), "Caress" (forefinger), "Hit" (middle finger), "Spread" (ring finger), and "Blow" (little finger). Each

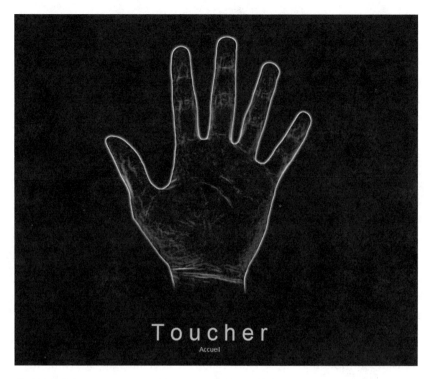

Figure 1.11
Serge Bouchardon, Kevin Carpentier, Stéphanie Spenlé, *Touch* (2009). © Serge
Bouchardon, Kevin Carpentier, Stéphanie Spenlé. Reproduced with permission.

textual sequence is entirely dependent on a continuing interaction with
the reader, who has to physically connect with the screen. Each textual
stage requires moving and clicking the mouse and, in one instance, blowing
into the microphone. Each mode of touching alluded to in each verbal/
audio/visual text is replicated in the tactile interactions mediated by the
mouse.

In the "move" section, scene permutations are triggered by mouse clicks
("Touch the words, replace them, move them"—"Do you touch me when
I touch you"); in "caress," the black outline of a female figure is gradually
revealed by dragging and clicking the mouse over the white screen along
sound-emitting paths ("Build a shape by caressing and following the
sound"); in "hit," a fly (figured by the word *fly*) moves across the screen
and leaves zigzag red lines of zzzz's in its wake, while the textual player
has to click on the fly in order to make the text legible again—this text
contains an excerpt from Aristotle "The History of Animals" about the

senses ("Hit the fly to be able to read the text"); in "spread," dragging the mouse creates a synesthesia between painted blot patterns on the screen and stereophonic musical sounds ("Move and click the mouse upwards, downwards, sidewards to create a musical painting"); finally, in "blow," the act of blowing into the microphone makes white letters of text fall into place, only to be covered by white flakes ("Blow to read the text, then to spread the words"). Writing scenes in *Touch* establish a conflicting relationship between manipulating and reading the text.

Touch looks at redefinitions of the act of touching produced by the development of tactile interfaces and places them in the context of verbal and literary allusions to the possibility of a human subject being touched by the world and by the word. Human–machine interactions mediated by the sense of touch are recontextualized through those literary uses of the sense of touch as metaphorical expression of the possibilities of connecting with others and with oneself. Epigraphs from Jean-Luc Nancy, Jacques Salomé, Helen Castle, and Walt Whitman intensify several layers of meaning in the word. The recovery of plural meanings for *Touch*—beyond the mere instrumental command-executing interaction with the machine— creates an affective mode of touching the screen through the manipulation of the mouse and through seeing, hearing, and breathing that ultimately celebrate human senses as doors of perception at each new encounter with the material world. The open hand that is used as the work's graphical interface is also a surrogate for other senses. Reading is experienced as reciprocal haptic and affective exchange: I touch the text, and the text touches me.

1.4 Assembling Pages

Reading acts can be simulated in writing in essentially two ways: they can be verbally represented and materially enacted. Verbal reference to reading acts, for instance, is a conventional feature of many early works of modern fiction that model the role of the reader within the narrative on the basis of social conversation and social interaction. An ongoing dialogue between writer and reader makes literary communication into a layer of the story, which usually functions as a protocol for interpretation that frames the fictionality of the narrated world. Reading is placed within a set of social and formal conventions that circumscribe the act of reading within the social semiotics of a particular genre, practice, or role. But the presence of reading in writing may also involve the graphic and bibliographic features of the work. In this case, the metaleptic oscillation of framing between being inside and being outside the narrative extends to the materiality of printed discourse. At this level, reading is enacted as a material act beyond the mere symbolic processing of meaning. The actual physical reading space of the codex becomes a space for rehearsing the mechanics of the book as a reading machine.

A good example of the relation between these two levels of simulation (representation and enactment) is Laurence Sterne's novel *The Life and Opinions of Tristram Shandy, Gentleman* (1759–1767). Self-reference to writing, reading, and publishing as social practices, as well as the description of typographic layout and codex structure as material elements in the production of narrative, sustain the continuing tension between plot and discourse in *Tristram Shandy*. Thus, its metanarrative unfolds as a meta-book, a sustained self-reflection on its own formal and social materiality as a codex. By "speaking of [his] book as a *machine*," the narrator brings the conditions of production and reception of the printed book, as well as its bibliographic syntax, into focus. Narrative interruption is not only the consequence of digressions, interpolated stories or secondary plots, but also of the foregrounding of the book's internal and external structure as a device for meaning production and communication. In several passages, reflections on narrative continuity bear on the connection between discourse organization and codex sequence:

"—NO doubt, Sir—there is a whole chapter wanting here—and a chasm of ten pages made in the book by it—but the book-binder is neither a fool, or a knave, or a puppy—nor is the book a jot more imperfect, (at least upon that score)—but, on the contrary, the book is more perfect and complete by wanting the chapter, than having it, as I shall demonstrate to your reverences in this manner—I question first by the bye, whether the same experiment might not be made as successfully upon sundry other chapters—but there is no end, an' please your reverences, in trying experiments upon chapters—we have had enough of it—So there's an end of that matter." (vol. 7, chap. 1, p. 1)

The codetermination between discourse and story is further stressed by the codetermination between book and discourse. In other words, Sterne thematizes bibliographic codes as signifying elements in his novel.

One of the best examples of the determination of narrative content by material form is the treatment of chapter divisions. In *Tristram Shandy* the relation between chapters as typographic units and chapters as reading and narrative units is repeatedly disturbed. New chapters interrupt the narrative and discursive sequence of ongoing chapters, thus splitting the unity between typographic divisions and content. This can happen within a narrative sequence of action, time, space, and character, but also within a merely verbal sequence: some chapters are a continuation of the dialogue of the previous chapter, others open in the middle of a sentence that was interrupted in the previous chapter. Chapters tend to have heterogeneous and unexpected lengths, ranging from a line up to fifty pages, often with one- or one-and-a-half-page chapters alternating with much longer chapters. A chapter has completely disappeared and left a hole of ten missing pages, two chapters are out of order, and one is partially blank, urging the reader to a "do it yourself" approach to character description (respectively, vol. 4, chap. 24; vol. 9, chaps. 18 and 19; and vol. 6, chap. 38) (figure 1.12). In addition, chapters can be multiplied indefinitely by mere association of

[146]

-- Let my old tye wig, quoth my uncle *Toby*, and my laced regimentals, be hung to the fire all night, *Trim*.

CHAP.

Figure 1.12
Laurence Sterne, *The Life and Opinions of Tristram Shandy, Gentleman* (1761), vol. 4, chap. 23, p. 146, chap. 25, p. 156. The missing chapter (chap. 24) and the missing pages (pp. 147–155).

[156]

C H A P. XXV.

-- No doubt, Sir -- there is a whole
chapter wanting here -- and a
chasm of ten pages made in the book
by it -- but the book-binder is neither a
fool, or a knave, or a puppy -- nor is the
book a jot more imperfect, (at least upon
that score) -- but, on the contrary, the
book is more perfect and complete by
wanting the chapter, than having it, as
I shall demonstrate to your reverences in
this manner -- I question first by the bye,
whether the same experiment might not
be made as successfully upon sundry
other chapters ---- but there is no end,
an'please your reverences, in trying experiments upon chapters -- we have had
        L 2   enough

Figure 1.12
(continued)

ideas and transform themselves into their own subject matter. Reading becomes scripted as the material conflict between the semiotic codes of typography, on the one hand, and the semantic and interpretative expectations of narrative, on the other.

Readers of *Tristram Shandy* are periodically reminded of their interaction with the writing marks that they are deciphering. The codex as a narrative organizer and mediator becomes a protagonist of the novel, and the novel is redefined as a certain kind of book by recurrent references to its printed codes (i.e., its particular graphical features) and the social codes used for reading them (e.g., its particular interpretative communities, which are divided into clergymen, aristocrats, middle classes, and women readers).[4] Hypermediacy, or the presence of the medium, is so pervasive that narrative continuity is postponed or interrupted by the evidence of the production of its discourse (the writing act) and its bibliographic materiality (the printing act). Discourse and book get in the way of narrative and show how the semantic import of what is said is a consequence of how it is being said, how typography is setting the text on the page, and how chapters are bound in a codex structure. This self-reference to the materiality of the printed page even uses page breaks as narrative and affective intensifiers at certain moments. Sterne is concerned with the physiology and sociology of writing and reading in its material, semiotic, bodily, emotional, and social details.

Consider, for instance, the writer-narrator's diagrammatic engraving of the way he has been telling the story in the first five volumes (figure 1.13). As a topographic and schematic mapping of Tristram Shandy's narrative journey, this visual representation is also a record of the heterogeneity of writing as an assemblage of diverse and discontinuous signifiers. The irregularities in the lines reflect the writer-narrator's awareness that narrativity is a function of discourse and the fictional power of language. His desire to find an inner and necessary logic for the story conflicts with the self-perceived evidence, in his own writing experience, of the myriad possibilities of connecting words and sentences, and thus connecting characters, events, times, and places as elements in a determinable plot set on the pages of a book. This symbolic productiveness is also the economic and social productiveness of the book as a literary commodity and reading machine for virtualizing events. The more the writer writes, the more she or he has to write. The more the reader reads, the more she or he will have to read. The failed attempt at plotting and narrating his autobiography highlights the arbitrariness of narrative as an ideologically motivated association of events.

[152]

C H A P. XL.

I Am now beginning to get fairly into
my work; and by the help of a
vegitable diet, with a few of the cold
seeds, I make no doubt but I shall be
able to go on with my uncle *Toby*'s story,
and my own, in a tolerable straight line.
Now,

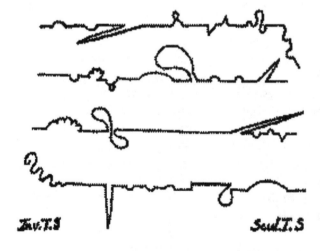

These

Figure 1.13
Laurence Sterne, *The Life and Opinions of Tristram Shandy, Gentleman* (1759), vol. 6,
chap. 40. (The zigzag lines, pp. 152–153.)

[153]

These were the four lines I moved in
through my first, second, third, and
fourth volumes. ---- In the fifth volume
I have been very good, ---- the precise
line I have described in it being this :

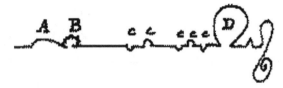

By which it appears, that except at the
curve, marked A. where I took a trip
to *Navarre*, -- and the indented curve B.
which is the short airing when I was
there with the Lady *Baussiere* and her
page, -- I have not taken the least frisk
of a digression, till *John de la Casse*'s
devils led me the round you see marked
D. -- for as for *c c c c c* they are nothing
but parentheses, and the common *ins*
and *outs* incident to the lives of the great-
est ministers of state ; and when compared

Figure 1.13
(continued)

Tristram Shandy combines the representation of reading acts as narrative elements (in the writer-narrator's dialogue with readers about the writing, publishing, and reading of the novel) with the enactment of reading motions that choreograph haptic and optic interactions triggered by transformations in the work's bibliographic materiality. The use of the marbled page is one striking example of this loop between representing and enacting the reading act. The marbled pages (vol. 3, chap. 36, pp. 169–170) are presented as yet another challenge to readers, recalling the black pages of the previous installment (vol. 1, chap. 22, pp. 73–74):

Read, read, read, read, my unlearned reader! read,—or by the knowledge of the great saint *Paraleipomenon*—I tell you before-hand, you had better throw down the book at once; for without *much reading*, by which your reverence knows, I mean *much knowledge*, you will no more be able to penetrate the moral of the next marbled page (motley emblem of my work!) than the world with all its sagacity has been able to unravel the many opinions, transactions and truths which still lie mystically hid under the dark veil of the black one. (vol. 3, chap. 36, p. 168)

As in several other places in the book, ironies are aimed at the practice of reading for hidden meanings, but they are also directed at the typographic form of the novel. The work's emphasis on its visual and graphical surfaces as an integral part of the narrative is achieved by means of verbal references and graphical markers that call attention to discursive and bibliographic conventions. Readers are intermittently reminded that they are reading in a certain way a book that has been written, printed, and published in a certain way. Narrative content is split into a narrative of discourse and a narrative of the printed codex as co-plotters of semiotic and semantic relations between different kinds of signs. The marbled pages are Sterne's ironic answer to critics who mocked the black pages in the first installment, and so they are part of the actual dialogue between the writer and his readers. More important, they create a disruption in the codex's material structure, and thus another instance of a conflict between book design and narrative content. Instead of being used as endpaper attaching the quires to the cover, the marbled leaf is resignified as a textual element that can be placed inside the narrative. The conventional distinction of textual, extratextual, and paratextual that establishes the reading protocols for a given printed genre is momentarily interrupted.

Since each page has to be individually marbled, the marbling patterns will vary even from copy to copy, introducing an element of singularity in a printed edition (figure 1.14). This singularity can be read as an image of the singularity of reading itself as a social and individual performance

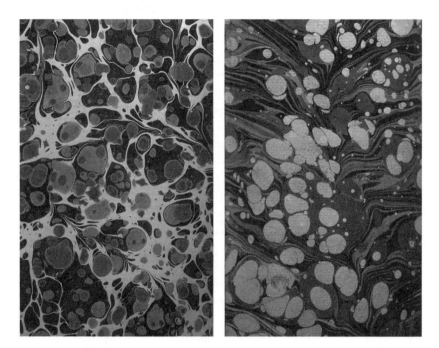

Figure 1.14
Marbled pages in early editions of *The Life and Opinions of Tristram Shandy, Gentleman* (vol. 3, chap. 36).

of traces and marks. The continuing interruption of stories by digressions, which happens at a verbal level, has been extended, here and elsewhere, to the material layer of printed signs, highlighting what Jerome McGann (1991) has called the double coding of the codex. It is as if the codex layers could interrupt the story layers, and consequently, the book's material properties could interact, on the same level, with the semiotic and semantic relations maintained by the text's verbal networks. Graphical layout, pagination, binding, and other book properties code verbal and narrative signifiers by displaying and relating them on the page in particular ways. Interruption of the linguistic textual elements by the marbled paratextual or extratextual elements calls the reader's attention to the structural function of endpapers in holding quires and cover in place, that is, they remind him or her of the book as concept and artifact.

This discreteness of the codex as a material and discursive unit is a running theme to which the writer-narrator keeps returning throughout the novel. His inability to order narrative events and determine narrative content and his inability to order chapters and finish the book are parallel and coterminous events. Textualization of the colored marbled pages has other semantic implications because the writer-narrator explicitly symbolizes the singularity of the work on the page's visual textuality, defined as "motley emblem of my work." Sterne's ironic textual semiotics depends on this playing of narrative conventions against printed codex conventions, resulting in chains of interruption, deferral, open-endedness, and arbitrariness. Random blots, points, and lines of color on each of the marbled pages can be read as a visualization of the indeterminacy that results from interplay between codex signifiers and narrative signifiers. The interaction between writing and reading is vividly expressed through those randomly produced abstract patterns—patterns that have to be produced anew for each single copy of each new edition, thus guaranteeing that the singularity of the reading event becomes materially and symbolically marked in each marbled page. Dissolution of verbal and linguistic form in the pure visuality of colored patches of ink shifts the consciousness of reading away from its grammatological and semantic nature to the visual processing of marks through the viewer's ocular system.

1.5 Embodying Books

The notion of bibliographic code was developed as part of the social theory of editing in the 1980s and 1990s. Jerome McGann (1991) foregrounded the social and material aspects of textual construction by positing a dynamic relationship between the linguistic and bibliographic materiality in literary artifacts. He described the semiotic function of the bibliographic codes and showed how they can function as an integral part of autopoietic processes in textual fields. This semiotic and social theory of textuality eventually led him to digital editing experiments that attempted to remediate the material and linguistic dynamics of books and other artifacts by means of the hypertext rationale (McGann 1996, 2001, 2004). Critical remediation of codex codes implied exploring the radiant textuality of the electronic medium in order to understand the dynamics of reading sustained by the bibliographic inscription of language. Books were turned into networks of marked-up digital facsimiles and electronically encoded textual transcriptions, which were structured as relational databases available to algorithmic processing through various kinds of tools. Hypertextual networked representations of the bibliographic and linguistic features would historicize meaning production in its material and social forms yet also also foster a new critical modeling of bibliographic codes and of their signifying function.

Remediation of print bibliographic features according to a social editing paradigm became the theoretical basis behind scholarly electronic archival and editing projects devoted to literary artifacts for the past two decades. In these projects, a critical mapping of the bibliographic codes of particular editions involves the creation of complex networks of digital surrogates and the placing of those surrogates within a large ensemble of production and reception documents. The new reading environment is built as a critical and interpretative space where the remediated disembodiment and reembodiment of codex works has contributed to our awareness of the dynamics between linguistic and bibliographic codes. This remediation of codex forms in digital space establishes a tension between emulation and representation that is useful for our understanding how verbal inscriptions become bibliographically codified, a topic that I address at greater length in chapter 2.

The evidence of bibliographic codes as elements of signifying processes can also be illuminated by same-medium translations and recodifications. An interesting case for observing the intertwinedness of linguistic and bibliographic codes is the genre known as the treated book. As the name implies, treated or altered books are books that result from various kinds of material interventions on a specific copy. These interventions can take the form of drawn, painted, written, and collaged reinscriptions over the original pages, but they can also alter the format and structure of the source book by redefining the size and order of its constituent parts. Relationships between inscriptional marks and codex spaces are restructured in ways that highlight the function of the book's bookness as a material signifier and a reading device. The interaction between the verbal and bibliographic layers of the artifact is made reflexively present: new signifiers tend to point to themselves as a reembodiments of that interaction in the altered book. Deformations and transformations of the source codex make readers experience the correlation between verbal or visual text and codex space. Changes performed on the source signifiers create a layered perception of both levels of encoding, as if the two books (source and altered) could occupy the same material and conceptual space.

In *A Humument: A Treated Victorian Novel* (1970–1975), by Tom Phillips, one or more visual layers are painted on the original printed text, leaving out scattered words and phrases across the pages.[5] Each page is treated as a graphical and verbal unit with the overlaying pictorial patterns reinforcing either the autonomy of the single-page text or the affinities between contiguous groups of pages. The elliptic, ambiguous, and semicontinuous character of the resulting verbal and visual structure allows *A Humument* to be read as a collection of poems, a fictional illustrated narrative, or an artist's journal. Visual poem, graphical novel, and artist's journal are placed in formal and generic contiguity as a consequence of verbal fragmentation and visual association, on the one hand, and of the constant tension between single pages/openings and page sequence and codex syntax, on the other. The bibliographic and typographic codes of the original print novel have been radically transformed, creating entirely new paths for reading its verbal discourse.

The generally loose verbal structure is given cohesion and coherence by means of recurrent verbal echoes, which include the appearance of characters (toge, a new character, and also Irma, Grenville, and other characters preserved from the underlying text), the visual definition of spaces (rooms, windows, streets, parks), and the representation of events. The same is true for the pictorial style, as patterns begin to recur in various pages at various points in the codex. Often the vagueness of words has a contextualizing element in external references contained in the visual representations. This multilayered verbal and pictorial structure is given further depth by means of intertextual and parodic echoes of other texts and other paintings and drawings. The treated book gradually becomes an encyclopedia of verbal and pictorial techniques and styles, documenting its own desire to assimilate modern literature and modern art.

Visual styles, literary techniques, and codex codes are used as an artistic repertoire available for reuse and resignification in much the same ways as language provides the self with the possibility of saying himself or herself (figure 1.15): "I myself am made of / reference to myself, / I—I, / Eternal—I / depth I / think I / I mean / Do I / I do / time / I am / I laugh? I am / which I / I have / soul—I / what I" (Phillips 1987, 194). This voice is also the voice of the book referring to its material condition as an attempt at embodying meaning. The self of this book mirrors the self of the codex, and the self of the speaking voice mirrors the self of language, and both, book and language, offer new possibilities for meaning in their inscriptional interactions. The description of its own method of composition is made in the very first treated page, the title page (figure 1.16): "volume And / side I shall lie, / bones my bones / A HUMUMENT / A HUMAN DOCUMENT. / INTRODUCTION. / The following / sing / I / a / book. a book / of art / of / mind art / and that / which / he / hid / reveal I" (1).

The relation between the two texts (Mallock's and Phillips's) is described as a relation between two books, and the speaking voice becomes the voice of the book itself. The author's self is self-consciously present as the voice of the medium, a product of the palimpsestic condition of writing as

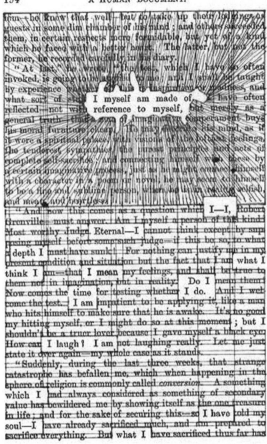

194   A HUMAN DOCUMENT.

Figure 1.15

Tom Phillips, *A Humument*: p. 194, Tetrad Press Edition, 1971–1975. © Tom Phillips.
Reproduced with permission.

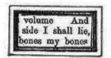

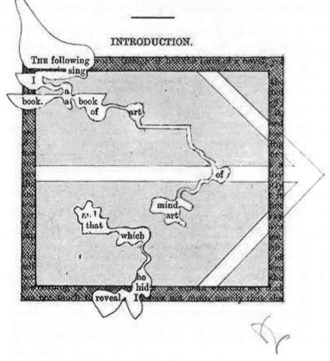

Figure 1.16
Tom Phillips, *A Humument*: p. 1, Tetrad Press Edition, 1971–1975. © Tom Phillips.
Reproduced with permission.

writing over previous writing. This title page alludes to the dialectics of veiling and unveiling that determines the relation of this book to the underlying book and to other books, and also of its discourse to the underlying discourse. The visual layers in each page work as formal operators that transform the linguistic and bibliographic codes to produce a new text and a new book: "a book exhumed from, rather than born out of, another" (Phillips 1987, afterword). As a procedural work, it also offers a model for the inscription of individual acts of meaning production in the general forms, patterns, and artifacts of culture. Individual acts of creation are enabled by material and discursive transformations on a prior body of forms and codes.

The first twelve pages of *A Humument* have been inscribed over the source book's title page and introduction and contain a self-description of the work as a treated book (figure 1.17). However, the peritextual function of the introduction in the original volume, which framed the 1892 naturalist novel by W. H. Mallock, is now fulfilled by a series of pages that are verbally and pictorially identical to every other page in this book. In this way, there is no formal and rhetorical difference between introductory text and novel/poem/journal text. This fact is a defining feature in Phillips's struggle with the previous fixed discourse and graphical layout in order to materialize his linguistic and visual signifiers. All the typographic elements in the source book—titles, epigraphs, page numbers, running heads, white spaces within letters and words, spaces around sentences and around text blocks, margins, and so on—are reactivated as part of the signifying field of the new work. The systematic conversion of the so-called paratextual and peritextual elements into fully textual elements is one of the many changes made by this work's recoding to its source codex.

The operation of recoding Mallock's printed novel as new kind of visual book originates a continuing semantic layer that reflects on the codex as a particular mode of embodiment of verbal text. Page 2 introduces the female character—"is / The woman we are speaking of / over her ankles / in / the storm and fire / an desire of art; and the / art of / art /, and / would have given us a humument / or two" (2) , page 3 establishes the relationship between male and female character, while pages 4 and 5 discuss the problem of literary form and genre: "A HUMUMENT / attempt to / cripple sentences / reality, / broken by / quivering / peculiarities / part / poken / the artificial / fiction / broken / in the imaginary / Journal" (5). Verbal and visual structure attempt to mirror one another, and both describe the intermedia method of composition of the work, a fragmentary journal that matches broken sentences and broken pages in its production of new

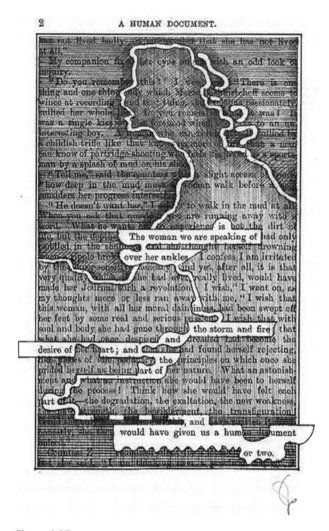

Figure 1.17
Tom Phillips, *A Humument:* pp. 2–3, 4–5, 6–7, Tetrad Press Edition, 1971–1975.
© Tom Phillips. Reproduced with permission.

A HUMAN DOCUMENT.   3

possess a certain something, and I am thinking whether I will show it to you. Tell me," she went on with a laugh, "do you think you would care to see it?"

To this riddle only one answer was possible. "Anything which you think worth showing me I am sure I shall think worth seeing."

"Ah," she replied, "but you will have to do more than see it. This is something which you will have to pore and puzzle over, and if you don't take enough trouble about it to thoroughly try your temper, I shall discover how apathetic you have been, and consider you have abused my confidence. You are perhaps prepared to hear that what I speak about is a collection of manuscripts."

"Are they yours?" I asked.

"Only," she said, "in the sense that they are my property. They were left me by the writer, who died a few months ago. She was a beautiful woman, and you know something about her; but not much, or I can't tell what would have happened to you."

"Go on," I said; "this is indeed interesting."

"If you really mean," she replied, "what you were just now saying, it ought to be far more interesting to you, than you have the least reason to suppose. Shall I tell you what the manuscript is? It is an imaginary continuation of Marie Bashkirtcheff's Journal, in which she is represented as undergoing the exact fate you were wishing for her. I suspect, too," she continued, "that it is something more than that. Indeed, I am certain that it is; but you must read it first, and I will talk it over with you afterwards. If you care to have it, it shall be sent to your room to-night."

Countess Z—— was as good as her word. I was tempted for a moment to think she was even better, when, on going up-stairs to bed, I saw lying on my table, not what I had pictured to myself—a small unpretending packet, which I could have held in my hand, and put with my pocket-handkerchief under my pillow, but a great folio volume bound like a photographic scrap-book, the sight of which filled me with dismay. When, however, I opened it, I was at once reassured and puzzled. It was a scrap-book in reality, not in appearance only; and its bulk was explained by the fact that its leaves were of thick cartridge-paper, and that the manuscript, whose sheets varied in size and appearance, had been

Figure 1.17
(continued)

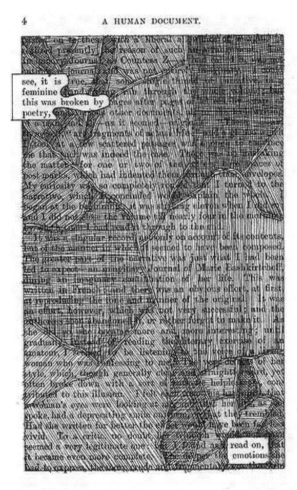

Figure 1.17
(continued)

Figure 1.17
(continued)

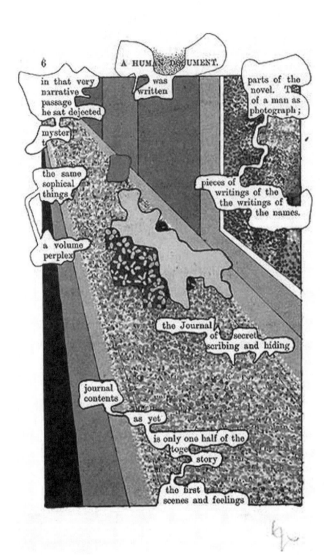

Figure 1.17
(continued)

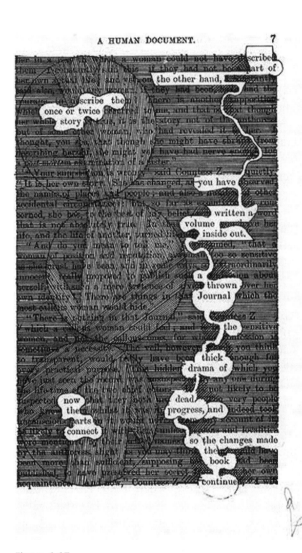

Figure 1.17
(continued)

signifiers. Making a new book by drawing and painting over the surfaces of a previous book provides many occasions for reference to the verbal and visual forms of the new book: "broken / the / besides / journal, and / poken / the impression / Journal / The first / discrepancy / Journal / the / Journal" (5). Meanings emerge through this process of systematic verbal fragmentation—"fragments fragments" (5)—and visual contextualization of the fragments cited and iterated.

Through this complex linguistic and pictorial layering, the new inscriptions are used to register themselves as signifying acts. Phillips uses the original prefatory text as a source for a fragmentary description of the nature of *A Humument* as an intermedia and intergeneric book that combines poetry, fiction, journal, graphics, illustration, and painting. Representation of its compositional method is achieved through reference to its verbal, visual, and bibliographic structure, placing readers within the codex's material form: "a volume perplex" (6); "pieces of / writings of the / the writings of/ the names" (6); "the Journal / of secret / scribing and hiding" (6); "scribe / art of / the other hand, / you have / written a / volume / inside out. / a / thrown / Journal / the / thick / drama of / dead progress, and / so the changes made / the / book continue" (7); "now / the / arts / connect" (7); "and a little white / opening out of / thought" (8). The visual and textual form of each page is made to mirror its verbal description. These self-descriptions are locally valid as descriptions of the particular form of the text or graphical pattern or picture on the page on which they occur, but many of them are also globally valid as descriptions of the features and method of this whole codex.

The doubling of self-reference (from page to book, and from page-over-page to book-over-book) gains an extra level when it also refers to other parts of the work, as happens on page 9, which refers back to the treated dedication on the title page, and forward to the occurrence of the same words on the very last page (367): "Look at this, / her book; /fulfilling her / book as her / 'Dedication / volume.' And / side I shall lie, / bones my bones" (9). These embedded layers of reference explicitly connect (1) *A Humument* to its source text, *A Human Document*; (2) the local form of each page to the entire form of the codex; and (3) the fictional narrative to the intermittent autobiographical reflection on the composition of the work: "A HUMAN DOCUMENT. / you in / mine / fused / in witness of my love for you, every page" (10); "I foresee / a book / which / which, / might / disguise / name. / admit / explain / perfectly indicate / mention / convince might, / most completely, / change" (10); "A HUMUMENT. / That book accordingly is now offered to the reader. As to what the changes are which I have been obliged to make, I cannot say more, / but / it is / a humument" (11).

This double reference to codex and to self is stressed by the repetition of phrases and words, echoing the whole process of genre, style, and codex resignification that is taking place with each material intervention on the book: "meaning / losing its meaning when / it follows / any picture of the / part of a / half of a / picture / details are not / representation / question / whether the book is / this—it is as / If it is / and / exists in the / purposes it / does" (12). Representation of this book's bookness is also achieved through the ghostly and palimpsestic presence of the former book. The original pages sometimes show through the layers of paint and ink. This presence of the printed paper body of the earlier book is generally conspicuous in the actual painted pages, but it can also be felt in the print trade edition, particularly when the underlying text is present in larger cut-ups or excerpts. That is the case of pages made by cutting from and pasting parts of other pages from the book (34, 73, 81, 105, 328), and generally of those pages where most of the text has not been completely painted over and remains readable, such as pages 99, 109, 178, and several others.

The margins of *A Human Document* and of *A Humument* do not always coincide (106, 124, 314), the running title is often integrated into the design of the page, and the original chapter divisions are sometimes present (for instance, 92, 103, and 110) and sometimes absent. The ambivalence of those markers of page, codex, and narrative structure also contributes to reinforce a tension between the original and the new bibliographic codes. Collages made with paper strips cut out from other copies of the book, the use of large excerpts from the original text, and the use of transparent layers of paint or partial crossing out of the underlying words—all of these contribute to the ghostly presence of the earlier codex in the constitution of this metarepresentation of book form. The material presence of the earlier book is gradually transformed into the presence of a large corpus of codex codes, particularly of illustrated books, from medieval illuminations and early printed books to twentieth-century artists' books. Tom Phillips (1987) explores the potentiality of each printed page as source for new verbal and visual meanings, the "inexhaustibility of even a single page" (afterword) becoming an instance of the inexhaustibility of the codex itself as signifying machine, and of the endless iterability of writing embodied in books.

1.6   Performing Codes

A related but also very specific meaning for code is captured in the concept of digital code, which implies automatic processing of numerical representations. N. Katherine Hayles (2005) highlights the specificity of code as an executable language for which neither the Saussurean semiotic definition of the differential and arbitrary nature of the linguistic sign nor the Derridean grammatological emphasis on the indeterminacy of the writing trace provides a proper account. The cascading processes that link electromagnetic voltage differences to high-level object-oriented languages are described as "interlocking chains of signifiers and signifieds" (45). However, the material constraints required for machine processing of voltage signifiers as signifieds at machine-code level limit the arbitrariness of the computer sign. Even if the digital computer works on the basis of differential relations between signals, code is highly constrained because the relation between signifiers and signifieds has to be stabilized if the machine is to work properly.

On the other hand, grammatological citability and iterability of writing emerge only at high-level object-oriented languages. Object-oriented programming languages have shaped the computer into an expressive medium. Considered as mediators between natural languages and binary code, programming languages foster an interactive dynamics between speech, writing, and code: syntax, grammar, and lexicon of natural language are incorporated into programming languages while algorithmic processes generate new forms and uses of language. The regime of computation depends on this machinic semiotic process, which in turn feeds back onto the practices of speech and writing (figure 1.18). Hayles (2005, 2008)

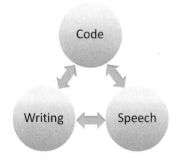

Figure 1.18
A diagrammatic representation of the performative dynamics of speech, writing, and code, according to N. Katherine Hayles's model (2005). © Manuel Portela, 2011.

captures this general interpenetration of human and computer languages (and of print and digital media) through the concept of intermediation.

Machinic processes of interpretation and execution imply that code is strongly performative since execution is an inherent feature of code as a form of language. The performativity of digital code acts is a consequence of the fact that at the machine level, writing and reading operations are executable behaviors performed by code, from high-level to low-level layers of operation. Material instantiations of visible, listenable, touchable, and readable forms result from the performance of the code at the machine-processing level. In turn, these material forms offer themselves for a perceptual and reading performance, suggesting the dual dimension of the performativity of electronic codes as a series of injunctions that links machine and human performance.

Wendy Hui Kyong Chun (2011) has offered a nuanced and granular description of the performance of code, looking at the material interactions of source code, machine code, and hardware. She has argued against the reification of software as the essence of new media, calling attention to the contingent and spectral condition of both code and interface. The prevailing understanding of software as the conflation between written command and execution ignores the differences among the various instantiations of code. Automatic executability of code depends on cascading processes between the symbolic and electronic levels of the machine. Its performativity is contingent on those processes. Readability of source code, for instance, implies that it can be compiled or interpreted by the machine as series of machine-readable commands, but also that its English-based commands are readable by humans. Through analysis of the performance of code in the machine and of the relations between code, user, and interface, a critique of the autonomy of the program becomes viable.

Philippe Bootz (2005b, 2006) has proposed the concept of performative sign, later substituted by the notion of "dual sign" (Bootz 2010, 2012), to account for the particular function of the machine in programmed literature. The work's material instantiation is partly generated as a response to the performance of the machine/program triggered by a reader's interaction with the work's algorithms. The layer introduced by the processing ability of the machine changes the role of the reader, splitting it between reading, as an affective and aesthetic perception of forms, and metareading, as a cognitive knowledge of the work's algorithm and overall structure. Bootz stresses the fact that the work/program is incomplete and depends for its actualization on data introduced by the reader during its execution. Programmed interactivity thus creates a semiotic gap between the author's text/program and the transient observable states displayed on the screen.[6]

Self-reflexive tropes and interactions in digital works attempt to highlight the particular semiosis of programmed works—the awareness that transformations that produce a domain of signs for the reader are the result of the technical processing of the domain of signs for the author. The machine processing connects these two sign domains, but reader's field and author's field remain partially unknown to each other. Authorial data and reader-introduced data have to be performed by the machine in its own nonhuman language before the reader can reperform them. Authorship and readability are iteratively mediated by the machine and the program. Reading interventions in programmed works thus take place at the levels of the textual instruments that generate new forms and interpreting the verbal and graphical semantics of the observable written and audiovisual forms. Machine performativity and reader's performativity are part of an entangled system: while the machine performs the code encapsulated in the program and in its array of interactions, the reader performs the codes as expressed through a particular interface and in the unique instantiations of relations between collections of signs originated by this machine-reader performance.

Increasingly embedded in objects, tools, and everyday activities, code is giving new forms to our social, cultural, and political practices. The present historical situation is characterized by our belief in the power of digital code for describing and modeling natural and social processes. This encoding of continuous processes in discrete machines becomes a self-fulfilling encoding of the human experience of the world, which in turn tends to be seen, apprehended, and modeled through iterations of code. Mark Marino (2006), Wendy Hui Kyong Chun (2006, 2011), Matthew Fuller (2008), and others have developed a software studies rationale concerned with the interpretative and ideological analysis of code. Code languages are seen as cultural texts that can be analyzed at the levels of both their programmability and their signifying and social effects.

Turing may have imagined computers as universal machines for decoding and producing human language, but programming languages show the fundamental and inescapable difference between code and language. Digital writers and artists have been experimenting with the complexities of the relations between code and language, offering a material critique of softwareness in human–machine interactions. The expression *codework* is generally used to describe works that explore programming and human language in ways that illuminate their relations and inflections. It can include the presence of formal programming languages within verbal text or uses of code that foreground software processing as an inherent element of the work. Code may appear as scripts that can be run—for example, in Nick Montfort's "ppg256" poetry generator series (started in 2007),[7] as pseudo-codes that conflate programming and verbal languages as in Mez's Mezangelle language system (1995 to the present),[8] or as both code and code-generated natural language—for example, in Talan Memmott's *Self Portrait(s) [as Other(s)]* (2003). Formal processes in those works direct attention to the relations and translations between various layers of code and language. They point to code as both a functional and a rhetorical tool in digital literature and highlight the coded nature of natural languages.

Codeness and programmability are used as explicit expressive elements in order to illuminate their function in the material production of text. Reflexive uses of digital codes can take the form of an explicit poetics of code in which verbal language and computer instructions are placed side by side. For instance, in *Sea and Spar Between* (2011), Nick Montfort and Stephanie Strickland have made extensive use of the comments field within the code in order to intersperse the executable language of the program with the nonexecutable English language that describes the program. Readers are brought into contact with the source code and are led to experience the layered, nested, abstract, and cascading nature of artificial languages. Reading the JavaScript program that implements the work, along with the comments on the functions and parameters that determine permutations and graphical structure, is a way of experiencing the multilayered poetics of networked programmable writing.

An aesthetic and cultural critique of the social functions of code objects permeates many artistic and literary works in new media. Several kinds of defamiliarization strategies have been used for showing the functions embedded in the software and, generally, in our networked practices with programmable media. Serge Bouchardon, for instance, has defunctionalized a whole range of interface and Internet practices, expectations, and experiences by turning them into playable textual games (*The 12 Labours of the Internet User*, 2008; *Touch*, 2009a). John Cayley's database poetics has defunctionalized Google searches by querying the servers for unindexed word strings and then generating new linguistic combinations (Cayley 2011; Cayley and Howe 2009–2011).

Of particular significance for the study of the performativity of reading acts are those codeworks whose reflexiveness is directed at general processes of reading inscriptional forms, including coded and multimodal forms of writing. Awareness of codes emerges from a process of affective attention to a performance of reading. A structured bodily and conceptual awareness of the interaction with the signifying codes is achieved through formal operations on the material signifiers. Formal interventions deconstruct the transparency of the electronic codes, making visible their algorithmic nature or graphical metaphors. Denaturalization of reading conventions can be achieved by creating a conflict between iconic layout and interface structure and genre expectations or designing an experience of the algorithm that shows how the work's material instantiation responds dynamically to reading inputs. Reading opens up to its own dynamic presence in exploring the programmed possibilities of association of signifiers at material surface.

The series "Petits poèmes à lecture inconfortable" (Uncomfortable reading little poems) (2005–2011) by Philippe Bootz is based on a conflict between noematic and ergodic readings. Readers have to manipulate textual elements in order to make them legible, but the act of manipulation produces new instances of illegibility. Unveiling and veiling are correlative operations, and reading is performed as a partial, fragmented, and untotalizable encounter with an ensemble of transient signs in motion. The first poem in the series "Le rabot poète" (The woodworking plane poet) (2005a) is only partially legible: words appear and disappear as the reader peels the various layers of text as she or he rotates, clicks, and drags its different elements, which disappear or dissolve into colored or white backgrounds (figure 1.19a). Words also disintegrate into their constituent letters, leaving readers suspended between visual patterns and verbal meanings. In the second poem in the series, "Petite brosse à dépoussiérer la fiction" (Small brush to dust off fiction, 2007), each writing scene generated by the program is covered by a textured gray opaque layer that the reader has to dust off to be able to read the underlying text (figure 1.19b). The foreground visual layer, however, keeps recovering the text, and the white dusted-off areas are only temporarily visible. Reading is expressed as a constant struggle with the dust that renders the text invisible.

In "Les amis sur le seuil" (Friends on the threshold) (2011), the third poem in the series, the production of meaning through reading acts also takes place at this threshold between illegibility and legibility. The wholeness of the text becomes inapprehensible, and the conflict between dexterity in manipulation and symbolic processing enacts the act of reading as a frustrating experience beyond the reader's control. The experience of liminality sustained by this conflict between manipulation and legibility leaves readers in between the inside and the outside of the text:

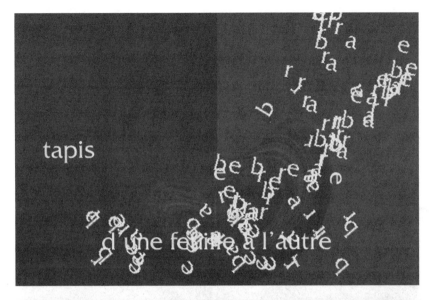

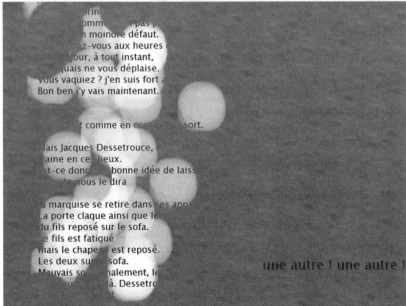

Figure 1.19
Philippe Bootz, (a) "Le rabot poète" (The woodworking plane poet) (2005), (b) "Petite brosse à dépoussiérer la fiction" (Small brush to dust off fiction) (2007), (c) "Les amis sur le seuil" (Friends on the threshold) (2011), from the series "Petits poèmes à lecture inconfortable" (Uncomfortable reading little poems) (2005–2011) (screen captures). © Philippe Bootz. Reproduced with permission.

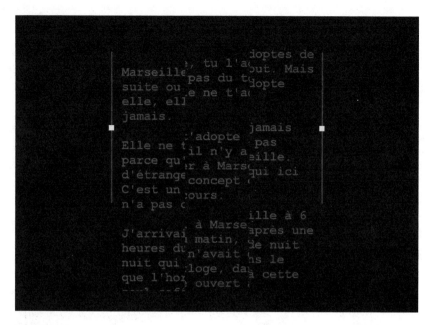

Marseille, tu l'adoptes de
suite ou ... pas du tout. Mais
elle, ell... e ne t'a... dopte
jamais.

Elle ne t... :'adopte jamais
parce qu'... il n'y a pas
d'étrange... :r à Mars... eille.
C'est un concept qui ici
n'a pas c... :ours.

J'arrivai... à Marse... ille à 6
heures du ... matin, après une
nuit qui ... n'avait de nuit
que l'hor... :loge, da... ns le
... ... ouvert ... à cette

Figure 1.19
(continued)

Friends on the threshold are thus within this inbetweenness of the encounter that constitutes the threshold: a place which is not really outside but which is not inside either, place of exchange, place of passage, undecided place. (Bootz 2011, my translation)[9]

Three unsynchronized strips of text move at different speeds across the screen. The middle one runs from bottom to top, independent of the reader's intervention, but the speed and direction of left-hand and right-hand strips can be controlled by the reader's hand. Two cursors can be moved along a line. The role of the reader is to move these cursors and change the speed and direction of the motion of the outer strips of text so that they match with the inner strip and make the text legible. However, the three strips never seem to quite fall into place, either because the outer strips of text run in opposite directions or at different speeds relative to the inner strip and relative to each other. Even when their velocity is more or less synchronized, they do not seem to verbally connect to each other or to the inner strip. It is as if the three strips did not belong in the same text, although the reader is under the constant impression that they are part of a coherent piece of writing, since similar lexical items and similar syntactic structures do run across the three cut-up segments (figure 1.19c).

The attempt to synchronize and fit the three running strips never really changes the player's uncomfortable reading position. Legibility and illegibility are in constant tension, and the reading of the text remains partial and fragmented. This conflict of eye motions, hand motions, and textual motions is Bootz's poetical way of undoing the act of reading and calling attention to the relation between ergodicity and interpretation in programmable works. This programming of reading rehearses the human physical and cognitive processing involved in recognizing codes and translating those codes into meanings. It also offers a simulation of the programmed text itself as an emergent network of interactions between author and reader mediated by algorithms. In the final textual sequences, the flickering and transient association of signifiers are shown through the decomposition of word and letter forms into their constituent black and white pixels.

In the following chapters, I look at codex and digital works that have been conceived and materially designed to make readers aware of their act of reading as a dynamic intervention in a field of signifiers. Disruption of typographic and bibliographic conventions has been used to show the presence of reading as an active element in the emergence of perceived form. Similarly, operations on software interfacing conventions and text-generating algorithms have been used to show the inflected nature of computer codes as meaning-generating practices that are codependent on reading inputs. The iterability of writing and the iterability of code are cognitively and affectively experienced through material interventions that choreograph the motions of reading as if they were scriptable in the works. I believe the analysis of reflexive uses of codes in codex and digital forms illuminates the performativity of reading acts in the constitution of signifying fields within each medium and also across media. This book is concerned with formal and material operations on bibliographic and electronic codes that attempt to capture the relational, interactive, and performative production of reading spaces.

1.7 Charting Fields

The aesthetic speculations and critical investigations contained in this book reflect my long-term fascination with the inner and outer workings of reading and writing. Many brilliant writers, artists, and researchers have examined the material, cognitive, and social semiotics of acts of reading within the current context of changing media ecologies. This section briefly describes the main fields of research that I have drawn on. My

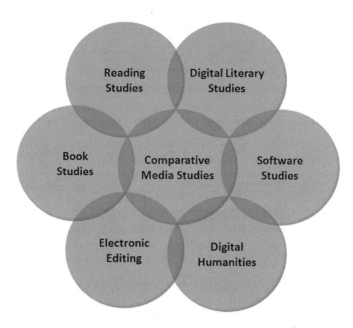

Figure 1.20
Intersections: A tentative chart of research field intersections in this book.

analysis of self-reflexivity and reading in print and programmable net-worked media is situated at the intersection of book studies, digital literary studies, and software studies. Other related fields, which have been equally relevant, include studies of reading, electronic editing, and comparative media studies (figure 1.20). Methods used combine close readings of print and intermedia works with graphical readings, characteristic of digital humanities methods, and they attempt to integrate cognitive, social, historical, and aesthetical perspectives into the material and formal analyses of artifacts.

At a moment when the codex form as the dominant model for the symbolic representation of the world and of human experience seems to be coming to an end, books emerge as one of the most powerful objects for the study of human cultures and societies, both ancient and modern. By means of book history and book studies, the codex recovers its pivotal role as a machine for knowledge. After witnessing the magic word revealed in religious experience, the rational word demonstrated in scientific experiment, and the poetic word embodied in literary experience, the book has become an archeological trace for all kinds of social and cultural transactions. The appearance of the book, described by Lucien Febvre and Henri-

Jean Martin in their seminal work, *L'apparition du livre* (1958), became the appearance of the book as an object of study and a privileged image of cultural processes in research carried out during the past fifty years. If this cultural history hypostasized the typographic codex as the materialization of the concept and form of the book, the invention of the electronic screen of multiple reinscription remediates and reconfigures long-established bibliographic codes. It opens up a new literary ecology that calls for a rethinking of the materiality and readability of the codex within the expanded writing and reading spaces of the digital age.

The expansion of book studies that began in the 1990s reflects theoretical developments internal to the field, but also this new context of networked digital media that fostered a heightened perception of the conditions of production and reception of books. Studies of the book published since then have produced detailed descriptions of its function in particular historical processes, resulting in a more complex conceptualization of its multiple dimensions as material and social artifact. Perhaps the most significant aspect has been the interdisciplinary integration of those dimensions, which enable the material artifact to be seen not only as the bearer of economic and social traces of a given mode of production, distribution, and reception but also as a powerful engine that interacts with its own embodied discourses (McKenzie 2004; McGann 1991; Johns 1998; Finkelstein and McCleery 2002; Darnton 2007, 2010; Price 2009). The methodological productivity of this integrated approach has been amply demonstrated in the history of reading (Chartier 1995; Saenger 1997; Cavallo, Chartier, and Cochrane 2003; Stewart 2006; Ablow 2010; Price 2012) and the study of artists' books and bookworks (McCaffery and Nichol 2000; Smith 1995; Drucker 1995, 1999, 2006a; Frost 2005; Stewart 2010, 2011).

Another component in this tentative charting of intersections between research fields can be identified rather loosely by the expression reading studies. I am not referring here to the study of reading as a historical or social practice, which could be subsumed in a broad definition of book history, but to cognitive studies about the processing of written signs. My analysis of codex and digital works as reading machines requires consideration of the cognitive and physiological processes involved in acts of reading perception. Sometimes formal operations are bibliographically and digitally materialized in ways that give readers awareness of their visual and haptic processing of those forms, as seen above. This feeling of reading has an evolutionary, cognitive, and neurological dimension that has been extensively studied in psychology and other disciplines (Snowling and

Hulme 2007; Wolf 2007; Dehaene 2009), for instance, in the context of studies of vision, attention, and perception (Rayner 2009) or in the context of electronic hypermedia literacy (Kress and Leeuwen 2001; Kress 2003; Mangen 2008; Hillesund 2010). Semantic processing of language and discourse in its relation to other material and intermedia features create a cognitive system in which an embodied self performs an embodied work through physical manipulation and affective interactions (Freeman 2008; Angel and Gibbs 2009, 2010).

Processes of remediation and intermediation between bibliographic and electronic technologies of inscription have been the focus of a large body of theoretical and critical work. This body can be subsumed under the general heading of electronic editing theories. The development of a rationale for editing and publishing our literary archive in the digital medium has direct relevance for the intermedia recoding issues considered here (McGann 2001; Schreibman, Siemens, and Unsworth 2004; Shillingsburg 2006; Frost 2008; Drucker 2006b, 2007, 2009a; Deegan and Sutherland 2009a ,2009b). The process of designing digital remediations of print works provides a new research context for testing our understanding of the functionalities and codes of book forms and conceptualizing the specific affordances of digital textuality beyond the mere contrast between print space and pixel space.

A third field of inquiry and research, which can be described as digital literary studies, originated with artists and theorists of electronic literature. Digital-born artifacts posed descriptive and theoretical challenges to traditional literary modes of perception and analysis. Programmability of networked media was adopted as a material basis for the production of new aesthetic experiences, such as generative text, animated text, interactive fiction, or network art, among many other forms and genres (see Hayles et al. 2006; Borràs et al. 2011). Medium-specific analysis has accounted for digital textuality and computer-mediated interactions through new concepts and new critical tools (Aarseth 1997; Murray 1998; Douglas 2000; Koskimaa 2000; Glazier 2002; Montfort 2003; Hayles 2002, 2005; Morris and Swiss 2006; Cayley 2004b, 2005, 2012; Bootz 2006; Engberg 2006, 2010; Gendolla and Schäfer 2007; Funkhouser 2007, 2012; Bouchardon 2007, 2009b; Saemmer 2007; Schreibman and Siemens 2008; Ryan 2008, 2010; Bootz and Baldwin 2010; Schäfer and Gendolla 2010; Simanowski, Schäfer, and Gendolla 2010; Simanowski 2011; Rosario 2011; Eskelinen 2012). Equally important, analyses of intermediality, programmability, variability, hybridism, and participation have been instrumental in the formulation of digital media theories (Bolter 2001; Bolter and Grusin 1999; Manovich 2001; Hayles 2008, 2012; Kirschenbaum 2008; Murray 2012).

Another related field is defined by the theoretical research that addresses programmability and the specifics of code in digital literary and artistic practices and also in the culture at large. A number of relevant books and articles could be placed within a software studies approach. Programming languages and algorithms, technological affordances of different platforms and programs, and the functional and rhetorical aspects of interface design, graphical metaphors, and data visualization are an integral part of the material and cultural layers of digital media. These and other software structures and practices are established objects of cultural and critical analysis (Cox, McLean, and Ward 2004; Cramer 2005, 2007; Marino 2006; Chun 2006, 2011; Vesna 2007; Fuller 2008; Manovich 2008; Wardrip-Fruin 2009). Discussion of the forms and functions of code in digital literature has also been taken up by various authors during the past decade (Raley 2002, 2006; Cayley 2002, 2003, 2006a, 2011; Glazier 2002, 2006; Baldwin 2003; Mateas and Montfort 2005; Bootz 2006; Pressman 2007; Engberg 2010; Bork 2009; Memmott 2011; Johnston 2011).

Analysis of information through automatic processing has expanded the methods of humanistic inquiry. Database building, algorithm design, textual encoding, structured searching, automated pattern and statistical analysis, data mining, and data visualization have been adopted across several disciplines. These and other technocultural practices are constitutive of the methods and modes of knowledge production known as digital humanities (McCarty 2005, 2010; Kirschenbaum 2010; Hayles 2010; Bartscherer and Coover 2011; Berry 2012; Gold 2012). Aggregation of information and collaborative online environments are also fostering new models of research organization and new scholarship practices (McGann et al. 2010; Deegan and McCarty 2012). In literary and cultural studies, computational techniques have been applied to both new and traditional corpora, enabling the formulation of new questions and new methods, such as distant reading (Moretti 2007), cultural analytics (Manovich, Douglass, and Huber 2011), and algorithmic criticism (Ramsay 2011).

Digital humanities is a mode of inquiry that explores the representational, modeling, and processing capabilities of digital media for marking up texts, visualizing natural and human landscape, visualizing data, simulating phenomena, and aggregating, structuring, searching for, and retrieving information. McCarty (2003) describes humanities computing as a common methodological ground that works in retroactive feedback with each discipline. Computational models receive methodological and theoretical input from specific disciplines. Conversely, the act of formalizing and designing digital models and analytical tools feeds back into the discipline. Moreover, computational methodologies are exchanged across disciplines. Interdisciplinary exchanges, which take place through what he describes as a "methodological commons," call on broader areas of knowledge. Intersections, feedbacks, and feedforward map the ensemble of knowledge exchanges that define humanities computing.

One of the consequences of the ubiquity and pervasiveness of digital media in our current social and artistic practices has been the emergence of comparative media studies within arts and humanities programs. The study of the literary and visual arts, for example, is being recontextualized within the ongoing transformation of art and cultural practices brought about by digital technologies. New teaching and research practices have already assimilated the comparative media studies approach in the study of artistic and cultural forms. The cross-over between new media theory and literary analysis that readers find here is the result of several years of teaching and researching literature, digital media, and book history. As an instance of comparative media studies, this book rehearses an intersection of those six briefly charted fields: book studies, reading studies, software studies, electronic editing, digital literary studies, and digital humanities.

My readings of codex and digital works experiment with the dynamics between machine and close reading at three related levels. First, focus constantly alternates between semiotic transactions and codex manipulation, thus objectifying the text and making the object readable at different scales of perception. Second, attention is directed at works engaged with digital textuality through reflexive operations that expose their condition as executable and readable forms dependent on code and interface manipulation. Third, this investigation examines remediation and intermediation retroactions between bibliographic and electronic codes as another source of insight into the workings of the performativity of reading. Bibliographic works and computer works that self-reflect on their readability, on the one hand, and theoretical and critical works that deal with forms of material reflexivity, on the other, circumscribe the creative and research fields most relevant for this study.

2 Codex Codes: Mapping a Choreography of Reading

2.1 Writing the Type

Despite containing many highly original creative investigations into the relations among narrative language, typography, and book form, Johanna Drucker's artist's books have received little critical attention. They constitute a remarkable aesthetic experiment in linking narrativity in language to narrativity in codex forms and typographic media. Her poetic exploration of the materiality of the printed codex is based on a large set of self-reflexive operations. As material investigations of the possibilities of print layout and narrativity, they show an impressive cultural and technical mastery. She has assimilated many print traditions, from modernist and postmodernist poetics to the popular press and the history of printing. Mostly self-produced in limited editions, her works cover a wide range of production techniques, including letterpress, offset, etching, and digital printing. Her stylistic and technical repertoire includes collage, drawing, illustration, poetry, fictional prose, and different styles of experimental typography. Typographical design is work specific (and sometimes even page specific), from typeface choice and paper selection to page layout and binding format.

Drucker's aesthetic engagement with print—and with written marks and visual codes in general as visual embodiments of language and signs—bridges her artistic and theoretical work. During the past decade, she has applied her deep poetic knowledge of the workings of print and codex forms to the digital medium in a sustained attempt to explain the relations between its material instantiations and its computational codes (Drucker 2009a, 2010, 2011). This reflection about signifying processes as functions of material mediations, including a sense of the self as a sign-produced site of experience and perception, has been repeatedly explored in many of her artist's books. In the catalog for an exhibition of her work held at Granary

Books, New York City, in June 1994, she offered this overview of her own work:

Books offered a private arena in which to express an ambitious and yet secret, intensely personal, investment of energy. My desire to make books combined a drive to write the world into being, to claim experience through its representation in language, with the desire to make closure and containment, to shut the word within the covers of a finished work held, saved, retained. Two themes run through the works: the first is the exploration of the conventions of narrative prose and the devices by which it orders, sequences, and manipulates events according to its own logic; the second is the use of experimental typography to expand the possibilities of prose beyond the linear format of traditional presentation. (Drucker 1994)

She conceives the ensemble of book materialities as this self-enclosing mirror where self and world come together in an intelligible order of signs. Experiments in typographic presentation and narrative prose have developed as codependent elements in her books, and both are part of a more general material investigation of the book as an experiential container and organizer of lived experience.

In her artist's books, she investigates the relation between the visuality of language as embodied in typography (typeface, type size, type style, typesetting, page layout) and narrativity as an effect of verbal montage within the full dynamics of codex structure. Page surface, page opening, and page turning offer further material dimensions in which the relations between typographic design and verbal narrative extend from the visual to the tactile and kinetic fields, in which eyes, hands, and body interact with the sign field maintained by codex space. There are many examples in her work in which recursive echoes among those three levels draw the reader's attention to the performance of reading as a particular embodiment of a given codex-typography-narrative dynamics. By means of specific formal operations, the book becomes a machine for creating self-awareness of codex codes through a self-referential rhetoric. Their bookness points to the specificity of their material form as books—the fact that as a signifying space, they cannot be reproduced by or translated into other media—and marks the codex as a signifier that repeatedly attempts to signify itself as a particular kind of experiential event.

I briefly analyze Drucker's aesthetic engagement with the materiality of the typographic book in two works: *From A to Z* (1977) and *The Word Made Flesh* (1989). Metareference to the material form and modes of production of letterpress books, one of the typographic and bibliographic tropes of those works, is also a feature in several of her works, which are structured on the basis of specific formal relations among typeface, page layout, paper properties, and book binding. Relations between verbal signs are strongly mediated by the way her works constantly display the dynamics of the printed book as manifested in the tensions among single page, page opening, and page sequence. She has developed a personal visual prose in which typographic and bibliographic structures become important narrative signifiers.

From A to Z (1977), a coded narrative about the community of artists and printers with whom an autobiographical narrator is working, contains a procedural restriction that makes narrative productivity a function of the individual sorts and pieces of type available in the type cases:[1]

The premise of this book was to take the type in 48 drawers of type, make a text that made sense, and use all of the elements in the fonts once and only once.

The type drawers were full and composition, though it often required moving from drawer to drawer, was fairly straightforward for introductory sections. Picking type faces to match character styles and then setting the original "poems" on the recto of the sheets was the next step, and editing was often required as type ran short. The setting of the back sides of each character page required three steps. First, all the sorts left in the case had to be set up and proofed, then they had to be arranged on paper, as in a scrabble game of punning sense. The setting into a final form came after, with pressure to use as many of the sorts as possible. (Drucker 1977, project statement)

Thus, the frequency of occurrence of any given letter in the text mirrors the quantity of sorts available for uppercase and lowercase type in each drawer. The effect of the procedural constraint becomes clearer in the recto pages, where scarcity of available type results in character omissions, abbreviations, and visual and phonetic puns. The representations of words through letter or number sounds and of letters through number shapes are two instances of the typographic and orthographic recoding of typesetting and spelling conventions caused by the work's procedure. This reference to the mode of production points to the formal features of type (face, size, style), its materiality as a metal piece that leaves an inscriptional mark on paper, and also its economic nature as a given amount of available production capital embodied in one of the tools required for printing.

As a procedural work, it turns the typographic alphanumeric characters, including punctuation signs and other special characters, into one of the content layers of the book. Its self-imposed constraint of using only a limited set of type means that its narrative content has to be adjusted to its typography. Linguistic combinations will be partially determined by typographic possibilities, thus translating the medium back into narrative content and structure. The writing alphabet is reframed as typesetting alphabet: letters are not only an abstract inked mark on paper but also the individual metal types used for making those marks. In *From A to Z*, the visual layout (the topographic organization of the page, the syntax of pages, and the montage of its narrative sequences) inscribes the materiality of the mode of production within the text's narrativity. Its exploration of the combinatorial potential of the written alphabet as an extension of the syntactic nature of verbal language is experienced as a fully material encounter with typography as material artifact. Language is embodied as writing, and writing is embodied as typography, thus heightening our perception of the material determinants of printed narrative as a particular mode of production of language as writing.

The generative power of the constraint can be seen, for instance, in the subversion of orthographic spelling, which is either replaced by characters that are partially similar in terms of visual or sound form or simply omitted and inferred from set sequences: "Sum' SORtS (...) WAS, US'D, UP, AND, SUM, WAS, LeFT, OV'R, AND. OF, A, HUNN'RD, COPI'S. ZIS. ON', IZ, NUMB'R::::::": (figure 2.1). This principle of simplification eliminates orthographical redundancies and produces readable sequences that recode writing conventions. The act of setting type and the quantification of its economic value as a given number of set pages is sometimes referred to in the verso of several folios: "$9.=,25Pps." (p. 10) "$15$.--,,29Pp." (20). As a personal autobiographic project, *From A to Z* contains marks of its production at formal, biographical, and economic levels. Texts are forced to acknowledge their limitations in telling themselves through self-reference to typographic availability and scarcity. Self-description and marginal annotations split the narrative into several layers of ironic commentary that constantly downplay the text's own authority (figure 2.2).

The fact that the work contains running marginal notes adds a parodic dimension to its form as a book, mocking its own descriptive pretensions while signaling a particular kind of annotated book: the annotated bibliographic list. Because its narrative attempts to describe the relations between the individuals in the print workshop, and particularly an imaginary love "nonrelationship" between A and Z, its reference to the means of production may be said to include the social and affective relations of production. Letters are metaphorical embodiments of the dramatis personae of the story: "A: Miss East Coast uptight hot shit coed—just so smart and attractive and well educated and able to play it all right"; "Z: Very Ivy League graying prematurely and into the distinction it lent him—good family, good education, & good prospects, nice inheritance—poor fellow" (Drucker 1977, 65). A careful reading of its coded allusions also highlights the power

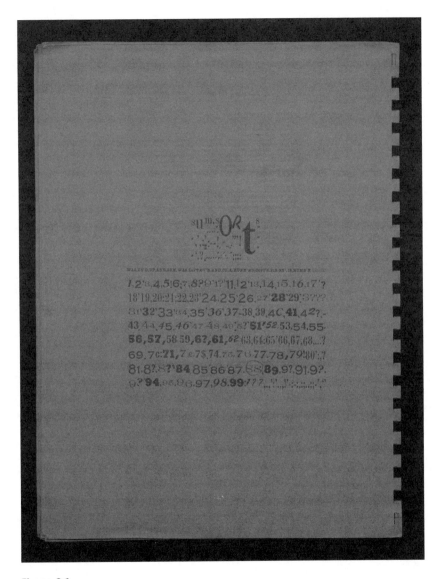

Figure 2.1
Johanna Drucker, *From A to Z* (1977), colophon, p. 66. Original size: 7.375 × 12 inches. © Johanna Drucker. Reproduced with permission.

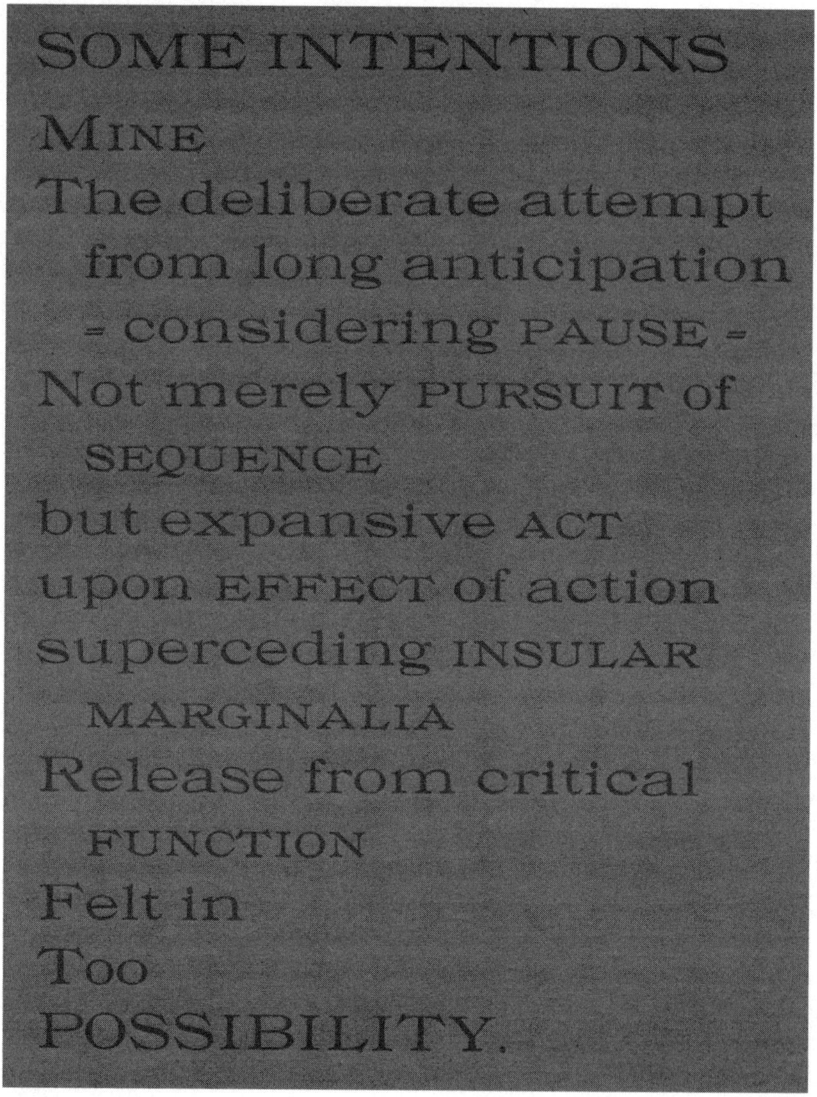

SOME INTENTIONS
MINE
The deliberate attempt
from long anticipation
= considering PAUSE =
Not merely PURSUIT of
SEQUENCE
but expansive ACT
upon EFFECT of action
superceding INSULAR
MARGINALIA
Release from critical
FUNCTION
Felt in
Too
POSSIBILITY.

Figure 2.2
Johanna Drucker, *From A to Z* (1977), p. 9, detail. © Johanna Drucker. Reproduced with permission.

relations that structure the affective and productive positions within this print community. *From A to Z* narrates the print workshop as a catalog of typographic types and human types. Narrative content of the description is a function of the symbolic power of type.

The tension between description and self-description never allows the reader to entirely leave the surface of the page. This visual anchor is the source of recurrent formal echoes between medium and content, that is, for constructing the reader's awareness of the semantic value of visual difference. Typographic layout and book structure become crucial elements in the work's meaning as readers are forced to notice again and again the recodification of spelling and typesetting conventions that is taking place as they try to read. Changes in type and layout are the result of the constraint imposed on the number of fonts, styles, and characters available at each stage of composition. Thus, the deciphering of coded allusions to the various relationships between the characters in the story is mirrored in the deciphering of the phonetic and visual puns as each piece of available type can be made to stand in for various letterforms. The drawers of type and the letterpress itself are written into the narrative.

2.2 Fleshing the Word

In *The Word Made Flesh* (1989) the layering of verbal and typographic meaning is equally complex (figure 2.3). The text offers several typographic reading paths that superimpose on the page. Paths are created by a basic rectangular grid that governs the arrangement of type on the page. This grid has about 19 (horizontal) × 14 (vertical) character positions on each page, or about 266 possible positions. Spaces between the grid's intersection points are sometimes distributed unevenly, which adds to the dynamism within and between the red and black layers of type. The use of two print colors (red and black), and the expressive use of other font properties create two reading trajectories: a background same-size-capital red text, of which each letter is symmetrically set at the grid's points of intersection, and a foreground varying-size black text that is set over the grid, thus interrupting and breaking the background pattern. Because the foregrounded text uses contrasting type sizes and styles, the result is a dynamic engagement of readers in deciphering words and sentences while moving between the background and foreground plane. This play with the materiality of type forms (font, size, style, kerning, leading, baseline, height) enacts the meaning of the title in the experience of trying to make sense of words and sentences at their basic material level.

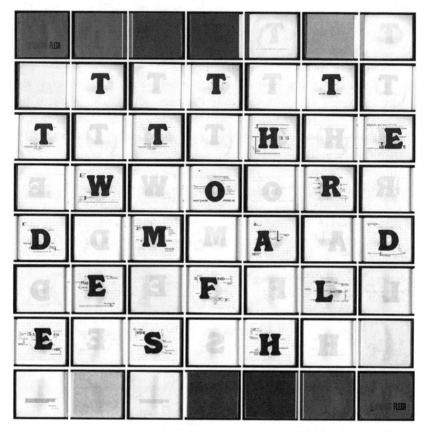

Figure 2.3
Johanna Drucker, *The Word Made Flesh* (1989), page sequence. Original size: 12.6 × 10.6 inches. © Johanna Drucker. Reproduced with permission.

The Word Made Flesh further denaturalizes print by combining different fonts, sizes, and styles in the same words and sentences, a stylistic feature called *paragonnage*. Several words are made to share the same character, which runs across two or more lines, as happens with all the letters in the phrase "THE WORD MADE FLESH." These sixteen characters (which are in fact twenty, because the *T* occurs five times) define diagonal reading trajectories within the basic horizontal and vertical typesetting grid. Large-scale letters themselves become the material center of this typographic narrative as they spread across the pages. The tension between letter sequence and letter constellation on each page increases the verbal tension between the lyrical and narrative/reflective threads in this work. At the same time, readers are forced to pause and consider the particular shape of the letter as if they were looking for the type to set the text. Reading becomes a typographic experience because it emulates part of its particular production history.

The setting of type is made present in the reading of the text. The typographic embodiment of the word becomes a figure for the creation of the human through language. Drucker (1989) stresses this dialectics between the word-made-flesh and the flesh-made-word: "This project worked as a book on the strength of the typographic argument. The theme of word made flesh and the counter theme (written in the red copperplate field) of the flesh made word, are so completely integrated into the presentation, and in such an unequivocal, graphically striking manner, that the theoretical issues are rendered explicitly." Drucker also refers to her page design as a relationship between field and figure, stressing the visuality of the *T* as an emblem of the cross: "The black texts are meant to 'figure' against the red ground, as the images of Christ, a cross, or other devotional images are called out in *carmina figurata*."[2]

Readers experience the temporality and spatiality inherent in codex structure as a syntactic arrangement of folios and pages as they shift back and forth between a self-enclosed constelled page and a continuing typographic narrative. Because the title-sentence is written across twenty recto pages ("TTTTTHEWORDMADEFLESH"), the work suggests a homology between syntactic structures in language and syntactic structures in codex. Page sequence establishes the basic syntax of codex forms, while type variations are a specific occurrence or instance of an abstract system of differences that guarantees the identity and semantic productivity of typography as a semiotic system. The initial sentences of the text echo the Saussurean conceptual dichotomy between langue/parole, and the Chomskian distinction between deep and surface syntactic structures: "A l'interieur de la/du langue/age" (3), "I" (5), "I/T" (7), "I/T / LAY / the tongue" (9), "The tongue LIES ON THE TABLE" (11), "The tongue LIES ON THE TABLE / writing, writhing, spelling out THE breath of its efforts in an unseemly desire to be seen / A stick taken up in defense of THE world marks THE struggling back of THE folds of skin" (13, 15). The corresponding background red text (which appears for the first time on page 15) reads: "ALL THE WATERS, ELEMENTS AND PRIMAL FISHES BROKE THROUGH AIR AROUND US INTO TONGUES. HOW WAS THE TRACE OF DISPLACEMENT INTO PALE AIR MADE INTO SPEECH BY A BREAKING WAVE OF CHANCE? ALL TH NIGHTS, BROKEN GLAS." This running red text on language concludes: "SIGNS OF MONUMENTALITY, SUGGESTIONS AND

RECONDITIONED BODIES MANIFEST THEMSELVES LONG ENOUGH TO
BE RECOGNIZED ACCORDING TO THE DELICATELY NUANCED PACE OF
ARTICULATION OF A RAW AND PASSIONATE TONGUE" (45).

Drucker is thinking about typography and codex in terms of a system
of differences that has a fully syntactic expression. The syntactic recursivity
of language is made to mirror the syntactic recursivity of typography as a
combination of type units and of the codex as a combination of page units.
The productivity of the recombination of those units is shown through a
process of accretion that, at each turning of the leaf, keeps adding new
verbal elements to form sentences and new typographic patterns that
eventually extend to the full space of the page. The act of being inside
language (and inside the printed book as a reliving of the origin of language) is dramatized in the work's generative development from blank
page to one character, to a few words, to full sentences, to an entire discourse. Furthermore, the production of self in language and its inscription
within the codex has been objectified in the initial transition between *I*
(5) and *IT* (7). The codex transubstantiates the word by giving it, as it were,
a visual and material existence that seems to give flesh to meaning. The
very consciousness of self emerges as a linguistic function, that is as a
particular product of the empty flesh of signifiers.

In *The Word Made Flesh,* the incarnation of the word is obtained by self-
referring to its typographical layout through a given reading performance.
But this embodiment of the word is made to take the flesh of paper as well.
The inscriptions of ink on the surface of paper are experienced not just as
a series of abstract formal differences that replicate the differential system
of language or a given discourse as a specific cultural and narrative instance
of language structures and ideological content. Folios are printed on the
recto side of a semitransparent paper, which allows the following recto
page to show through and also for the recto to be seen from the verso
(figure 2.4). Instead of a printing error, the printed matter that can be seen
from the other side of a leaf projects type and word onto codex space. The
typographic layering of the two main reading trajectories extends to
the three-dimensionality of leaf and codex. Semitransparency has made
the visibility and tactility of paper into another semantic layer of the work.
Printed words can be experienced not just as inked inscriptions but as
paper objects. In *The Word Made Flesh,* type and paper are structural components of the meaning of the text. To read *The Word Made Flesh* is a
renewed optical and tactile relation with its self-consciously crafted printness and bookness.

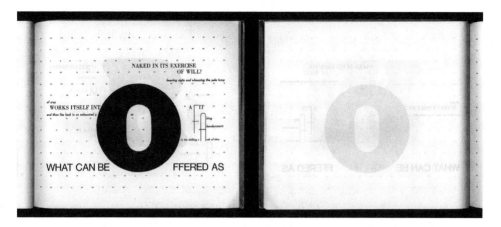

Figure 2.4
Johanna Drucker, *The Word Made Flesh* (1989), pp. 23, 24. Original size: 12.6 × 10.6 inches. © Johanna Drucker. Reproduced with permission.

Self-reflexivity in codex works contains useful critical insights about the semantic possibilities opened up by formal interventions at the various levels of a book's materiality. Drucker's aesthetic experiments with the materialities of codex codes call attention to the various ways in which they choreograph readers' interactions with the ensemble of codex inscriptions and structured motions. Her use of visual space, tactility, and typography points to their function as bibliographic notations for performing specific reading motions. They enable readers to experience the role of material differences in sustaining the virtual imaginary space created by the feedback between language and book forms. A general theory of self-reflexive formal operations in books as they have been explored in artists' books will provide a more powerful description of writing and reading acts as they are constituted through codex and other book codes.

2.3 Bibliographic Codes

The concept of bibliographic code that I am using here may be said to have two genealogies: one was formulated within the fields of historical bibliography and the social theory of editing, which examined the symbolic functions of the material aspects of text (McKenzie 2004; McGann 1991, 1993; McLeod 2004); the other developed in the field of book art studies, focusing on the expressive function of book forms and structures

(Smith 1995; Drucker 1995), including in its "demediated" bookwork embodiments (Stewart 2010, 2011). Intersections between textual criticism and book studies were also favored by the practice of electronic editing during the past two decades. Expansion of electronic textuality and the ongoing massive remediation of printed and manuscript books as digital files have furthered the critical modeling of books. Awareness of the semiotic functionalities of bibliographic forms stems from this historical combination of textual research and aesthetical investigation with digital technology.

The possibility of editing books (i.e., specific editions and copies with all their bibliographic markers) instead of just editing texts was claimed by Jerome McGann in "The Rationale of Hypertext" (1996). Bibliographic codes (the material semiotics of the book) are part of a text's social and historical dynamics, performing specific expressive and signifying functions. The bibliographic rationale of electronic representations of books would raise our awareness of the specific function of bibliographic elements in their relation to linguistic and other visual codes. Through remediation of the multiplicity of material forms that constitute a book, subject to the double logic of character and pixel codes of electronic representation, the "double helix of grammatological and bibliographical codes" (McGann 1991, 154) could be studied through the differential dynamics created by remediation. It also followed from this hypertext rationale that archival hierarchies between types of documents could be freed from fixed relations and become decentered and reconfigurable: "As with the nodes on the Internet, every documentary moment in the hypertext is absolute with respect to the archive as a whole, or with respect to any subarchive that may have been (arbitrarily) defined within the archive" (McGann 2001, 73–74).

The use of books for modeling books, which had been the basis for the critical edition rationale in textual and bibliographic studies since the Renaissance, was thus challenged by the use of networked computers for modeling books. Digital representation of codex texts became a thriving field, as testified by many scholarly archival and editing projects in electronic media. The need to edit texts for digital environments has led textual and literary critics to reexamine the bibliographic codes of literary texts in order to produce more accurate models of book structures and books forms. McGann has described the dynamics of textuality in autopoietic fields according to six dimensions: linguistic, graphical/auditional, documentary, semiotic, rhetorical, and social (2004). Historical and theoretical analyses of the socialization of texts have also contributed to a representation of editing and reading acts as performative practices constitutive of literary events.

Borrowing from speech-act theory, Peter L. Shillingsburg (2006) proposed the concept of "script act" to account for the multidimensionality of any inscriptional and reading event. The performativity of "script acts" refers to both acts of reproduction and acts of reading. Conceptualization of inscriptional practices in terms of the pragmatics of speech acts means the integration of the formal and social materialities of writing and reading interactions. His theory of electronic scholarly editing is based on this view of scripting practices. An electronic infrastructure for script acts becomes an interactive metarepresentation of complex networks of genetic and social documents. Shillingsburg ascribes four major functions to this electronic infrastructure: "textual foundation," "contexts and progressions," "interpretive interactions" and "user enhancements" (101–102). One important realization of this model is that the representation of print and manuscript corpora as a network of interrelated script acts becomes inscribed with the affordances and functionalities of the new medium and its own contexts of use.

The hypertext rationale generally implies digitizing and structuring the materials in ways that give a metarepresentational function to the process of decentering and reconstellating digital modules as image and text files. Digital surrogates of book parts point to both their analog originals and their condition as digital remediations. The electronic edition becomes reconfigured as an archive that attempts to make explicit the editorial frames that have produced each textual form in its past bibliographic materiality. Texts are pluralized in their various authorial, editorial, and material forms. They are also renetworked within large ensembles of production and reception documents, which in turn are subject to the affordances of computer-mediated analysis and communication. The representation of texts and images as a networked, aggregated, and socialized archive is a way of testing a theoretical approach by exploring specific features of the electronic writing and reading space as simulatory environment. Metarepresentation of codex forms through markup tags, metadata, and database models provides the occasion for a critical encounter with both the bookness of the book and the digitality of the hypermedia database, including its procedural, encyclopedic, navigational, self-documentary, participatory, and socializing affordances.

Several scholarly electronic textual editing projects of the late 1990s and early 2000s have generally adopted a hypertext rationale in which the source bibliographic codes are at once enhanced and metamorphosed by the new environment. This is the case of text-and-image digital archives such as the *Rossetti Archive* (McGann 1993–2008), *Dickinson Electronic Archives* (Smith 1994–2012), *The William Blake Archive* (Eaves, Essick and Viscomi 1996–2012), *The Walt Whitman Archive* (Folsom and Price 1995–2012), and *Artists' Books Online* (Drucker 2006c). The representation of texts and books in *Artists' Books Online* combines bibliographic and textual criticism with the hypertext rationale, which has become a standard approach for electronic textual editing:

> The core of *ABsOnline* is the presentation of artists' books in digital format. Books are represented by descriptive information, or metadata, that follows a three-level structure taken from the field of bibliographical studies: work, edition, and object. An additional level, images, provides for display of the work from cover to cover in a complete series of page images (when available), or representative images. (Drucker 2006b)

Johanna Drucker has eloquently argued for the importance of modeling the functionality of e-space in ways that reflect a thorough understanding of the dynamics of book structures, but also in ways that go beyond the structures of the book and take full advantage of the capabilities of digital materiality in networked environments. These include continuing reconfiguration of data, possibility of tracking and marking changes in electronic documents, aggregation of documents and data, and creation of intersubjective exchanges (Drucker 2009a). Designing a digital archive for books depends on the best possible articulation between presenting and representing the source materials and inscribing that representation in the specifics of the database ontology and algorithmic functionalities of networked digital materiality. Digital representation of books is where bibliographic codes confront the specifics of digital codes.

The representation of texts and images as a networked, aggregated, and socialized archive is also a way of testing new theoretical approaches and exploring heuristic features of the electronic writing and reading space. Matthew Kirschenbaum (2008) has produced a complex and inflected understanding of the cascading forensic and formal processes within the digital computer and of the ways in which these programmed signifying processes become subject to multiple social materialities. Engagement with bibliographic and electronic materialities in the act of creating digital archives has contributed to a better understanding of the nature, functionalities, and autopoietic features of each medium.

Despite the ambitious research projects of the past twenty years, we still lack a model of bibliographicality that can be adequately translated into electronic codes. Most projects have been based on a documentary facsimile principle: they use image files to represent pages in digital format and a hypertext structure to emulate codex structure. The codex is virtually disassembled into its constituent single pages or, less frequently, into openings, which are then represented as single image files. The book's internal table of contents is usually supplemented by a Web table of contents that links to individual pages. This mode of remediation results from the fact that the tridimensionality and multiple materialities of book forms have to conform to the planographic inscriptional surface of photoelectronic screens. Screen-conformant books thus have to virtualize the codex's third dimension and its physicality. Visual layers and interactive simulations are sometimes added in order to emulate the tactile and kinetic space of the book.

The transparency effect obtained by the remediated digital facsimile obscures the difference between image file and paper page, but this transparency functions in a hypermediated tension with a more or less elaborate graphical and critical apparatus for electronic manipulation. Electronic manipulation requires disassembling the codex into the modularity of its pages, stored as image files and restructured as a database that readers can access through particular interface functionalities, including search parameters and hypertext navigation. To the extent that graphical space and codex space perform signifying functions, textual transcription of written language as character strings is usually combined with its textual inscription into bitmapped image files that capture the page's graphical dimensions. Additionally, the codex dynamics of openings and turning pages has to be translated into a hypertext navigational structure. Electronic representation of book forms seems to depend on an adequate interaction among those three layers: character strings, graphical spaces, and book structures.

If bibliographic codes are part of a book's signifying process, representing books in electronic archives requires adequate modeling of page dynamics and codex structures. This attempt at translating book codes into electronic codes has become a major theoretical and technical issue in digital archives devoted to imaginative works. Modeling books for electronic presentation provides an opportunity for engaging with the various formal material codes that constitute the book as a signifying artifact. Because artists' books often make their bookness part of their meaning, they are particularly useful for understanding the nature of the codex and other book structures as signifiers. Electronic modeling of bibliographic operations in artists' books raises our awareness of the complex dynamics between material and conceptual spaces in book forms.

2.4   Recoding Bookness

As a specific art form, artists' books originated in the early twentieth-century historical avant-garde and came of age in the second half of the century. Johanna Drucker singles out the work of Swiss-German artist Dieter Roth (1930–1998) in the 1950s and 1960s as the first full realization of this new concept of the book as artistic form:

> Roth is the first artist to make books the major focus for his work and to engage with the book as an art work—not a publication or vehicle for literary or visual expression, but as a form in itself. Though early avant-garde artists had experimented with books, stretching their conventions, they did not take these conventions of format and structure as the subject matter for the making of books in the way Dieter Roth does. There would be no way to translate a Dieter Roth book into another medium—the idea of the works is inseparable from their form as books and they realize themselves as works through their exploration of the conceptual and structural features of a book. (Drucker 1995, 75)

The notion that in artists' books the entire dynamics of the book becomes an art form of its own is a crucial critical and aesthetic criterion in Drucker's historical survey. In her poetics of book forms, what makes an artist's book an artist's book is its degree of self-referential bookness. It is precisely this integral treatment of the book form that makes artists' books useful for thinking through the problem of representing or migrating book forms to digital forms.

If artists' books are so medium specific that they cannot be translated into any other medium, what happens when we remodel or re-create them for a digital environment? How can we represent a book's bookness in electronic form? Can we represent what an artist's book tells us about book spaces and about book structures in general? Or what it tells us about its own bookness by means of its internal echoes between meaning and structure, between conceptual space and material form, between verbal content and graphic form? How do we model a book's bookness so that it can be recoded, represented, and simulated in electronic format? What elements of its artistic form cannot be electronically emulated, marked, or described? What elements of its bibliographic code can be recreated, preserved, or evoked? These are some of the questions embedded in *Artists' Books Online*, a digital archive possessed of the paradoxical desire of remediating what cannot be remediated.

As part of the current migration of bibliographic forms into new media, *ABsOnline* partakes of the general belief in the power of digital representation as a technology for knowledge production. The mode of knowledge production fostered by computers is driven by the aggregation of vast corpora of files structured as databases. And this is also what happens to the digital surrogates of books: they are segmented into a series of constituent parts according to the possibilities of the digital archive and the imagined taxonomies required for search, analysis, and retrieval. The syntactic articulation established by a given book structure has to be broken down for the bitmapping of its visual surfaces. Once these page surfaces become separate files in the database, they become available for reconfigurations available at the metalevel of the archive. These archival reconfigurations are made possible by the particular mode of the existence of book works as digital files. Reproducibility takes the form of digital surrogates that tear the book apart and allow various types of analysis and manipulation. The particular connection between tactile and visual space embodied in the works' formal operations on their own codes as books has been substituted by visual emulations and verbal descriptions of those connections.

A book is an ensemble of interrelations between thematic and material concerns that make up a discrete entity, whose structure, in its codex form, is conventionally composed of standard-size pages fixed in a rigid sequence. Hence Johanna Drucker's point about the basic idea of the book: "the presentation of material in relation to a fixed sequence which provides access to its contents (or ideas) through some stable arrangement" (Drucker 1995, 123).[3] Several types of variation on these conventions of uniform and intentional sequence have been explored in artists' books: variations created by binding structures that change the sequence of or access to the pages; variations in the degrees of translucence in the paper or materials used that can create other internal spaces within or across the pages; variations achieved by changing the structure of signatures into folds; variations produced by the use of hybrid structures, which combine binding and folding and by the use of spatial forms that extend beyond the limits of the codex; and variations created by interior spaces within the codex structure, such as books within books or books that contain discrete interior spaces, for example, as folded or cut-out pages.

One of the basic dualities of codex semiotics is the duality between flow (the scroll-like continuous reading surface) and break (the discontinuity between pages). Drucker (1995) refers to this duality as the "basic internal dialogue of a book form" (140). One of the most productive features of codex structure is the fact that pages and openings can be accessed at any point in the sequence, a property that Lev Manovich (2001) describes as the random access property of codex forms and is one of the reasons for the enduring appeal of the codex form as a perfect integration of design and function. The tension between discreteness of page surface as a unit and sequence of the codex structure as a whole provides the basic syntactic articulation for the book's material spaces. The relation between this material syntax and its thematic and conceptual content is what may be described as the semantics of a specific codex form. Mark Danielewski's novel *Only Revolutions* (2006) is a recent example of a systematic use of this tension between codex sequence and page unit to produce narrative and poetic tension. In *Only Revolutions*, bibliographic coding and narrative coding illuminate each other and they have to be deciphered, played with, and interpreted in conjunction (see chapter 5 in this book).

In artists' books, meaning is also a function of the dynamic relation between a specific operation at the level of codex structure and the way that operation feeds back (or forward) into the book's visual, verbal, tactile, and spatial dimensions. Readers are required to read the form of the book and experience their particular interaction with its form as part of the signifying process. From a social text perspective, the interaction between linguistic and bibliographic code takes place by the very existence of a material book even when its code is not subject to expressive authorial interventions. Bibliographic codes do not have to be explicitly thematized in order to work: various social agencies manifest themselves in the ways texts become codified in certain bibliographic forms. Those codes, which express themselves through the choice of materials, formats, layout, binding, and other elements, function as a set of subconscious conventions in the social and individual performance of reading. In the case of artists' books, reading bibliographic codes becomes a conscious and explicit element in the pragmatics of reading: authors explore those codes as cognitive, expressive, and rhetorical devices, and readers are expected to read those embodiments of bookness into the meaning of the work. The book has to be read as a total material artifact that sustains the virtuality of its world of meanings through reading interactions with its multiple inscriptional spaces.

Self-reflexivity in artists' books can take the form of both an interrogation of the structure of the book and a conscious record of its production process. Besides, artists' books often combine self-reflection on their condition as books with self-reflection on their condition as artistic objects. Self-reflexivity directs our attention to the ways in which the materials used, page size and shape, page structure, letter forms, images, binding, and other material and formal properties interact with the work's visual and verbal meaning. By pointing to the particular syntax, semantics, and pragmatics of codex, and other book structures, bibliographic coding in artists' books reveals how complex the topological structure and conceptual space of books can be. Because they make the book itself an expressive medium deeply entangled with its verbal and visual codes, the use of bibliographic codes in artists' books challenges the possibility of media translation.

2.5 Translating the Codex

Digital media have been used as tools for representing all sorts of books from our collective bibliographic archive and as tools for remaking the forms of the book. The representation of book forms as digital files that are to be accessed through screen interfaces forces us to think through the specificity of each medium. Another way of looking at the interaction between digital media and codex forms is to examine the ways in which the use of digital tools, such as desktop publishing, has affected the visual and physical form of the actual artifact. In fact, this interaction is marked in artists' books produced since the early 1990s. While artists' books produced in the 1960s, 1970s, and 1980s used mostly analogical composing and printing techniques and media (such as offset, letterpress, linoleum cuts, etching, engraving, photocopying, collage, montage, and assemblage), in recent decades we find that the use of digital media has given new artistic form to codex structures, particularly in relations between image pixels and character pixels at the page surface level. Digital tools are being used to reform codex language and expand the visual vocabulary of page layout. Besides, desktop publishing has made it easier for artists to gain full control over the execution stages, particularly for those not trained in offset, letterpress, or etching media.

The use of digital photography and digital printing to produce limited editions is one instance of this conflation between old and new media, as we can see in *abecê: Mexico City Book 2* (2004), by Joan Lyons. This book, which represents graffiti as a sort of linguistic and cultural entry into a foreign language, combines traditional production techniques with digital printing of digital photos. The effects of digital page layout and digital page setting are evident in many artists' books. In Drucker and Freeman's *Emerging Sentience* (2001), for example, the graphical possibilities created by digital design (at the level of image, letterforms, and page design) have become a central focus of the work. Its many-layered image effects obtained by algorithmic filters and the compositional plasticity afforded by digital type are used as a self-reflection on the work's materiality as both paper codex and computer product. Self-awareness as an emergent property of intelligent systems thus becomes embodied in its material form, which points to the exploration of new forms of book embodiments provided by digital intermediation.

If this kind of self-reflexivity is such an important element in artists' books, how can there be an adequate electronic representation of the manifold codex dimensions, such as materials, structure, physicality, dimensionality, and texture? If we look at the electronic editions of Tom Phillip's *A Humument* and Lewis Carroll's *Alice's Adventures Under Ground*, we will see that in both cases, this representational dilemma has been addressed by means of a slide projection of digital facsimiles that simulates the act of turning over the pages (figures 2.5 and 2.6). This kind of interactive and animated graphic interface is now used by many libraries, museums, and publishers and has become a conventional application in mobile devices. While they are intuitive and suggestive as electronic rep-

Figure 2.5
The book as slide show: Tom Phillips, *A Humument: The Complete 4th Edition*, online edition, 2008. (screen capture) © Tom Phillips. Reproduced with permission.

Turning the Pages may take more than a minute to load.

Figure 2.6
Clicking the pages: Lewis Carroll's *Alice's Adventures Under Ground* (1864) (screen capture). British Library Add. MS 46700, online edition, 2006. © British Library. Reproduced with permission.

resentations of the abstract function of sequence in codex structures, they also show the limitations of electronic media for accommodating other physical materialities—for example, the textures of paper, ink, and paint that are so important in those two works—and, generally, the three-dimensional topologies of codices and other book structures. Medium-specific tactile and topological features tend to become flattened and homogenized in screen presentation. Body motions particular to certain book forms can be captured when a video clip is used to choreograph a reader's embodied engagement with the physical object, but they are hardly translatable into screen refreshes.

Screen simulation has the potential to bring to light hidden bibliographic codes, but it can also lead to a transparency effect that obliterates the distinction between paper and screen textures and leads to the reduction of a book's multidimensionality to the smooth surface of electronic screen and mechanistic simulations of its form. Because of these formal and material specifics, digital recoding of artists' books may help to clarify how bibliographic codes, and particularly codex codes, work. Failures of representation highlight those features that cannot be represented in digital media, thus contributing to a better modeling of both codex dynamics and digital materiality. The ongoing mass digitization of books takes advantage of the storage and simulacral capabilities of digital media for turning books into modular units of an ever-growing archive. Once the various textual and file modularities exist in a electronic network, connections within and between them can be variably reconfigured according to the associative logic of hypertext. These migration and translational processes open up the forms and structures of the book, which becomes a virtual field of connections and possibilities beyond the hierarchical relations of book and hypertext archive.

Drucker's critical work on digital media (2008a, 2009a, 2009b, 2010, 2011) can be described as an attempt at freeing the new medium from its dependence on a mechanistic emulation of the book and as a way of realizing the potential inherent in the medium's specific mode of virtuality. This engagement with electronic space implies a more complex modeling of the book's functionalities, that is, a conceptual and technological move that imagines electronic spaces beyond both the horizon of book forms and the current design of computer forms. It is precisely at this crux of modeling books for the electronic space and exploring the plasticity of electronic codes for creating nonbibliographic interactive spaces that we may place her poetical and critical claim for speculative computing. The difficulties of realizing this critical imagination of an autopoietic space in the electronic medium can be illuminated by looking at how artists' books are being represented and simulated as an aggregate of annotated and marked-up text and image files.

2.6   Remediating the Codex

How can we make an adequate digital representation of an artist's book? Three sets of interrelated problems have to be addressed. The first concerns the ways in which we represent the discreteness and modularity of the codex (and other book forms) to make intelligible not just the sequencing but the moving back and forth from parts to whole and from whole to parts, that is, the random access that defines the codex navigational structure. The second concerns the representation of the different materialities and visual textualities that compose artists' books by means of the simulation power of digital image representation. The third concerns the representation of the formal operations that perform self-referential functions—at the material, visual, and structural levels. The following questions spell out those three kinds of problems: How can digital files model the modularity of books? What happens when book units are redefined by the modularity of digital objects? What material, visual, and structural features can be represented by digital facsimiles? What self-referential codex operations can be represented in digital form? What is the relation between the formal materiality of artists' books as digital display and their metadata structure? What aspects of bookness are representable or simulatable?

Because textual strings inscribed on a page never function without a specific visual function as well, facsimile representation has become the norm for representing graphic codes in digital media. Digital facsimile documentary editing authenticates digital images by its photographic referentiality: a given edition and a given specimen of that edition are identified as the source for the digital replicas. Several scholarly digital editions and archives combine the documentary and textual critical approach, presenting both an electronic facsimile and the diplomatic alphanumeric transcription. In facsimile editing, the photographic and planographic surface of screen pixels is made to emulate the book as a sequence or syntax of surfaces: the codex is converted into a series of image files, in various formats, hypertextually organized in a sequence that emulates its codex equivalent. Such digital facsimile pages can be structured in various forms: as single-page or double-page openings; as recto only or recto and verso; as groups of pages arranged in specific patterns determined by the original object and also by the needs of hypertext file structure and data stream transmission (with two or more versions of image files, in small and large formats, with low or high resolution, for instance). In turn, these digital facsimiles can be seen and manipulated at various scales (from thumbnail image to actual size and to enlarged picture).

Representation of codex structure in digital media is also a problem of navigation, as we can see in *ABsOnline*. Digitization decomposes the continuous sequence of any given codex into a series of discrete digital objects defined by the modularity of image bit maps and character codes. As image files, they retain an indexical correspondence to single pages or page openings, but they unbound the pages from their original order. As text files, they free the verbal text from its particular inscription on a paper surface. Image-based digitization adds the modularity introduced by single-surface scanning to the organizing modularities that originated in the external and internal structures of the codex, such as quires, folds, chapters, and sections. Text-based digitization adds the modularity of searchable character-based strings to the compositional modularities of graphical layout, word order, sentence order, and style.

Once pages are freed from bound sequence and texts are freed from their particular layout on page surface and from their verbal order, each codex is reconfigured as a database of image and textual codes. And once they exist as part of an environment of other digitized representations of books, they become digital objects in this large archival database of book databases. In *ABsOnline*, the tension between digital modularities and codex modularities is expressed through a series of embedded frames of reference whose aim is to preserve and contain the identity and integrity of the digitized codex. At the same time, the interface aims to open up each individual codex to the critical relations made possible by the discreteness of the digital surrogates and the metadata and critical discourse marking up and describing the facsimiles. The conceptual and material space of the digital archive is made visibly present through these multiple framings.

Representation of book structure within this environment depends on the containment of the digital modularity within the limits of the modularity of the original codex. The representational tension between similarity and difference has to be resolved, at least temporarily, in favor of similarity. Possibilities opened up by remediation have to refer back to the unity of the codex, producing an immediacy effect that leads the user from the surrogate back to the object itself. Otherwise the recombinant potential of the database would dissolve the codex into the network of constellations made possible by the archived juxtaposition of pages and texts. *ABsOnline* has designed a display interface that resolves the problem of representing codex structure as a navigational problem. The hierarchical structure of the interface display establishes four frames of reference that allow users to answer questions such as these: (1) Where am I within the archive? (2) Where am I within the work-edition-object-image? (3) Where am I within the codex? and (4) Where am I within the page? (respectively, figures 2.7a, 2.7b, 2.7c, and 2.7d). This four-level framing (text-page-codex-archive) is a sign not just of the presence of scholarly archival standards, but also of the archive's anxiety about the power of digital textuality to dissolve the bookness of the codex. These features highlight the ambiguous relation between digital facsimiles and their source hard copy: facsimiles emulate the document, but they also map the document by making simultaneously available replicas that can be seen at various scales.

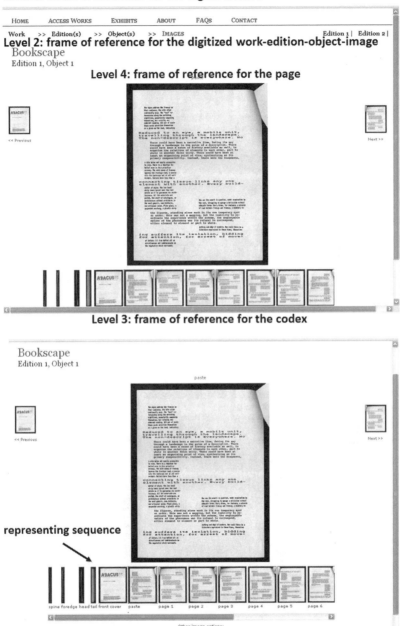

Figure 2.7

The book as digital facsimile: four frames of reference (1); representing sequence (2); frame of reference for the text (3); the screen page as a map of the print page (4). Johanna Drucker, *Bookscape* (1988), in *Artists' Books Online* (screen captures). © Johanna Drucker. Reproduced with permission.

frame of reference for the text

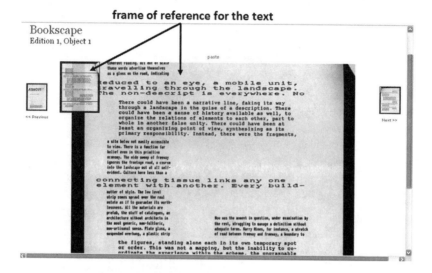

metarepresentation: the page as a map of the page

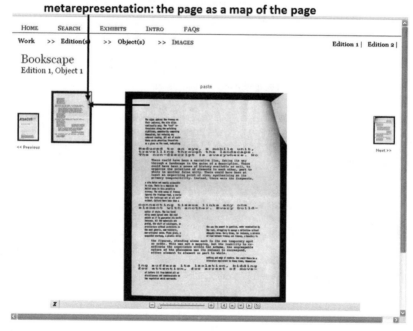

Figure 2.7
(continued)

In general, digital facsimiles make it possible to re-create most of the visual dimensions of pages and books, but they fail to represent tactile features that depend on the three-dimensional space of the structure and materials of the codex. In Drucker's *The Word Made Flesh* (1989), for instance, transparency is a crucial element in the self-referential layer that points to paper itself as a material signifier in the embodiment of the word (figure 2.8). Digital scanning has attempted to capture this feature of the work, but the pixelation of screen images tends to homogenize visual textures, such as degrees of opacity or transparency, and transition areas between textured surfaces. Tactile impressions will generally be translated

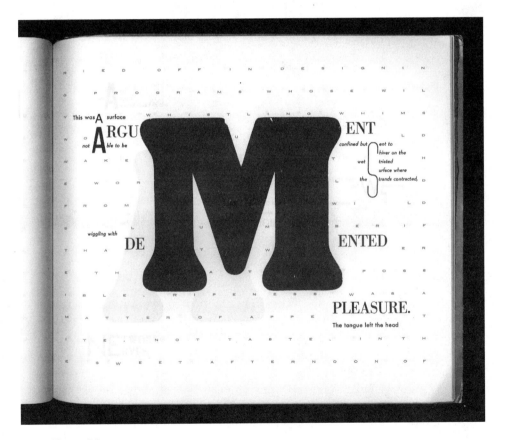

Figure 2.8
The book as digital facsimile: Johanna Drucker, *The Word Made Flesh* (1989), pp. 29–30, in *Artists' Books Online* (screen captures). © Johanna Drucker. Reproduced with permission.

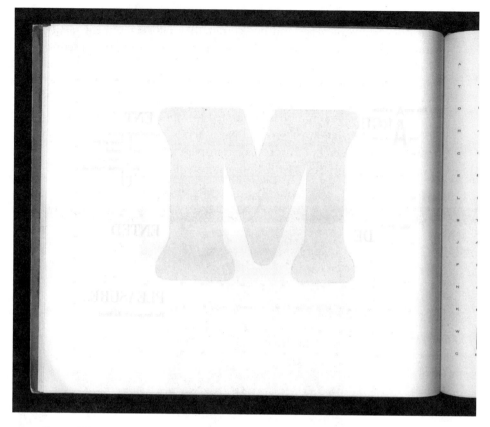

Figure 2.8
(continued)

into visuality: folds, for instance, will be experienced as visual rather than sculptural space. Although virtual three-dimensional environments may be conceived as new kinds of digital spaces for emulating codex forms, the physical experience of the materials will be difficult to emulate even in immersive environments. Digitization changes the sensory ratio between the various materials, often reducing visual-tactile and visual-kinetic perceptions to merely visual perceptions.

Although electronic hypertext has developed from the codex's organizational and navigational features—particularly from structures such as the marginal annotation, footnote, index, table of contents, page numbers, and chapter and section markers—digital textuality dissolves the three-dimensionality of codex spaces in the multiple inscriptional surface of screen display. The features of the screen in turn depend on the automatic processing of various types of data by various programming languages at the different levels of abstraction that define digital machines. Electronic pages are mimicking paper pages as devices for visual presentation of hierarchical information, but they are also hiding their nature as coded objects and their interfacing potential, that is, the fact that they can structure access to other data and inscriptional spaces that are different from themselves.

When used to emulate codices, electronic facsimiles attempt to conflate the new digital image file structure with the paper pages and thus create a transparency effect aiming at reducing the difference between electronic facsimile and paper page. The use of viewing interfaces that allow minimizing and magnifying the page facsimiles or moving them around for inspection enhances the page as main unit of digital representation and visuality as the main channel in the sensorial experience of books. Digital translation of book forms changes the ratio between visuality and tactility: a number of tactile three-dimensional interactions have to be emulated visually, often through the use of both mouse and mouse pad and the keyboard as mediating tools between the hands and the digital version of the book. This disconnection between visuality and tactility is perhaps the major change in the ergonomics of codex spaces when they are digitally remediated.

2.7 Mapping the Codex

Drucker has used graphical design to map different textual and discursive spaces in her works. In *The History of the/My Wor(l)d* (1990), for instance, different areas in each page are set with different type (with variations in face, color, size, and style), and they establish different kinds of relation between text and images (figure 2.9). She has used layout and typography as a critical instrument to map the ideological and discursive content that sustains the work's verbal and pictorial representations, many of which are sampled from popular media. This book's self-consciousness of its material form is achieved through a multilayered visual articulation of the narrative in page openings and page sequences and also through its recycling of images from magazines, newspapers, and other media. In this case, typographical design has been used to break up verbal and visual representations and expose the rhetoric of their constituent elements. They are used with a narrative function to create reading paths that offer continuity and discontinuity within the multilayered and fragmented threads (world

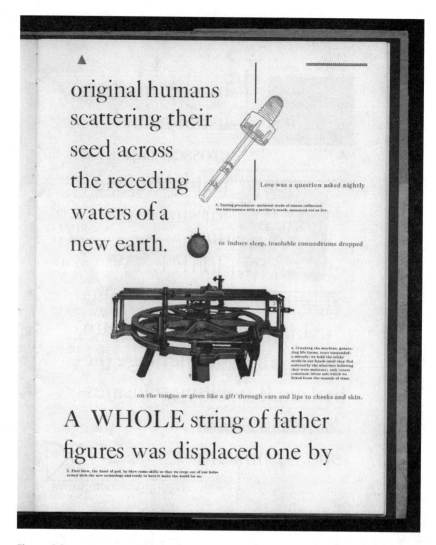

Figure 2.9
Johanna Drucker, *The History of the/my Wor(l)d* (1990), p. 7. Original size: 10 × 13 inches. © Johanna Drucker. Reproduced with permission.

history, family history, individual history, image captions), but they also work as markers of familial and personal memories and of various social, media, and religious discourses in the constitution of the subject.

A digital mapping of artists' books should proceed with a similar critical rationale: it should be able to both mark and represent the experience and the rhetoric of bookness. Digital mapping of bibliographic codes in *ABsOnline* creates a critical space in which the conceptual and perceptual experience of the artist's book as metabook can be explored. In the context of rapidly evolving transliteracy technologies, this understanding of self-reflexivity may contribute to a better understanding of the nature of bibliographic writing and reading acts as both material and social events. Digital representation in *ABsOnline* takes the form of a map that reproduces the books as navigational spaces and as objects of knowledge.

In *ABsOnline* the representational and modeling relation between book map and book object seems to imply the following rematerialized transcodings:

1. Electronic space simulates bibliographic space (with corresponding changes in scale, dimensionality, materiality, texture, and so on): the photographic principle as a mode of inscription of a real object guarantees its indexical link with the book object.

2. Three-dimensionality is flattened into the two dimensions of the screen plane: pages become page images, and volume becomes volume image.

3. Tactile qualities have been translated into visual properties: the texture of different kinds of materials is smoothed out in the homogeneity of pixel properties, and the book's internal tactile spaces are translated into visual perspectives presented on a display screen planographic surface.

4. Electronic facsimiles are framed within sets of coordinates for navigating different kinds of codex spaces (within and between pages, from the fragmentary detail to the entire codex sequence), while the book's internal navigational structure (table of contents, page numbers, index, and so on) is further supplemented by associations between the modularities introduced by individual files and by structures linking the files.

5. The codex's particular syntax has been translated into the specifics of graphical user interface, that is, into a Web site's hierarchical structure, which reframes the book's spatial sequence within its own classificatory and navigational arrangement. Codex frames of reference are emulated within the archive or Web site frames of reference, and image files participate in two orders of representation: in the electronic archive order (internal reference to the book as a set of codified elements in an archive) and

in the codex order as subsumed by the archive order (external reference to an actual book or codex being simulated and described in the archive).

6. The abstract and conceptual aspect of the codex form, as opposed to its multisensorial aspect, is stressed by the particular formal materiality of digital representation: the book is made simultaneously present, through its digital emulation, and absent, since the object is distanced by this spectral appearance as a representation of itself.

7. This modeling of artists' books through digital remediation creates a map of codex surface and codex structure. The fact that page images are scalable stresses the representational and modeling function of digital facsimiles and XML encoding of metadata as maps of codex forms. Since magnification and filters can reveal details that would elude unaided observation, facsimiles foreground the computer's power as a simulation environment and cartographic tool.

8. Topographicality of digital representation directs our attention to the formal operations performed by codex forms at the syntactic, semantic, and pragmatic levels. The digital spatialization and modularization of codex elements becomes an analytical tool for engaging reflexivity within the new order of representation.

Discussing the problem of digital representation, Dino Buzzetti (2002) has proposed two criteria for assessing the adequacy of digital representations of nondigital forms: "the exhaustivity of the representation" (61) and the "liability of the digital representation to automatic processing and its functionality with respect to the critical operations of reconstructing or interpreting the text" (62). The adequacy of digital representation in *ABsOnline* conforms to the criteria that Buzzetti outlined. The authors of the archive have expanded the metadata so that they include not only standard cataloging and indexing fields but also additional fields containing artistic, historical, technical, and critical data.

Digital representation combines descriptive information with facsimile reproduction. Many features are represented conceptually as categories in the database and as verbal descriptions expanding on those categories. As happens in several remediation processes that reproduce bibliographic objects in electronic space, artists' books in *Artists' Books Online* become a second-degree representation. This representation is a combination of bitmap images and machine-readable text, organized as an intricate web of files. This web includes images, verbal descriptions, textual and bibliographic models, document type descriptions (DTD), XML markup of those DTDs, a hypertext structure that provides access to the different levels of the archive, and search tools. Digital remediation thus takes the form of the scholarly annotated edition that establishes itself as a metarepresentation of previous textual and bibliographic forms.

What we access is a simulacrum of the object as remade by the mediation of a representational technology and by knowledge schemata embedded in a particular use of the technology. This knowledge structure is, above all, the structure of the archive whose classificatory system reenacts certain institutional forms of documentary validation within the digital space. Digital archiving on the basis of facsimile representation, XML modeling, hypertextual graphic interfaces, and the use of digital search tools is part of the current aestheticization of knowledge. It also reflects a growing belief in the power of digital representation technologies as a means for knowledge production and in the database as the best way of modeling the multiple material and critical dimensions concerning an object.

If self-reference in artists' books tries to contain a representation of the experience of the book within the book, *Artists' Books Online* attempts to escalate that representation into an extra level. However, self-reflexivity to the work's bibliographic code is one element that resists remediation because it depends on the actual material interaction with a book artifact. The attempt at re-representing the bookness of artists' books also demonstrates the ultimate untranslatability of their codes and the representational limits of the digital archive rationale. The recodification imposed by the specifics of digital materiality means that migration of codex codes into electronic space can be achieved only by mapping rather than by recreating or remaking the object. The syntax, semantics, and pragmatics of bookscapes are reframed by the syntax, semantics, and pragmatics of screenscapes. This technological difference is the reason that this form of translation of physical paper codex into physical electronic facsimile may prove a decisive critical contribution for our understanding of the verbal-visual-tactile-spatial-biblio feedbacks that take place each time we make and read a book.

3   Digital Transcreations: Transcoding a Poetics of Reading

3.1   The Poem Is the Medium

Looking at the emergence of digital literature, studies of the past decade have highlighted the connection between concrete and oulipian poetics and digital poetics (Glazier 2002; Simanowski 2004; Cramer 2005, 2007; Emerson 2006; Wurth 2006; Block and Torres 2007; Funkhouser 2007; Block 2010; Schaffner 2010; di Rosario 2011). Aesthetic investigations of the relations among language, writing, technology, and literary forms have been programmatic in concrete and oulipian poetics. Similarly, the signifying materiality of the computational medium has been systematically probed by digital poetics. Concerns with intermediality, visuality, permutation, and algorithms, and with technocultural self-reflexivity in general, are common features across those literary practices.

Reflexive operations related to language structures, writing codes, and literary forms have been remediated and transformed in order to address digital mediation as a new kind of literary space. This historical connection is present, for instance, in the use of concrete poems as storyboards and scripts for electronic texts, both in composing text for graphic interface static display and for animation. It is as if the concrete and oulipian approaches to language and form, because of their constructivist, conceptual, mathematical, and objectivist emphases, anticipated the kind of reflection on media set in motion by the electronic page and automated algorithmic procedures. Close attention to the visibility of language and the materiality of reading, two reflexive functions in concretist texts, also underlies many of the poetic attempts to make self-referential use of the properties of electronic textuality in digital forms. The same applies to the combinatorial constraints and gamelike procedures of oulipian aesthetics and to the ways in which they lend themselves to exploration and expansion in programmable media.

The adoption of computers as a means for literary creation has been fostered by those poetics. Because of its internalization of a theory of language as a structural system of signs, the concrete poem laboratory explores the projection of the paradigmatic axis into the syntagmatic axis. A probabilistic game with phonetic and semantic similarities and differences is spatialized on the page in ways that foreground the fact that a text is also a set of instructions for reading itself. Consequently, the combinatorial procedures that generated the rhetorical and typographic code of the poem become visible on the textual surface. In retrospect, the poem appears as a script for meaning production, even if this meaning remains unstable and undeterminable.

Despite their reliance on the ambiguity that results from superposition of sense and sound states, many concrete poems focus on language and print as technical devices for encoding and exchanging information. An early example is Edwin Morgan's poem "Message Clear" (1965), where the bits and bytes that produce verbal meaning have been decomposed, as if the poem intended to present us with the machine code for the miracle of transubstantiation that occurs in linguistic signs. This is the kind of metalinguistic analysis that signals concrete self-reference to the poem's information code. For concrete aesthetics, the dynamics of syntactical combination originating in phonetic and graphical attractions and lexical cross-breeding is the guiding principle of composition.

Its conscious and subconscious workings may be observed both below and above the word level: in the first case, in the agglutinations, prefixes, infixes, suffixes, and various types of fragmentation of lexemes, morphemes, and graphemes; in the second case, at the higher level of syntactic units, sentences, and texts. The semantic and ideological level of language is subject to a combinatorial art that destroys and reconstructs the structure of inferences and recurrences that upholds textual cohesion and discursive coherence. Concrete poetics models the structural and psychic materiality of the sign by linking its formal linguistic properties with the ear-eye-mouth-hand-and-mind processing of those properties. It is a poetics of spoken and written language as much as it is a poetics of reading and cognition. Its hermeneutics starts at the physiological processing of audiovisual input, which transmutes the poem into a cyborg, that is, a cybernetic simulation of meaning as a specific processing of subjectively apprehended and constructed bits of information.

From this point of view, concrete intermedia verbivocovisuality and oulipian permutational playfulness are language generators that provide a laboratorial microcosm for linguistic invention, from the level of phonetic, lexical, and syntactical parsing to the semantic and pragmatic functions that produce language as social action. Contextual references contained in print and verbal discourses, through allusions obtained by typeface choice or discursive citation, situate the formal audiovisual dynamics of difference in particular social and historical spaces. Language is not a mere repertoire of given elements, classes of elements, and combinations of those classes, but it is above all the possibility of expanding elements, classes, and combinations in ways that rearticulate our social construction of the world through signifiers.

Virtualization of the infinity of language implied that poetical production had to take place also at the more fundamental levels of the linguistic sign and written signification. Language as a means of production had to be pulled apart and scrutinized in its microscopic materiality, and not only at the level of an inherited repertoire of forms, genres, and discourses. Peeling of words and phonic fracture, for example, were proclaimed as programmatic principles by Haroldo de Campos in his early series of five poems *O â mago do ô mega* (1955–1956). As happened in *Konstellationen constellations constellaciones* (1953) by Eugen Gomringer, this semiotic phenomenology of language explodes the phonosemantic units that were crystallized in lexemes and morphemes by means of fragmentation and unexpected recombination. Revealing the mathematics of language that turned poems into structures of metadata, the concrete poem often remains entrapped in the self-reflexivity of its verbal and iconic tools.

It is not a matter of coincidence that the poem about the poem (always a serious candidate to being the most frequent topic in the history of any tradition of poetry) has become perhaps an architheme of concrete poetry, as if every single poem had to be an ars poetica at the same time. That is certainly the case with Haroldo de Campos and Augusto de Campos, who, over the years, have been parodying, translating, and quoting a large constellation of authors and texts in order to write about the act of producing poetry—a list that extends from classical Hebrew, Greek, Latin, and Chinese texts to medieval, Renaissance, romantic, and modernist writers in the Portuguese, French, Italian, Spanish, English, and Russian languages (*Canticles, Ecclesiastes*, Homer, Vergil, Chuang-Tzu, Li Po, Guido Cavalcanti, Dante, Camões, Goethe, Novalis, Poe, Dickinson, Mallarmé, Mayakovsky, Khlebnikov, e. e. cummings, Pessoa, Ezra Pound, James Joyce, T. S. Eliot, Sousândrade, Oswald de Andrade, Mário de Andrade, João Cabral de Melo Neto, John Cage, and others).

Concrete aesthetics was trying to extend and redefine the typographical and topographical objectivity of earlier modernist conceptions in a new technological context. That the program or script for the meaning of a text can be or has to be formalized is perhaps the price to be paid for the theoretical dimension of a language poetry that defines itself in those terms and puts most of its emphasis in intersemiotic and intermedia processes. In their attempt to unify the activities of criticism, poetry, and translation—by means of "the critical devouring of the universal legacy" (in the words of Haroldo de Campos)—concretists developed a poetical consciousness of language that matched the science of linguistics and the science of cybernetics of our own time. More important than reifying the poem as a finished object, concrete poetry has contributed to the writing and reading of the poem as a process for the production of meaning.

This never-ending attempt at making the poem a mirror of itself is one of the poetechnical consequences that follow from the concrete emphasis on the objective, autonomous, and self-enclosed nature of the poem. The concepts of intersemiotic translation, untranslation, and transcreation developed out of an acute sense of the mediated nature of the poem as a material and informational artifact. Concrete aesthetic investigations establish a poetics of the medium that provides critical tools for experimenting with the intermedia and permutational nature of digital artifacts in their interactions with language structures. Translations between languages and translations between media are articulated as complex semiotic processes with autopoetic layers.

The smooth, and almost inevitable, transition from page to screen in Brazilian visual poetry has been wonderfully captured in a special issue of the online journal *Artéria*, edited by Omar Khouri and Fábio Oliveira Nunes.[1] This issue of *Artéria* brings together pre-Web and post-Web authors, linking the digital artists to an earlier generation of Brazilian visual poets. Its remediation strategies are particularly useful for thinking about the relations between the dynamics of page layout and screen display. Graphicality and digitality are presented as being contiguous rather than in opposition. Works included in this online edition of *Artéria* date from 1962 up to 2003. Some of the early print (and video) works have been remade for Web presentation by the editors of this issue. As remediated works, those digital concrete texts highlight the historical and material continuity between constellated experiments in print layout and the open-ended possibilities of refreshable screen display.[2]

Another recent instance of digital remediation of visual and concrete texts appeared in the special issue of the online journal *Errática*, whose issue number 104 (February 2011) contains digital recreations of works by Augusto de Campos, several of which were made by the digital artist André

Vallias.[3] Vallias has produced intersemiotic translations for the digital medium that transform reflexive features of the original text into multimedia and interactive tropes of the remediated kinetic version. Animation scripts are sometimes used in these media translations in ways that make explicit the function of the mouse as an embodied reading device for linking hand and eye movements to constellated signifiers. By suggesting a synchronicity between the Web writers of the 2000s and the concrete and visual poets of earlier decades, both issues of the journals *Arteria* and *Errática* focus our attention on the materialities of signification and on the poem as an investigation into its own medium.

Three properties justify the connection between concrete and oulipian texts and digital texts: first, the intermedia visualization that occurs in the concrete text is similar to the iconic and kinetic writing of digital interfaces; second, the spatialized creation of nonsequential reading paths (with multiple trajectories resulting from the breaking up of language and discourse units through constellated arrangements) anticipates the multisequential writing of hypertext; and third, constrained and rule-based permutations, a defining principle of oulipian poetics, already imply algorithmic formalization. To these, we can add the explosion of texts into networks of collages and allusions. By means of multiple cultural associations and literary allusions, densely packed in minimal graphical elements, the concrete poem often appears as a cluster of palimpsestic references and meanings.[4] The opening up of text to the probabilities of meaning through language permutations and media integration has allowed writers to investigate reading acts through the specific affordances of the digital medium. Poetic remediations provoke a new reflexive engagement with writing and reading codes.

3.2 Topographies of Reading

The confluence of concrete and digital poetics can be found in works by digital artists, but also in works by concrete and visual poets. Augusto de Campos and E. M. de Melo e Castro, pioneers of concrete poetics in the 1950s and 1960s, were also among the first to integrate computers into their creative processes in the early stages of personal computing in the 1980s. The ways in which they have transposed their own works into the digital medium suggest that there may be continuity between concrete space and digital space as constituted by topographic structures and algorithmic processes. Interaction between self-descriptive texts and acts of reading as perceptual processing is apparent in the way several works make the act of reading the text the central reference of their textual semantics. Visual reference coincides with graphicality, and aural reference coincides with phonetics. Those texts seem to create a feedback loop between the semantic signified and the audiovisual material signifiers.

A few examples will illustrate this seamless transition between kinetic paper page and kinetic computer display. *SOS*, by Augusto de Campos, was originally written in 1983 (Campos 1994, 27) (figure 3.1). The title word *SOS*, which in Portuguese is also the plural form of *só*, which means both alone and only, stands at the center of seven circles of letters and words. At once a cosmological and psychological constellation, the ideogram can be read clockwise and counterclockwise, from the outer to the inner circle and vice versa, and in various combinations of those four movements. The outermost circle is made of eight words, in eight different languages, for

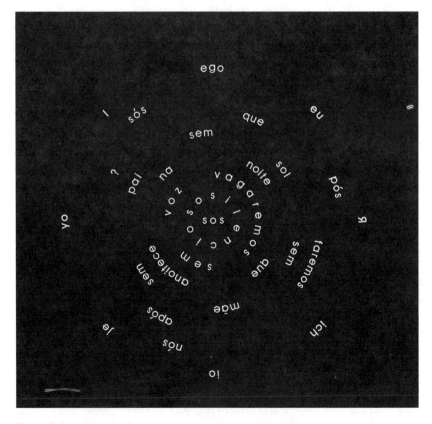

Figure 3.1
Augusto de Campos, *SOS* (1983). © Augusto de Campos. Reproduced with permission.

the personal pronoun *I*. The text seems to reenact the process of awareness from individual consciousness to collective human consciousness, by reference to the cosmological mystery of origin and also to human mortality and universal entropy. This diagrammatic reflection on human solitude in the universe mimics planet orbits (through allusion to scientific and literary diagrammatic representations) and also the pattern of electromagnetic waves spreading outwards from a source. The oppositions "night"/"sun" and "voice"/"silence" are visually translated to the black and white surface of the page.

The second poem is a computer animation of *SOS* (2000) developed by Augusto de Campos using Flash (figure 3.2). It was first published in the CD-ROM *Clip-Poemas* (1997–2003), which was included in the book *Não*

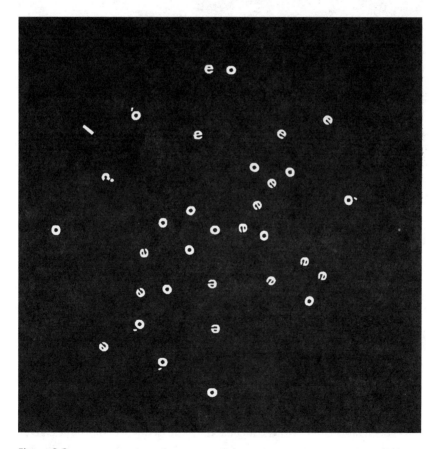

Figure 3.2
Augusto de Campos, *SOS* (2000) (screen captures). © Augusto de Campos. Reproduced with permission.

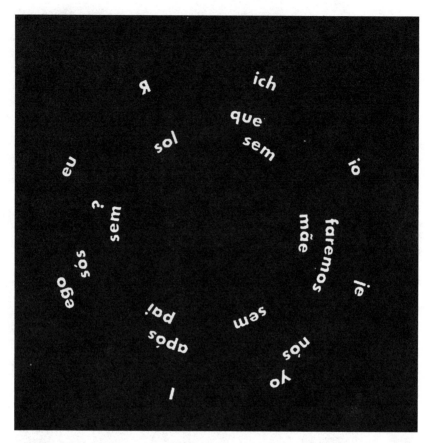

Figure 3.2
(continued)

Poemas (2003). The intermediation between the two technologies is marked by the fact that book and CD-ROM converge and diverge in their content: some print-born poems have digital versions, and at least one born-digital poem has a print version. The digital version of *SOS* adds color, movement, and sound to the original text, using it as storyboard or notation for its digital remediation. The individual appearance of letters suggests points of light in the night sky, while the successive appearance of each circle accompanied by a reading voice establishes a temporal sequence for our engagement with the topographic structure. Some of the possible reading paths have been animated, which means that the sequence of frames gives viewers a privileged reading sequence, providing a cinematic resolution for the ambiguity of the dehierarchized printed page dynamics.

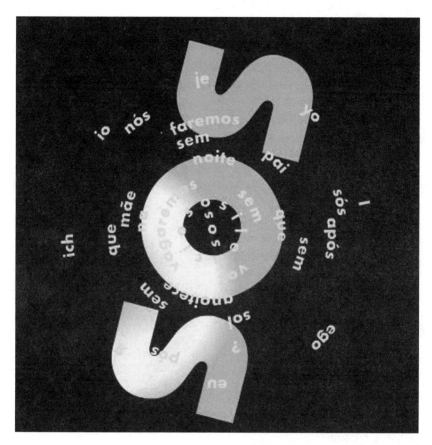

Figure 3.2
(continued)

The simultaneity of the spatially organized written signifiers has been broken down by cinematic temporality, which is now a simulacrum of reading movements, directing the viewer's attention to textual movements, word recognition, and syntactical operations. As the text unfolds reading itself, readers become aware of the powerful associative mechanisms that its ideogrammatic structure contained, including the way in which the act of reading the poem was designed so that it could be experienced as a cognitive replica of the cosmological questioning of the universe. While the animation silently reads the text, voices materialize the human horizon of self-consciousness, interrogation, silence, death, and oblivion. Echoes and reverberation of voices further stress this individual-collective cosmological ontology of hope and despair. The textual tension

Figure 3.2
(continued)

between visuality and readability functions as an embodied cognitive
analog of the cosmological reading and writing of the universe.

What is most striking about Augusto de Campos's digital works is the
translation of reflexive layers across media and also the ways in which
digital versions make explicit the bibliographic codes of printed texts.
Self-reflexivity of his visual texts—their metalinguistic engagements with
the typographic, ideographic, and phonographic materiality of signs—is
carried over into his digital versioning. Because many of them were originally set as typographic constellations on the page, animation has to deal
with the openness of simultaneous reading trajectories. In its turn, the
sequencing of trajectories and events on the screen creates a material simulacrum of reading movements, which appear as the cinematic temporiza-

tion of what were topographic spaces waiting for reading interventions. His media translation of print texts enacts the temporal nature of reading through the motion of frames. Textual motion created by frame refresh is a kinetic re-creation of eye movements across textual fields. Readers see the digital text reading the print text, but they also continue to see themselves reading the digital text.

The concrete aesthetics of turning language into a material object available for semiotic processing is emulated by this digital use of kineticism as a model for reading codes and reading acts. Campos's visual texts are extreme instances of a complex layering of the intertextual multiplicity of writing and its potentiality for generating meaning. His works develop what he himself has described as intersemiotic translations: translations that work across different media systems, as happens when semantic layers dependent on lexical signs are translated or transferred to semantic layers dependent on iconic or visual signs. His typographic and visual translations already explore several transcoding formal operations (across languages and across media) that he later used for his own digital poems.[5]

The GIF animation of his visual translation of "Rã de bashô" (Basho's frog, 1998) gives us an extreme instance of the relations between translation and transmediation (figure 3.3). Matsuo Basho's seventeenth-century haiku is verbally and visually translated, and this print translation in turn is recodified as a five-frame GIF animation. The motion of the frog described in the original haiku has been semiotically inscribed in the graphic form of the text, which becomes an iconic representation of the perception synthesized in the haiku. The movement of the eyes reading the letter becomes an echo of the movement of the eyes seeing the frog jumping from the water lily into the pond. Immersion is obtained by making the reader hallucinate the letters, the code itself, instead of the object of the world evoked by the letters. The motion of the letter is the motion of the reader reading the letter. The text self-reflects on the cognitive process embedded in its own material forms as they are perceived by a reading subject.

The graphic pattern of the three groups of four letters is an alphabetic iconic rendering of the water lily, evoking at the same time a visual affinity with the ideograms and stanza structure of the Japanese haiku. The green-colored *a*, which becomes an icon for the frog, is replicated in each of the letter groups but in different relative positions. When turned into an animation, the implicit motion of the letter in print form becomes an explicit image of the motions of reading. Seeing the frog and reading the letter that is the frog analog are placed in perceptual contiguity. The ability of

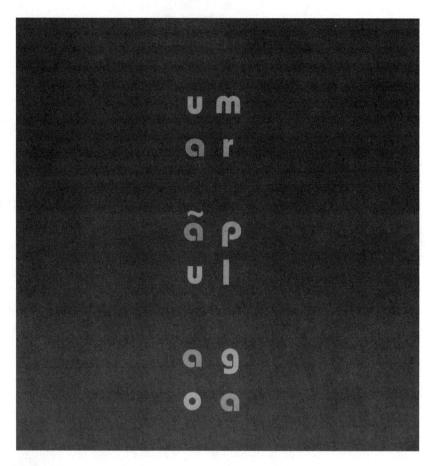

Figure 3.3
Augusto de Campos, "Rã de bashô" (Basho's frog) (1998): translation of Japanese
ideograms into visual text and translation of visual text into digital text (screen
captures). © Augusto de Campos. Reproduced with permission.

Figure 3.3
(continued)

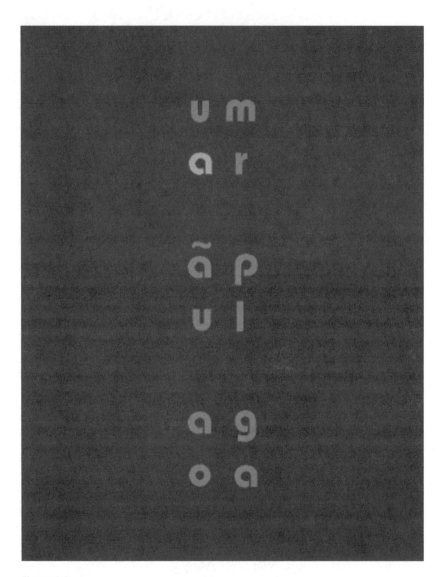

Figure 3.3
(continued)

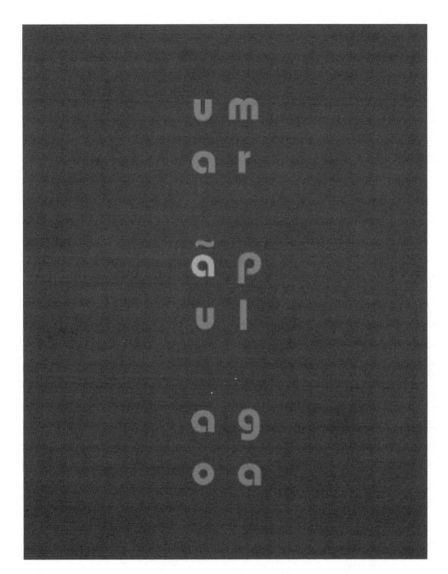

Figure 3.3
(continued)

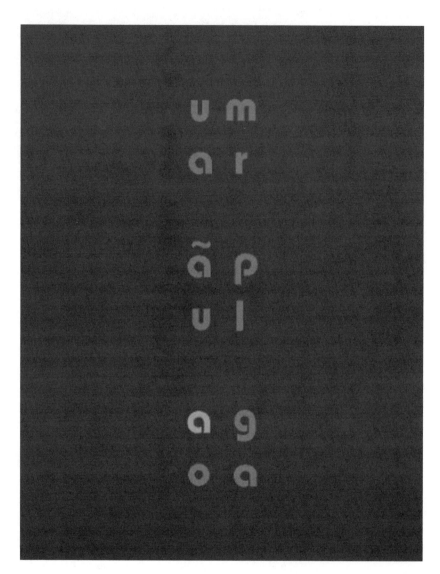

Figure 3.3
(continued)

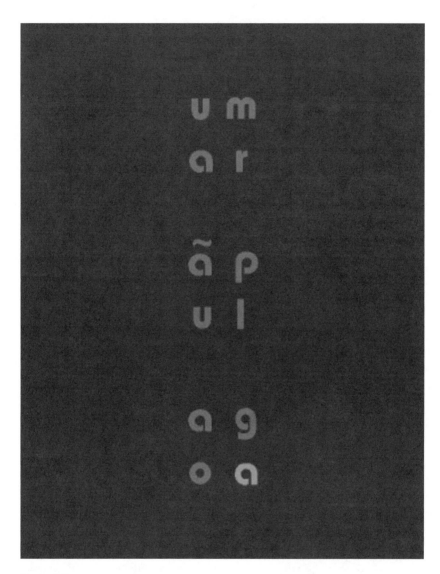

Figure 3.3
(continued)

Figure 3.4
Augusto de Campos, "Tensão" (Tension) (1956) (screen capture). © Augusto de Campos. Reproduced with permission.

language to evoke the memory of experience is simulated in the actual perception of the textual surface: the textual event of the jumping letter is a semiotic emulation of the perception of motion that reenacts lived experience in the textual surface. Reading, seeing, and seeing reading become entwined as the major textual reference of the textual experience. In this digital version, translation is taking place at the level of language, writing systems, and media.

The digital sound version of "Tensão" (Tension, 1956) is another good example of the notational function of typography and spacing in concrete texts (figure 3.4). The multivoice, multiechoed reading enacts the typographic and visual tension between pattern and meaning. It also stresses the structural tensions between sound and sense, between sequence and permutation, between word and sentence, and between syllable and word. Constellating signs in symmetrically displayed structures randomize reading paths into their factorial horizon. Readers have to decide how to move among the various textual strings—in other words, they have to construct a reading code. Reading is experienced as an embodied perception, a kinetic, haptic, and vocal interaction with material signifiers.

A similar intersemiotic translation has been achieved in the GIF animation "Coraçãocabeça" (Hearthead, 1980): the throbbing interference of the two alternating texts, reinforced by animation, adds extra reading difficulty to the parenthetical interruptions that require readers to read out from the center linking words and phrases. In both cases, digital versions of print texts contain powerful formal solutions for exposing the motions

Figure 3.5
Augusto de Campos, "Coraçãocabeça" (Hearthead) (1980, print; 1997, GIF animation) (screen captures). © Augusto de Campos. Reproduced with permission.

of reading in the production of sense, thus laying bare their original typographic codes (figure 3.5). Reading codes become tangible in Augusto de Campos's constellated works. The signifier loops on itself by making readers aware that they are performing what the notation requires of them: the actual act of reading becomes its own reference. The work's metapoetic function takes the form of an exercise in typographical notation whose performance contains a minimalist reflection on the technologies of writing and reading.

Portuguese poet E. M. de Melo e Castro is the author of an early series of computer-animated poems, *Signagens* (*Signages*, 1986–1989), which can be described also as media translations. Those sequences adapt twenty-one of his concrete and visual texts, and they were originally presented by Melo e Castro as VHS video poems.[6] Treating the paper version of each poem as a storyboard, animation rewrites the reflexive layers of those texts using the properties of the new production technology. In some cases, what the viewer sees is the actual accomplishment of what were suggestions of movement in the original paper version. However, a careful analysis of the suggestions of movement will note that his textual kinetics contains two different types of reverberations: while one type is a function of imagining an iconic mimetic between ideogram and external reference, the other type is a function of the physical and semiotic act of reading the ideogram. Many visual poems contain this double rationale of movement: a movement that is symbolically and mimetically associated with the object represented by the ideogram and a movement that is an enactment of the act of reading. What this means is that poem-object and reader-subject are split and rejoined in the field of perspective created by the consciousness of reading as a movement in the outer space of the page and the inner space of the mind. Recognition of the object and recognition of the perception of the signifier of the object are the two sides of those iconic motions.

Animated versions, when they are but sets of instructions for reading constellated poems, can offer a poorer viewing and reading experience than the paper original. Digital versions of concrete texts add signifying layers by integrating specific properties of digital reproduction technologies, such as the use of color and texture, three-dimensionality, framing and point of view, suggestion of camera motions, human voice, music, sound effects, and interactivity. The syntax of movement and sound, as well as the editing of image frames and the emulation of camera angles, enable texts to acquire the material and formal properties associated with cinema. Melo e Castro's first experiment was a film-poem with animation and voice, "Roda-Lume" (Wheel Light), produced in 1968–1969; a computer reconstruction of this text was later included in the series *Signagens* (figure 3.6).

Melo e Castro's computer text animations are early electronic and video explorations of the visual space of writing as a reading field for media performances. One example is the video poem version of his 1962 ideogrammatic poem "Objectotem" (figure 3.7). While the frames of the computer version remake the reading sequence, highlighting the internal echoes between new words and the words contained in agglutinated word-object that makes the title, they also add a vocal interpretation (chorus and drums) that reinforces the representation of the poem-object as a collective totemic icon celebrated through ritual acts. Objectivist aesthetic theory is related to the archaic magical use of language whereby the computer video poem becomes a sort of ethnographic record of concrete forms. Vocalization and iconicity are used to suggest primeval body rhythms and primeval forms of writing, presenting the poem as an object of magic where signified and signifier can coincide.

Figure 3.6
E. M. de Melo e Castro, "Roda lume" (Wheel light) (1969) (screen shots from the 1986 reconstruction). © E. M. de Melo e Castro. Reproduced with permission.

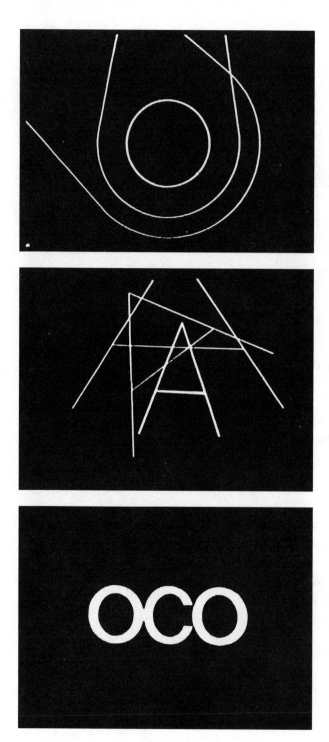

Figure 3.6
(continued)

```
O B J E C T O T E M
    T E T O
    T E T O
    T O T E M
    T A C T O
   ,A C T O
   ,A C T O
        T O T E M
        T A C T O
        A C T O
        A C T O
            T O T E M
            T A C T O
            A C T O
            A C T O
                T O T E M
```

Figure 3.7
E. M. de Melo e Castro, "Objectotem" (1962). © E. M. de Melo e Castro. Reproduced
with permission.

3.3 Performing Inscriptions

The concrete poem is one specific instance of the experimental intermedia
aesthetics of the 1960s. A concrete poem can be defined as a self-referential
poly-sign that, through fractal self-similarity between graphic form and
semantic form, seeks to enclose its field of reference in its own materiality.
From this point of view, the concrete poem is the linguistic equivalent of
abstractionism and minimalism in its desire to refer to its own objectness—
even if the external contexts of words and graphical forms often make
signifiers return to the space of social interaction from where they were
collected and isolated. In its more extreme forms, the poem becomes an
abstract conceptualization that aestheticizes signifiers enclosing them in
the sensoriality of their own graphic and typographic forms, as if sign and
referent could somehow coincide.

A digital reflection on the presence of the signified in the signifier is
the basis for Tiago Gomez Rodrigues's film *Concretus* (2002), a six-minute
narrative that contains digital animations of five ideograms: "Tontura"
(Dizziness, 1962) by E. M. de Melo e Castro; "Arranhisso" (Spidery, 1964),
by Salette Tavares (1922–1994); "Cascata" (Waterfall, 2002), "Cubo" (Cube,
2002), and "Esfera" (Sphere) (2002), by Tiago Gomez Rodrigues, who is
also the author of the digital soundtrack (figure 3.8). This film is a brilliant
essay on the marriage between concrete aesthetics and digital technology.

CONCRETUS

Figure 3.8
Tiago Gomez Rodrigues, *Concretus* (2002) (screen captures). © Tiago Gomez Rodrigues.
Reproduced with permission.

Figure 3.8
(continued)

In *Concretus*, the reflection on the specific properties of the medium takes place in the ingenious foregrounding of three-dimensional digital animation techniques (e.g., shot angles, surface textures, light sources, shadows). *Concretus* is not simply illustrating the objectivist principles of concrete poems in a three-dimensional environment, since its elaborate suggestion of camera movement around and inside the word-objects turns optical consciousness of the cinematic illusion into a central element of this narrative about the nature and possibility of concreteness in written representation.

The tension among iconicity, mimesis, and self-similarity, on the one hand, and the abstraction provided by written signs and synthetic sounds, on the other, is the driving force of this work. This tension shows how a specific digital intermedia form has adopted concrete poetics to explore its own material possibilities for meaning. The distance between signifier and signified cannot be overcome, even when the signifier is the signified, because that is the interval that makes meaning possible. Considered as a narrative, this digital film poem points to the paradoxical nature of its objects as concrete abstractions that exceed the pictographic and logographic logic that seems to contain them. The movement suggested by the sequence of frames, shots, and angles is a radical rewriting of the original ideograms, asking for a whole new level of cognitive and narrative engagement with the concreteness of text.

Another digital performance of concrete visual constellations can be found in the works of Argentinian poet Ana María Uribe (1951–2004). Her minimalist animation sequences *Tipoemas* (Typoems) and *Anipoemas* (Anipoems), produced between 1997 and 2003, recode her earlier visual poems. Letters and words are re-created as cinematic audiovisual ideograms (figure 3.9). Iconic and cinematic redefinition of type forms and structures depends on the use of the vocabulary of optical and phonographic media. Manipulation of the features of type (such as face, size, color, and style) transforms single letters into icons for human characters and human actions, which are further personified by suggestive motions (dancing, jumping, running, walking, conducting, playing, acrobatics). The use of a soundtrack creates a referential context for the ideographic alphabetic symbols: circus acts; train journey; lovemaking; music playing; dancing. Her minimal and joyful transmediations enact the objectivist and self-referential games about reading acts and the ideogrammatic iconization of alphabetic signs that defined concrete visual poetry.

The performative character of reading motions can also be apprehended through the treatment of topographic layout as a notation for the

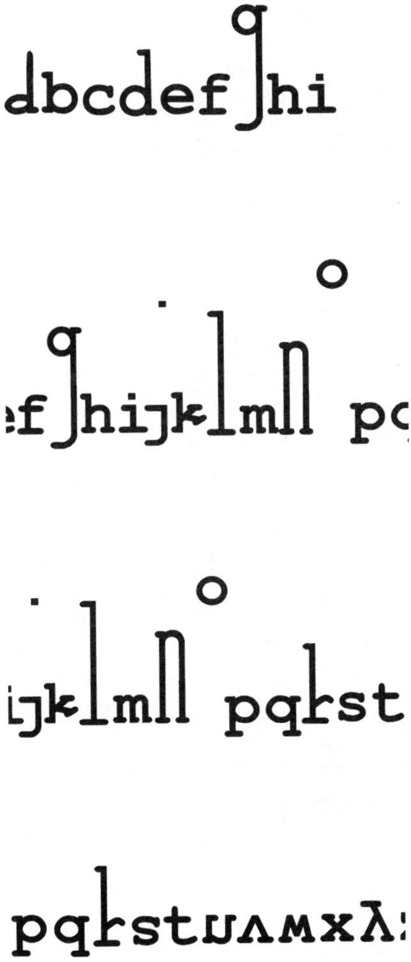

dbcdef ghi

ef hijklmn pc

ijklmn pqrst

pqrstuʌʌxλ

Figure 3.9
Ana Maria Uribe, *El gran desfile/The grand parade* (2001) (screen captures). © Ana
Maria Uribe. Reproduced with permission.

Figure 3.9
(continued)

articulation of sounds and silences. In his reading of a selection of "Ideo-gramas" (Ideograms, 1962a), by E. M. de Melo e Castro, sound poet Américo Rodrigues (2006) interprets the page layout of words as musical notation, combining the reading of horizontal lines with vertical columns in various iterative and repetitive patterns. The syntagmatic axis of syntactical asso-ciation and the paradigmatic axis of lexical replacement, as structural properties of verbal language, become probabilistic operators of poetic sequences. On top of that vocal permutation, which is but one actualiza-tion of many possibilities offered by graphical spatialization, Américo Rodrigues freely inserts variations in pitch, duration, and rhythm. Changes in tempo, dynamics, and expression allow him to emphasize different intentions and emotions. Such iterations and reiterations define patterns and recurrences constructed by reading on the entire semiotic ensemble formed by written signs and their typography and topology. Codependence between writing and reading is unequivocally clear in this exercise: reading recodifies writing through its own protocols. Its enactment in a unique performance of the text reveals signification as a single event resulting from the act of reading as a material and embodied performance.

It is as if the notational function of written marks were defined only after the fact, when the vocal interpretation gives them a sonic, emotional, and conceptual value. When written text consists solely of black dotted lines and blank spaces, for example, what Américo Rodrigues does is to find prelinguistic vocal equivalents that may be said to read dots, traces, and blanks. The relationship between dash/trace length and white space length works as a marker for relative duration of sound emissions and pauses, both interpreted in a fairly free and improvised manner. Sounds are grouped by the articulatory affinities of their distinctive traces, with variations in increasing or decreasing respiratory rhythm and sound intensity. The relationship of these changes with graphical variations is almost entirely arbitrary, since their vocalization has an internal order that resignifies graphic marks, as if vocal sound preceded and originated the semiosis of graphical representation. The conventionality and arbitrariness of the written sign depend on an act of production and an intention that is realized through an act of reading as an unrepeatable occurrence of a vocalization. Voiced in this way, the ideograms become an experience of the performativity of inscriptional marks.

In "Ideograma No 1," as in the other ideograms in the series, the voice rewrites the marks in the act of reading them. This vocal exercise by Américo Rodrigues shows the codependence between reading and writing: both the sound and the meaning seem to operate in a feedback loop between the forms of textual reading and textual writing. Vocal interpretation gives meaning to the notation, and the notation gives meaning to the interpretation in ways that are always asymmetrical and inexhaustible. Notationality becomes a function of interpretability, and vice versa: the vocal repertoire coextends the written repertoire. This seems to be a feature of the disseminative mode of meaning production through writing: the presence of the absence of meaning, which must be made present at each new reading, can occur only through the temporal inscription of the interpreter´s voice and mind in the eventuality of its own interpretation. The sound recording, in its performative singularity, is an occurrence of the phenomenological codependence between reading and writing. It is as if the algorithm that determines the verbal and conceptual structure of the elements in the text remained incomplete without the cognitive intervention specific to the act of reading.

3.4 Language Machine

Knowledge of the generative and recursive properties of language structures favored the development of algorithmic approaches to textual creation. In "A máquina de emaranhar paisagens" (The machine for entangling landscapes) (1964), Herberto Helder rewrites the initial chapters of *Genesis* using permutations and recombinations of words and phrases. The work suggests the coextensibility between creating the text and creating the world in the text and shows metaphoric attraction as a form of creation of the world as language. Words, in their metaphoric substitutions, display the mechanism of language—its limitless capacity for meaning transfer and generation. The generative productivity of the landscape of language enables it to evoke the whole metamorphosis of creation from a limited set of interchangeable elements.

The transformational syntax that sustains lexical permutations is a correlative of morphological variations of organic matter in the world. To reveal the genetic code of the poem is to reveal the poem as self-replicative machine, capable of expanding and transmuting in accordance with its own program of instructions. In the digital re-creation of this poem, Pedro Barbosa makes explicit the algorithm for entangling landscapes by using his automatic text generator "sintext" for recombining texts from the books of Genesis and Revelation and from poems by François Villon, Dante, Camões, and Herberto Helder (figure 3.10).

This means that Barbosa has formalized the procedure used in the original text and programmed it: once the syntactic structures of sentences have been defined and word classes have been assigned their position reference within those structures, permutations and combinations can be guided by an algorithm that selects in a randomized sequence the words from each of the subsets and then inserts them into a syntactical string. Metaphorical attractions show themselves as the result of the genetic process of textual creation, less dependent on a subject's intentionality as such than on the iterability and productivity intrinsic to language. In a paradoxical quantum effect, language appears as the creator of the creation that creates it. The self-replicative property of life manifests itself through the generative property of language. This mode of critical knowledge of language developed out of the antiexpressive and antireferential project of the experimental

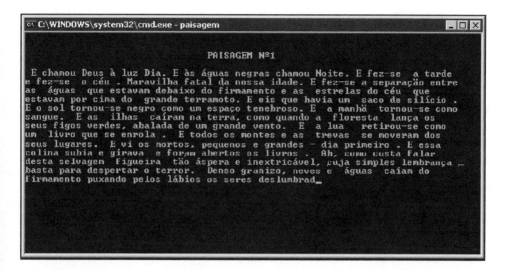

Figure 3.10
Pedro Barbosa, sintext version (2008) of "A máquina de emaranhar paisagens"
(The machine for entangling landscapes) (1964) by Herberto Helder (screen capture).
© Pedro Barbosa and Abílio Cavalheiro. Reproduced with permission.

poem as verbal mechanism. Self and referent emerge as functions of language in its proliferative way of presenting and representing world to self and self to self.

The double articulation of language explains its digital nature: it is the phonological machine code that sustains, at the morphological, lexical, and syntactic levels, the system of differences that originates meaning. This revelation of the basic code of language in its written form is the compositional principle of "Homeóstato 1" (Homeostate 1) (1967), by José-Alberto Marques: graphemes contained in a single line (placed at the beginning or at the end of the line sequences) repeat themselves in the same relative positions and become minimal units in other lexemes and morphemes, which in turn recombine at the syntactic and semantic levels (figure 3.11). Self-replicative, self-referential, and recursive properties of the linguistic code are shown as similar to permutations in electronic code. Much like the phoneme-grapheme differences that enable language permutations, the machine code sustains the semantic and syntactic level of programming languages. The generativity of both codes is evident in the digital version by Rui Torres and Eugenio Tisselli, who use a Processing script to delete one letter at random each time the textual display is refreshed. The concept of homeostasis is suggested as a dynamic balance between signal presence and signal absence (figures 3.12 and 3.13). José-Alberto Marques,

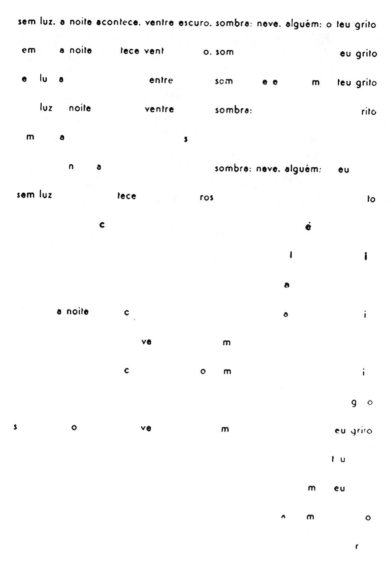

Figure 3.11
José-Alberto Marques, "Homeóstato 1" (1967) (first string of words: "without light. night happens. dark womb. shadow: snow. someone: your scream"). © José Alberto Marques. Reproduced with permission.

sem luz. a noite   c nte e. ven re e curo. so   bra neve.   lguem o teu g ito

sem luz. a noi e   contece. ve tre escuro. sombra: neve.   I uem: o teu grito

sem lu . a oite conte e. vent   e curo. sombr : neve. algu m: teu   r o

sem luz. a noite acontece. ven r   escuro. som   a: n ve. alguem o teu grito

sem lu . no te aco tece. ventre escu o. ombra: neve. alguem: o teu rito

sem luz. a noite acontece. ve tre e curo. sombra: neve. alguem: o teu g it

sem luz. a oite aco tece. entre escuro. ombr : neve. alguem: o teu gri o

sem luz. a noite acontece. v   tre escu o. s mbra: ve. algue : o teu grito

sem luz. a noite acontece. ventre escuro. so bra: neve. alguem: o te g ito

sem luz. a noite acontece. v ntre es uro. sombr : neve alguem: o teu grito

em luz. a noite acon ece. ventre escuro. sombra: nev . alguem   teu grito

sem luz. a noite contece. ventr e curo. sombra   eve   lguem: o teu rito

sem luz a noite aconte e. ventre esc o. sombr : neve. a guem: eu grito

sem uz. a noi e aconte   . v ntre escuro. somb a: neve. a gu m: o teu   o

sem luz. a no te ac ntece. ventre escuro. s mbr : neve. alguem: o te   grito

sem luz. a noite acont ce. ventre escuro. sombra: ne e. algu m: o teu grito

sem luz. a noite acontece. v ntre scuro. sombra: neve. algue   o teu grito

em luz. a noite acontece. ventre escu   . sombra: neve. alguem: o teu grito

sem l z. a no te acontece ve tre esc ro. s m ra: neve. algu m: o eu grito

Figure 3.12
Rui Torres and Eugenio Tisselli, digital version (2008) of "Homeóstato 1" (1967) by José-Alberto Marques (screen capture). © Rui Torres and Eugenio Tisselli. Reproduced with permission.

like Edwin Morgan in his topographic permutations, seems to demonstrate the double articulation of language as the way in which natural language is already digital.

In the digital version of "Dois fragmentos de uma experiância" (Two fragments of an experianxious) (1966), a poem by José-Alberto Marques re-created by Rodrigo Melo, the programming consists of highlighting the continuity of lines, in which letters are a string without word spaces. The possibility of reading—which depends on spaces that mark beginnings and endings of words and reconstitute syntactic hierarchies in sentences— seems to have become even more remote in this digital translation. Strings of letters run in opposite directions and at different speeds, making it impossible to understand more than a few fragments of meaning. The fragmentariness of the original experience, whose nonrepresentability was emulated in both the continuity of unspaced text and the difficulty of deciphering caused by the lack of spaces between words, is now translated

```
PFont font;
java.util.Vector letras;
int deleteLetter = -1;
int cColor = 0;
int nColor = 0;
int dir = 1;
void setup() {
  size(600,600);
  font = loadFont("Arial-BoldMT-16.vlw");
  textFont(font,16);
  textAlign(LEFT);
  letras = new Vector();
  loadText();
  if (notFinished()) {
    deleteLetter = chooseLetter();
    saveText();
  }
  fill(0,0,0);
}
void draw() {
  background(255,255,255);
  drawLetters();
}
void drawLetters() {
  letter l;
  for (int i=0;i<letras.size();i++) {
    l = (letter)letras.elementAt(i);
    if (l.state==1) {
      fill(0,0,0);
      text(l.letter,l.x,l.y);
    } else if (l.state==0 && i==deleteLetter && nColor < 256) {
      if (dir!=1) {
        fill(255,nColor,nColor);
        text(l.letter,l.x,l.y);
        nColor ++;
      } else {
        fill(cColor,0,0);
        text(l.letter,l.x,l.y);
        cColor ++;
        if (cColor==255) {
          dir = 2;
        }
      }
    }
  }
}
void loadText() {
  letter l;
  String URL = "http://www.po-ex.net/homeostatos/h/iso.txt";
  String lista[] = loadStrings(URL);
  for (int i=0;i<lista.length;i++) {
    String valores[] = split(lista[i],",");
    if (valores.length == 4) {
      l = new
letter(int(valores[1]),int(valores[2]),valores[0],int(valores[3])));
      letras.addElement(l);
    }
  }
}
```

Figure 3.13

Rui Torres and Eugenio Tisselli, code for the digital version (2008) of "Homeóstato 1" (1967) by José-Alberto Marques. © Rui Torres and Eugenio Tisselli. Reproduced with permission.

```
void saveText() {
  letter l;
  String URL = "http://www.po-ex.net/homeostatos/change.php?c=" +
deleteLetter;
  String lista[] = loadStrings(URL);
}
int chooseLetter() {
  int r;
  letter l;
  r = int(random(letras.size()-1));
  l = (letter)letras.elementAt(r);
  while (l.state == 0) {
    r = int(random(letras.size()-1));
    l = (letter)letras.elementAt(r);
  }
  l.state = 0;
  return r;
}
boolean notFinished() {
  letter l;
  boolean ret=false;
  for (int i=0;i<letras.size();i++) {
    l = (letter)letras.elementAt(i);
    if (l.state==1) {
      ret = true;
      break;
    }
  }
  return ret;
}
```

Figure 3.13
(continued)

into the undecipherability caused by the motion of letters. The anxiety of experience as fragmentary representation is experienced in the motion of the text and the movement of reading a text in motion. The reader is not only at a loss in isolating words and in remaking phrases and sentences, but cannot help experiencing the incessant motion of the very language with which he or she tries to make sense.

The remediation of "Mapa do deserto" (Desert map) (1966), by E. M. de Melo e Castro, in a version by Rui Torres, and ActionScript code by Jared Tarbel, also suggests the permutational processes of linguistic structures. Each set of letters permutates with all the other letters of the alphabet until lexicalized forms (those recognized as word strings in the dictionary) appear. The combinatoric potential of alphabetical writing (as graphic translation of phonological permutations) is a simulation of the possibilities for replication and mutation capable of generating new words. Permutations are timed and predefined, but they also respond to interaction with the mouse cursor: clicking on a letter triggers a new sequence of letter permutations. Permutations stop only when letters vanish or a lexicalized string is formed, suggesting that the word, that is, the pair signifier-signified, is a temporary stabilization of the flux inherent in the natural language code. Replication and transformation are the two main consequences of this generative property, with sequences appearing and disappearing consecutively. This digital transcoding maps the genome of language with the probe of writing in what may be described as a digital extension of one of the principles of experimental poetry: the coextensibility between world and poem that produces the real as the real of the poem in the poem (i.e., the linguistic and graphic forms that realize its mode of existence and signification).

In "Edifício" (Building) (1962), by E. M. de Melo e Castro, the digital rereading by Rui Torres and Jared Tarbel, represents the potentiality of form through the potentiality of a structure under construction (figures 3.14 and 3.15). Its printed ideogrammatic structure, which evokes reinforced concrete, has been transformed into a dance of materials in search of form: to

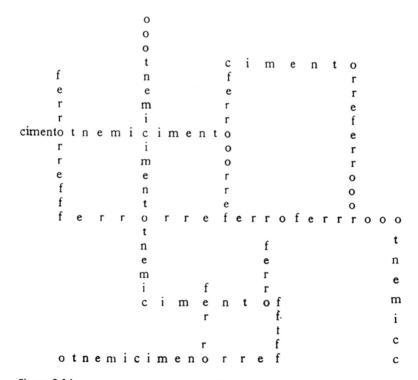

Figure 3.14

E. M. de Melo e Castro, "Edifício" (Building) (1962). © E. M. de Melo e Castro. Reproduced with permission.

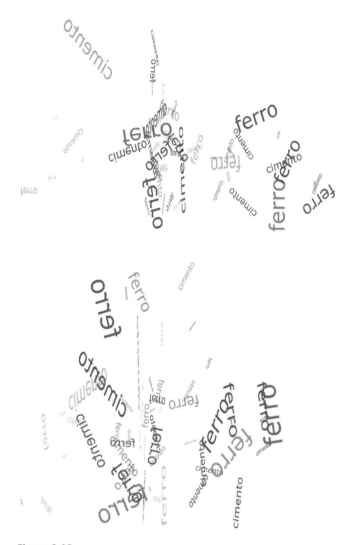

Figure 3.15
Rui Torres and Jared Tarbel, digital version (2008) of "Edifício" (Building) (1962) by E. M. de Melo e Castro (screen captures). © Rui Torres and Jared Tarbel. Reproduced with permission.

the iconic similarity between graphic structure and referent, the digital version adds an image of the potential of structure as a combination of materials—cement and iron, paper and printing, electronic screen and animation. Kinetic translation of a static layout turns the movement of reading contained in the original text into an actual motion of signs. It induces coalescence between the materiality of materials, creating a sensory perception of the flow and arbitrariness of structure as hypothetical construction. Such fluidity is made possible by refresh and multiple reinscription on the same writing space, a feature of the optoelectronic screen. The building of writing is evoked by the potential of drawing for the invention and manipulation of forms. As in other animations of constellated poems, decisions for animating certain textual objects seek to make kinetically explicit the process of writing as a live act of thought and as prosthesis to the imagination.

3.5 Galaxies of Signifiers

Other processes, which are no less procedural, arise through random collage or so-called found texts. Visual poetry made with preexisting materials (extracted from newspapers, magazines, and other kinds of printed materials) functions on the basis of a tension between the original meaning of assembled materials and resignification obtained by recontextualization. In these texts, unlike what happens in constellated and ideogrammatic concrete poems, in which the text appears as an allegedly self-sufficient microcosm, signs retain their material contiguity with the contexts of communication and discourse from which they originated. This is one of the strategies for representing discourse within the poem, that is, as a ready-made documentary evidence capable of reappropriation and critical recycling.

The series "Poemas Encontrados" (Found Poems, 1964) by António Aragão is exemplary in the resignification operated on the language of newspaper headlines (figure 3.16). They expose the social and political nature of language through appropriation of the graphics and semantics of fragments of phrases and words found in the press. Pointing to the infosphere as social and political space of collective representation, they establish a record of its particular historical moment. The random collage of those headlines seems to refer to an alienating effect that makes readers and writing strangers to each other at the very moment of their encounter. To reencounter those pieces of text as a poem is to be confronted with the proliferative materiality of language in the written press. It is to see again

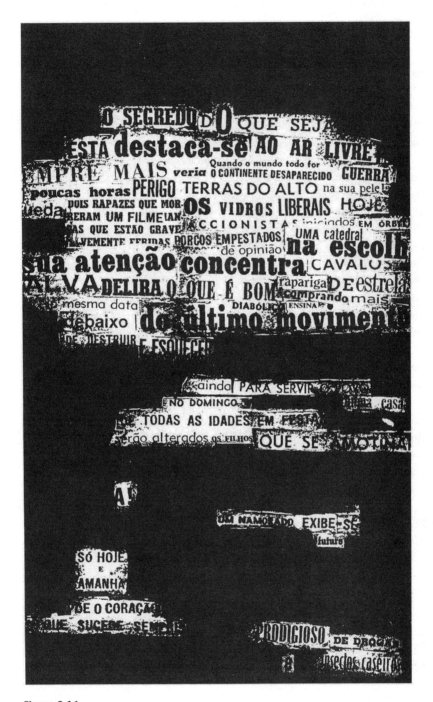

Figure 3.16
António Aragão, "Poemas encontrados" (Found poems) (1964). © António Aragão.
Reproduced with permission.

its signifying materiality outside the reading protocols of newspapers and of their mode of production of a daily agenda for public consumption. By doing this, these "found poems" also expose the unspeakable in the public sphere of the 1960s Portuguese press and make an indirect statement about the absence of political freedom.

The original "found poems" cut out words from newspapers in order to appropriate their alienated language in an expressive collage. They proposed a counterreading that liberated language from the discursive and graphical structures of the printed newspaper, opening up those structures to new associations resulting from fragmentation and juxtaposition. Two digital re-creations of "Poemas encontrados," authored by Rui Torres, Jared Tarbel, and Nuno Ferreira, adopt different strategies, both of which stress the timed and temporal condition of writing, exploring the nature of language and code. As rereadings, they are analyses of the compositional procedure of the original and an occurrence of reading as an algorithmic recombination of signs.

The randomized combination of printed headlines on the pages of periodicals is performed, in one case, on a set of words and phrases taken from the original collage. Typographical differences in face, size, and style, as well as the progressive layering of white letters on black background across different areas of the screen, emulate the indiscriminate collage of title fragments in the original. Instead of digitally replicating topography and typography, what is re-created is the compositional and procedural principle of aleatoric combination of a predefined set of elements (figure 3.17). As the program runs, the reader is faced with a certain correlation of verbal elements taken from the database of the original, whose visual distribution originates a black and white pattern of legible and illegible words or groups of words.

In the second instance, the ActionScript code works in conjunction with Hypertext Preprocessor (PHP) programming and with RSS feed in real time from online editions of six news sites: *La Vanguardia* (Spain), *Expresso* (Portugal), *Folha de São Paulo* (Brazil), *Google News Brazil*, *New York Times*, and *Público* (Portugal) (figure 3.18). The combinatorial collage of newspapers' headlines has been applied to the current online press, mining the language of Web pages to build a mechanism for real-time digital collage. The production of "found poems" has been formally scripted and automated, generating a defamiliarized sample of Web newspaper language. By displacing the particular historical content and historical reference of the original collage, this digital recoding decontextualizes and breaks the chains of meaning that bind text and context, a rhetorical move comparable to the

Figure 3.17
Rui Torres, Jared Tarbel and Nuno Ferreira, digital version (2008) of "Poemas encontrados" (1964) by António Aragão. © Rui Torres, Jared Tarbel and Nuno Ferreira. Reproduced with permission.

Figure 3.18

Rui Torres, Jared Tarbel, and Nuno Ferreira, digital version 2 (2008) of "Poemas encontrados" (1964) by António Aragão. Screen captures of iterations made with RSS feeds from *Folha de São Paulo, New York Times,* and *La Vanguardia* (August 8, 2011, c. 2.30 p.m. GMT). © Rui Torres, Jared Tarbel, and Nuno Ferreira. Reproduced with permission.

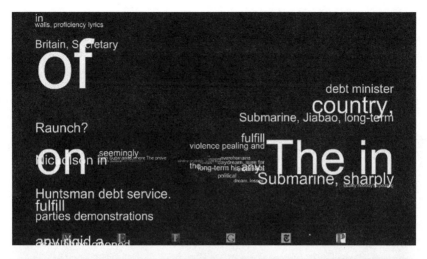

Figure 3.18
(continued)

Figure 3.18
(continued)

one occurring in the original. Indeed, this is one of the main effects of the collage by António Aragão: its original sources and references have been abolished, or they remain only as a distant echo. As found poems, they have broken the verbal and graphic markers of discursive cohesion and coherence that ensured a pragmatic function in their textual source. Its signifying emptiness, that is, its potential for meaning, is transcoded and reembodied in the arbitrary network of relationships between words and sentence fragments, which continuously overlap and repeat in different scales and at various points of the screen, resembling statistical clouds of occurrences.

As the program runs, the layout begins to resemble the graphical pattern of António Aragão's "Poemas encontrados." In the meantime, the reader has been able to observe the formation of constellations of news fragments in a process that delights in the randomness and automated nature of the final result, an entirely contingent and temporary effect of an iteration of the program's code at a particular moment, and from a particular corpus of textual sources. Even more so than in Aragão's text, meaning appears as an accident of reading and of its processes for filling in gaps and ellipses and establishing links that are at once unique and patterned. Such links, however, have lost the hierarchy characteristic of either newspaper or poem structures: they have lost the whole function of producing linguistic and graphical cohesion and coherence. They emerge rather as live wires of semantics and chaotic appearances of the proliferation of signifiers in a world saturated with letters and inscriptions. The black background is the negative space from which an almost illegible galaxy of signifiers emerges— a galaxy that algorithmically reconstellates the original analog collage and turns its generative process into the main reference of the text.

We find here a materialization of the distributed and weblike nature of digital materiality: the fragments that make up the text, like the addresses of files in computer circuits, have to be transferred and reassembled from multiple servers in accordance with the hardware and software properties of the machine that displays them. The automatic feeding of headlines from news sites—which, in turn, is overdetermined by the code that generates the graphic layout of the transferred textual fragments—also refers to the materiality of distributed electronic reproduction as a machine for finding poems. The semidetermined and random nature of the graphic and linguistic output, which can be printed, means that this second digital version of the original poem is ergodic and interactive: the final instantiation of this work depends on an intervention by the reader, which is unique and temporary. The introduction of temporality into the writing occurs at two levels simultaneously: as a predefined timing in the source code that correlates with the machine clock and as the temporality of acts of reading that respond to newly generated text. Time of writing and time of reading attain material expression in textual animation and generation and in the interaction with the animation and generation mediated by the mouse cursor.

This textual engine gives readers the possibility of seeing the combinatorics of text generation and understanding how this process is a function of the automated tools of electronic writing. It is perhaps here that the transcoding shows a fundamental difference between Aragão's original text and its digital re-creations. In the first case, the random combination of words and phrases found in the press still contains the mark of the subject who found them. In the second case, the association is generated by a randomized programmed procedure whose historicity seems alien to the human subject who activates its generation, as if the texts were constructed independent of his or her participation. In effect, this is one aspect that resists conceptualization in the phenomenology of electronic hypermediation: the semiautomatic nature of text generation, although subject to decisions that affect its enfolding, appears to offer the text as a kinetic spectacle, disconnected from its interpretive remediation by a reader. Considered as a reflection on the nature of writing and reading, the experimental poem located the dissemination of meaning in the relationship between semiotic intervention and hermeneutic intervention, drawing our attention to visuality and topographicality as textual markers, and therefore as particular sets of reading instructions. In this respect, digital transcodings further extend a poetics of reading—typical of both ideogrammatic texts, and of collage- and assemblage-based texts—into a poetics of machine reading. Self-consciousness of reading plays out also as awareness of the readings of the machine.

3.6   Kinetic Translations

The use of kinetic properties of electronic writing for rereading and rewriting experimental poems makes visible the operations performed by programming codes on the graphic codes that configure language in visual and concrete poems. In electronic remediation of the printed page, the digital re-creation of typographic and topographic markers usually consists of projecting a sequence of movements onto the constellated poem. These motions frame the printed text constellation as either final, or initial, or an intermediate frame within a temporal sequence of other related frames.

The original layout enfolds as a storyboard for animation. Motion of letters and words actualizes through specific sequences the multiple reading paths featured in the spatialized field of signifiers, which the eye follows from point to point, exploring the possibilities created by a radial distribution. The hermeneutic potential of the original text, that is, the interpretive possibilities arising from the proliferation of paths for reading a topological space, is converted into a new semiotic set by means of animation.

This conversion of hermeneutic space into semiotic marks presupposes the conversion of an act of reading (e.g., eye movements that connect letters or words along certain paths) into an act of writing (the explicit presentation of that perceptual linking as a property of the kinetic sequence). This writing of reading in turn is poised on an intersemiotic translation, which involves, among other things, implementing operations characteristic of film codes (e.g., definition point of view, shots, cuts, angles, zooms, travelings) that stand for (and transform) the original graphical code. This kinetic revisualization of the visual text also implies a geometrical shift from paper plane to screen space. The bidimensionality of planographic writing sometimes makes way for the tridimensionality of electronic writing: to the x- and y-axes of the surface gridlines, we have to add the z-axis of the third dimension of electronic space. In this process of transcoding the experimental poem, it is the electronic space itself that opens up as a laboratory for forms released from paper. Certain self-referential and self-similarity operations can now be extended to the new electronic environment, creating loops that are specifically addressed at the digital medium.

Let us take a look at the digital remakings of "Transparência/oblivion" (Transparency/oblivion) (1964), a poem by E. M. de Melo e Castro, digitally redesigned by Rodrigo Melo; "Hipopótamos" (Hippopotamuses) (1964), a poem by Herberto Helder, digitally recreated by Rodrigo Melo; "Poemas em efe" (Poems in f) (1964), by Salette Tavares, re-created by Rodrigo Melo and Pedro Reis; and "Al gar ismos alfinete" (Fi g ures pin) (1966), by Salette Tavares, re-created by Rui Torres and Jared Tarbel. In "Transparência/obliv-ion," the procedure is to build a kinetic narrative, of which the original visual text becomes a kind of compressed version. The letters first appear and distribute themselves according to the spatial axes of the paper version, but they soon extend beyond that grid as they accumulate and become denser all over the screen in order to suggest a rapid explosive expansion and the shrapnel scattering after the blast. The sentence "a pax evita a explosão" (pax avoids explosion), which was set along axes parallel to the scattered letters, has now become the culmination of the sequence, offering in a much more explicit way its pacifist message as textual closure. Narrative sequencing of elements that were simultaneously present on the plane of the paper page is, in some cases, a factor that reduces the diagrammatic ambiguity of the original.

Reduction of combinatorial possibilities functions, to some extent, as a hermeneutic action that performs a particular interpretation on a multi-layered set of verbal and visual signs. This explains why these re-creations also present themselves as rereadings: in many cases, they are actually exercises of electronic interpretation applied to written or printed texts. In other words, what we see on the screen is not only the potential of electronic tools as a new way of writing but also what these tools reveal about how written language and bibliographic codes produce meaning. In the re-creation of "Hipopótamos," the exercise of separating letters, required for reading the original text, is mediated by the mouse cursor, which allows readers to speed up or slow down the circles of text and to move them back or forward. This is a frequent cinematic trope in the rewriting of printed visual poems: the physical movement of reading is transferred to the movement of the text itself, and the cursor is made to perform part of the work of the eye by acting on sets of signs in order to make them legible. Digital transcreations seem to change the ratio between optic, haptic, and symbolic operations when compared with print originals.

In both poems by Salette Tavares, the layout of word lists is set in columns: in "Poemas em efe," they have to be read in several directions, and they come in various typefaces, sizes, and styles; in "Al gar ismos alfinete," there are two directions for reading and a single typeface and type size. In the digital version of "Poemas em efe," the movement of words starting with *f* has been set along a diagonal axis, with relative variations in speed causing multiple and overlapping patterns and several patterns of movement, which suggest the phonic, semantic, and graphic attractions of the original combinations. The typographic contiguity between groups of words that are distributed along horizontal and vertical axes, which form subsets in the original text, is turned into a weblike and radial contiguity. Their animated motion enhances the relations of contiguity between any one element and the other elements in the set. Any act of reading this digital text reflects its random association of words by forcing readers to fix their eyes at random on a particular element. Although it lacks some of the play with the graphic materiality of the letter *f* in the graphic layout of the original, this re-creation brings digital materiality to the fore: the kineticism of words on the screen is an intersemiotic translation of the topographicality of the printed layout.

In the digital version of "Al gar ismos alfinete," the original words have been radially reconstellated in a way that suggests three dimensions, emphasized by differences in size and tonal shade of characters, with words superimposing each other in four or five successive planes (figure 3.19). The words are programmed to increase in size and to move continuously toward the forefront of the picture until the extreme close-up falls outside its framework. As this cinematic trope enfolds, the reader has the possibility of clicking on one of the words, which automatically causes it to shift to the central area of the screen, thus recentering the moving word constellation. Both effects (kinetic radial distribution and repositioning of the three-dimensional word cloud when one element is brought to the center) convey in a more powerful way one of the effects of the original: the perception of the coexistence of words in a network of phonetical and lexical affinities, indicated by either their common etymological origin or their sound similarity.

If, when reading the print version, the eyes are moving between each of the words, and momentarily demoting or erasing peripheral elements, in reading the digital version, the network of constellated words remains present even when eyes move to the word, which temporarily functions as the central focus for reading. The movement of the text toward the viewer activates peripheral vision and does not allow the eye to isolate the word, where it is momentarily fixed, from the others surrounding it. This means that the original effect of decentering, which presented words as a kind of musical lexicon score, is emphasized in this animation, in which each word appears as a link in a web of language units without center, at the same time decentered and recentrable from any one point. The first and last planes may change their respective positions in a loop with neither beginning nor end. In each of these media translations, motion performs a reading movement on the source printed constellations and creates its own mouse-mediated reading choreography.

3.7 Reflexive Remediations

Experimental poetry of the 1960s and 1970s inflected the reflexiveness characteristic of modernist aesthetics toward a critique of discursivity. This critique involved a double rationale: it was a critique of discursivity as part of the social modes of production of self and of a certain order of political representations of the real, and it was a critique of discursivity in poetic discourse itself (i.e., of the discursive modes of poetic production). *Experimental,* in this particular historical context, meant performing a critique

Figure 3.19
Rui Torres and Jared Tarbel, digital version (2008) of "Al gar ismos alfinete" (Fi g
ures pin) (1966) by Salette Tavares (screen captures). © Rui Torres and Jared Tarbel.
Reproduced with permission.

Figure 3.19
(continued)

of language by means of both combinatorial syntax and semantics and by means of visualization and sonification of the poem. Graphic, diagrammatic, and ideogrammatic materiality of spatialized signifiers on the page and pictorial, intermedia, and sculptural three-dimensionality were constituted as poetical resources, thus redefining the materiality and form of the poem.

Stressing the acoustic, aural, oral, and gestural materiality means recovering the poem as temporal and temporary event. As an instance of writing, its visuality is made to imply a voice and a body in the body of the poem. Whether sound or visual, the text on the page in these operations reveals itself as mere notation or record for a poetic interpretation that has to reenact itself again and again as a unique performance, which can happen only through situated and concrete acts of reading. This is perhaps the particular contribution of experimental poetics: a systematic use of several modernist and postmodernist processes and techniques (procedural writing, serialism, randomness, fragmentation of the signifier, critique of referential transparency, medial self-referentiality, the poem as a sonic event, the poem as visual figuration, objectuality, intermediality, performative presence of reading in the poem itself) in order to investigate the conditions of meaning production in language and of poetic meaning production in particular.

Animated versions make clear the multilayered movement that takes place in the mind of the reader of a constellated poem. What often baffles readers of concrete texts is the paradox of finding themselves before minimal signs that are at the same time highly charged of references and desires for meaning. What appears as an impenetrable self-descriptive surface-only sign opens up its single-word palimpsests of echoes and allusions to the discursive and graphical forces of social language. The fact that many poems attempt to break the discursive chains associated with the elements contained in the poems, often discarding syntactic connectors, turns texts into a challenging notation that readers have to learn how to read. The word, written or spoken, is never entirely taken for granted in its material form, and iconic referentiality is not necessarily a trivial poetical device, sometimes originating complex ideogrammatic texts.

Two formal and material features explain the apparent ease with which many visual and concrete poems lend themselves to digital rereadings and re-creations: their intermediality (or intersemioticity), especially their triple verbal, visual (both typographical and topographical), and sonic coding, which tends to associate voice and writing in new graphophonetic patterns; and their cinematicity, that is, the suggestion of graphemic motion between letters and other word elements. Spatiality and temporality are incorporated into the poem, resulting in a poetics of reading and language as cognitive practices. By embodying this experimental poetics, texts show themselves as products of their own generative procedures and the perceptual and cognitive motions of reading.

The text becomes the place of its own effects, which are structured in a series of intersemiotic echoes between the phonetic, the semantic, the syntactic, and pragmatic levels of verbal language, on the one hand, and of the representational and nonrepresentational dimension of writing, on the other. Mimetic and expressive effects are displaced to the inside of language and of its codes and practices, calling into question discursive modes of reference to self and world. A correlative of that type of metatextuality of writing is precisely the attempt to represent the materiality of reading in its neurological and mental motions. It is this awareness of reading and writing codes that gives digital properties to many experimental texts.

As mentioned above, digital rereadings of experimental and concrete poetry of the 1960s and 1970s were, in several instances, initiated by the authors themselves. In these digital transcodifications of texts originally made for books and exhibitions, multiple reading paths are transformed into animation sequences, which temporize the appearance and motion of letters, actualizing a set of combinatorial and associative possibilities. The text foregrounds itself as a performance of its own writing and its own reading: once the text is animated, it becomes clear to readers how the movement of the letters-as-writing replicates in its own specific algorithm the combinatorial rules of language and how the movement of the letters-as-reading embodies the physical and cognitive motion of interpreting a verbivocovisual notation. Readers experience the materiality of reading and the codependence between meaning and particular semiotic trajectories and hermeneutic operations. Denaturalizing pragmatic uses of language, including expectations of poetic communication, experimental poetics explores the probabilistic and stochastic nature of language for meaning production.

Digital transcreations seem to make clear that releasing poems from paper-based bibliographic coding is not so much a way of showing the limitations of the printed page as it is a demonstration of the astonishing complexity of its topology as a signifying mechanism. In fact, digital re-creations often fall short of the signifying potential contained in the paper text, undermining the so-called linearity of one medium versus the multilinearity of the other. Considered as a critique of poetical codes, the experimental poem rightly sought to augment its knowledge about the specific materiality of graphic and verbal mediation and about the nature of reader participation. The point was to show how the medium was the poem and how meaning was produced through an embodied interaction with the probabilistic presence of the poem. Being a technology for writing and reading, electronic tools extended this research through self-awareness of the semantic effects of their specific modes of mediation and reader participation.

In digital re-creation of visual and concrete poems, we can see the relationship between a reading function, which reveals the complexity of the graphic source code on page, and a rewriting function, which explores the potential of the computational source code. If some properties are directly derived from the first, others are specific to the formal operations of electronic digitality. It is through that dialectical relationship that we can reassess the prospective value of the experimental poem as anticipation of a new technology for writing and as an exploration of the digital properties of natural language. In other words, it is not only digital technology that allows us to reread the experimental texts: experimental texts also help us to understand digital mediation in its intrinsic intermediality and generativity. These transcreations are remarkable demonstrations of the digitality of the concrete poem, that is, of the profound relationship between computer codes, print codes, and language codes. In these works we can see digital transcoding as an extension of the machinery of writing and print and a renewed engagement with the complexity of reading acts.

Experimentation with the codes of writing and reading, a central feature of the experimental poem of the 1960s and 1970s, and experimentation with a new technology for writing and reading, characteristic of electronic literature in recent decades, occur in the context of a deconstructionist conceptualization of writing and reading, for which both poetic practices continue to contribute. More than mere repositories of visual and concrete texts, *Po.Ex: A Digital Archive of Portuguese Experimental Literature* (2013), *Concrete Poetry: The Verbivocovisual Project* (2008), *Artéria* number 8 (2003–2004), *Errática* number 104 (2012), and other reflexive remediations of experimental texts are part of the ongoing process of research into the experiences and codes of signification. Reflexive remediations explore print textual programs as a cognitive poetics of reading. Two strategies for a critical remediation of print graphicalities as scripts for reading motions are the performance of inscriptions through kinetic translations and algorithmic permutations. Specific affordances of the new medium are used to heighten our sense of the interactive eventuality of meaning production through acts of reading.

4 Moving the Mind: The Motion of Signifiers

4.1 Poetic Engines

The important European group of electronic literature, L.A.I.R.E. (Lecture, Art, Innovation, Recherche, Écriture) (Reading, Art, Innovation, Research, Writing), was formed in France in 1989.[1] Philippe Bootz, a founding member, has developed a procedural model of digital textuality for describing the reconfigured relations of author's field, work's field, and reader's field in programmed works. His semiotic approach addresses the pragmatics of writing and reading programmed works, establishing the dual nature of programmed signs (2004, 2005b, 2006, 2012), the splitting of reading (2010), and the lability of the device (Bootz and Saemmer, 2012). Those properties, particularly the relation between ergodic and noematic readings, are also structural tropes in the interactive scripts used for sign manipulation in his own work.

Bootz describes the materiality of the display, the multimedia screen features of works, as "le transitoire observable" (observable transitory), and he uses the concept of metastylistic forms to refer to programming codes. Transient observable forms are material instances produced by metastylistic implicit forms, code that is not immediately accessible to readers. Authors of programmed works move between these two levels: on the one hand, the physical process of executing the program, and, on the other, the pragmatic reality of the reader's activity. The grammatical productivity of computer code and the perceptual display of transient signifiers should be studied in their interrelations. Electronic literature requires the consideration of both programmability and the material instantiation of code in a given form:

Programming is a new material sculpted and modeled by artists. In the perspective of Transitoire Observable, this modeling implies work on the form. It is a formalist approach to the duality algorithms/process that constitutes programming. What we are aiming at in this approach is not the program considered as an ensemble of lines of text or well-formed code, nor the event produced by the execution as audiovisual reality, but the relation between this event to, on the one hand, the algorithmic reality of the code, and, on the other, the pragmatics of reading. (Bootz 2004, my translation)[2]

This poetics of programming explicitly engages with the level of code rather than simply with the metaphors, graphically embodied in software tools. Bootz's aesthetic position highlights one important aspect of digital literature: a software layer that scripts its interactive tropes and its audio-visual materiality and is part of a poetics of digital media that "relocates programming at the core of electronic art" (Bootz 2005b). Writers of pro-grammed works should move beyond predefined expressive features embedded in a given program and instead consider programming itself as their material. It is through this conscious intervention at the programming level that the specificity of the *transitoire observable* may be grasped and fully explored. The pragmatics of authoring electronic literature engages with its algorithmic nature, and not merely with transient screen effects.[3]

The model further attempts to capture the specifics of the relationship between the performativity of the program, as executed by the machine, and the performativity of reading, as a recursive loop between the reader and the transitory states of the work's process. Reading acts cogenerate the *transitoire observable* by feeding back data during the execution of the work. As acts of reading, they become scripted in the work's virtual field at the metatextual level. Through programming, reading can be put inside the work itself and becomes an internal function of the metatextual device that instantiates the text: "the work is a system whose reading is one of its internal functions" (Bootz 2004, sec. 4, my translation).[4]

In the procedural model, reading is split between affective and analyti-cal reading (Bootz 2010), which leads Bootz to conceive of a metareading position that reframes the internal reading of the observable transitory within an external cognitive understanding of the whole programmed process of the work. This mode of presence of reading in programmed works can offer new insights into the nature of reading in general and also about the particular performativity of reading in programmable media. The notion of scripting the reading act through material operations triggered by the program has been a major concern for several new media artists, but the specific freedoms and constraints of the reader of programmed works have yet to be properly accounted for.

Bootz's model also provides a nuanced theoretical account of the role of the author in light of the changeable and ephemeral conditions for the execution of works. The role of the author as expressed by the program is further determined by the lability of digital devices. If electronic materiality consists of a series of cascading abstractions with several layers nested on each other, it is clear that certain properties at the level of the formal materiality will depend on specific codes and hardware capabilities. Execution and display depend on machine instructions that cannot be entirely controlled by the author but are constitutive of the digital communication environment required for programmed and networked media. The whole dynamics of author-program-machine-screen implies the incompleteness of the program itself:

> The program that the author writes contains only a part of the instructions used for its execution: the author is only a coauthor of what happens on the screen, even if his program is only a description of what he wants to see appear on the screen. The transitoire observable changes with time. The same program produces a different transitoire observable when it is executed in a different technical context or on a different machine, and this is true even when it consists of just a basic description of what can be seen on the screen. The relationship between the diverse transitoires observables made by the same program is called "procedural transformation" in the model. (Bootz 2006)

These three notions—the duality of programmed signs, the incompleteness of the program and the presence of reading in the constitution of the work—seem useful for grasping the singularities of author-machine and reader-machine intermediation.[5]

In *Ré-veille poétique* (2007), it is possible to identify the central tenets of Bootz's poetics of the programmed text (figure 4.1). This work contains a timed sequence of French words that use the string *ré* as a morphological element in their formation and form a combinatorial poem. There is also a second timed sequence of words that is independent of the random *ré* string combinations and forms a love poem in three stanzas. The motion of the seconds' clock hand has been replaced by the appearance and disappearance of word elements. Words pulsate at the clock rhythm of a one-word element every second: the prefix or character string *ré* appears at even seconds and the word or remaining part of the word at odd seconds. Although *ré* works as a prefix for most words, it is also used as an initial string without a morphosemantic function for some words. Thus, in the random sixteen-second sequence between 10:10:04 and 10:10:19 we would read the following prefixes and words: "ré" "animer" (re animate) + "ré" "sonne" (re sound) + "ré" "arranger" (re arrange) + "ré" "parer" (re pair) + "ré" "création" (re creation) + "ré" "activer" (re activate) + "ré" "acteur" (re actor) + "ré" "incarner" (re incarnate).

The use of *ré* as an autonomous string creates a tension between repetition and difference, since each word is perceived in both its prefixed and

unprefixed forms. Morphological division reinforced through word animation points to the function of the prefix as a remaking of the semantic
content of each word in its unprefixed form. The repetition suggested by
the prefix and the measured passage of time also works as a self-reflexive
and metalinguistic device at various levels: it is a doubling of each word
within itself (as *creation* within *re-creation*), a repetition of the author's
program within the reader's machine, and evidence of the presence of
reading within the transient state textual display on the screen. The work
explicitly alludes to the incompleteness of the author's program by integrating the real-time machine clock of the reader's machine into the internal timing of the text. As a textual instrument, it also depends on reading
interventions for playing out its double-structured program. For instance,
deactivating or activating the alarm of the clock causes the display to
alternate between the combinatorial poem of the first sequence and the
three-stanza love poem of the second sequence. The pulses of the seconds'
hand make the passing of the time a material reference of its verbal
content, which describes love as a cycle of "erotic desire, common construction, separation."

```
t =
["incarner","insérer","essayer","intégrer","mission","occuper","orchestrer","organiser","orienter","
ouverture","parer"]
  repeat with i = 1 to t.count
    p_poeme.add(t[i])
  end repeat
  t =
["pression","primer","public","unifier","union","vêler","diction","partie","pis","pondre","pression","
conforter","créatif"]
  repeat with i = 1 to t.count
    p_poeme.add(t[i])
  end repeat
  p_texte = []
  t = ["moi","ouverture","elle","ferrer","moi","introduire","elle","moi","jouir","fort","","veille",""]
  p_texte.add(t.duplicate())
  t = ["elle","inviter","moi","installer","elle","moi","unir","inventer","","veille",""]
  p_texte.add(t.duplicate())
  t = ["elle ment","elle","embobiner","moi","moi","capituler","partir","","veille",""]
  p_texte.add(t.duplicate())
  member("texte").text = ""
  sprite("veille").loc = sprite("point 30").loc
  p_old_nb = 0
  p_etat = 0
  p_re = true
  sprite("veille").blend = 0
  p_en_cours = 0
end
```

Figure 4.1
Philippe Bootz, *Ré veille poétique* (2007) (code and screen captures). © Philippe Bootz.
Reproduced with permission.

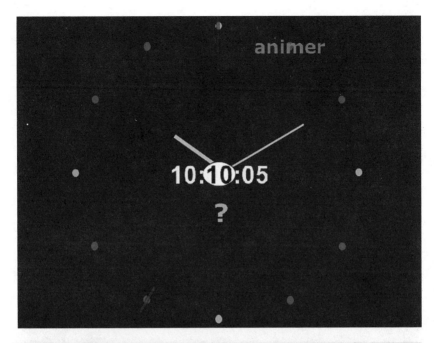

Figure 4.1
(continued)

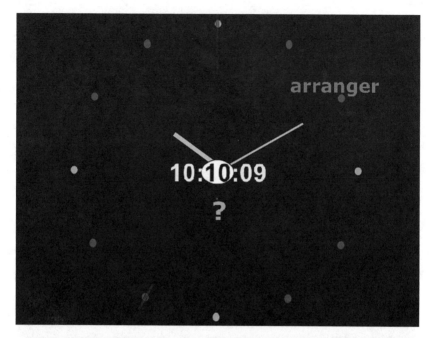

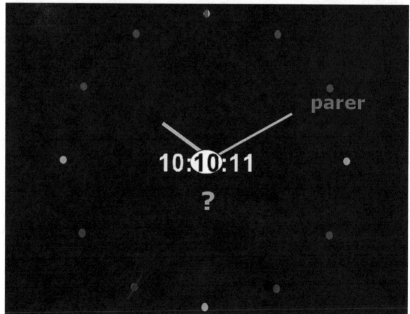

Figure 4.1
(continued)

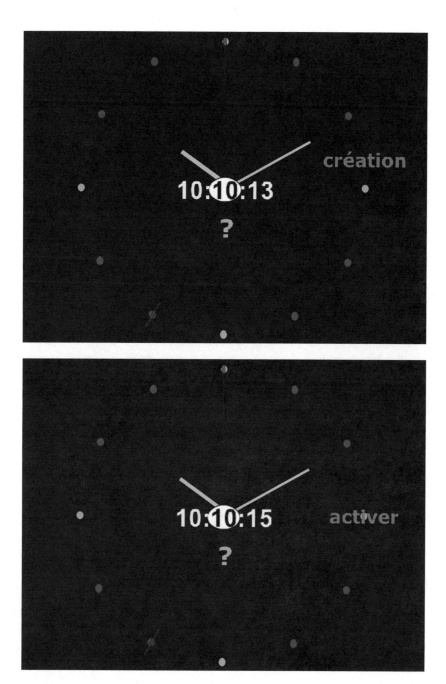

Figure 4.1
(continued)

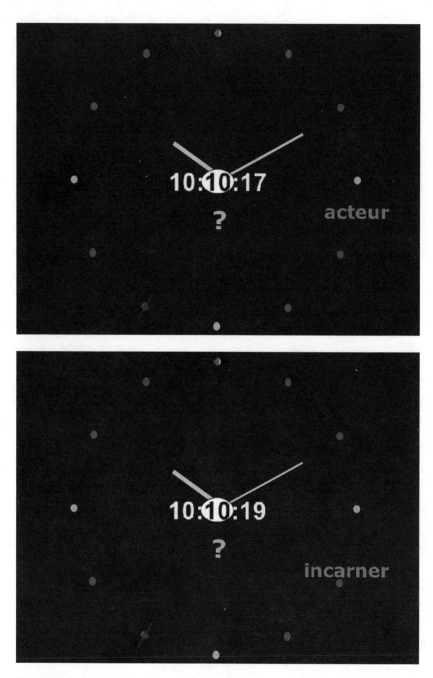

Figure 4.1
(continued)

Figure 4.1
(continued)

```
global g_reveil_actif
global g_langue -- langue active
global g_old_etat -- n° de strophe enregistré dans le fichier de préférence re_veille.txt

property p_texte
property p_poeme
property p_re -- true si "ré" visible
property p_old_nb
property p_etat --état du poème : 0 (courant), 1(érotique),2(engagé),3 (déçu)
property p_en_cours -- mot en cours (pour les états non nuls)
property p_old_etat -- ancien état activé par le réveil
--property p_fileini


on endsprite
   -- result = bawriteini("etat","p_old_etat",string(p_old_etat),p_fileini)
   -- put result
   g_old_etat = p_old_etat
   texte = g_langue&","&&string(p_old_etat)
   _player.setpref ("re_veille",texte)
end


on beginsprite me
   --  p_fileini = _movie.path&"re_veille.ini"
   --  p_old_etat = bareadini("etat","p_old_etat","",p_fileini)
   -- p_old_etat = integer(_player.getpref("re_veille"))
   p_old_etat = g_old_etat
-- if p_old_etat = "" then
   --  p_old_etat = 0
-- else
   --  p_old_etat = integer(p_old_etat)
-- end if

   p_poeme = []
   t = []
   t = ["spire", "sonne","frein","de
lumière","d'heure","dire","son","sonner","absorber","acteur","action","activer"]
   repeat with i = 1 to t.count
     p_poeme.add(t[i])
   end repeat
   t = ["adapter",
"admettre","ajuster","alité","animer","apparaître","arranger","chaud","citer","clamer","concilier","
confort"]
   repeat with i = 1 to t.count
     p_poeme.add(t[i])
   end repeat
   t =
["création","écrire","embarquer","entendre","engager","équilibrer","fléchir","crier","former","essa
yer","fraction","galet","imprimer"]
   repeat with i = 1 to t.count
     p_poeme.add(t[i])
   end repeat
```

An excerpt from the Lingo syntax used for defining the text generation behavior in *Ré-veille poétique* gives us a glimpse into the layered nature of digital works. Objects and behaviors are defined according to a program that describes their graphic, audiovisual, kinetic, and interactive properties as the work enfolds in processing time. This excerpt expresses hierarchies between various files and behaviors, the relation of the current state of the poem with a previous state, the response of the text to the preferences set by player, and the eighty-eight textual strings that will be combined with *re* every two seconds. The author's comments describe the functions of each element in the generation of the textual events, including the four textual states of the poem: 0 (*courant*) (current), 1 (*érotique*) (erotic), 2 (*engagé*) (committed), and 3 (*déçu*) (separated).

States 1, 2, and 3, describing a three-stage love relationship, will be displayed if the reader sets the alarm clock; otherwise the program will perform only state 0, combining *ré* with character strings that form words related to *creation* or *bed*. While the difference between code and display shows the dual nature of programmed signs, the actual display will depend on both the distributed execution of the program across a network by a particular machine and specific data input by a reading interaction. The machine clock-time measuring the passage of the time of love in its electronic circuits becomes a reflexive expression of the changing material conditions of writing and reading through programmable media.

4.2 Machine Texts

This section contains examples of textual instantiations of the workings of the machine, usually through visual and kinetic metaphors that emulate machinic processes. Works by Alexandre Gherban, for example, are based on the generative use of programming codes as grammars for producing visual, audio, and kinetic instances of computer textuality. Gherban is concerned with the modularity of digital elements: codes for computer characters, codes for colors and other pictorial elements, codes for spatial coordinates and motions, codes for sounds, and more. His factorial poetics makes codes apparent by refusing to work with clearly defined semantic units or recognizable visual and sound patterns. Character strings, image fragments, and sound pulses take on a machinic, abstract, and purely formal character, as if they were meant to create a sensory emulation of the numerical changes that happen at the level of code when instructions are executed. His works contain visual and sound metaphors for the code itself by means of randomized permutations and transformations.

Robolettries (2007b) is a series of programmed texts that play with random permutations of graphic signs and sounds in ways that call attention to the purely abstract character of their forms. Some texts in the series generate arbitrary sequences of character signs, and others are based on letter permutations from a short sequence of words. This is what happens, for instance, with the letters of the names of the authors used in "Robolettrie 2 (Hommage à jean pierre balpe)" and "Robolettrie 9 (Hommage à Tibor Papp/70)." In "Robolettrie 9," two characters appear continuously at different points of the black screen grid, as if we were looking at a catalog of special characters, diacritics, and punctuation signs. At the center of the black screen, we see permutations of the letters contained in the name "Tibor Papp" that result in multiple phonetic combinations of vowels and consonants. These texts perform the machinic factoring of all the possible combinations of signs, suggesting the strangeness of machine language but also its relation to human language.

In *Essayeur sémantique* (2007a), each click activates a brief sequence of signifiers that include letters, graphic patterns, fragments of synthetic images suggesting landscapes, and synthesized sounds (figure 4.2). Automated textuality is experienced as a modular collage of fragments that can be apprehended only as an abstract sound and visual pattern. Seeing and reading are conflated in a way that resists both the semantics of verbal language and the semantics of images. *Robolettries* (2007b) and *Essayeur sémantique* (2007a) stress the role of the program as a genetic code for unpredictable and chaotic associations, based on the factoring of its constituent mathematical entities. Readers experience meaning and resistance to meaning as functions of the associative probability of signifiers, which depends on random iterations of the program. Although the lines of code remain inaccessible, readers are given a graphic and sonic correlative of machine generativity.

Antero de Alda is the author of *Scriptpoemas* (Scriptpoems, 2005), an ongoing series of kinetic texts based on recursive explorations of animation techniques using ActionScript and JavaScript. Like some of the examples in chapter 3, his digital remediations of visual texts on paper show how collages and visual texts already accommodated the kind of intermediality that digital codes have encouraged. Each of the *scriptpoemas* is a short looping sequence, usually accompanied by a musical soundtrack. The word *poem,* which is used in the eighty-one titles of this sequence, turns visual self-reference into a major signifying layer of these works. Iconic self-similarity is presented as a catalog of multimedia and animation tropes of scripted texts that illustrate expressive possibilities of the program tools.

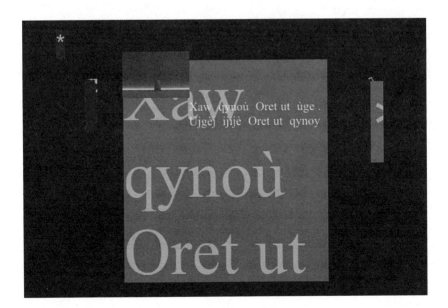

Figure 4.2
Alexandre Gherban, *Essayeur sémantique* (2007) (screen captures). © Alexandre Gherban. Reproduced with permission.

Figure 4.2
(continued)

As a digital ars poetica, they show the animated poem as a function of the program scripts and their enabling displays. Scripts for animation and other visual effects are used to evoke objects, motions, and sensory impressions through the graphic and multimedia interface of the screen, playing with the relation between concrete (aural and visual) and abstract (semantic) modes of reference. Conceptual and perceptual effects are obtained through the sensuous manipulation of the iconicity and graphicality of the word and other visual elements.

One of the most self-reflexive texts in this series is titled "Poema em código" (Poem in code) (figure 4.3). The screen is split into two halves: the right half of the screen runs a long sequence of lines of code, while the left half shows large-size fragments of those lines. The speed of presentation in each half of the screen is not controllable, and it seems to have been designed to suggest machine writing and machine reading. In both halves of the screen, code lines run too fast to become completely legible for a human reader without resorting to more invasive actions such as zooming in and taking screen captures. Readers can, however, hint that the code they are only half-reading is self-descriptive: those lines belong to the JavaScript and HTML source code required for the effects and properties that they are seeing on the screen. Motion of code lines and recognition of alphanumeric strings as expressions of code perform the rhetorical function of miming the digital materiality of programmable signs as they are processed by artificial languages for relaying instructions to the machine, which are then performed as screen displays.[6]

Motion of signs thus becomes an emulation of the motion of the source code as it is being executed. Readers are faced with the double articulation of high-level programmable signs as half-human and half-cybernetic, and with the poem itself as a coded and enigmatic device that refunctionalizes the uses of discourse, including the alphanumeric forms of writing that constitute a coded language. The only sentence that is not in motion contains the ironic warning: "pode ser perigoso descodificar o poema" (decoding the poem can be dangerous). *Decoding* refers to the consequences of removing the code out of the text, which would compromise its machine executability, but it also refers to the human interpretation of the text, which may open up uncontrolled and unanticipated meanings in a probabilistic and emergent manner. In the conflation of display and source code, readers encounter the dual nature of programmable language and the fundamental difference between code performativity and natural language performativity. The code is and is not the text, at once excessive and defective in its processing of itself.

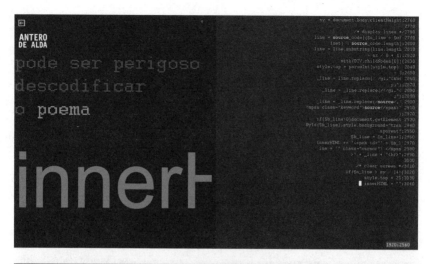

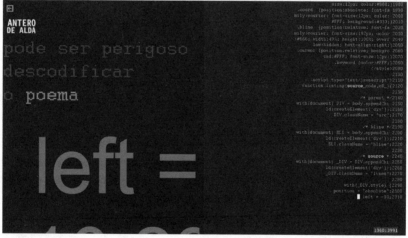

Figure 4.3
Antero de Alda, *Scriptpoemas:* "Poema em código" (Scriptpoems: Poem in code)
(2005). Script by Gerard Ferrandez (adapted) (screen captures). © Antero de Alda.
Reproduced with permission.

Figure 4.3
(continued)

A similar reflection on the instrumental function of code can be found in works by Brazilian poet, translator, and digital artist André Vallias, who has played a major role as programmer and Web designer in the transcoding of Brazilian visual and concrete texts for the digital medium (Wiese 2012). His own works are hybrids of digital art and digital poetry that foreground the screen as a Cartesian space. In *Nous n'avons pas compris Descartes* (We have not understood Descartes) (1991), for instance, there is a level of interpretation suggested by the relationship between the two-dimensional flat space "page" and three-dimensional curved space "poem": the deformation of the page enacts the dynamic function of the poem in activating its inscriptional space by either reconfiguration of material relations among its elements or the intervention of the reader in making sense of this dynamic space. Its close relationship with analytical geometry (i.e., with the possibility of translating the symbolic language of algebra into the visual language of geometry, and vice versa) becomes a reflection on digital three-dimensional representations as aesthetic renderings of Cartesian principles. The program translates numerical representation into a geometric visual instantiation. Metaphorically, the poem is visualized as an expression of the variable geometry of written language that projects its force field onto the page.

Another example of his graphical poetics of the mathematical space is the digital work *De verso* (The verse) (2003). Vallias created a three-dimensional graph in which each visual pattern is linked to a metrical foot. He thus produces a graphical visualization of sound patterns associated with four metrical feet, which readers and users can freely recombine (figure 4.4). Each foot is metaphorically associated with a concept: running for the trochee; throwing for the iamb; striking for the anapest; the finger for the dactyl. The traditional metaphor of writing as plowing is visualized through deformations of the graphic space that are equated with making furrows. Rhythmic structure is thus visualized as an entirely abstract graph whose visual pattern translates the traditional notation for long/stressed and short/unstressed syllables as they are combined in fixed rhythmic units of two or three elements. The graph can be visualized as structured on the basis of just one metrical foot or on the basis of any combination of two, three, or four feet. Inflexions created by sound patterns are translated into three-dimensional visual patterns that have abstracted and translated their combinatorics as particular deformations of the graphical surface.

The kinetic play with legibility and visuality in *Caosflor* (Chaosflower) (2004) by Pedro Valdeolmillos is another simple and effective meditation on machine text and on machine-mediated reading (figure 4.5).[7] As hinted by the warning that introduces this text—"(si lees lo suficiente) Las cosas se acelerarán a medida que advances. Lo qual significa que podría instaurarse el caos. A veces es así" ([if you read long enough] Things will speed up as you go. Meaning chaos might take over. Sometimes it's just like that.)—this text stages the complexities of reading acts as producers of meaning. The work's retroactivity depends on a forward button that readers click in order to access the following page, a simple device that mimics page-turning interfaces. Each click triggers a rapid succession of textual fragments that move either toward or away from the reader. When this three-second movement ceases, a sentence fragment in white becomes readable at the top of the blue screen. Each fragment is part of a series of longer sentences that gradually cohere into a daydream meditation on the strange nature of fractals. The text's voice reflects on the randomness of thought associations and asks whether it is possible to empathize with a fractal. Later in the short narrative, we learn that this apparently random series of thoughts originated in the narrator's observation of the fractal structure of the flower of a cauliflower while preparing a salad. Readers are then given the recipe for the dish and are invited to share a meal.

Up to this point, the text seems to illustrate the incremental process of reading as a linear accretion of new signs to form complex discursive and narrative structures. The illegible or partially legible sentence fragments that zoomed in and out of the screen were nothing but textual fragments

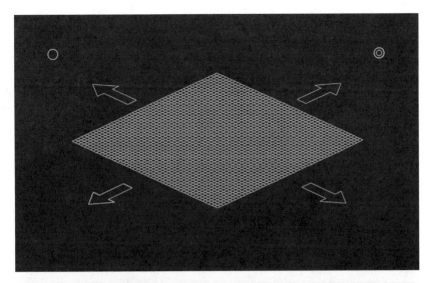

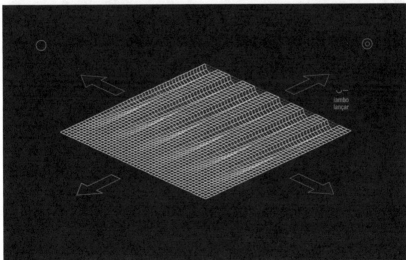

Figure 4.4
André Vallias, *De verso* (2003) (screen captures). © André Vallias. Reproduced with permission.

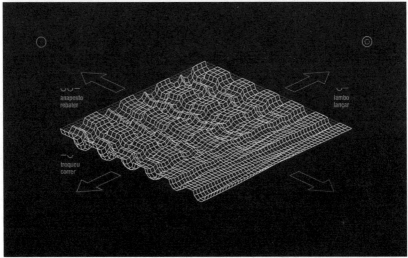

Figure 4.4
(continued)

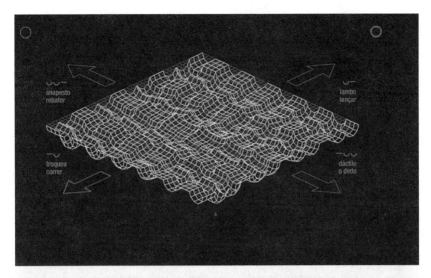

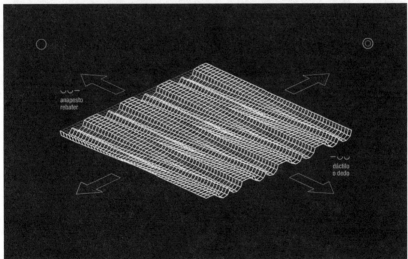

Figure 4.4
(continued)

Figure 4.5
Pedro Valdeolmillos, *Caosflor* (2004) (screen captures). © Pedro Valdeolmillos. Reproduced with permission.

**me di cuenta
de lo difícil**

**que debe ser en
realidad el ser**

Figure 4.5
(continued)

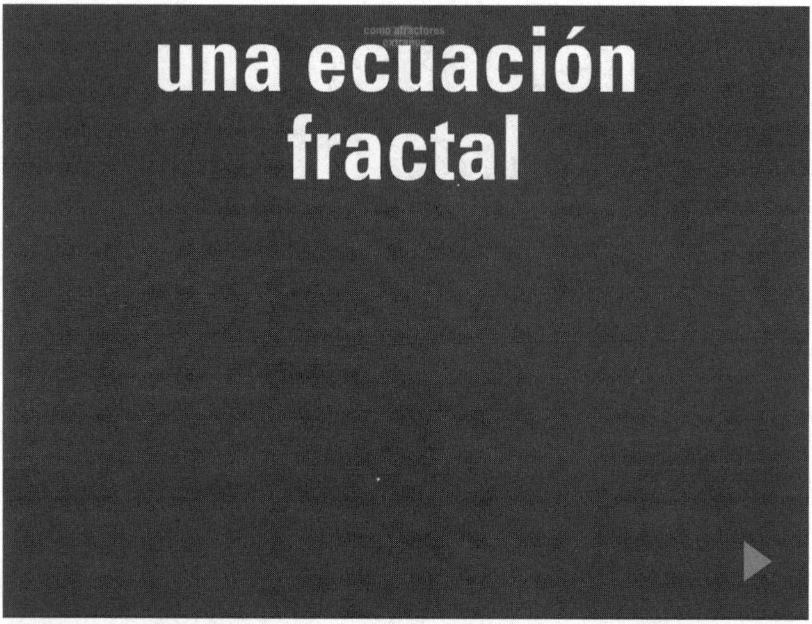

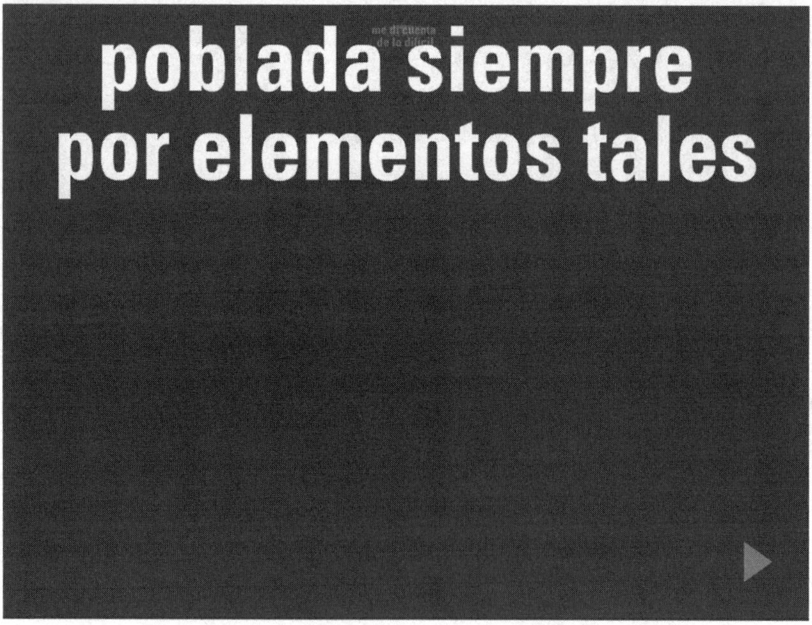

Figure 4.5
(continued)

como atractores
extraños,

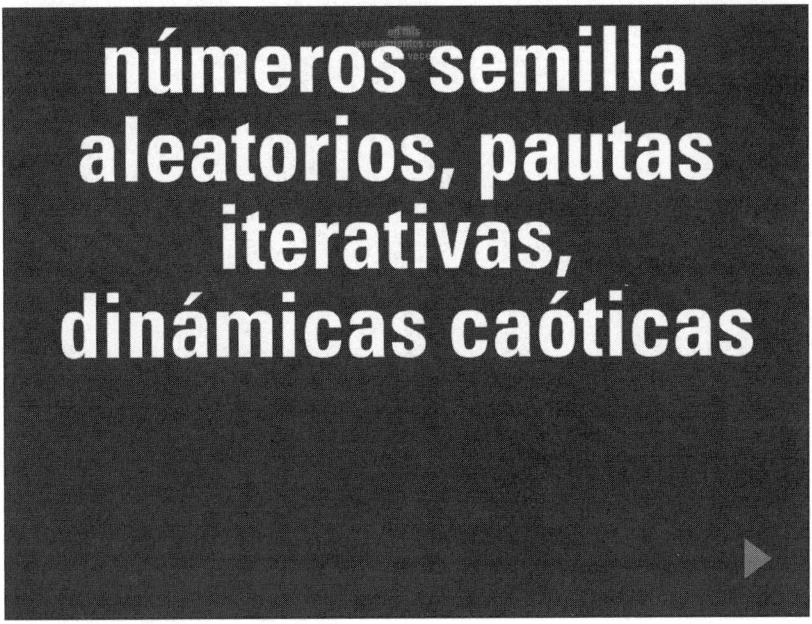

números semilla
aleatorios, pautas
iterativas,
dinámicas caóticas

Figure 4.5
(continued)

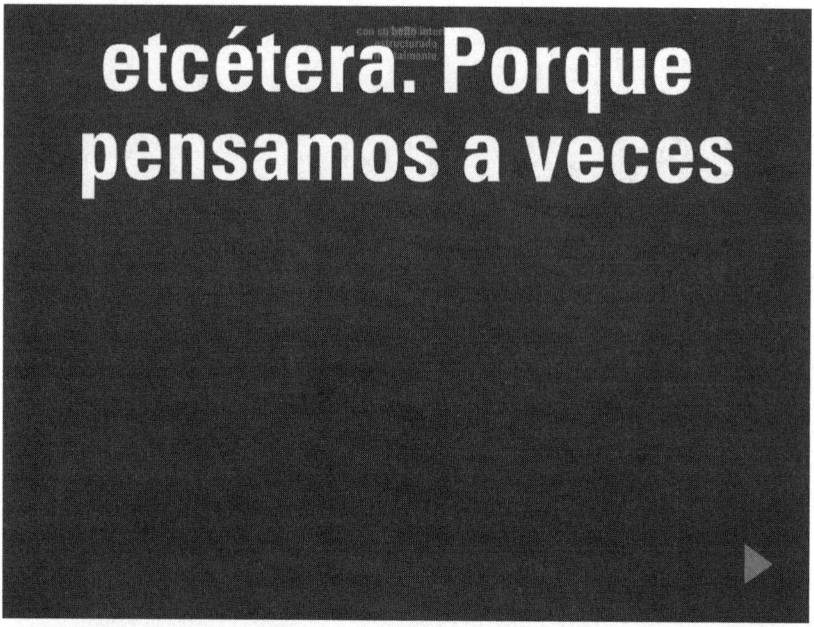

etcétera. Porque
pensamos a veces

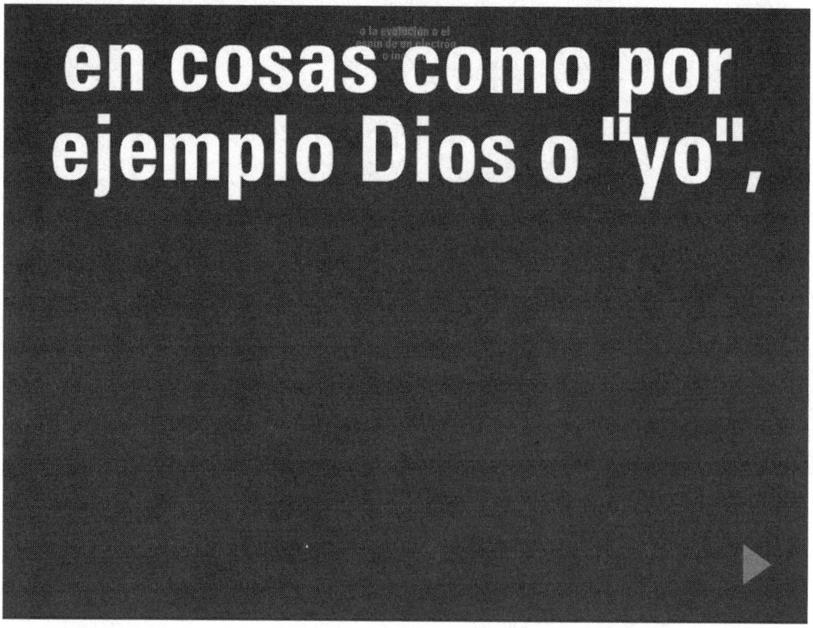

en cosas como por
ejemplo Dios o "yo",

Figure 4.5
(continued)

that were to become legible in future screen refreshes or had already been traveled through. They represented the past and future memory of the text as a syntactic and semantic cohesive and coherent discursive whole but that readers access locally only as short, readable segments one at a time. However, as reading and clicking continue, readers will have less and less control over the sequence and speed of what happens on the screen. The motion of substitution accelerates and moments of stasis and legibility are increasingly rare, while syntactic and narrative coherence becomes more difficult to achieve. Sentence fragments are still the same, but their order has been randomized. The motions and visual effects also become more erratic and varied. The overall effect is to suggest the motions on the screen as the rapid and inapprehensible associative motions of thought and also as the rapid algorithmic processing of the machine itself.

These reading motions become unstoppable and illegible. Clicks are no longer able to produce changes or control the self-sustained motion of the machine. The human order of discourse and narrative has been disrupted by the mathematical chaos of the machine's code, which produces combinations that resist readability and signification. The recursiveness of the fractal and the possibility of human empathy with a mathematical concept, the initial seed for this narrative, have been embedded in the recursive structure of the program and of its display. The "flower of chaos" unfolds as a self-reflection on digital meaning production as a semidetermined looping process dependent on random and fragmented associations of signifiers. Human and machine are intertwined in this playful meditation on the productive chaos of thinking and reading. Through these animation scripts, the motions of reading are materially simulated within the work. The reading self has to confront modes of textual kineticism that model the dynamic chaos of iterative associations.

4.3   Self-Assembled Databases

The "I" of the author is dissolved in the writing. The so-called personality of the writer exists within the very act of writing: it is the product and the instrument of the writing process. A writing machine that has been fed an instruction appropriate to the case could also devise an exact and unmistakable "personality" of an author, or else it could be adjusted in such a way as to evolve or change "personality" with each work it composes. Writers, as they have always been up to now, are already writing machines; or at least they are when things are going well. (Calvino 1987, 15)

Rui Torres has been using computer programming to investigate rules and patterns embedded in particular writing processes. In fact, his works seem to prove Calvino's and OuLiPo's conjectures about writing as a material exploration of rules and constraints that are internal to the linguistic code. If the writer already is a literary machine, then using a computer to emulate the writing process means using one literary machine to probe into another literary machine. Most of Torres's computer works may be said to function, at the same time, as a new work and as a critical analysis of his source texts. Considered as metatexts, structural and stylistic descriptors of their source texts, they are particularly useful for understanding generative procedures at the level of grammar, discourse, and narrative. His "poetic engines," as he calls them, invite readers to recombine textual elements taken from preexisting literary corpora, revealing the potentiality of meaning contained in those textual bodies.

Starting from texts by other twentieth-century authors, Torres's generative works recode their source texts by opening up their syntax, semantics, and pragmatics to digital materiality and programmed signification. Most of his works start from actual texts produced by Portuguese and Brazilian authors. During the past decade, he has used poetry and fiction texts written by Clarice Lispector, Sophia de Mello Breyner, José-Alberto Marques, António Aragão, E. M. de Melo e Castro, Herberto Helder, Raul Brandão, Florbela Espanca, Fernando Pessoa, and Salette Tavares. Randomized algorithms, permutational procedures, and interactive functions are applied to sets of digital objects consisting of verbal text, video, voice, music, and animation. His hypermedia poems foreground the pragmatics of reading programmed works in ways that show the rhetoric and poetical function of codes. I will analyze his database poetry by looking at the algorithmic play between writing and reading in three of his hypermedia works: *Mar de Sophia* (*Sophia's sea*, 2005b), *Amor de Clarice* (*Clarice's love*, 2005a), and *Húmus poema contínuo* (*Humus continuous poem*, 2008).

Torres's source texts are digitally recoded by means of specific algorithmic operations: a few syntactic structures, collected from his source texts, are used as matrices for iterating permutations of lexical items that have been XML-encoded and fed into the database. This lexical database can start off as the product of statistical analysis of a given author's vocabulary, but it can also be supplemented by new items added by readers for each grammatical class. Lexical items from the various classes (nouns, adjectives, adverbs, and verbs) are then parsed and recombined according to timed sequences or readers' interventions in the textual field. These semirandom permutations, which are open to rearrangement determined by readers' choices during their reading acts, make readers experience the productivity of the original structures and a given author's lexicon. Writing is apprehended as a rule-constrained exercise, dependent on recursive structures and open-ended permutations, whose creative properties derive in part from automatisms in the grammar of language, which are then overdetermined by discursive constraints, cultural patterns, and stylistic preferences that favor certain kinds of association.

These matrices or templates can be either a single poem or, more frequently, a small set of textual fragments. In *Mar de Sophia*, for example, one of the templates Torres uses is the poem "Retrato de uma princesa desconhecida" (Portrait of an unknown princess) by Sophia de Mello Breyner. In *Um corvo nunca +* (One raven never +, 2009), the matrix is Fernando Pessoa's 1924 translation of "The Raven" by Edgar Allan Poe. In *Do peso e da leveza* (On weight and lightness, 2009), the matrix is a set of lines collected from poems by Sophia and by Pessoa according to topics of its title. In *Húmus poema contínuo* (Humus continuous poem), his source texts are both *Húmus: Poema-montagem* (Humus: Montage-poem, 1967) by Herberto Helder and *Húmus* (1926) by Raul Brandão. This work is a kind of *mise-en-abîme* of his programming tropes, since he programs a 1960s text that was already a permutational collage of a 1920s text:

> *Húmus: Poema-Montagem* starts from *Húmus* by Herberto Helder (which is based on "words, phrases, fragments, images, metaphors taken from *Húmus* by Raul Brandão") in order to create a combinatorial poem that is re-fed by the lexicon of Brandão. The combinatorial rule that has been applied to it responds to the dictum of "freedom, freedoms," as in Helder's text. Readers can trigger the textual combinatorics by interacting with certain words, and they also have the possibility of changing the lexical lists. The sound texture is dynamically generated. (Torres 2008, my translation)

Húmus poema contínuo is also typical of his programmed works because reader-generated textual occurrences can be added to author-generated combinations. Torres's transforms texts into textual instruments for producing further texts, thus distributing authorship among the author of the algorithm, the rules of the grammar of language, and the interventions of the reader. This work is explicitly affiliated with combinatorial and metaphorical processes formalized by Herberto Helder in his early works, such as "Máquina de emaranhar paisagens" (Machine for entangling landscapes, 1964a) and in *Electronicolírica* (Electronicolyric, 1964b). In *Húmus poema contínuo*, the work's algorithm expands, through automation, the compositional principle that Helder used for his printed text. Torres reapplies this method to lexicon taken from the work of Raul Brandão in a way that automates the production of unexpected associations through serial permutations. Because Helder's poems are used as matrices, we can say that

Helder's montage is used as a data structure for organizing Brandão's textual corpus.

Helder's original montage consisted of freely selecting phrases and words from Brandão's textual fields and linking them in new associations. *Húmus: Poema-montagem* operates on the basis of juxtaposing elements from *Húmus*, sometimes arranging white spaces on the page in ways that point to elements that were left out. Most of its vocabulary and some of its syntactic structures come from its source text, as many texts can be thought of as a particular editing and rearrangement of preexisting linguistic and discursive repertoires. Its lyric energy derives in part from bringing into closer proximity words and phrases already contained in its source text's lexical and semantic fields. Rui Torres's analysis of Helder's rewriting of *Húmus* has uncovered several types of operations on its source text, including connecting, separating, repeating, restructuring, omitting, adding, and transforming (Torres 2010). Helder and Torres have performed the meanings in their source texts through acts of reading that become acts of rewriting and, in turn, create metareading situations—those that show the productivity of reading as an interaction with the textual field. Both works call attention to the iterability of textual artifacts endlessly looping in reading and writing processes that readers and writers have to perform anew each time they encounter the world in language.

After identifying the source text Helder used (extracted from the 1926 version of the novel), Torres's generative work selects eleven excerpts from Helder's poem (ranging from two to fifteen lines) as syntactic matrices for permutations (figure 4.6).[8] These permutations are fed by lexical lists compiled from Helder's source work. This means that Torres's metatextual return to the 1926 version of Brandão's modernist prose is mediated by Helder's selection and collage of fragments, but it is also an entirely new montage made with many different elements that can be randomly inserted into each of the permutational positions in the eleven matrices. *Húmus poema contínuo* rewrites Helder's rewriting of Brandão while offering itself as a critical reading of both Helder and Brandão and of Helder reading Brandão. Helder's appropriations and transformations of Brandão's text demonstrate the power of language for telling the world anew. It is a matter of showing language as a genetic event in which telling and generating the world are commensurate. Writing turns into reading, which turns into writing as part of the general processes of substitution that make meaning possible.

Rui Torres's generative text is a text upon another text that was already a text upon another text, showcasing citation and iteration as exponential

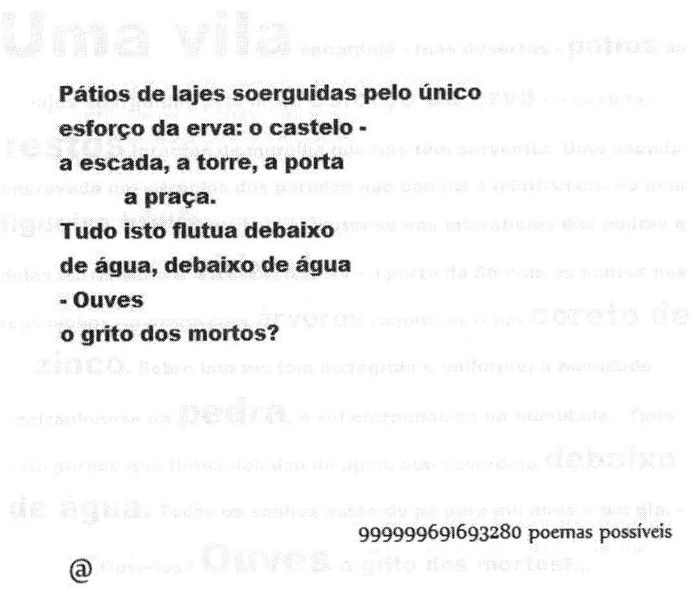
Uma vila
Pátios de lajes soerguidas pelo único
esforço da erva: o castelo -
a escada, a torre, a porta
a praça.
Tudo isto flutua debaixo
de água, debaixo de água
- Ouves
o grito dos mortos?
999999691693280 poemas possíveis
@

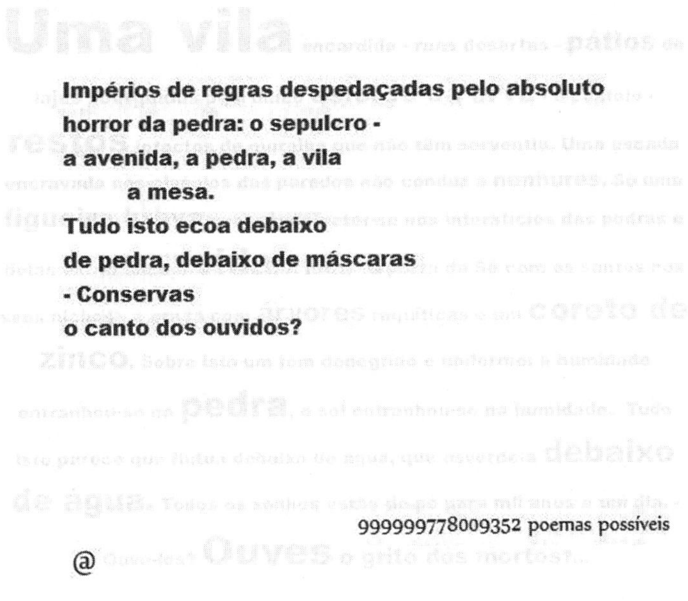
Uma vila
Impérios de regras despedaçadas pelo absoluto
horror da pedra: o sepulcro -
a avenida, a pedra, a vila
a mesa.
Tudo isto ecoa debaixo
de pedra, debaixo de máscaras
- Conservas
o canto dos ouvidos?
999999778009352 poemas possíveis
@

Figure 4.6

Rui Torres, *Húmus poema contínuo* (2008), first textual matrix (lines 1–8 from Herberto Helder's *Húmus*), followed by iteration of one substitution in each of the seventeen positions (screen shots). © Rui Torres. Reproduced with permission.

functions in the production of literary meaning. *Húmus poema contínuo,* *Húmus: Poema-montagem,* and *Húmus* are placed in a complex intertextual web, suggestive of the endless signifying chains of language, discourses, and genres. *Humus,* the noun that describes these three individual works, can be read as a metaphor for the continuous deposition of textual layers that give literature its infinite iterability, depth of allusion, and signifying potentiality. Readers of Herberto Helder will know that in 2001, he collected his poetry under the general concept of "continuous poem," as if all of his individual poems and books of poetry were part of a continuous and endless process of verbal genesis. Citation of this idea of continuity becomes a way of claiming Helder's views on the permutational nature of language as a principle of poetic creation and on literary production as a self-conscious palimpsestic process of writing upon writing upon writing.

Generativity of language, metaphorical substitution, and iterability of written signifiers as means of production of literary experience are further contextualized within the domain of machine-generated and machine-read literature. Each historically existent text and each potential virtual text are placed in a continuum in which every textual occurrence adds to the existing strata of written signifiers. Human–machine intermediation is just another form for the social and historical nature of writing and reading acts. In his latest works (including the online version of *Húmus poema contínuo*), Rui Torres has introduced an e-mail tool that enables readers to record and publish textual instances of their own choice in a blog, *Poemário.*[9] Reader-edited or reader-authored instances of particular machine iterations become part of a continuous process of textual proliferation, with each permutation subtracting one poem from the total number of possible poems. Textual instances, as writings and readings, seem to have been released from any definite authorial origin. They are left to the signifying and resignifying flux of emergent associations produced by the interplay of programmed rules, database structure, machine processing, and reading events. Inscribed and registered as an actual expression of an affective choice of a particular set of signifiers, they become available for future rereading and rewriting iterations: a machine-writing is read by a human and registered by another machine as a new piece of writing available for further human and machine writings and readings.

Torres's generative works do not limit themselves to a syntactical and lexicometric analysis of their source texts. They recode their source printed texts by reinscribing the verbal texture in the multimodality of digital materiality. Randomized algorithms and permutational procedures are applied to sets of digital objects consisting of verbal text, video, voice,

music, and animation. Thus, linguistic signifiers are aggregated in a multimedia database consisting of sounds, images, and animations that reinforce the virtuality of sense as a combinatorial instantiation of modular
elements. By making the paradigm explicit and the syntagm implicit,
digital culture profoundly interferes with narrative modes of producing
meaning. In effect, this tension between narrative logic and database logic,
which Lev Manovich (2007) describes as a structural element in digital
media, is the very aesthetic axis of Torres's works. A textual sequence,
coincidental with either a poem or a narrative fragment, is treated as a
generative matrix for many other possible textual occurrences, now recontextualized in a three-dimensional audiovisual immersive space. Treated as
a particular actualization and single instance of a potential textual state,
the source text is opened up again to the turbulent potentiality of signifiers
and signifieds and to processes of remediation and resignification characteristic of digital literacies.

Mar de Sophia can be described as both a computational analysis of the
poetry of Sophia de Mello Breyner Andresen and as a digital poem by
Torres. In this work, Torres used a set of data mining tools for analyzing a
corpus of her works, including automated searches, aggregation of online
poems, and statistical analysis of lexical occurrences.[10] The *sea* in this
work's title contains an allusion to the most frequent word in the collected
corpus of 450 online poems (showing the prominent place of that word
in the lexicon of the poet) and a metaphorical allusion to the sea of online
poems by Sophia de Mello Breyner Andresen. These online poems document acts of reading and appropriation by the Portuguese and Brazilian
readers who transcribed and published them. Torres's source texts are also
the texts of Sophia de Mello Breyner Andresen as mediated by acts of
reading reflected in their transcription and sharing. In this sense, *sea* may
be taken to refer to the socialization of meaning production that occurs in
literary communication. *Mar de Sophia* demonstrates the disseminative,
derivative, and intertextual nature of the processes of reading and writing
by turning a structured corpus of evidence gathered from other readers
into the dictionary and grammar for a new work. *Mar de Sophia* is, at a
certain level, an essay on the poetry of Sophia and on the Internet as a set
of reading and writing practices.

As a digital work *Mar de Sophia* also contains a digital ars poetica, since
the work is preceded and accompanied by an explicit description of
the method of composition in its various technical stages, exploring
what the author defines as the relationship between hypermedia, poetry,
and criticism in digital poetics. Torres describes the poem as an algorithm,

that is, as a function that associates elements according to a formalized process. Designating the text chosen for syntactical matrix as "virtual text" emphasizes the signifying potentiality of the substitution process that associates and reassociates signifiers (figure 4.7). This substitution process takes place within a syntactic structure created by the source-author and uses a dictionary derived from a large sample taken from her work as collected by readers. The automation of the production of new associations has the effect of virtualizing the text, that is, of returning it to the associative chains of language. The modularization that is inherent in digital objects results in the inversion of the relationship between the axis of presence and the axis of absence. It is the presentification of the paradigm (the axis of lexical substitutions) that turns the poem into a database whose mode of presentation highlights potentiality, mobility, and transformation.

To the lexicon of Sophia de Mello Breyner Andresen, Torres has added the lexicon of a sample taken from *Alice's Adventures in Wonderland* by Lewis Carroll, thereby suggesting the connection between his process-poem and the surreal and unexpected associations of Alice's adventures.[11] Those improbable metaphorical links are also a hypermedia simulation of the dynamics of language in its process of continuous differentiation and endless resignification. As a hypermedia poem, its linguistic permutational logic is extended to those other material elements, such as image, sound, and animation, that run in a constant counterpoint to the merely verbal visuality. Hypnotic recurrence of synthetic sounds, overlapping verbal layers with various degrees of transparency, asynchronous behavior of the voice, which keeps repeating the verses of the textual matrix independent of the graphic changes that make new words appear on screen—all of these elements contribute to the objectification of the verbal and digital mate-riality of the work, which turns signs into sensory and sensuous objects. Assimilating the verbivocovisual postmodernist experimentation and the programmed literature of the past two decades, Torres continues, in the context of digital reproducibility, the experimental program of transform-ing poetry into experience.

4.4 Semiotic Gaps

To write in order to dialog with a text: to admit of the possibility that re-creating the texts that we read is one of the nodes of literary criticism is a strategy that I am invested with and use it to present a poem that was written with the intention of reading the short story "Amor" by Clarice Lispector, expanding rather than limiting

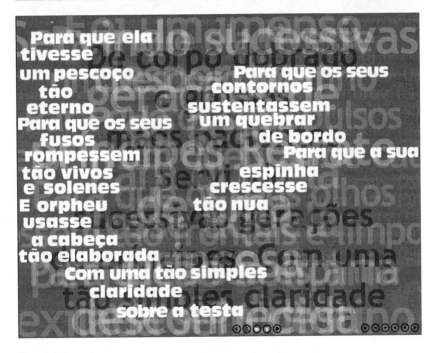

Figure 4.7

Rui Torres, *Mar de Sophia* (2005), first stanza followed by one random iteration of lexical substitutions (screen shot). © Rui Torres. Reproduced with permission.

the signifying energy that potentially exists in the Brazilian author's text. The reading-poem *Amor de Clarice* thus belongs to the devouring and "plagiotropic" tradition of experimental poetry. (Torres 2006a, my translation)

In *Amor de Clarice*, a hypermedia rewriting of Clarice Lispector's short-story "Amor," originally published in 1960, the protagonist's dark epiphanies about her inner life are re-created in hypnotic images and rhythms. The twenty-six sequences that constitute this hypermedia work are made up of fragments of the original story that gradually appear over superimposed textual layers and over inset images and videos. Each textual sequence or screen is attached to sound files that loop its own musical piece. Each textual element (word or group of words) within a sequence or screen is also indexed and linked to a voice file that reads the written fragments as they appear on screen or as readers click on or drag each item, thus interfering in the pretimed sequence. The text runs according to its own pretimed sequence, but lines and screens can be clicked on and changed at any given moment. Readers can move strings of words around, altering the internal textual structure for each screen. Permutations within each screen and across the entire network of screens result in numerous possible actual sequences of its hypnotic verbal, visual, and sound layers.

The inset videos, for instance, contain metonymic representations in which objects and spaces are recognizable, but they appear more like patches of light and color, blurry or backlit, and not as clear, identifiable photorealistic images (figure 4.8). The objects chosen for video sequences are represented fragmentarily and decontextualized (bus window, lemon, plants, high-heel shoe, lamp) and are obliquely linked to the text. Their contribution to suggest a location (home, public transport, street, garden, kitchen, living room, bedroom) is usually obtained by an oblique and strongly metonymic effect. This process allows for an expressive re-creation of the disturbed state of mind of the character through its cyclical repetitions (looping text, video, sound, and voice), suggesting the insidious presence of the real as an arbitrary and unjustifiable order about to disclose itself and overwhelm the female self at any moment.

Each textual element can be clicked and dragged: each click on a textual element immediately activates its corresponding sound file. Layers of sound (background music and human voice) overlap very much like layers of text on text or of text on video. The virtual immersive space created by Rui Torres is the machinic space of automatic processing and pixelated screen display. The palimpsestic fragmentation of meaning is embodied in the textual layers with various shades of color and transparency and with different typographical fonts and sizes. Clarice Lispector's source text

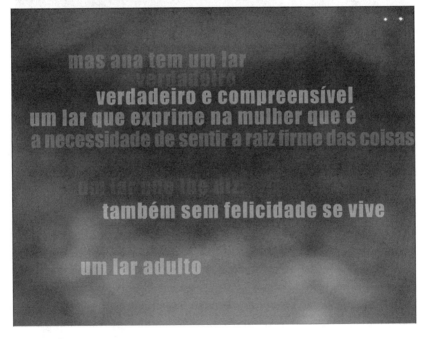

Figure 4.8
Rui Torres, *Amor de Clarice* (2005), "Aos filhos" (For her children), "Mas Ana tem um lar" (But Ana has a home), "E sim, pergunte-se, porquê escolher" (And yes, ask yourself, why choose) (text over video) (screen shots). © Rui Torres. Reproduced with permission.

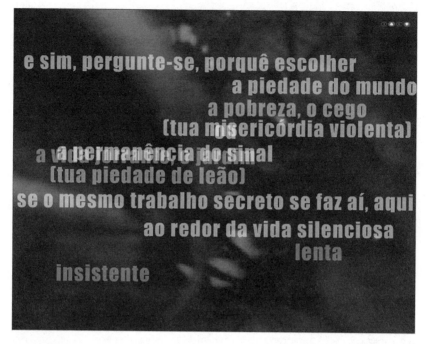

e sim, pergunte-se, porquê escolher
a piedade do mundo
a pobreza, o cego
(tua misericórdia violenta)
a permanência do sinal
(tua piedade de leão)
se o mesmo trabalho secreto se faz aí, aqui
ao redor da vida silenciosa
lenta
insistente

Figure 4.8
(continued)

resurfaces in the form of a collection of scattered fragments, as if the original text had been disjointed and its lexias had reassembled separately into
nodes of sense whose association gives consistency to the ideological and
discursive web of the story and to Ana's emotions and memories. *Amor de
Clarice* is, in a way, a reading of the short story that, like Roland Barthes's
experiments with Balzac's *Sarrasine*, shows the productivity of reading
through processes of inputting and outputting the multiple nodes of
meaning.

Victor Shklovsky's fragmented quotation, which appears as a sort of
prelude to the poem, recalls the formalist conception of the literary act as
an intensification of the experience of the world through verbal operations
of defamiliarization that return objects to their intrinsic thingness: "Habit-
ualization devours works, clothes, furniture, one's wife, and the fear of
war. . . . And art exists that one may recover the sensation of life; it exists
to make one feel things, to make the stone *stony*. The purpose of art is to
impart the sensation of things as they are perceived and not as they are
known" (Shklovsky 1965, 12). *Amor de Clarice* digitally re-creates the expe-

rience of Ana, transferring the character's perception and confrontation with the violence and strangeness of everyday life to the level of signs themselves. The nausea and vertigo experienced by Ana, who feels the arbitrariness of the order of the world and of her own life as a human subject and a female self, are translated into the reader's experience of nausea and vertigo in confronting the mobility and proliferation of verbal, audio, and visual signifiers.

As readers interact with successive screens, the writing field produced by the writing machine is perceived as correlative to their haptic motions of clicking and dragging. Readers feel their own motions being scripted as a specific textual and sound display, a consequence of the dynamic programming of all the work's elements. New reading sequences, based on the rearrangement of individual lines, interfere with pretimed looping sequences that automatically generate textual layers and in turn are linked to voice files reading those lines and phrases. This recursive play within the field of signifiers provides a sensory experience of the database as a series of organizable discrete elements. Writing is staged as a programmed kinetic display of written and spoken lines, whose kinetic properties are reperformed by the eye and haptic motions of the reader. Through those material interventions, the text is (re)constituted. The spatial and temporal structure of writing as programmed animation (which sequentially fills the screen from top to bottom) are subject to a restructuring in space and time by the cinematics of reading. All of these effects are amplified because the entire hypermedia work already is a reading of a previous print work.

Programming codes are a fundamental resource of digital rhetoric and digital poetics, which appropriate interactive functions in menus and in graphic environments and treat them as tropes with literary, cognitive, and affective effects.[12] While the cinematic animation of signifiers is a formal property of digitality, the representation of writing and reading as signifiers in motion points to eventuality and performativity as general properties of processes of signification and interpretation. Describing his creative process, Torres (2006a, 2006b, 2010) explains his method for virtualizing texts as an integration of the creative, research, and learning functions. He sees his programmed poems as both hypermedia textual environments and tools for analyzing literary texts and learning more about them. This interpretational encounter between textual creation and textual analysis shows how computer tools can be used for critical purposes in ways that foster humanities modes of knowledge. His works offer a speculative and aesthetic engagement with computer codes as envisioned by Johanna Drucker (2009a):

The event of interpretation in a digital environment includes many steps: creating a model of knowledge, encoding it for representation, embodying it in a material expression, and finally encountering it in a scene of interpretation. Each is part of a performative system governed by basic principles of second-generation systems-theory, in particular, codependence and emergence. These can be used to describe an aesthetic experience grounded in subjective judgement just as surely as they can be used to describe formal systems. (xiv–xv)

Readers can see how texts are constituted and reconstituted. At a first level, they see them as the result of a set of programmed instructions. At a second level, they see them as the consequence of a particular response to new instructions introduced during the moment-by-moment interactions between readers and the text's graphical, sound, kinetic, and verbal fields. The set of textual and metatextual operations that we find in Rui Torres's hypermedia poetry can be apprehended by the tripartite conceptualization of textual fields in computer-assisted literature developed by Philippe Bootz. Bootz has attempted to clarify the relationship between what he calls "the incompleteness of the program, the activity of the reader and the intermedia transitoire observable" (2006) by proposing a specific performativity for programmable signs. Programmed performativity creates a metareading position, that is, a position of reading that is able to access all aesthetic layers that compose the entire construct of the programmed work, including signs that are not displayable:

There are signs in the "texte-auteur" that don't have any corresponding trace in the "texte-à-voir," no elements of it there are present as an hint of these signs. We can conclude that the reader is not the destined recipient. I don't mean the person who is reading, but the role of the reader in the situation of communication. In other words, reading does not allow one to access all of the aesthetic layers of the programmed work of a digital medium. In order to fully access the work, another position must be maintained: that of the meta-reader. A meta-reader is one who knows the "texte-auteur" or its properties and who observes someone else in the process of reading. He is thus able to interpret what happens during this reading. (Bootz 2006)

In my view, Rui Torres's works may be described as a consistent investigation of this metareading position (figure 4.9). As we have seen, source texts in his works are subject to lexicometric, syntactical, and discursive analyses. As acts of reading, they make formally explicit their own reading strategies and protocols, establishing a strong critical distance from a merely affective and aesthetic relation to their source texts. As programmed texts, his works function on the basis of a tension between immersion in virtual panoramic textual audiovisual spaces and the reader's cognitive

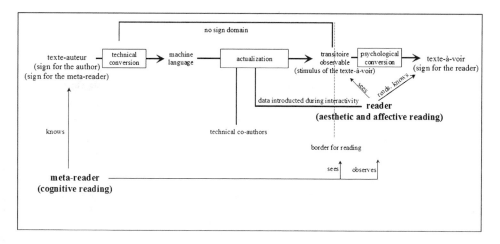

Figure 4.9
Bootz's diagram: *The Status/Position of the Meta-Reader in Programmed Digital Poetry* (2006, 8). © Philippe Bootz, 2006. Reproduced with permission.

awareness of textual algorithms and database structures. Sometimes readers can add items to database content, access the work's back office in the form of a text editor, and record and publish online particular instances of their own interventions. Through these interventions, the act of reading is split between reading the signs and reading the reading of the signs as a particular relation between author's program and reader's text.

Programmability of signs in automatic generation of text sustains the illusion of textual self-assembly. However, the workings of these open-ended databases are also experienced as resulting from interferences between programming algorithms and readers' responses to those algorithms through the mediation of the work's interface. Textual iterations are instantiations of both the writing potential contained in the coded algorithm and specific acts of reading that topicalize a set of elements from the evolving database of the poem. Between the author-text (texte-auteur) of the author and text-to-be-seen (texte-à-voir) of the reader, there is a semiotic gap created by automated processing of data entered during interactivity and this gap makes texte-auteur and texte-à-voir incoincident. Ultimately this algorithmic interactive game serves to simulate the turbulent motions of writing and reading as codependent functions in the production of meaning. The incompleteness of program and the endlessness of text are material expressions of that writing-reading and reading-writing turbulence.

4.5   Immersive Spaces

Readers' interventions in the work's semiotic field are mediated by the interface, which functions as an organizing and narrative principle that imposes order on a database made of sets of modular signs. This mediating interface creates a privileged reading sequence or calls forth several reading sequences that result in specific instantiations of the work's formal materiality. Computer interfaces may be said to work in a similar way to page layout in typographic design: both codify a series of reading instructions. As reading instructions, they define a horizon of expectations for the reader and establish a specific genre. In this case, however, the experience of reading the work becomes an explicit part of the work because the text is made to exist in several superimposed states and strata that are only partially identical. Because the material form of the text is not entirely immune to the actions that we have to perform for making the text visible or legible, we may say that reading motions have been scripted into the form of the text. The material instantiation of text, and our perceptual consciousness of it, respond to and reflect our own haptic and visual interaction with the interface.

All reading acts deform their objects in the sense that they foreground and background elements of the textual field according to the reader's perceptual attention, cultural disposition, intentionality, and affectivity. We may say that reading, as visual perception and semantic representation, always coproduces its object. Except under highly controlled, disciplined, and closed systems and conventions, coding and decoding do not entirely coincide. The symbolic productivity of natural language and other semiotic systems tends to exceed the intentionality embedded or encoded in its form, which has to be remade and reenacted in every new act of reading. What is particular about ergodic works (those whose instantiation is only partially determined prior to an actual material intervention by the reader/player) is that readers can experience this instability and multiplicity at the perceptual level as a correlative of the instability and multiplicity at the conceptual level. The reader sees the emergence of meaning as an effect of that semidetermined game with signifiers in the turbulence of their material associations and substitutions.

Of course, such material changes in the text are themselves subject to further acts of interpretation, and these cannot be scripted or simulated in the text itself since they depend on actual historical and social conditions and practices. Thus, the feedback loop between writing and reading breaks down since as a material artifact and historical event, the poem cannot be self-sufficient. As a material artifact and historical event, it partakes of the heterogeneity and alterity of all social practices. However, by reproducing itself in response to the program and to interventions of readers in their turbulent signifying field, it shows the literary device or poetic engine as a virtualized sensorial and conceptual space. This space is increasingly characterized, in the case of digital hypermedia poetry, by the accumulation of multimodal signifying strata. The programming of writing, text, and reading in combinatoric automated devices intensifies the sensorial experience of indeterminacy and processibility.

The principle of cinematic montage of visual elements echoes the permutational logic observed in verbal elements that become semantically linked by virtue of their temporary syntactic association. The device of metaphor, responsible for the motion of resignification within the semantic layer of language, is given a visual analog in the actual verbal and multimodal juxtapositions and substitutions. In Torres's generative works, metaphor is visualized as the signifying and resignifying motion that enables the production, reproduction, and transformation of meaning. The poem is turned into a database of written and spoken words and phrases, still images, video clips, and synthesized sounds that exist as a series of potential superimposed states rather than a single actual syntactic instance. This potentiality follows from the act of making explicit the algorithm of the text—the conceptual mechanics that may produce its material instantiations. Since these instantiations are subject to further material interference by the reader, we can say that the text reveals in its material behavior the quantum dimension of reading—a dimension that is more often located at the level of interpretation (McGann 2002, 2003, 2004; Drucker 2009b). John Cayley (2006), Philippe Bootz (2006), Pedro Barbosa (2001, 2006), and others have emphasized this material fluctuation and the ensuing virtualization of text as a determining factor in the rhetoric of generative electronic literature.

Through this process of material transformation and virtualization, Torres's hypermedia poems produce a critique of the belief of their source texts in the necessary nature of their own unique forms. A text's belief in its own form (i.e., the possibility of matching form to meaning) is shown as a mere combinatoric instance or snapshot in the verbal flux. The ability to continue to say itself or to say itself in other ways, which the text's program has automated on the basis of the grammar of language, exposes the discursive and ideological limitations of the poem as an utterance that is able to say itself and to say the world. Those operations generated by the machine code question the reification of expression and style. Through this automation of textuality, the reification of the uniqueness of expression is perceived as part of the ideology of poetry and the ideology of fiction. It is as if the text could no longer coincide with itself and the heterogeneous forces of language and discourse had reopened the tension created by its desire to fix itself in a singular verbal form. The apparent autogenesis of a self-sufficient and self-contained writing is exploded by the alterity created by the programming code, which makes the text different from itself and opens it up again to the force fields of discourse.

We find in generative literature a simulacrum of the author function embedded in the works' code by virtue of its self-assembling and self-organizing properties. The text auto-authorizes itself by being generated automatically. Subjectivity is no longer anterior to particular associations of signs and words, as marks of a self writing himself or herself, but instead it is brought to bear on the signs a posteriori by the intentionality of readers, who respond as interpreters to the stream of machine-generated associations. The constitution of self in language is textually experienced as a self constituted in and by the mechanism of language. The author function, a historically constituted discursive function, is still intact at the level of programming the text: the author is now the author of the metatext (texton) that creates a second-degree representation of the original text. However, part of its internal mechanics is shown as a mode of producing new associations of language and signs in general, which derives from modes of formal articulation of the codes themselves. While preferred associations and preferred meanings for those associations establish the stylistic and hermeneutic identity of a given individual's use of language, computer-generated associations break up that identity by making its discursive possibilities, including some of the most improbable, simultaneously present.

The use of lexical databases derived from the actual lexicon of a particular author has a double effect. On the one hand, it means that randomly generated texts bear a certain resemblance to an author's style and use of language. Certain textual occurrences could even be said to be part of the future or potential repertoire of that writer. Poetic and narrative rules have been inferred from a corpus of that writer's works, and they have been fed as iterative constraints in the rules of the program. Some combinations may be said to perform a certain mode of writing or, at least, some features of a unique style. At this level, what we have is the beginning of an analysis of the works that makes explicit the expressive singularity of a given use of signs. On the other hand, the multiplication of textual occurrences calls into question the privileged status of a single textual instance. By suggesting a continuum of possible associations, each of which with its own semantic import, generative texts show form as ideology. Multiplication undermines the reification of meaning, authorial presence, and textual and interpretative stability in the production of meaning. Meaning, crystallized by successive repetition of a poem's formal identity and its dominant readings, is reopened to associations between signifiers that make it possible to think and say other things.

Torres explores the database as a new framework for knowing and experiencing literature. His integration of text generation with hypermedia and social media creates multilayered intermedia online forms that point to the emergence of new genres. In his programmed networked poetry, aesthetic and critical functions feedback on each other in ways that shed light on writing and reading loops as literary processes. His database poetics also contains a critical investigation of the database as a cultural form and an expressive tool for new media art. *Mar de Sophia*, *Amor de Clarice*, and *Húmus poema contínuo* instantiate the aesthetic and critical productivity of the database for perceiving the signifying chains that link author, text, and reader as particular functions of semiotic and discursive structures.

4.6   Procedural Signs

Another highly reflexive exploration of intermediality and programmability in current digital literature can be found in Jason Nelson's work. The visual, kinetic, and sound textualities become procedural signs designed for the interactor to experience the algorithmic nature of the work. Multimodal programming is used to reflect on digital materiality and the nature of cognitive perception of form and meaning. Random permutations and iterative processes, combined with hypermedia fragmentation, place readers in the midst of a labyrinth of visual, verbal, and aural signs. Readers have to engage with the chaotic and probabilistic nature of algorithmic and machinic processes of meaning production. Intermediality and indeterminacy challenge the medium boundaries and the discursive consistency of conventional literary and artistic genres. In Nelson's technotexts, digital technology foregrounds the specificity of its mode of computational and electronic inscription. This foregrounding testifies to his extraordinary formal inventiveness in the aesthetic use of codes and programming tools. He is a database and interface artist who has turned the multimodal modularity of computer materiality into an aesthetic structural principle for combining drawings, collage, photography, video, words, sounds, music, and other forms in multilayered and multitextured compositions and textual games. His cybertexts emulate electronic space itself, and they redefine the poem as a plaything that reflects on algorithmic culture, database aesthetics, and interface conventions.

Nelson's intermedia digital works are a late product of the interaction between writer and computing machines in which programming cannot be thought of as separated from graphic, kinetic, or sound display. In *Hymns of the Drowning Swimmer* (2004), the reader encounters a complex reticular hypermedia structure. Readers are exposed to this hypermediated space and the symbolic hyperphagia of contemporary global communications networks. This sign-saturated work emulates the constant generation of multimedia signifiers that defines electronic semiosis as part of our current technosocial semiotics. The work's sequences and frames are generated from a randomized collection of fragments, grouped into eighteen sections. They are organized in multiple iterations, branches, loops, and redundancies. Because progress and recurrence have to be constructed by the reading self without any clues, reading assumes the figure of the networked labyrinth. Most elements in this work are organized on the basis of looping permutations. These include sound files, video files, graphic icons, drawings, different types of images (drawings, printings), linguistic fragments, and simultaneous layering and patterning of the various elements on the screen. Random numbering of the eighteen sequences, absence of any narrative or discursive continuity, diverse visual patterns, and varied biographical, cultural and technological references in each sequence—all of these contribute to the experience of nontotalization, (i.e., for the difficulty in stopping the play of or with signifiers). Readers experience the cognitive disorientation as a drowning in the overloaded system of the electronic work.

Nelson's *Hymns of the Drowning Swimmer* combines the hyperstructured and the hyperfragmentary in ways that are typical of postmodern cybernetic culture. Once the database structure of a work is subject to algorithmic processing, the result is a truly recombinant poetics—a poetics of literature as potentiality that projects automated signifiers onto individual consciousness in search for meaning. Bill Seaman's (2007) description of subject-object interaction in algorithmic works seems entirely adequate for Nelson's work:

As we explore material in interactive work, meaning arises out of a subject/object unity. The participant draws on past experience and defines his or her own approach to understanding the connections between media fragments selected from the database as these fragments fall together in a context that is being constructed in an ongoing manner. Thus, meaning is always involved in a human process of becom-

ing. Such work is accretive in nature and open in terms of ongoing meaning production. (132–133)

Context building, accretion, and openness could be used for describing how meaning is produced by readers' interactions with each of the eighteen sequences in *Hymns of the Drowning Swimmer*. Modularity is used at various scales to make the structure of each section or subsection a mirror of the overall structure of the work. There is no set order for choosing between behaviors or attributes associated with each digital element. Readers/players have to decide at random which paths they want to take and how and when to move the cursor to activate a specific behavior or move to a different section or level of the work. As they explore each sequence, they will learn the connection between their own actions and the appearance of linguistic fragments, visual patterns, or video animations on the screen. Figuring out how to play or read the work is one important element of its form.

In "Hymn: Eighteen: Perhaps We Were Never Entertained," for instance, the first screen includes the general menu, moving windows containing video fragments, looping sound files, and four textual fragments that read (from lower left, clockwise) "remote vitamins 5," "smokey array," "sex with a clear utility and electrics," and "more like floods for the year, the correct scene" (figure 4.10). Each of these four fragments contains an active link that launches a new layer of textual fragments containing longer sentences or sentence fragments, which are presented as rectangular numbered boxes that readers can drag around the screen, thus composing the four sentence boxes into a larger textual unit. One of the textual fragments for this second layer reads: "Each of the new and outdated gadgets are represented by the same five films. To her the image's content is less vital than the variant methods the electronic bits swim their way to her eyes." Readers then realize that this sentence describes the video fragments looping as moving, opening, or closing windows in the background layer. The words *five films* contain yet another link to a description of the way those video bits were obtained. Similarly highlighted links appear in the remaining sentence boxes, providing further information on those image-producing technologies.

As readers realize that Nelson's work may be a complex meditation on various media technologies, they begin to frame the various elements within this ongoing context. As they proceed, other references introduce more topics and experiences, such as the various references to water and rain. The ensemble of interconnections is never immediately clear or

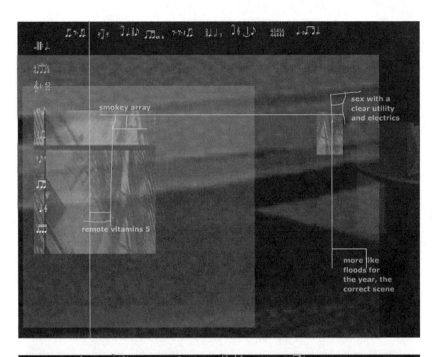

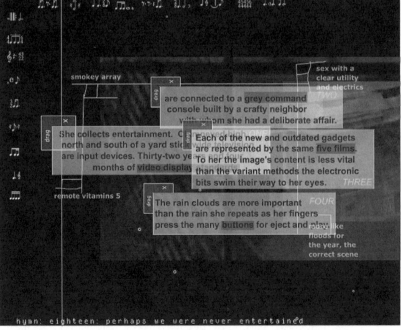

Figure 4.10

Jason Nelson, *Hymns of the Drowning Swimmer* (2004): "Hymn: Eighteen: Perhaps We Were Never Entertained" (screen captures). © Jason Nelson. Reproduced with permission.

straightforward. In the end, meaning arises from the recombination created by this exploratory juxtaposition of elements that become materially associated by virtue of the way signs have been programmed and as a result of ongoing choices made by the interactor. Multiplicity of media and media convergence depend on digitality as the ultimate abstraction of inscription and reproduction technologies. A system of potential choices will produce unanticipated associations through actual choices, which in turn generate new fields for meaning.

The work is a machinic assemblage that suggests the shifting nature of meaning through media-element substitutions. At the same time, it seems to emulate the multimodal materiality of hypermedia that has come to dominate contemporary electronic writing space. The variety of interfaces, textual content and media elements used in *Hymns of the Drowning Swimmer* can be seen as both reflection on new media as remediation and an aesthetic exploration of algorithmic procedures, database culture, and interface conventions. Variability as a defining feature of digitality can be appreciated, for instance, in the display screens and database structure of the following sections: "Hymn: Eight or Five: Concerning Mobility," "Hymn: Seventy and Seven: Technology from a Distance," "Hymn: Three Hundred and Three: Aquatic," and "Hymn: One Hundred and Twenty: Rain Drawn" (figure 4.11). In their variations, they suggest the arbitrary relation between a given graphical interface and the database of media objects that constitute each section of the work.

4.7   The Play of Reading

Dimension Is Night Is Night (2007) by Jason Nelson (with text by Christine Hume) is a virtual three-dimensional literary Rubik's cube, a playable work which the reader has to learn "how to play/read/recreate." In this ergodic work, the relation between the act of reading/playing and the production of text is given a fractured and disjointed expression. The reader/player, immersed in the field of signs, has to coproduce his or her textual experience. Textual immersion takes place not at the semantic level of a fictional possible world, but at the material level of the graphical user interface itself. Readers are caught in a field of signifiers that have to be related to each other by virtue of their simultaneous presence but whose semantic relations are not obvious. Verbal discourse and the electronic objects themselves (sound, image, and text files) are defamiliarized. The $3 \times 3 \times 3$ rotating mechanism of the cube works as a texton, a generative algorithm that produces a very large number of textual occurrences. Once activated

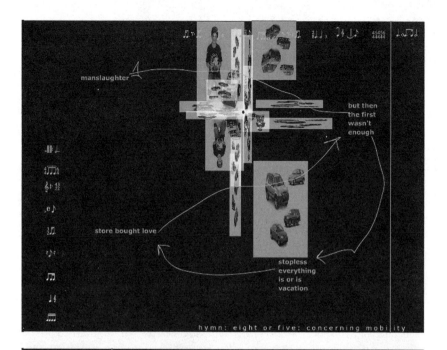

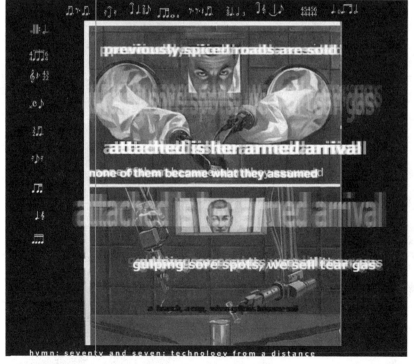

Figure 4.11
Jason Nelson, *Hymns of the Drowning Swimmer* (2004): "Hymn: Eight or Five: Concerning Mobility," "Hymn: Seventy and Seven: Technology from a Distance," "Hymn: Three Hundred and Three: Aquatic," and "Hymn: One Hundred and Twenty: Rain Drawn" (screen captures). © Jason Nelson. Reproduced with permission.

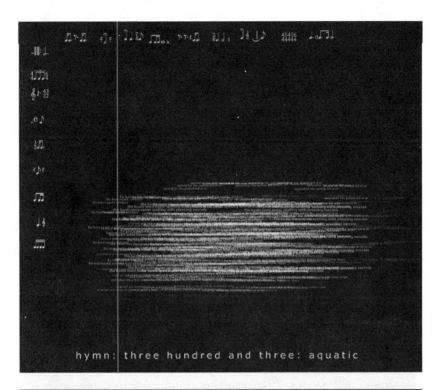

hymn: three hundred and three: aquatic

hymn: one hundred and twenty: rain drawn

Figure 4.11
(continued)

by the reader, the texton will be displayed as a scripton, a particular textual sequence.

A particular textual sequence or occurrence generated by readers' actions never completely loses its fragmentariness, since no totality emerges from the recombination of textual units. The resulting text is always partially illegible because layers with various colors can be simultaneously present, and rotating cube sections will unscramble some lines while scrambling others. Because of the fragmentary, associative, and ambiguous nature of the source text, solving the digital puzzle (i.e., unscrambling the same-colored lines that make up each cube face) will not make way for a coherent or final textual experience. Fracture, incompleteness, multiplicity, and uncertainty of digital sign fields in Nelson's work enact the motions of reading as always an attempt at reading, never to be fully realized. Textual associations produced by rotations and translations of the inscriptional faces of the cube become a geometric model of the metaphorical intersections created by syntactic hypotactic and paratactic juxtaposition within the original text.

Nelson's *Ars Combinatoria* is based on Christine Hume's text "Nocturnal Dimensions of the Future."[13] In its original form, each poetry sequence was followed by a short prose text. Nelson organized his "plaything" on the basis of fifty-four units (nine possible positions on each square face × 6). Five cube faces contain lines from Hume's poems, and the sixth face contains one image divided into nine parts. The image, which could be a filtered color photograph or a painting, suggests an indoor space with a door opening to the outside. The indoor space is structured on the basis of darkness and light contrast, incoming light possibly coming from the sky as reflected by the sea. Nelson broke up Hume's four poems into five groups of lines. The five groups follow the original line sequence, with only two exceptions: the lines "your lordish hours form unknown conduits/ and unknown songs empty into my lungs" (lines 16–17, third sequence) were left out. They were replaced by the lines "is a way of worship if smashing waves / do not listen for where the sound ends" (lines 14–15, fourth sequence; in Nelson's cube, these lines were interpolated in the third sequence). Groups are distinguished by color (red, black, blue, green, and yellow) and are composed of nine units (usually two or three lines per unit). Each unit is linked to one of the nine squares on each face. Only the yellow group has eight units, which means that there is one vacant position on the corresponding cell of the nine-square table of the yellow face. Table 4.1 identifies each unit and its place in the original text. Table 4.2 describes the cube's structure and the distribution pattern for the various textual units.

The metaphoric associations in the original text already contain a relatively high degree of randomness resulting from elliptical associations and oblique references. However, the prose texts that follow each poem sequence establish a referential and, at times, what feels like an autobiographical context for the contorted symbolic and metaphoric displacements of the lines. The continuing presence of the pronoun *I*, in particular, gives those prose fragments a textual coherence that is absent from the verse sections. The print text seems to live from this tension between determined and undetermined referential meaning. Several lines can be read as relatively autonomous syntactic units or as part of larger discursive units formed by groups of lines. Repeated metaphorical displacements result in a dense symbolic texture.

Nelson has increased the semantic and syntactic autonomy of the source text's fragments by breaking up each text further into groups of one, two, or three lines and by programming permutations according to the cube's multiple rotational axes. When played by readers, his cubic textual machine generates thousands of random combinations in which line groups change position, superimpose, and mix. Rotating the virtual cube along its axes will sometimes expand and sometimes contract textual interlineations and textual transparency, resulting in different degrees of legibility (figure 4.12). Sentences, words, and letters are often only partially legible. This layering of textual position, transparency and opacity, as well as the combination of image and character textuality, emulate the graphic environment of digital space itself.

Readers experience digital text as an assemblage of palimpsest fragments, where sense emerges from changing and transient patterns generated by the player's interaction with the digital object. Nelson's algorithmic organization of the square units works by exponentiating the principle of juxtaposition and association, already present in the metaphoric displacements of the original text. Readers play with the semantic and syntactic gap that prevents immediate textual cohesion and textual coherence. In this turbulent associative mechanism, the programmability of signs is used for choreographing the reading of cybertexts. The gaming element of this choreography is the work's main reflexive device. Its playing mechanism is a material program for experiencing machine-produced meaning as an open-ended permutational and stochastic process.

Embedded in the algorithmic culture of the digital age, Nelson's electronic poem redefines the role of the reader as player. Readers become aware of the role of the interface as a mediator in connecting the various textual layers constituting the work and of their own manipulative role in combining them. Three-dimensional combinations of column and row

Table 4.1
Segmentation of Christine Hume's "Nocturnal Dimensions of the Future" in Jason Nelson's *Dimension Is Night Is Night* (2007)

"Nocturnal Dimensions of the Future"		*Dimension Is Night Is Night*	
Original sequence	Lines	Text colors	Text on each of the squares
1st	1–2	Red 1	Once I drew a line around myself dug my shape into a rich field Some night fell in, bruising itself
	3–4	Red 2	The fresh dirt was a muscle stowing away years It wasn't dead, it just couldn't sleep
	5–6	Red 3	I stuffed night's hem into my mouth to stay shut Night also buttoned up when it couldn't find a thing to adorn
	7–8	Red 4	When it couldn't find a fly to swallow If I keep my eyes quiet, if it mistakes me for blind
	9–10	Red 5	I dry heave fits of impure air One night, until I had it all to myself
	11–12	Red 6	If I could retrieve that night from a dream Its air wakes up inside my lung, bearing amplifications
	13–14	Red 7	Shovels score the dark and damage allergies When I am awake back and forth for so long I can't remember
	15	Red 8	Being left or not being left alone, I fall bed to bed to bed
	16–17	Red 9	If I could move toward it while moving away Night kills what it shifts into; I pine for what I alight
	17 lines	9 squares	

Table 4.1

(continued)

"Nocturnal Dimensions of the Future"			*Dimension Is Night Is Night*
Original sequence	Lines	Text colors	Text on each of the squares
2nd	1–2	Black 1	Nine stiches and liquid morphine cannot keep it closed Lunar halo runs circles more than hollow
	3–4	Black 2	Still birds fly from clocks Striking the same hour in rounds
	5–6	Black 3	A freak disease tears across the vista You've been told this is the year of medicine
	7–8	Black 4	Lunar halo must bother you tonight with some life Stronger than satellites with strong melancholies
	9–10	Black 5	The situation of radar gone deaf War shine and flare lit in the lips
	11–12	Black 6	A ring of unknown men waiting To think of it is a tourniquet
	13–14	Black 7	Embracing you to the point to the point of Sugar awake in the animal disaster
	15–16	Black 8	Vaccinations break and they bother you The situation of its waves
	17–18	Black 9	Puts catheters in blather-mouths Time for you to ride
	19–20	Blue 1	Time for you to ride Even when it acts hypnotic or botched Tornado hanged in example
	20–21	Blue 2	Eye sticking to its guns It must bother you with oblong torment tonight
	23–24	Blue 3	Between your deserts and escaped stars Messes of radial spoils steal on you

Table 4.1

(continued)

"Nocturnal Dimensions of the Future"			*Dimension Is Night Is Night*
Original sequence	Lines	Text colors	Text on each of the squares
	25–26	Blue 4	Recognize your continuous tattoo Lunar halo casts your face in harassments
	27–28	Blue 5	It dissolves former weather in your ear Takes up with your hexes
	29–30	Blue 6	Ice becomes gas blasting into a foam hole Out of which zodiac carcasses crawl
	31–32	Blue 7	Under lunar halo, anyone who waits For sleep waits to be seen to
	32 lines	16 squares	

"Nocturnal Dimensions of the Future"			*Dimension Is Night Is Night*
Original sequence	Lines	Text colors	Text on each of the squares
3rd	1	Blue 8	you may pound this night as much as you please
	2–4	Blue 9	you will never pound into me what you think you say the contrary and the lashings madden night thinks you should pay for it
	5–7	Green 1	pound at your belief until it's empty of you loaded with lords aft and boxes of forward lucifers but how could a lucifer get fire in this crying night

Table 4.1

(continued)

"Nocturnal Dimensions of the Future"			*Dimension Is Night Is Night*
Original sequence	Lines	Text colors	Text on each of the squares
	8–9	Green 2	you could fill buckets with your drenched hems no lightning rod will channel this night
	10–11	Green 3	(it will pound me no matter) and better than a stormbird on its last wing
	12–13	Green 4	you pound this metal against my skull defang the dark's thunderstalk swerves
	14–15	Green 5	words pound at me because I won't use them night gnaws and unknots the anchor
	16–17	[excluded lines]	your lordish hours form unknown conduits and unknown songs empty into my lungs
	18–19	Green 7	only to drag dark after me and lurk it in my orders it pounds its meaning into me
	20	Green 8	that blankness packed with impressions I will not salvage
	21–22	Green 9	I endure the irate backpounding endure the obsessions that stand in for you
	22 lines	10 squares	

Table 4.1

(continued)

"Nocturnal Dimensions of the Future"			*Dimension Is Night Is Night*
Original sequence	Lines	Text colors	Text on each of the squares
4th	1–3	Yellow 1	let the ocean uptake shape your cover if by memory foam, if on a dream-fast do not use a sleep mask because of your thoughts
	4–5	Yellow 2	snuff out the count with an open mouth let your night cape have a gas-hole
	6–7	Yellow 3	lie grovelling in your belly the lead body lies down with the feather body
	8–10	Yellow 4	you are not one of the guards even if you can still feel if your position is diagonal enough
	11–13	Yellow 5	a dark ball rolls void into you hasten to make use of that freed dark empty it the way fatigue
		Yellow 6	[empty square]
	14–15	Green 6	is a way of worship if smashing waves do not listen for where the sound ends
	16–18	Yellow 7	if smashing waves consolidate you then night never finishes even if fully in it would you be unable to
	19	Yellow 8	as undertow takes the child think
	20–21	Yellow 9	of each part of your body vanishing skin as the dark stares and stares back
	21 lines	9 squares	

Table 4.2

Fifty-four textual (juxta)positions: Diagram for the cube in Jason Nelson's *Dimension Is Night Is Night* (2007).

r7	r4	r1	g1	g2	g3	b3	b6	b9
r8	r5	r2	g4	g5	g6	b2	b5	b8
r9	r6	r3	g7	g8	g9	b1	b4	b7
			b1	b2	b3			
			b4	b5	b6			
			b7	b8	b9			
			y1	y2	y3			
			y4	y5				
			y7	y8	y9			
			i9	i8	i7			
			i6	i5	i4			
			i3	i2	i1			

Note: key to initials in the table—r, red; g, green; b, blue; **b, black**; y, yellow; i, image.

imply that this work's formal materiality can be instantiated in many textual and visual combinations. The high number of permutations and the openness of the connections create a haptic and cognitive experience of the modular, variable, and interactive properties of the medium. It is as if the database had become present at the level of the interface, and readers, like the machine, had to perform operations on data. As in computer video games, the reader/player experiences the codependence between machine actions and operator actions (i.e., the fact that they are part of the algorithmic system of an "active medium") (Galloway 2006, 3).

Writing and reading are shown as events of the cybernetic system that produces the algorithmic poem in response to programmed interactions. Reading has been scripted as a series of actions that are required to make the text readable. Through their gaming action, players explore new possibilities for natural and computer language opened up by algorithmic machines: programmability of language and signs; discovery of complex surfaces for writing and reading; multimedia materiality of electronic signifiers; presence of the reading or playing act in dynamic displays; and temporal transience of forms and meaning. Recursive loops between the motion of signifiers and the play of reading suggest the emergence of a reflexive interface poetics that addresses digital literacy itself.

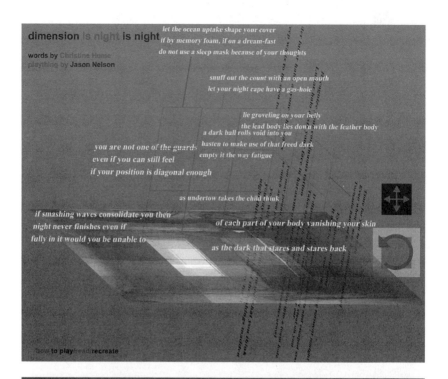

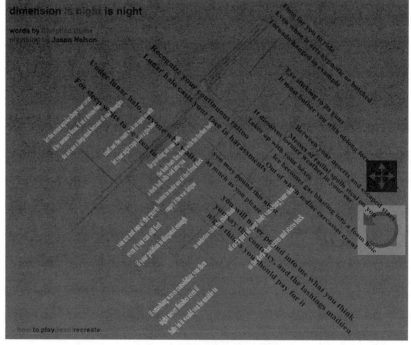

Figure 4.12

Jason Nelson, *Dimension Is Night Is Night* (2007): twelve textual configurations of one-color cube faces in contracted and expanded forms (screen captures). © Jason Nelson. Reproduced with permission.

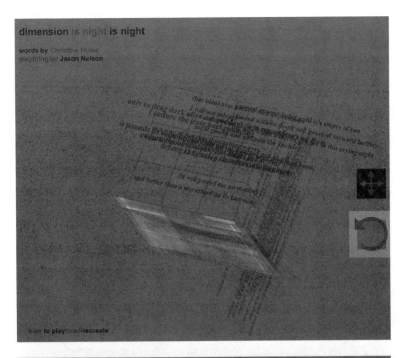

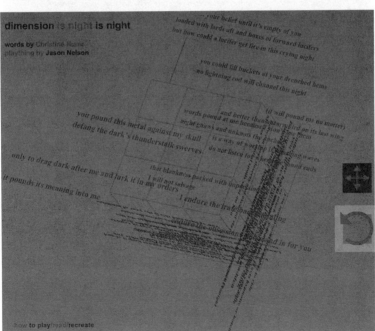

Figure 4.12
(continued)

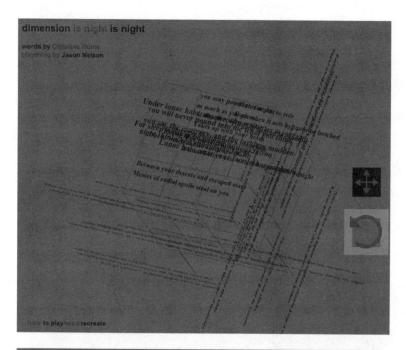

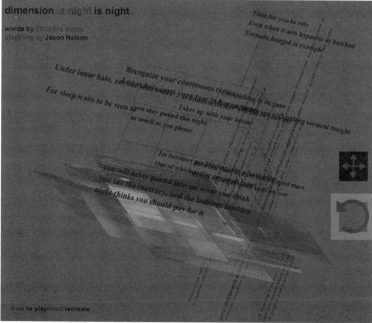

Figure 4.12
(continued)

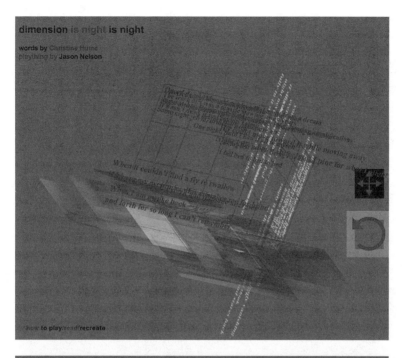

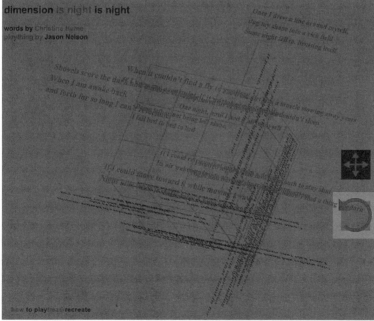

Figure 4.12
(continued)

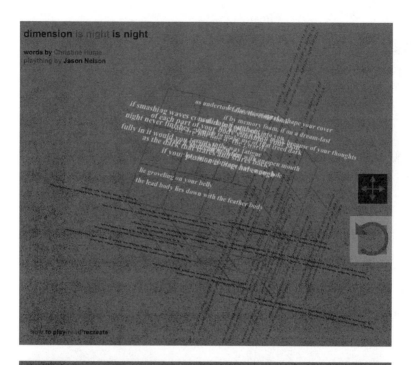

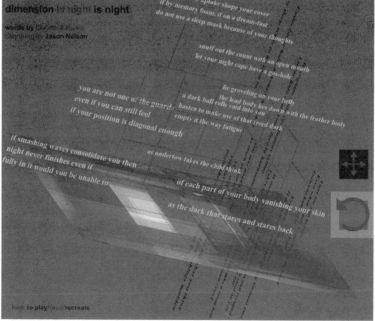

Figure 4.12
(continued)

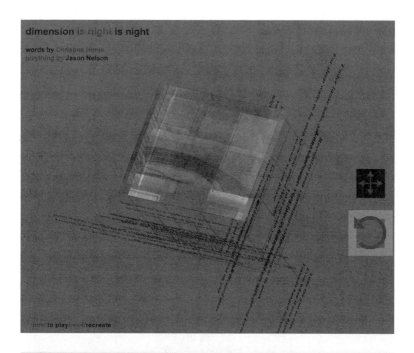

Figure 4.12
(continued)

5   Loving the World: The Codex as Computer

5.1   Infinity Is Round

Potential literature can be defined as the process of textual generation by the formalization of permutational rules at various levels of language: from the microlevel of grapheme, phoneme, morpheme, and sentence to the macrolevel of narrative sequences. The structural syntax of language, with its double articulation, is projected onto narrative syntax, creating isometries between linguistic sentence and narrative discourse. The fundamentally combinatorial nature of both language and narrative is enhanced by a method that reveals meaning as the genetic product of permutations and recombinations. Permutations and recombinations are formalized by rules or algorithms that determine constraints, iterations, substitutions, and transformations of elements. In oulipian literature, writing is redefined as a program for inventing and applying constraints and algorithms, thus laying bare generative mechanisms on which semiotic and hermeneutic productivity depend, as if the world were a mere effect of the engine of language.

The novel-poem *Only Revolutions* (2006), by Mark Danielewski, is a challenging exploration of the probabilistic potentiality of literary and bibliographic devices in the production of meaning. Two features stand out in this work: the link between typographic materiality and the world of hypermedia digital technology, and the inventiveness of its writing, whether at the level of words and sentences or at the level of narrative sequences.[1] Danielewski's obsessive and meticulous typographic and bibliographic construction of text and book matches an equally acute sense of the combinatorial possibilities in the materiality of language and writing. The result is a work that blends a numerical and algorithmic logic—descendant from oulipian mathematical procedures, with its formalized rules and constraints—to a Joycean paranomastic associationism—with its verbivocovisual revelations of the unconscious of language by means of phonic, graphic, and semantic attractions that explode into unexpected combinations. Whitmanian parataxis, with its uncontainable drive for ever-increasing enumerations, joins a Rabelaisian humor, replete with genital allusions.

Operations of metatextual organization add an ergodic and cybertextual layer to the discursive and bibliographic structure of Danielewski's work.[2] By suggesting several reading trajectories, they enlarge the set of syntactic and narrative permutations that readers can perform in its universe of signifiers. This compositional process turns the text into a machine for revealing the mechanism that makes the production of meaning possible. *Only Revolutions* exposes the mechanism that generates its particular bibliographic structure, that is, its material code. Through this device, it displays the intertwined mechanics of writing, language, and codex and of the novel itself as printed and narrative genre. Designed as a textual machine, the text shows the abstractness of signs and culture— the combinatorial nature of discourse and representation. Those features enable us to investigate the connectivity and the physicality of the forms language and writing as producers of meaning: "A lot of *Only Revolutions* is interested in the mechanisms that are underlying things, the grammar, the physics of things. We're not talking about particular words but the relationship between words. Not the particular names of planets, but the nature of an ellipse and the effect of gravity on the orbit" (Danielewski, quoted in Miller 2007).

Only Revolutions confirms the architectural and stylistic ability that Danieleswki showed in his first novel, *House of Leaves* (2000). Both works are remarkable feats in the representation of various internal and external spaces, the typographic spatialization of voices and discourses on the page, and, above all, the act of creating correspondences between the different scales and patterns into which those internal and external spaces are articulated. Whereas *House of Leaves* was written and page-set on the basis of labyrinthine ramifications, *Only Revolutions* is materially structured on the basis of symmetric and recursive circularity.[3] A set of rules and algorithms translates the space-time of fiction into the space-time of the codex. The correspondence between referential spaces (spaces in the fictional world) and self-referential spaces (spaces within the book itself) results in a heightened awareness of mediation that defines the experience of reading in both works. Danielewski is trying to create a homology between bibliographic form and narrative content in order to show how recursivity works in the process of meaning production. Meaning is experienced as the result of feedback between sequences of signifiers and their mode of material inscription.[4] Considered in its literal configuration on the page, the text takes on an iconic and indexical dimension, which creates a constant tension between a mimetic and a self-reflexive self-descriptive effect.

Like *House of Leaves*, *Only Revolutions* is not only a print emulation of the electronic writing space. This work interrogates the very topology of the codex as a multidimensional space for meaning, exploring the articulation between the page as a unit and the motions from page to page. Self-awareness of the ergonomics of codex spaces is achieved by means of internal symmetry axes at each level (graphic and bibliographic, verbal and narrative). The articulation between material spaces and conceptual spaces works through the topological and algebraic mediation of a set of geometric shapes and patterned numbers that stand out as a metacode. In this way, the codex reveals itself as a computational engine, a mechanism that governs the distribution of letters and blanks on the page surface. Its signifying power depends on various layers of symbolic inscription.

The symbol or logo of the work (figure 5.1), for example, can be read as a sign of those multiple inscriptions. It is a symbol at once for the two characters, for stasis and motion, for union and separation, for the circularity of narrative, and even for the orbital relations between the bodies of signs and the bodies of readers created by the mechanics of book rotation and book translation. By linking graphical space to narrative space, this logo marks its own materiality as an archeological and technological record of itself as a signifying trace. This ideogram may be said to contain a double reference: to the circle, represented in the outer ring, and to the Möbius strip, represented in the two traces. The figure of the circle is also used, in the body of the text, as a symbol for the eyes of each character—gold for

Figure 5.1

Only Revolutions' ideograms. © 2006 by Mark Z. Danielewski. Used by permission of Pantheon Books, a division of Random House, Inc.

Hailey and green for Sam. The ring imitates the shape and color of the pupils of Hailey and Sam's eyes, while the two traces suggest the point of entry for light. As ideograms for the eye and for the act of seeing, they are symmetrically structured as reflections of each other and representations of the specular nature of the organ of sight. Their presence is multiplied and echoed in the colored letters and numbers in the text, and also in the doubly circled page numbers. The alphanumeric sign (as the number 0 and letter *o*) gains an ideographic and pictographic content by turning this particular logographic form into an identifying sign for each of the two individual characters. The color-coded O's and 0s become pictograms referring to the individual characters and suggesting the presence of the eyes in the act of reading. They are part of a series of graphical strategies for adding a visual layer to the alphabetic coding of this novel, and for involving readers in its semiotic circles.

In fact, the circle is not only a circle. It is also a model for a Möbius strip. Interior monologues of the two characters are laid out on opposite sides of the strip, as if each of them were written on the surface of the other. Inside and outside become entirely relative coordinates. Once you get to the end, the journey begins again, restarting a new circular cycle. This endlessness is expressed through the lack of hierarchy in narrative focus: each perspective has an exact counterpoint on the opposite point of the circle. Danielewski has attempted to make linguistic and narrative forms symmetrical, as if they were mirroring one another. The symbols 8 and ∞ recur as numerical and geometrical tropes of the novel.[5] On both title pages, ∞ is used to symbolize infinity. It can be read also as a two-dimensional representation of the Möbius strip. By emulating a Möbius strip, page layout re-creates the topology of this structure in the reading surface of the codex. The topographic relationship between 8 and ∞ is established by a rotation that transforms one symbol into the other. In fact, ∞ was often made in printing by typesetting an 8 on its side. Like verbal language, which has a mathematical expression, numbers have a geometric expression, and vice versa. Besides, the symbol ∞ is also a graphic representation of both time and space within the narrative and of the trajectory of reading motions. Infinity (∞) is thus a representation of the manifold dimensionalities of the codex as topological and semiotic space.

The circle and the Möbius strip are used not only metaphorically but also as a model or metadescription of the bibliographic and typographic form that determines the linguistic and narrative composition. There is a continuous process of calculus that projects a topographical and numerical structure onto a bibliographic and typographical structure and, as well, a linguistic and narrative structure. Topographical and numerical correlations work at different levels: they structure the book, the chapters, and the pages; they structure the strings of alphanumeric characters and the number of lines; they structure the font, size, style, and color of type; and they work at the level of syntactic structures, narrative sequences, and chronological history. They have been codified so that the structure and spaces of one level are mapped onto the structure and spaces of another level. This set of correlations can be described as the metadata for writing, page setting, and reading the work. As a device, it shows the technological nature of the book as a machine for linking writing to reading, and language to narrative. Like its predecessor, *House of Leaves* (2000), *Only Revolutions* may be analyzed as a technotext in the sense proposed by N. Katherine Hayles: "literary works that strengthen, foreground, and thematize the connections between themselves as material artifacts and the imaginative realm of verbal/semiotic signifiers they instantiate" (2002, 25).

The circle and Möbius strip, in their multiple material and symbolic occurrences (including the shape of alphanumeric characters), are the main organizers of this universe of signs. This is done by using both their geometry and a large set of numbers derived from their properties. Typographical composition and page layout make possible at least three major reading trajectories, according to three axes of symmetry. Circularity can be experienced at the level of the book as a whole, at the chapter level, and at the page level, all structured as symmetrical halves. Thus narrative space desires to fully coincide with the paper space of the page and with typographical composition, that is, with the exact shape of written characters (typeface, type size, type color, type style, line distribution, and constellation of character strings). Readers have to acquire a new kind of literacy through this secondary reading code. In the following sections, geometrical and numerical circularity will be mapped considering the book as a whole: chapters, openings, single page, columns, lines, alphanumeric character strings, and type.

5.2   The Book Is Round

5.2.1   Recursive Layout

This book's pagination and page layout are based on the projection of 360 degrees of the circle onto its bibliographic structure. There is a large set of numbers that can be projected onto that structure, which works at both a numerical level and a geometric level, according to several axes of symmetry. The numbers used to generate the linguistic and typographical combinations are mostly multiples and submultiples of 360 (1, 2, 3, 4, 5, 8, 9, 10, 36, 40, 45, 60, 72, 90, 180, 360, 720 . . .). In certain instances, such numbers can be used to generate additional numerical sequences with circular and recursive properties. The book has 360 pages split into two symmetrical layouts, which establish two directions for reading: half of each page is read in one direction and the other half in the opposite direction. The book has two identical title pages, each identifying one narrative voice. The story is told from the perspective of Sam in one direction and Hailey in the other. Thus, the end of Sam's narrative coincides with the beginning of Hailey's, and vice versa. Like a Möbius strip, there seems to be no exit. The inner surface gradually becomes the outer surface, and vice versa, generating a recursive movement around itself.

This form of recursivity in the act of reading becomes a material experience of the recursivity between graphic and conceptual space within the codex and a choreographic embodiment of the hermeneutic circle created by the relationship between sign and interpreter. The need to choose between paths among constellations and networks of signs confronts readers with their role in the coconstitution of the object that they interpret. The act of rotating the book embodies the eventive nature of meaning production. If a computational work has to be executed by a program before it becomes readable by a human reader, this bibliographic work follows a code that shows the semiotic import of the reading operations coded in its various material levels. Reading is being produced by reproducing its object as a series of coded fields. The number 8, which works as a symbol for infinity and a planar representation of both the circle and the Möbius strip, also functions as a diagram for the reading motions of the novel. Circularity and infinity are captured on the book's algebraic expression, repeated at each end: "Volume 0: 360: ∞," a formula that should be read as a mathematical representation of the endless proliferation of meaning relations generated by this codex as a discursive machine.

As happens with the successive levels of abstraction that link forensic materiality to formal materiality in a computer (Kirschenbaum 2008), these procedures make explicit the multiple layers of coding contained in a printed book. This layering includes the levels of articulation of language (phonological, syntactic, lexical, and semantic), its recoding by writing (which makes it possible, for example, to explore the combinatorial and recursive structures of language with a higher degree of complexity), its recoding by modes of production of cohesion and coherence in discourse (manifest, for instance, in stylistic patterns, cultural archetypes, and narrative genres), and the typographical and bibliographic coding of all those elements (according to particular planographic and three-dimensional layouts). By giving explicit semiotic functions to all these material levels of the codex form, *Only Revolutions* delights in the multiplicity of its levels of encryption.

It activates as part of its literary form the double set of codes (linguistic and bibliographic) that characterizes the book as an artifact. It should be noted that bibliographic codes work even when they are not explicitly incorporated into the literary form of the work: their function is to socialize the text (i.e., to materialize it as an artifact). The text is dependent on a mode of production and a set of reading protocols established by its specific bibliographic condition. The paperback edition of *Only Revolutions* (June 2007), for example, contains praising quotations on both covers (from the *San Francisco Chronicle* and the *Washington Post Book World*), the phrase "National bestseller," an embossed silver seal that reads "National Book Award Finalist," and a note that identifies the author as "Author of *House of Leaves*" (figure 5.2). Those four markers are repeated in similar

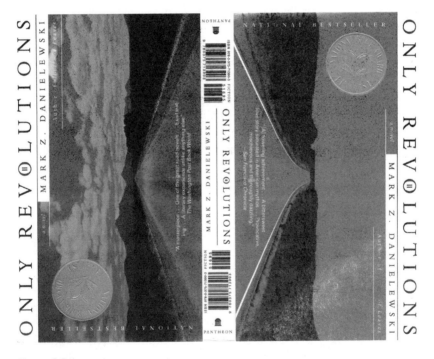

Figure 5.2
Mark Z. Danielewski's *Only Revolutions:* double cover and spine (paperback ed., 2007). © 2006 by Pantheon Books, a division of Random House, Inc., from ONLY REVOLUTIONS by Mark Z. Danielewski, copyright © 2006 by Mark Z. Danielewski. Used by permission of Pantheon Books, a division of Random House, Inc.

relative positions on both covers, accommodating themselves to the principle of symmetry used in the composition and pagination of the book. To these we should add two praising quotations on each of the book flaps (from the *New York Times Book Review* and from "National Book Award Finalist Judges' Citation"), typical of book blurbs. The graphic layout of this set of markers reenacts the principles of symmetry and circularity that are internal to the work's compositional rationale, but its pragmatic function is to promote the book as a commodity.

In this way, the whole institution of literature becomes present in the socialized artifact: through book reviewing in the periodical press, the system of literary awards, the network of bookstores, and the author's reputation—in other words, through the whole set of markers that produce the symbolic identity and commercial value of a book in the literary market. Those markers inscribe the work in the system of literary reception in the North American book market. They link the symbolic economy of discourse to the symbolic economy of monetary value. There are therefore elements in this book's bibliographic coding that go beyond what the author can control and depend on a broader system of signs that reinscribes his work in a particular mode of production and reception. These socializing elements recontextualize the edition's illusory autonomy as bibliographic artifact. Even with the most detailed authorial planning of all areas of the book (including colophon, flaps, spine, inside cover, and bar code), the ubiquity of the author cannot overwrite the ubiquity of the market. In other words, a representation can never exhaust itself, and no explicit metacodification can escape the general processes of socialization of meaning and the codes that determine it.

5.2.2 Symmetrical Strips

The circular structure, which organizes the ensemble of 360 pages, is replayed at each page. Each page is divided into four sectors or areas, whose limits are defined by two axes of articulation (inside/outside and upper/lower). Each of these four sectors contains an identical number of alphanumeric strings. The counting unit is the alphanumeric string of characters (not the word): for example, the punctuation sign that follows a given word (or precedes it, such as dashes) has to be counted as part of the letter or number string; numbers or numbers followed by letters are always one single sequence. Blank spaces set the boundaries of any unit. "22 Nov 1963," for example, is counted as 3 strings. Each of the four sections of the page has exactly 90 strings. This means that each page is an analog of the circle, with 90 + 90 + 90 + 90, or 360 strings.[6] By using character strings as counting units instead of word strings, Danielewski points to the code of alphabetic writing as a specific and arbitrary form of recoding language. That differential and generative function of the alphabetic code is also clear when he blends words or gives them a phonetic twist.

Each page has two columns divided into two halves, forming four sectors. The inner column always contains references to dates and historical events, and the outer column contains the interior monologues of each character. These four sectors can be read according to several horizontal, vertical, and diagonal sequences: for example, (hH1 + H1) + (hS360 + S360), or (hH1 + hS360) + (H1 + S360), or (hH1 + S360) + (hS360 + H1) (figure 5.3).[7] The page thus becomes a mirror of the book and another analog of the circle: the book's 360 pages are now the 360 character strings of each page. The three-dimensional space of paper gets translated into the bidimensional space of alphanumeric characters. An identical structure links the actual writing surface to the printed marks of writing. Each page is a replica of codex structure, thus establishing a homology between the movement within the plane (x- and y-axes) and the movement within space (z-axis). The three-dimensional circularity obtained by handling the sheets and the volume of paper also occurs on the two-dimensional

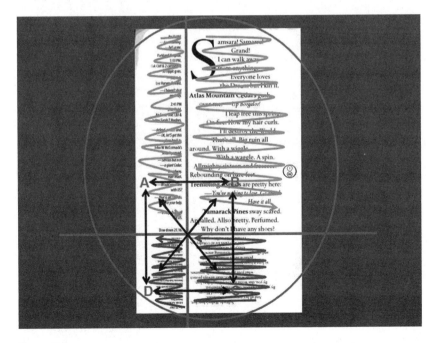

Figure 5.3
The page as a circle and twelve reading directions between the four sectors: AB/BA: CD/DC; AD/DA; BC/CB; AC/CA; BD/DB. © Manuel Portela, 2009.

surface arrangement of typographical layout in each page. Readers' body movements handling the codex mirror their eye movements traversing the page, and vice versa. Hand movements are symmetrical to eye movements.

5.2.3 Intersecting Circles

The use of initial letters organizes the 360 pages in groups formed by 8 pages. There are 45 chapters in each reading direction, so 90 in all. This means that motions of reading can trace three circular paths at the level of bibliographic structures: at the level of the book as a whole, at each chapter, and at each page. Reading can move around the four sectors of each page in different directions (left-right; right-left; top half/bottom half; inside column–outside column) and in various combinations, either clockwise or counterclockwise (H1[1/4, 2/4]//S360[3/4, 4/4]) (figure 5.3); those same paths can be made between diametrically opposite pages (H1[1/4, 2/4]/S1[1/4, 2/4] + H2[1/4, 2/4]/S2[1/4, 2/4] + …) (figure 5.4a); the reader

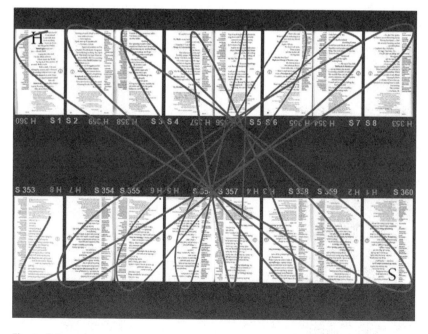

Figure 5.4
Symmetrical chapters: (a) reading as a circle in space (eight full translations); (b) reading as a Möbius strip (8 × 2, reverse directions); (c) reading as a circle and a Möbius strip. © Manuel Portela, 2009.

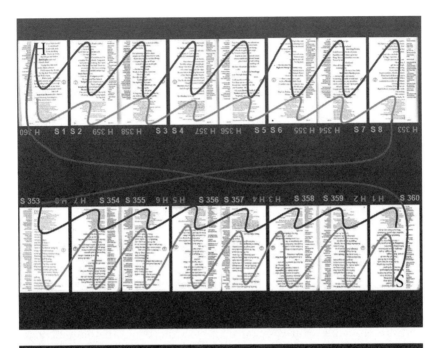

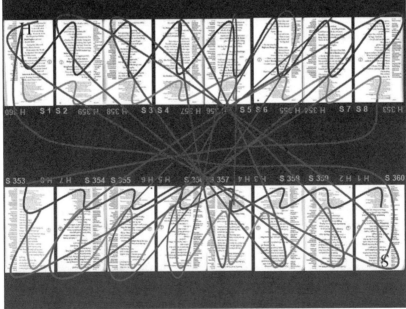

Figure 5.4
(continued)

can read 8 + 8 pages of symmetrical chapters (S1–S8 [1/4, 2/4] + H1–H8 [1/4, 2/4] . . .) (figure 5.4b); the full 360 pages of each sequence (S1–S360 [1/4, 2/4] + H1–H360 [3/4, 4/4]); or any combination of those reading paths, moving randomly between the scale of the column, the scale of the page, the scale of the chapter, and the scale of the book (in both reading directions) at any given moment (figure 5.4c).

Only Revolutions is thus both multilinear, in the sense that several reading trajectories have been produced in advance as preferred courses (such as H1–H8/S1–S8, or H1–H360/S1-S360, or even H1/S1, H2/S2, and so on), and multicursal, in the sense that many other trajectories are determined by readers according to regular or random patterns. As a constellated constrained hypernovel, one of the most constellated and constrained novels ever written (including electronic hyperfictions), *Only Revolutions* is an extreme instance of what Aarseth has called "cyborg aesthetics" (1997)—an aesthetic of textual machines. Figure 5.5 represents the triple circularity in the typographical and bibliographic structures of the work, showing in diagrammatic form the relationship of the character strings that define the circle on each page, the sequence of pages that makes up each chapter, and the ensemble of pages that makes up the book. In this schematic representation, arrows mark the trajectories of reading (turning the page + rotating the page + rotating the book), which materialize the experience of circularity in the act of crossing the work's field of signs by means of those combined motions.[8]

5.3 Typography Is Round

5.3.1 Generative Letters

Initial letters also form a numerical and recursive pattern that loops at each end of the book. Initial letters are legible when combined together, forming a recurring cycle that suggests the topology of the Möbius strip: "SAMANDHAILEYAND."[9] Reading can follow a clockwise or counterclockwise direction. Certain properties of the Möbius strip, whose structure may be described by a system of differential algebraic equations, are recreated in the material and symbolic space of the book:[10]

1. The reading of initial letters can start at either end and run continuously, as happens with the continuous unlimited surface of the Möbius strip: [SAMANDHAILEYAND**SAMANDHAILEYAND**SAMANDHAILEYAND **SAMANDHAILEYAND**SAMANDHAILEYAND**SAMANDHAILEYAND** SAMANDHAILEYAND**SAMANDHAILEYAND**SAMANDHAILEYAND]

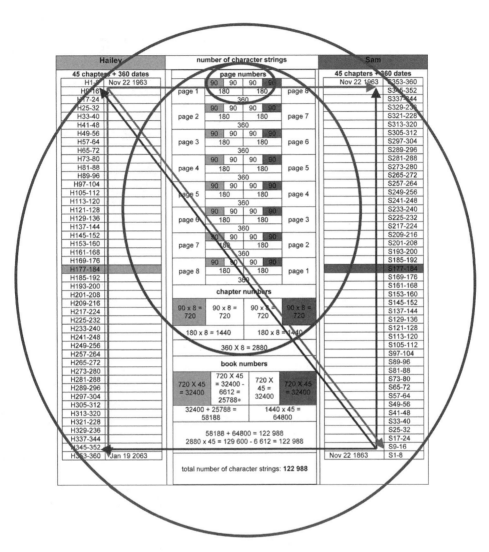

Figure 5.5

Circle analogs: page circularity, chapter circularity, and book circularity. Symmetrical reading sequences at the page level, chapter level, and book level. A numerical analysis of character strings in the novel. © Manuel Portela, 2009.

[HAILEYANDSAMANDHAILEYANDSAMANDHAILEYANDSAMAND
HAILEYANDSAMANDHAILEYANDSAMANDHAILEYANDSAMAND
HAILEYANDSAMANDHAILEYANDSAMANDHAILEYANDSAMAND].

2. The motion of the book when reading symmetric chapters or inverted pages emulates a half-turn needed to produce a Möbius strip out of strip of paper.

3. The boundary of the Möbius strip, when projected in three dimensions, is a topological equivalent of the circle.

4. The page works as the basic rectangle and its division into two parts, with reverse reading directions, is akin to the unlimited double-face of the Möbius strip.

5. The rotation needed to obtain a Möbius strip is made around a point outside the surface of the strip itself, and this is actually simulated by the rotation of the book in space.

Such symmetries (SAMAND/DNAMAS + HAILEYAND/DNAYELIAH) are a feature of the whole work, and they manifest themselves at the level of letter, number, and page sequences. This means that the bibliographic and typographical elements have a fractal structure: recurrences at the scale of the book as a whole are repeated at the scale of the chapter, the scale of the page, the scale of the line, the scale of the word, and the scale of letter and number strings. The textual machine that Danielewski designed produces iterations that are homologous in each of those levels of meaning production. What is performed by the surface of inscription is also being performed by the inscription marks. The overall structure becomes an embodied equation for deriving topological spaces from alphanumeric expressions, and vice versa.

Yet another marker associates chapters in groups of three, since the initial letters for chapters 1, 4, 7, 10, 13, 16, 19, 22, 25, 28, 31, 34, 37, 40, and 43 are set in a larger font. In the table with these chapter groups, we can isolate the four letter markers: S, A, H, and L (figure 5.6). The reading motion of the structure created by initial letters suggests the topology of the Möbius strip, in which the front side of Sam's story is also the back side of Hailey's story, and vice versa. The motions of reading make a retroactive path between one sequence and the other. This elliptical motion is the line drawing movement for the number 8 and the symbol for infinity. As mentioned above, the book actually describes rotations and translations that turn reading into a sort of gravitational orbit between reader and signs (see figure 5.21). The wavy line that reverses on itself suggests both a looping without beginning or end, like a Möbius strip, and an

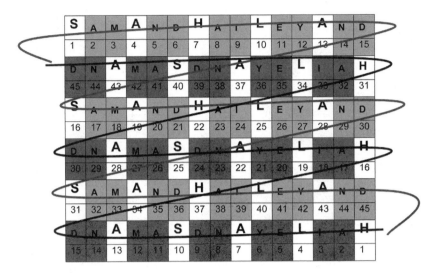

Figure 5.6
"SAMANDHAILEYAND" (H chapters) and "HAILEYANDSAMAND" (S chapters) as a Möbius strip. The initial letters form fifteen groups of three letters (45: 3 = 15 × 2 = 30). © Manuel Portela, 2009.

elliptical or circular motion. Danielewski's bibliographic device models reading and writing as gravitational fields. His book is an experiment on the physical and conceptual mechanics of reading.

These three-chapter groupings produce the palindromic equivalence "AND" = "DNA," which suggests that the numerical metacodification can also be read as a matrix or genetic code for generating certain textual occurrences and certain semiotic correlations between verbal language and mathematical language. The constraints (which determine the number of lines, number of character strings, font size, areas of the four page sectors, number of pages, and number of page sets) function as the code for the permutations and combinations. The productivity of this recursive replication for generating new textual segments is a consequence of that code. The established correlations, which link sequences according to the symmetry axes left/right and top/bottom, generate a periodic pattern 2–3–2–3–2–3 (figure 5.7). Anagrammatic and anacyclic patterns (palindromes) occur in both combinations of letters and combinations of numbers. Thus, the anacyclic principle (reading in reverse) works at the level of bibliographic structures (page, page groups, and entire codex), linguistic and narrative structures (each narrative can be read from first

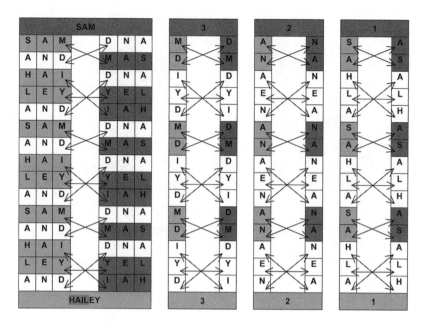

Figure 5.7

"SAMANDHAILEYAND" (H chapters) and "HAILEYANDSAMAND" (S chapters). Reflection symmetries between groups of letters. Initial letters as a textual genetic sequence. © Manuel Portela, 2009.

page to last, and from last page to first), and, in several instances, character strings (letters and numbers). The axes of symmetry that duplicate those structures operate according to specularity (mirror reflection) and self-similarity.

Besides mirror symmetries, each column provides various combinations of four or three letters. These letters suggest the DNA code and the possibility of factorial permutations of the base elements in new strings:

1. In the first columns S and H:

In groups of four (top-bottom), S-A-H-L, A-S-A-H, L-A-S-A, H-L-A

In groups of three (top-bottom), S-A-H, L-A-S, A-H-L, A-S-A, H-L-A

In groups of four in reverse direction (bottom-top), H-L-A-S, A-H-L-A, S-A-H-L, A-S-A

In groups of three in reverse direction (bottom-top), H-L-A, S-A-H, L-A-S, A-H-L, A-S-A

2. In the second columns S and H:

In groups of four (top-bottom): A-N-A-E, N-A-N-A, E-N-A-N, A-E-N

In groups of three (top-bottom): A-N-A, E-N-A, N-A-E, N-A-N, A-E-N

In groups of four in reverse direction (bottom-top): A-E-N-A, N-A-E-N, A-N-A-E, N-A-N

In groups of three in reverse direction (bottom-top): A-E-N, A-N-A, E-N-A, N-A-E, N-A-N

3. In the third columns S and H:

In groups of four (top-bottom): M-D-I-Y, D-M-D-I, Y-D-M-D, I-Y-D

In groups of three (top-bottom): M-D-I, Y-D-M, D-I-Y, D-M-D, I-Y-D

In groups of four in reverse direction (bottom-top): I-Y-D-M, D-I-Y-D, M-D-I-Y, D-M-D

In groups of three in reverse direction (bottom-top): I-Y-D, M-D-I, Y-D-M, D-I-Y, D-M-D

If initial letters are substituted for the equivalent chapter numbers, an identical generative structure can be applied to the chapter numbers (figure 5.8).

The bibliographic and typographical division based on the number 3 has a noticeable correspondence within narrative space, since it is possible to associate events in Hailey's and Sam's story as fifteen sequences of three chapters. Every three chapters (that is, every set of twenty-four pages) contains a core theme, expressed in action, time, and space. Figure 5.9 is an attempt at identifying those fifteen narrative sequences. In the center column, which numbers the fifteen sequences from each end of the book, it is possible to find other numerical associations. For instance, the number 8 stands out as both the center of the narrative and the center of the book, and the thirteenth sequence includes the car accident that precedes the death of both characters—Hayley from a bee sting (S321) and Sam from a fall (H321). The double circle and Möbius strip are further reflected on the wheels of the bicycle that Sam and Hailey use in their daily rides to work (the eighth sequence). There are references to cycles and cycling in the sixteen pages of chapters 22 (H169–H176/S169–S176) and 24 (H18 –H192/ S185–S192), and the word *Bike* is used eight times, on the first and last pages of the bicycle sequence (S169, S170, S191, S192; and H169, H170, H191, H192).

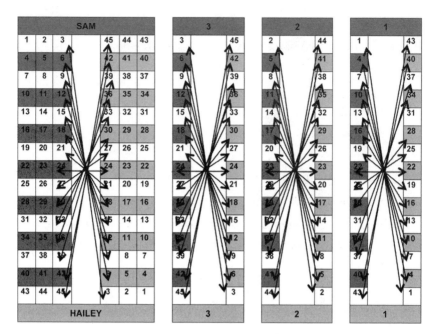

Figure 5.8

"SAMANDHAILEYAND" and "HAILEYANDSAMAND." Reflection symmetries between chapter numbers. Correspondences between chapter positions and chapter numbers. Chapters 22, 23, and 24 as a central axis. © Manuel Portela, 2009.

5.3.2 Looping Types

Numerical patterns also determine the number of lines in the two narrative sectors (outside column) in each page. The number of lines of the monologues by Sam and by Hailey always adds up to 36 lines. Therefore we have yet another submultiple of 360 and a reading path linking the reversed halves of each page as a projection of the circle. The number of lines is organized according to the following sums: 22 + 14, 21 + 15, 20 + 16, 19 + 17, 18 + 18, 17 + 19, 16 + 20, 15 + 21, and 14 + 22 (figure 5.10). The number of lines decreases when readers move toward the end of the book and increase when they move away from the end. These changes are symmetrical since the movement near the end of one narrative is toward the beginning of the other. In the central chapters, the number of lines is the same in each half column (18 + 18). In other words, the bibliographic pattern of the codex structure has a typographic equivalent in line layout.

			Center				
H A I 1 2 3	Sam and Hailey first meet **[1-24]** [S1-S8] [S9-S16] [S17-S24]	1	15	Hailey's lament for Sam **[337-360]** [H360-H353] [H352-H345] [H344-H337]	D N A 45 44 43
L E Y 4 5 6	Sam and Hailey reunited **[25-48]** [S25-S32] [S33-S40] [S41-S48]	2	14	Death of Sam **[313-336]** [H336-H329] [H328-H321] [H320-H313]	Y E L 42 41 40
A N D 7 8 9	First car journey **[49-72]** [S49-S56] [S57-S64] [S65-S72]	3	13	Car accident **[289-312]** [H312-H305] [H304-H297] [H296-H289]	I A H 39 38 37
S A M 10 11 12	Club party in New Orleans **[73-96]** [S73-S80] [S81-S88] [S89-S96]	4	12	Fifth car journey and fight against THE CREEP **[265-288]** [H288-H281] [H280-H273] [H272-H265]	D N A 36 35 34
A N D 13 14 15	Hailey in the hospital **[97-120]** [S97-S104] [S105-S112] [S113-S120]	5	11	Fourth car journey and marriage **[241-264]** [H264-H257] [H256-H249] [H248-H241]	M A S 33 32 31
H A I 16 17 18	Second car journey **[121-144]** [S121-S128] [S129-S136] [S137-S144]	6	10	Third car journey, Hailey and Sam try to get married **[217-240]** [H240-H233] [H232-H225] [H224-H217]	D N A 30 29 28
L E Y 19 20 21	Stay at St. Louis and work at the bar **[145-168]** [S145-S152] [S153-S160] [S161-S168]	7	9	Last days working at the St. Louis bar **[193-216]** [H216-H209] [H208-H201] [H200-H193]	Y E L 27 26 25
A N D 22 23 24	St. Louis, bike rides to work, Sam and Hailey in bed **[169-192]** [S169-S176] [S177-S184] [S185-S192]	8	8	St. Louis, bike rides to work, Hailey and Sam in bed **[169-192]** [H192-H185] [H184-H177] [H176-H169]	I A H 24 23 22
S A M 25 26 27	Last days working at the St. Louis bar **[193-216]** [S193-S200] [S201-S208] [S209-S216]	9	7	Stay at St. Louis and work at the bar **[145-168]** [H168-H161] [H160-H153] [H152-S145]	D N A 21 20 19
A N D 28 29 30	Third car journey, Sam and Hailey try to get married **[217-240]** [S217-S224] [S225-S232] [S233-S240]	10	6	Second car journey **[121-144]** [H144-H137] [H136-H129] [H128-H121]	M A S 18 17 16
H A I 31 32 33	Fourth car journey and marriage **[241-264]** [S241-S248] [S249-S256] [S257-S264]	11	5	Hailey in the hospital **[97-120]** [H120-H113] [H112-H105] [H104-H97]	D N A 15 14 13
L E Y 34 35 36	Fifth car journey and fight against THE CREEP **[265-288]** [S265-S272] [S273-S280] [S281-S288]	12	4	Club party in New Orleans **[73-96]** [H96-H89] [H88-H81] [H80-H73]	Y E L 12 11 10
A N D 37 38 39	Car accident **[289-312]** [S289-S296] [S297-S304] [S305-S312]	13	3	First car journey **[49-72]** [H72-H65] [H64-H57] [H56-H49]	I A H 9 8 7
S A M 40 41 42	Death of Hailey **[313-336]** [S313-H320] [S321-S328] [S329-S336]	14	2	Sam and Hailey reunited **[25-48]** [H48-H41] [H40-H33] [H32-H25]	D N A 6 5 4
A N D 43 44 45	Sam's lament for Hailey **[337-360]** [S337-S344] [S345-S352] [S353-S360]	15	1	Sam and Hailey first meet **[1-24]** [H24-H17] [H16-H9] [H8-H1]	M A S 3 2 1

Figure 5.9

"SAMANDHAILEYAND." Initial letters and the fifteen three-chapter narrative sequences (15 × 3 = 45)]. © Manuel Portela, 2009.

	outside column				
type size decreases	H	36 lines per page		S	type size increases
↑	H1-8	22	14	S353-360	↑
	H9-16	22	14	S345-352	
	H17-24	22	14	S337-344	
	H25-32	22	14	S329-236	
	H33-40	22	14	S321-228	S321
H41	H41-48	21	15	S313-320	
	H49-56	21	15	S305-312	
	H57-64	21	15	S297-304	
	H65-72	21	15	S289-296	
	H73-80	21	15	S281-288	S281
H81	H81-88	20	16	S273-280	
	H89-96	20	16	S265-272	
	H97-104	20	16	S257-264	
	H105-112	20	16	S249-256	
	H113-120	20	16	S241-248	S241
H121	H121-128	19	17	S233-240	
	H129-136	19	17	S225-232	
	H137-144	19	17	S217-224	
	H145-152	19	17	S209-216	
	H153-160	19	17	S201-208	S201
H161	H161-168	18	18	S193-200	
	H169-176	18	18	S185-192	
	H177-184	18	18	S177-184	
	H185-192	18	18	S169-176	
	H193-200	18	18	S161-168	S161
H201	H201-208	17	19	S153-160	
	H209-216	17	19	S145-152	
	H217-224	17	19	S137-144	
	H225-232	17	19	S129-136	
	H233-240	17	19	S121-128	S121
H241	H241-248	16	20	S113-120	
	H249-256	16	20	S105-112	
	H257-264	16	20	S97-104	
	H265-272	16	20	S89-96	
	H273-280	16	20	S81-88	S81
H281	H281-288	15	21	S73-80	
	H289-296	15	21	S65-72	
	H297-304	15	21	S57-64	
	H305-312	15	21	S49-56	
	H313-320	15	21	S41-48	S41
H321	H321-328	14	22	S33-40	
	H329-336	14	22	S25-32	
	H337-344	14	22	S17-24	
	H345-352	14	22	S9-16	
↓	H353-360	14	22	S1-8	↓
type size increases	H	36x360=		S	type size decreases
number of lines=6480		12960		6480=number of lines	
	outside column				

Figure 5.10

Number of lines (outside column) and correlation between decreasing and increasing type size in the half pages *Hailey-Sam* and *Sam-Hailey*. Changes in size as musical notation. © Manuel Portela, 2009.

This pattern is also replicated in font size, which decreases at regular intervals (figure 5.10). The font size decreases every five chapters, or every forty pages. This means that character size changes eight times in each direction of reading. Changes occur, respectively, on pages H41, H81, H121, H161, H201, H241, H281, and H321 and on pages S41, S81, S121, S161, S201, S241, S281, and S321. In each group of five chapters, the number of lines on Hailey's pages increases by one line, while the number of lines on Sam's pages decreases by one line, and vice versa. Font size and number of lines on Hailey's and Sam's half pages is identical in the five central chapters of the book (pages H161–H200 and S161–S200). It is only here that the surface area of the page is divided into two equal halves. This divides the page height, 22.4 centimeters, into approximately two halves of 11.2 centimeters. Changes in type size function as musical notation for a vocal performance of the monologues: they correlate with the changes in the general tone and emotional atmosphere of the various narrative sequences. The allegro vivace of the first sequences turns into the andante of the middle sections, and finally into the adagio of the last sequences. The joyful euphoria of love and car journey as filtered through individual consciousness gives way to Sam and Hailey's social transactions with other voices and other people, and finally turns into a melancholic lament for separation and death. Type size and type style are also making writing audible, and they can be read as prosodic markers.

It is not only the structure of the pages that is symmetrical. Symmetry is also a property of line layout, and font size variation. As we will see in the next section, such symmetry extends to the syntactic structure of sentences. Typesetting thus mirrors linguistic structure in the sense that typographical forms share topographical properties with the corresponding linguistic forms. Linguistic syntax becomes homologous to typographical syntax. The same syntactic structures are used by Sam and by Hailey, but with lexical variations that distinguish their voices. Moreover, each page (and, in some cases, groups of two pages) can be read as a poem, because they often function as an autonomous unit, more or less independent of narrative sequence. Their rhythmic and syntactic unity often allow a suspension of narrative continuity or, at least, a tension between the self-enclosed page and the open-ended sequentiality of the circular codex. Syntactic structures, text lines, page sectors, single page, and page groups produce what can be best described as a vocovisual and constellated novel.

5.4 Language Is Round

The mirroring of Sam's story in Hailey's, and vice versa, duplicates—in the
material space of language and in the conceptual space of narrative—the
material and conceptual space of the codex as a circle with one axis of
symmetry that divides it into two topological identical parts. The permutational principle that establishes the verbal symmetry between the monologues by Sam and Hailey can be seen in the symmetrical pages of each
sequence (H1/S1, H2/S2, and so on). The same syntactic and phonic structure sustains their voices, which suggests both the coincidence and the
uncoincidence of their consciousness (i.e., the possibility and impossibility
of union; the possibility and impossibility of identity between signifier and
signified; the necessary and the arbitrary logic of the verbal, narrative, and
bibliographic associations that generate meaning). The work's narrative
semantics displays itself as an effect of phonic, syntactic, and lexical repetitions and variations, in turn reinforced by a feedback between the material
and linguistic space in the book. The linguistic template that supports the
lexical variations has a graphic equivalent in the typographical template
that determines the parameters for typesetting (figure 5.11). Symmetry at
the codicological and typographical levels extends into the linguistic and
narrative levels.

Pages H33 and S33 (as would any other pair of symmetrical pages)
exhibit one of the central stylistic features of the work: the repetition of
the same syntactic and graphical structures in the discourses of Hailey and
Sam. Their interior monologues are like echoes of each other, and most of
the time they cancel out the possibility of determining their relative ante-
riority or posteriority. Although occurring at different places in the book
and at different reading times, perceptions of each character are given as
temporally and topographically identical. In this way, both symmetry and
asymmetry are suggested, giving readers access to shared experience and
the particular perspective of each voice. All references to flora that appear
in Hailey's monologue for example, are substituted by names of fauna in
Sam's monologue. Even the direct speech of each character or the sounds
of nature follow patterns of semantic and phonetic symmetry:

> New **Mountain Phlox** and **Wild**
> **Strawberries** praise pleasingly
> my racing breeze:
> —*Weeeeeeeeeeeeeeeeeee!*
>
> (H33)

New Mountain Phlox and Wild
Strawberries praise pleasingly
my racing breeze:
—*Weeeeeeeeeeeeeeeeee!*
Every smipering **Stickseed, Laurel**
and Toadstools by pool and gush,
Brewer's Bittercress offering up
from ground and bog, **Beech &
Spruce** whrrrring at clouds, all
creeeing my impossible rush:
—*Weeeeeeeeeeeeeeeeee!*
And I'm allready gonegoing,
their only one and on, feetbare
padpadding by leaps and rounds
of **Pawpaw Apple** and Wax
Currant with abounding **Clasping
Peppergrass** snippering zowns:
—*Weeeeeeeeeeeeeeeeeeeee!*
From escarpments and névé cwms,
by cirques, couloirs and slides,
I streak free, which Them allso
hazard, trailing after me,

Every **American Robin** and **Sage
Thrasher** chears admurringly
my tremendous blur:
—*Whirrrrrrrrrrrrrrrrrr!*
Newly fidgeting **Bats, Wrens**
and **Newts** by ponds and rill,
Hooknosed Snakes tumbling
over banks and logs, **Wolverines &
Moles** grrrrring by brittle rocks, all
breeeing for my impossible stir:
—*Whirrrrrrrrrrrrrrrrrr!*
And I'm allready gogone, their
only On and On, shooooshing
beyond these thickets and marsh.
By **Chorus Frogs** and
Western Turtles with a
Gyrfalcon circling above:
—*Whirrrrrrrrrrrrrrrrrr!*
From palisade and powdery saddle,
fumarole, flume and falls,
I hurtle free, even if Them allso
hanker to follow me,

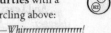

Figure 5.11
A textual motor: linguistic and typographic symmetry in Hailey and Sam's discourses. Lexical substitution takes place over a syntactic matrix. Typographical composition works according to a template that defines styles, justification, and position of lines (H33 and S33). © 2006 by Mark Z. Danielewski. Used by permission of Pantheon Books, a division of Random House, Inc.

> Every **American Robin** and **Sage**
> **Thrasher** chears admurringly
> my tremendous blur:
> Whirrrrrrrrrrrrrrrrrrrrrr!
>
> (S33)

When read continuously, these recursions and permutations are barely noticeable because of the vibrant phonic and oral nature of the writing. The complex relation between sound and visual patterning in the work can be appreciated when we compare a silent reading of the pages with the sound recording of the novel.[11] This recording alternates one chapter by Sam, read by a male voice, and one chapter by Hailey, read by a female voice. While it is still possible to recall echoes of Sam in Hailey's monologues, listeners will miss the highly constrained patterns visible to readers. Tracks (chapters) have been given titles, and in several passages, a musical soundtrack has been added to the voices. Conventions of audiobooks have framed the recorded reading in a way that stresses both the linearity of narrative syntax and the realist and romantic aspects of the work. Certain hierarchies are restored in order to navigate what is a highly decentered text. For instance, Sam's voice is given primacy, which turns his text into a template and Hailey's into a variation on that template. Reading the symmetrical chapters also stresses continuity of time, action, and place instead of the fragmentariness and incompleteness of each character's single consciousness. As the semantics of spoken discourse overpowers the semiotics of typography and codex, narrativity displaces poeticity, and visual spatial tensions are resolved as aural temporal sequences. Through this recording, one can see the relation between the potentiality of the novel's graphical layout, with its multicursal and multilinear possibilities as an open notation for semiotic and hermeneutic operations, and a particular vocal performance as a single interactive instantiation of an event that coconstitutes its own text. As with any other highly constellated work, several other equally valid performative trajectories would have been possible.

One experiment I made with my students consisted of reading aloud one sentence or a short sequence of phrases by Hailey and the corresponding symmetrical sentence or sequence by Sam. The result was a significant transformation of the lyric and narrative layers into a dramatic layer. The fact that each character's text is partially identical creates a powerful dramatic effect, as if they were arguing the representation of their own feelings and actions. This means that there is a reading scale below page level at which the quasi-symmetrical counterpoint of voices also works as a dramatic dialogue, particularly at those points where tension and difference between characters are marked. *Only Revolutions* thus seems to have created a bibliographic and linguistic notation for the voices of Sam and Hailey that embodies at least three modes of literature, since it can be read as novel, poem, and play according to specific trajectories and segmentations of the reading spaces made available through its constellated visual semantics.

Paronomastic associations, puns, elliptical syntax, truncated quotes, frequent use of parataxis, removal of connectives, and repeated use of metaphors based on slang and terminology (flora and fauna)—all of these techniques emphasize the presence of a character's specific point of view that creatively deforms the events through the sieve of his or her emotions and motivations. Ellipsis and juxtaposition of thoughts, speech, and memories emphasize the absence of a single focus, a narrative effect of the interior monologue technique. They also contribute to the narrative presence of objects in the uniqueness of their existence, and especially to the fullness of the rhythmic and objective presence of the words themselves. The use of many sentences without verb and the presentation of dialogue fragments require readers to deal with words and phrases in nonhierarchical form. Their sensorial dimensions (aural and visual) and semantic individuality are given priority over their logical place and syntactic function. This effect is replicated in the tension between the self-sufficient page and its projection onto the sequence of pages or chapters. The autonomy of the poetic dimension of verbal discourse has a visual equivalent in the visual patterning of each page, which can be read as either an independent unit or an echo of its correspondent symmetrical page.

The narrative dimension of discourse, in its turn, is projected onto the eight-page chapter, groups of chapters, and corresponding chapters, symmetrically placed in opposite positions in relation to the codex center. This tension between the plane of the page and the space of the sequence of pages also articulates the basic duality of the codex as a device for organizing information. Page unity and page sequence are the main organizational properties of the codex: the tension between the plane of the page and the space of the book, that is, the tension the page as self-contained area for simultaneous presence and the codex as a space for sequential presence.

This lexicalization of reading motions has a visual occurrence on the inside covers of the book, where circular and elliptical disks work as a diagrammatic echo of the bibliographic movements that determine lexical and narrative associations. A series of sixteen semantic and lexical fields is laid out in the shape of circular and elliptical disks (figure 5.12). These sets represent words not found in the novel or, in a few cases, found only once. Crossed-out words deliberately point out to the combinatorial nature of this work as an explicit exploration of the generative features of language: "~~The Now Here Found~~ Concordance" (which also contains the visual rhyme "The Nowhere Found") ~~Found Once Once Here~~ and ~~Found Once Once There~~. Each set of words is alphabetically ordered from A to Z, and they direct readers' attention to the dictionary and the grammar of language, but also to cultural patterns and abstract concepts as human constructs for making sense. Their circular and elliptical shape is an echo of the reading motions required for the production of meaning as a recursive path from sign to sign.[12] Because all of the inside cover is set in reverse,

Figure 5.12

~~The Now Here Found~~ *Concordance*. The codex as a mirror of language and narrative: inside covers contain a concordance lexicon (in mirror image) of words not used in the novel. The lexicon is organized into sixteen semantic and lexical fields. © 2006 by Pantheon Books, a division of Random House, Inc., from ONLY REVOLUTIONS by Mark Z. Danielewski, copyright © 2006 by Mark Z. Danielewski. Used by permission of Pantheon Books, a division of Random House, Inc.

the concordance can be read only by holding the book up to a mirror. This action is both an evocation of the history of typography as a specific inscription technology and a performative analog of the various forms of symmetry embodied at linguistic, bibliographic, narrative, geometric, and numerical levels.

Readers have to see themselves reading. Consciousness of the act of reading as a particular physical motion draws attention to the ways in which this codex is made to mirror its language and the ways in which its language is made to mirror its codex. The circular syntax of codex structures interacts with the circular syntax of language structures by bibliographically multiplying permutations that are inherent in grammatical structures. Page layout feeds back onto the language, opening up words and sentences to the potentiality of new and unexpected associations. These sixteen sets, which are composed of shapes that superimpose, intersect, and touch each other, are also evocative of various kinds of scientific graphic representations. They evoke diagrams that represent the workings within living cells and diagrams that represent both the cosmological forces of the universe and the quantum world of infra-atomic forces. One of the predominant semantic and lexical fields "found (t)here" at "the now here found concordance" is the field of language, literature, writing, and inscription technologies. Thus codex and language become equated with the basic magnetic and gravitational forces of matter and the genetic code of living organisms.

5.5   The World Is Round

In a work so full of self- and metareference, how does referentiality work? In *Only Revolutions*, reference is divided into two dimensions: the dimension of collective U.S. and world history, given as a chronological accumulation of facts, and the dimension of individual and personal story, given as an accumulation of thoughts, feelings, perceptions, spoken words, and memories. In terms of the circular topology of the work, Sam and Hailey's stories can be seen as two half circles. At the same time, the full circle of their joint story is but the half circle that relates individual story to collective history. There is an overlapping hierarchy between the two circles: circle 1 = Sam + Hailey, and circle 2 = (Sam + Hailey) + history, or, in a different formulation, circle 1 = US, and circle 2 = (US) + U.S.

The relationship between readers and characters to the world also contains isometries between the fictional space and the semiotic space. Capitalization of "the World" occurs many times, making it possible to think about the relationship between the two characters as their knowledge of and relation to the world. The movement from individual consciousness to collective consciousness is reflected in the double reference of the pronoun "US." For the reader, the journey in the graphical fields of the book simulates the geographical, historical, and symbolic journey in the territory of the United States. Similarly, the route of the reader in the universe of signs describing Sam and Hailey's journey has an equivalent in the journey through the history of the United States and the world since 1863. The natural and political geography traveled by the characters triggers a set of associations with historical events, broadening the scope of the term "the World" and also placing the historical world within the metafictional trope of circularity. However, one aspect clearly distinguishes story from history: although the facts entered in the history column show a significant number of patterns, similarities that would suggest history as repetition, history does not exhibit the same kind of circular recurrence that we find in the fictional narrative. History is shown as a linear, time-dependent, and open-ended process: dates after 2006, for example, are necessarily blank, and the verbal symmetries do not have corresponding historical symmetries, since historical facts resist accommodation within cyclical processes.

5.5.1 Inscribing History

Representation of history is also geometrically and numerically patterned, which links the modes of typographical and bibliographic construction of fictional narrative to those of historical references. Besides the constraint of character strings in each half column, it seems possible to infer another algorithm from numbers generated by the intervals between consecutive dates in the historical chronology. The numerical intervals between dates increase when we move from 1963 to 2063 and decrease from 1863 to 1963 (figure 5.13). These number sequences, obtained by placing the numbers of the same reversed half-pages side by side, can be related to concepts of symmetry, circularity, and recursion. In this case, number sequences are not the result of an arithmetic operation, but they can be used as a matrix for deriving further sequences of repetitions of which they are the elementary constituents.[13]

Digits or numbers generated by date intervals work as a kind of genetic code for generating larger numbers that have recursive structures, axes of symmetry, and circular patterns. The two arrays of numbers, obtained from the symmetrical double pages of Sam and Hailey, correspond to the double helix molecule of DNA and also to the doubling of language, narrative, and bibliographic structure. Their decoding by the act of reading—which implies reuniting what the actual page setting has set apart—is an equivalent of the replication of genetic material, when the basic building blocks of cells are put together according to a template that has to be translated by molecular mediation. In this instance, reading executes the algorithm of meaning encoded in language and typography. As far as concerns about this and other templates' ability to generate a large number of unpredict-

hH	dates	numerical intervals between dates		dates	hS
H1	Nov 22 1963	+ 1	0 +	Nov 22 1963	S360
H2	Nov 23 1963	+ 1	1 +	Nov 21 1963	S359
H3	Nov 24 1963	+ 1	2 +	Nov 19 1963	S358
H4	Nov 25 1963	+ 3	2 +	Nov 17 1963	S357
H5	Nov 28 1963	+ 3	3 +	Nov 14 1963	S356
H6	Dec 1 1963	+ 4	4 +	Nov 10 1963	S355
H7	Dec 5 1963	+ 4	5 +	Nov 5 1963	S354
H8	Dec 9 1963	+ 5	4 +	Nov 1 1963	S353
H9	Dec 14 1963	+ 5	7 +	Oct 25 1963	S352
H10	Dec 19 1963	+ 8	7 +	Oct 18 1963	S351
H11	Dec 27 1963	+ 7	6 +	Oct 12 1963	S350
H12	Jan 3 1964	+ 8	8 +	Oct 4 1963	S349
H13	Jan 11 1964	+ 9	7 +	Sept 27 1963	S348
H14	Jan 20 1964	+ 9	11 +	Sept 16 1963	S347
H15	Jan 29 1964	+ 9	10 +	Sept 6 1963	S346
H16	Feb 7 1964	+ 12	10 +	Aug 27 1963	S345
H17	Feb 19 1964 [l.y.]	+ 13	13 +	Aug 14 1963	S344
H18	March 3 1964	+ 11	12 +	Aug 2 1963	S343
H19	March 14 1964	+ 13	13 +	July 20 1963	S342
H20	March 27 1964	+ 15	14 +	July 6 1963	S341
H21	April 11 1964	+ 13	15 +	June 21 1963	S340
H22	April 24 1964	+ 17	13 +	June 8 1963	S339
H23	May 11 1964	+ 15	17 +	May 22 1963	S338
H24	May 26 1964	+ 16	16 +	May 6 1963	S337
H25	June 11 1964	+ 17	17 +	April 19 1963	S336
H26	June 28 1964	+ 17	18 +	April 1 1963	S335
H27	July 15 1964	+ 20	14 +	March 18 1963	S334
H28	Aug 4 1964	+ 18	24 +	Feb 22 1963	S333
H29	Aug 22 1964	+ 19	20 +	Feb 2 1963	S332
H30	Sept 10 1964	+ 24	21 +	Jan 12 1963	S331
H31	Oct 4 1964	+ 19	20 +	Dec 23 1962	S330
H32	Oct 23 1964	+ 27	24 +	Nov 29 1962	S329
H33	Nov 19 1964	+ 18	32 +	Oct 28 1962	S328
H34	Dec 7 1964	+ 25	17 +	Oct 11 1962	S327
H35	Jan 1 1965	+ 25	17 +	Sept 24 1962	S326
H36	Jan 26 1965	+ 25	29 +	Aug 26 1962	S325
H37	Fev 20 1965	+ 24	25 +	Aug 1 1962	S324
H38	March 16 1965	+ 26	29 +	July 3 1962	S323
H39	April 11 1965	+ 27	30 +	June 3 1962	S322
H40	May 8 1965	+ 30	24 +	May 10 1962	S321
H41	June 7 1965	+ 31	31 +	April 9 1962	S320
H42	July 8 1965	+ 27	35 +	March 5 1962	S319
H43	Aug 4 1965	+ 28	29 +	Feb 4 1962	S318
H44	Sept 1 1965	+ 32	22 +	Jan 13 1962	S317
H45	Oct 3 1965	+ 30	29 +	Dec 15 1961	S316
H46	Nov 2 1965	+ 35	36 +	Nov 9 1961	S315
H47	Dec 7 1965	+ 30	31 +	Oct 9 1961	S314
H48	Jan 6 1966	+ 35	34 +	Sept 5 1961	S313
H49	Feb 10 1966	+ 33	35 +	Aug 1 1961	S312
H50	March 15 1966	+ 34	39 +	June 23 1961	S311
H51	April 18 1966	+ 37	34 +	May 20 1961	S310
H52	May 25 1966	+ 35	36 +	April 14 1961	S309
H53	June 29 1966	+ 38	35 +	March 12 1961	S308
H54	Aug 6 1966	+ 36	40 +	Jan 31 1961	S307
H55	Sept 11 1966	+ 38	29 +	Jan 2 1961	S306
H56	Oct 19 1966	+ 42	48 +	Nov 15 1960	S305

Figure 5.13

Consecutive dates in the history column, listing numerical intervals between any two consecutive dates (pages hH1//hS360 to hH73//hS288, and hH352//hS9 to hH360//hS1). © Manuel Portela, 2009.

hH	dates	numerical intervals between dates		dates	hS
H57	Nov 30 1966	+ 39	39 +	Oct 7 1960	S304
H58	Jan 8 1967	+ 44	47 +	Aug 21 1960	S303
H59	Feb 21 1967	+ 40	37 +	Jul 15 1960	S302
H60	April 2 1967	+ 39	53 +	May 23 1960	S301
H61	May 11 1967	+ 43	34 +	April 19 1960	S300
H62	June 23 1967	+ 44	49 +	March 1 1960	S299
H63	Aug 6 1967	+ 43	32 +	[l.y.] Jan 29 1960	S298
H64	Sept 18 1967	+ 48	40 +	Dec 20 1959	S297
H65	Nov 5 1967	+ 45	60 +	Oct 21 1959	S296
H66	Dec 20 1967	+ 45	52 +	Sept 4 1959	S295
H67	Feb 3 1968 [l.y.]	+ 48	48 +	July 18 1959	S294
H68	March 22 1968	+ 45	37 +	June 11 1959	S293
H69	May 6 1968	+ 49	47 +	April 25 1959	S292
H70	June 24 1968	+ 49	52 +	March 4 1959	S291
H71	Aug 12 1968	+ 50	49 +	Jan 14 1959	S290
H72	Oct 1 1968	+ 53	51 +	Nov 24 1958	S289
H73	Nov 23 1968	+ 40	43 +	Oct 12 1958	S288
H74	Jan 2 1969	...	...	...	...
...	...	...	...	...	...
hH	dates	numerical intervals between dates		dates	hS
...	...	...	...	...	...
...	...	...	...	July 8 1871	S10
H352	April 27 2056 [l.y]	+ 307	+ 310	Sept 1 1870	S9
H353	Feb 28 2057	+ 307	+ 292	Nov 13 1869	S8
H354	Jan 1 2058	+ 308	+ 317	Jan 1 1869	S7
H355	Nov 4 2058	+ 307	+ 302	[l.y] March 5 1868	S6
H356	Sept 7 2059	+ 307	+ 330	April 9 1867	S5
H357	July 10 2060 [l.y]	+ 308	+ 306	June 7 1866	S4
H358	May 14 2061	+ 307	+ 299	Aug 12 1865	S3
H359	March 17 2062	+ 308	+ 319	[l.y] Sept 27 1864	S2
H360	Jan 19 2063	+ 0	+ 310	Nov 22 1863	S1

Figure 5.13
(continued)

able associations, we may say that they also offer a model for literature as a complex system and for meaning as an emergent phenomenon. The numbers generated by the matrix of date intervals further suggest the identity between numerical and verbal language in terms of both their permutational mechanisms and their abstract nature.[14]

With very few exceptions, date headers were chosen not for their particular symbolism (such as November 22, 1963), but for the numerical intervals between consecutive dates.[15] As between any two consecutive dates it is possible to include any events one wants to select, Danielewski makes allusions to a huge slice of history from a U.S. and world historical perspective between 1863 and 2006.[16] The choice of date headings is determined by the numerical pattern rather than by the selected events, which tend to fall within the period set by two consecutive date headings and not necessarily on the specific calendar day. Yet while giving the impression of randomness, the representation of history is powerfully framed within a general theme of political, social, and natural violence—history as an endless cycle of human and natural violence. The nightmare of history, with its brutal accumulation of violent events, is not so much the result of a random accumulation of dates, as it is the effect of bias for selecting certain types of events, particularly those that can be represented by death counts.

The juxtaposition of events follows a discernible set of patterns, which include references to hundreds of political revolutions and military conflicts of the past 150 years, references to many natural disasters and accidents of human origin, and references to important legal developments in the political order. Chronology seems dominated by political violence, natural disasters, and human accidents, all of which confront humanity with death and violence as the fundamental condition of individual and social existence. In the representation of the history of the United States, the violence within society and the imperialist design of the state stand out as part of the general pattern of a representation of world history. Despite factual referentiality, the history column embeds chronology in the bibliographic and narrative pattern of the story sections. Although facts and references are, in most instances, quickly identifiable, the history column follows a technique of montage and a fragmentary logic of association similar to the techniques governing the body of Sam and Hailey's interior monologues. This associative logic is clear in the fragments of quotes from various historical protagonists. The following excerpt exemplifies the discursive structure and the rhetorical function of the chronology in the narrative economy of *Only Revolutions:*

July 29 1914
1,200,000 troops.
Austria & Belgrade.
–consult her own.
Attack Germany,
Attack France.
–Neutrality.
–Impartiality.
–Fairness.
–I attack.
von Kluck, von Bülow
& The Marne.
–We have lost the War.
–clear out of my way.
U-9s.
Braves over Athletics.

–*woman's body belongs.*
Sydney's Emden.
Butte Mine Fight.
Hindenburg's Austro-
German forces.
Raggedy Ann.
Aerial battles over
Southend-on-the-Sea.
French to German
trenches. Fortino Samano.
Triple Entente.
River of Doubt.
–*going out all*
over Europe.
Italy quakes, 29,500 go.
Blücher down.
Coast Guard.
800,000 to Prussia.
Champagne attack.
Total Sub Warfare.

(hS66)

In this example, the early history and first battles of World War I are evoked through fragmentary and truncated quotes and names of historical significance (individuals, places, institutions). By means of an associative mnemonic, the reader provides a context for these references, a cognitive operation that reveals the contextual and fragmentary nature of the semantic mechanism for meaning construction. Such fragmentation can be read as a kind of interior monologue of history, as if causal relations in the historical processes could acquire the phantasmagoric nature of a stream-of-consciousness voice without narrative mediation. Thus narrativity shows itself also as a product of association by reading. Juxtaposition predominates over hierarchy, as if the facts of history were a mere lexicon available for syntactic recombination.

Even at this documentary level, Danielewski's novel is a product of digital serendipity, which has made all sorts of documents and sources available for search, citation, and cross-reference in the electronic networked environment. History appears as a mere reservoir of discursive representations available for automated searches and verbal sampling. Many historical references, perhaps the majority of them, have been quoted or taken not from printed sources but from electronic sources using electronic tools. This form of intertextual digital historiography, that is, the many quotations from speeches and written documents woven into the history column, results from access and reorganization of personal knowledge of the historical archive by the intermediation of the computer. Moreover, several items in the chronological lists were taken from an online forum where Danielewski's readers contributed references to their own local and national histories.

5.5.2 Inscribing Geography

If numbers constrain reading paths in the territory of the page, are there any numbers that determine the journey in geographic space? Reconstruction of the geographic itinerary of the journey follows the same principle of uniting the two symmetrical half pages. Readers have to intersperse the locations that Sam mentions with the locations that Hailey mentions in symmetric chapters, since their place references (towns, cities, buildings, monuments, streets, roads, natural landscape) are rarely identical. The journey goes from East to West, in several stages: it moves south from Pennsylvania and Maryland to New Orleans; then it continues from south to north, mostly along the Mississippi River and along meridian 90°W; after a prolonged stay in St. Louis, the center of the journey also coinciding with the center of the book, it continues north to Wisconsin; in the last stage, the characters travel west, to Montana, mostly along the interstate highway 90. Therefore the 90 degrees of the circle are projected onto the 90 degrees of the four cardinal points of the geographical coordinates. In this way, what is happening in bibliographic and linguistic space is translated into the fictional geographical space. The numerical infrastructure of the work has an equivalent in the geographic coordinates that map the territory.

The first toponymic references are "Passing through Gettysburg, / Route 30 East to 134" (H50) and "Passing through Gettysburg, / Chambersburg Pike to Taneytown Road" (S50). The last references are "Past Avon, Ovando and Apgar" (H304) and "Past Missoula, Polson and Kalispell" (S304). In between, several small towns, cities, streets, and roads have been mentioned. They run across fifteen states—Pennsylvania, Maryland, Virginia, North Carolina, Tennessee, Mississippi, Louisiana, Missouri, Illinois, Iowa, Wisconsin, Minnesota, South Dakota, North Dakota, and Montana—plus Washington DC. There are also mythical coordinates and references linking East and West. The Mountain, referred to at the beginning of the journey— "I'm leaving The Mountain. / East. I am The East. / Master of the Wheel. All mine." (S49) and "I'm leaving The Mountain. / East. I am The East. / Master of the Wheel. That's me." (H49)—reappears at the end of the journey, as the place where Sam and Hailey are separated by death—"The Wheel hers no more. / We're stuck but she's my West. / And we've reached The Mountain." (S312) "The Wheel his no more. / We're stuck and he's my West. / But we've reached The Mountain." (H312). Like the characters, human and natural spaces extend into a mythical and symbolic dimension. The Möbius strip is also echoed in the charted itinerary, as we can see when linking the compass points (figure 5.14).

This archetypal dimension is evident in another central element in the flow of images of the work: the Mississippi River. The Mississippi appears as yet another analog of the Möbius strip and the idea of recursion. Like the Liffey in *Finnegans Wake*, the river enacts a symbolic function in the psychic economy of the self narrating the world. The river is at the same time an image of the cycle of natural forces, in its long path between Lake Itasca and the Gulf of Mexico, an image of the flow of collective history, and an image of the force of desire within the self. Its mythical and historical place is echoed in the characters' road journey along the river. There are recurrent references to the river in both Sam and Hailey's monologues and the history column. The onomatopaic word *Mishishishi* (for Mississippi) appears in the inside and the outside columns. A major part of the journey (narrative sequences 6 to 10) runs from south to north along the course of the Mississippi, following approximately the meridian 90 degrees West, through Louisiana, Mississippi, Tennessee, Missouri, Illinois, Iowa, Wisconsin, and Minnesota. Several references to the natural and human history of the river are listed in the history column. That is the case of the historical floods of 1926–1927 (hS87: Feb 9 1927)—"Mishishishi's 30 million acres,"; 1967— "Mishishishi & Student riots" (hH61: May 11 1967); and 1993—"Mishishishi's 15 million acres" (hH235: June 5 1993); and a ferry accident in 1976—"New Orleans ferry, 78 go" (hH132: Oct 18 1976). The desire of the characters is sometimes personified in the river: "The Hudson L bucks on through, / around vermicular shores lapped with / waste, Our Mishishishi, hoisting a / low Paddleboat loaded with / Half a Ferris Wheel puppuppering for / Southern Fields. I am the South" (S121) and "The Ford Elite whines on / around caressing banks splashed with / refurse, Our Mishishishi, heaving a / low Barge loaded with / Half a Ferris Wheel tuttuggering for / Southern Pastures. I am the South" (H121); "The River, Our Mishishishi, / Rolling Along The Long Gone / Sadly Sliding On, / too slow to ever catch up with US" (S132) and "The River, Our Mishishishi, / Roaming Along The Long Way / Sadly Sliding On, / too slow to ever catch up with US" (H132); "And overcome by / no distances, surrounding, fastening US to / The City, Our Mishishishi and US. Just two / for the

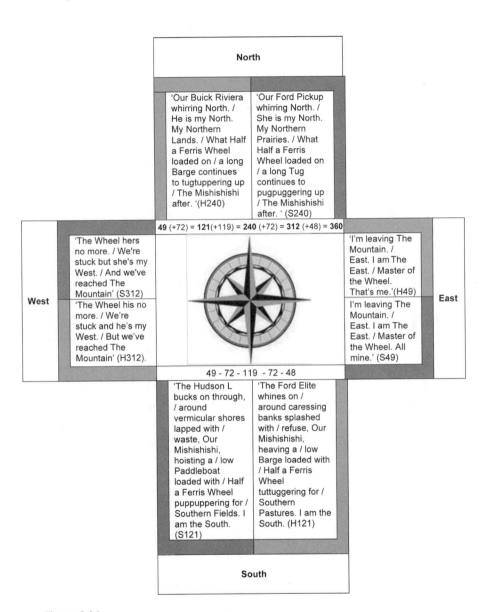

Figure 5.14

The four points of the compass as page numbers: east (H49 and S49), south (H121 and S121), north (H240 and S240), and west (H312 and S312). Number sequence: 49–72–119–72–48. © Manuel Portela, 2009.

World" (S176) and "And overwhelmed by / no distances, encircling, fastening US to / The City, Our Mishishishi and US. Just two / for the World" (H176).

The "Mishishishi" is one of the verbal and historical links between Hailey and Sam's story column and the history column. Other referential links between story and history are made more or less explicit through the natural and historical landscape of their journey. However, both columns seem to run on parallel sections of the page without any mutual awareness, at least from the point of view of the characters. It is up to readers to traverse this gap between the factual record of historical events and the fictional record of mythical events and find patterns of connection in the randomness of their co-occurrence on the same page. This representational gap increases the tension between the apparent timelessness of the fictional structure of this love narrative, on the one hand, and the timebound uniqueness of historical events, on the other. Although the principle of anacyclic reading applies to both columns, in the end human history breaks free from the symmetry patterns, since the future cannot be written in advance. The blank columns show the limits of cyclic representations of experience, and thus they point to the abstract and ideological nature of any mythical representation.

The tension between the absolute presence of the present in individual consciousness and the presence of signs of historical temporality may be observed in the modes of representation of the automobile. The car is metonymically transformed into many different models, as if it assumed a new identity with each new reference. Such mutations are a projection of the emotional states and desires of the characters at any given moment but also of the technological unconscious of history. The diachrony and historicity of America show through the relentless synchronic fullness of the present in the interior monologue. Here is the first reference to the automobile in each of the monologues:

For now here, weirdly, where my chainsawed **Green Ash** died by Sam's murdered ride waits a Shelby Mustang. Idling. (H48)	For now here, weirdly, where my butchered **Horse** died and Hailey's betrayed timber lies waits a Ford 999 Racer. Idling. (S48)

A sports car of the late 1960s and the first Ford sports car (dated 1902) seem to overlap in the same slice of time, evoking in their morphology the technological history of the twentieth century. In all the remaining occurrences, the car will assume many other forms: Cadillac One (H50) and Dodge Charger (S50); Oldsmobile Roadster (H56) and Pontiac GTO (S56); Imperial Baker (H57) and Corvette Sting Ray (S57); Model T (H57) and Corvair Monza (S57); Overland 71 (H65) and Buick Electra (S65). More important than the design of the individual vehicle, it is the archetype of the car and its mythology that are evoked. A journey in the present extends into a past that is both historical and mythical. Cars are thus one of the forms of linking American history and American myth to the story of these characters. Actual time and actual space overlap with mythical time and mythical space as the car becomes a narrative and poetical fetish.

This rhetorical operation juxtaposes historical strata to the layers of the present, linking the story column to the history column. At the same time, it also contributes to show the sixteen-year-old characters as myths and archetypes. Both characters always refer to themselves as US, a self-reference that generates a level of allegorical reading in which their actions and relations stand for a narrative of American history and the American nation. This mythological projection is enhanced by the paronomastic power of phonetic and lexical associations that agglutinate words. References to flora and fauna, which are associated, respectively, with Hailey and Sam, perform a similar function. They form a catalog of species and represent a large piece of natural history as a series of Americana items. Thus, the journey through the human and natural landscape of the United States and the psychology and actions of teenage lovers expose their mythical and ideological dimension as narrative-producing categories.

5.6   Love Is Round

The digit 8—also a symbol for mathematical infinity (∞),the Möbius strip (∞), and a double circle (oo)—functions as a numerical matrix that generates many verbal, narrative, and bibliographic permutations. It also works as the geometrical figure for structuring both the plane of the page and the space of the book. Each opening, for example, is divided into eight parts, projecting the infinity symbol in the duplication of the circle projected onto the four sections that make up each page. The retroactive function of the signs 8 and ∞ as figures for the circuits between the different levels can be exemplified by one of the refrains of the book (figure 5.15). This refrain consists of eight words, and it has ten occurrences in each direction of reading: it is thought eight times by Sam and another eight times by Hailey; it appears twice in direct speech at the center of the book, by both Sam (S180 and S181) and Hailey (H180 and H181). Its

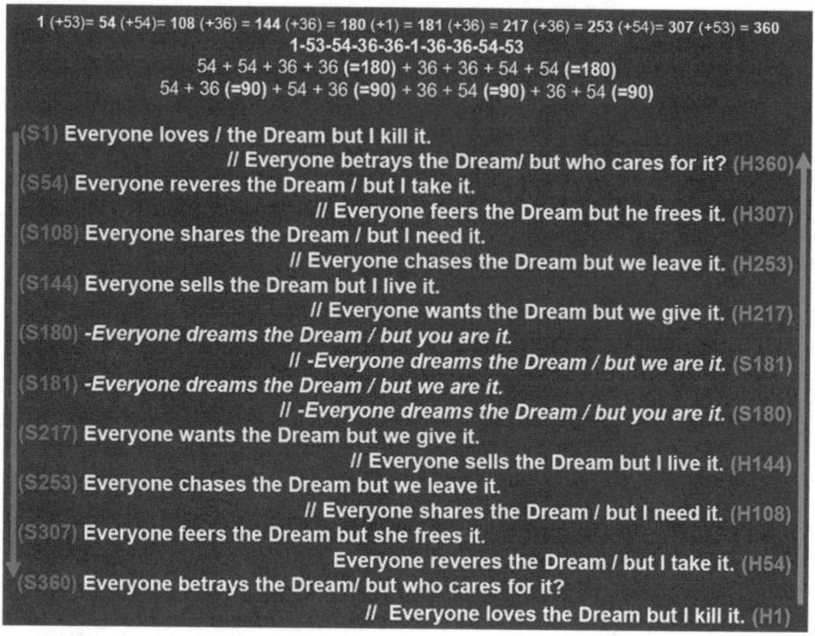

```
1 (+53)= 54 (+54)= 108 (+36) = 144 (+36) = 180 (+1) = 181 (+36) = 217 (+36) = 253 (+54)= 307 (+53) = 360
                            1-53-54-36-36-1-36-36-54-53
                    54 + 54 + 36 + 36 (=180) + 36 + 36 + 54 + 54 (=180)
                54 + 36 (=90) + 54 + 36 (=90) + 36 + 54 (=90) + 36 + 54 (=90)
```

(S1) Everyone loves / the Dream but I kill it.
                        // Everyone betrays the Dream/ but who cares for it? (H360)
(S54) Everyone reveres the Dream / but I take it.
                        // Everyone feers the Dream but he frees it. (H307)
(S108) Everyone shares the Dream / but I need it.
                        // Everyone chases the Dream but we leave it. (H253)
(S144) Everyone sells the Dream but I live it.
                        // Everyone wants the Dream but we give it. (H217)
(S180) -Everyone dreams the Dream / but you are it.
                        // -Everyone dreams the Dream / but we are it. (S181)
(S181) -Everyone dreams the Dream / but we are it.
                        // -Everyone dreams the Dream / but you are it. (S180)
(S217) Everyone wants the Dream but we give it.
                        // Everyone sells the Dream but I live it. (H144)
(S253) Everyone chases the Dream but we leave it.
                        // Everyone shares the Dream / but I need it. (H108)
(S307) Everyone feers the Dream but she frees it.
                        Everyone reveres the Dream / but I take it. (H54)
(S360) Everyone betrays the Dream/ but who cares for it?
                        // Everyone loves the Dream but I kill it. (H1)

Figure 5.15
Repetition and variation in the novel's refrain $(4 + 1 + 1 + 4) \times 2$. Symmetrical sequences: 54-54-36-36 | 36-36-54-54. © Manuel Portela, 2009.

double central occurrence symbolizes the coincidence of selves and bodies at the center of the circle, and they define an axis of symmetry with four occurrences at each side. This refrain undergoes transformations as the action progresses. Its initial form—"Everyone loves / the Dream but I kill it." (S1 and H1)—is an expression of adolescent rebellion against the world, and its last occurrence—"Everyone betrays the Dream / but who cares for it?" (S360 and H360)—seems to recast, in a collective and impersonal dimension, the experience of individual and social desire as imagined forms of the real.

The tension at the heart of desire as dream and at the heart of dream as desire is symbolized in the spelling change that turns "fear" and "free" into anagrams for each other: "Everyone feers the Dream but she frees it" (S307), and "Everyone feers the Dream but he frees it" (H307). Besides the dream cycle (ideation-realization-destruction), changes in the refrain's personal pronouns suggest a cycle for human union (singleness-union-singleness): *I* is the form used until the center of the book is reached; *we* is used after the center has been reached; and then *he* and *she* are used after the death and survival of both characters. The characters' narrative development suggests a movement poised between self-consciousness, consciousness of the other, and the possibilities and limits of personal and political union. Moreover, the numbers generated by page intervals in the occurrences of the refrain create axes of geometric and numerical symmetry: 54 + 54 + 36 + 36 + 36 + 36 + 54 + 54, a division of the circle into eight parts (which are equal in two groups of four). They also create a number with a central axis of symmetry, and this number shows recursion of the same elements (in units of two or four) on both sides of the axis: 54 54 36 36 | 36 36 54 54, or 5454 3636 | 3636 5454.

The passage of time and the duration of love and life are symbolized in the twelve jars of honey consumed as the story proceeds (figure 5.16a). Their duplication in both symmetrical and reversed pages can be read as a projection of the twelve (or the twenty-four) hours of the day (figure 5.16b). They function as a time-keeping device that measures the passage time. As the narrative moves on, readers are updated on the remaining fractions of honey jars. Hailey and Sam share all jars of honey. The fraction 1/2, being a narrative occurrence of half a unit, echoes the division of the page and the division of the circle. References to honey also occur on the reversed pages of Sam and Hailey (42//319, 43//318, 66//295, 123//238, 180//181), strengthening the connection between typographical signifier and narrative signifier. Honey jars also stand for the duration of love. Early on, honey is set up as a figure for the love relationship between Hailey and Sam:

Sunnyastounded kisses my mouth.
    Mistletoe whisks:
      –Consume only this.
      HONEY!'
      (H42)

Sunnyastounded kisses my mouth.
    Storks bliss:
      –Consume only this.
      HONEY!'
      (S42)

A dozen kisses unfinished.
    Half kisses.
      (H43)

A dozen kisses competing.
    Half kisses.
      (S43)

This association between honey and love is established during their first sexual intercourse on pages 42 to 48, and at the beginning of the car journey. It ends with their death and separation on pages 319 to 328, and with the end of the journey:

Impossibly still. Just gone. Dead.
To where I'm allready goinggone.
Though over her still bawling, kissing her, plugging

42 (+1)= 43 (+23)= 66 (+57) = 123 (+29) = 152 (+28) = 180 (+1) = 181 (+28)= 209 (+29) = 238 (+57) = 295 (+23) = 318 (+1) = 319 (+41) [= 360]
42-1-23-57-29-28-1-28-29-57-23-1-41

(S42) Jars! One dozen Jars! / (...) Honey!
　　　　　　　　　　　　　// savage separation. Our Jar over. (H319)
(S43) Half a Jar goes.
　　　　　　　　// and retrieves for US our last jar of honey. / (...) Just half. (H318)
(S66) Spooning up honey.
　　　　　　　// Even though he's my honey. My everything. My me. (H295)
(S123) Honey. / 8 ½ left. / One Jar for two. Halfandhalf.
　　　　　　　　　　　　　// 3 ½ left. Sweet / Honey. (H238)
(S152) Only for US. Honey. 7 ½.
　　　　　　　　　　　　// 4 ½. Honey. Only ours. (H209)
(S180) Our honey. With just 6 ½ Jars left.
　　　　　　　　　　　// With just 5 ½ Jars of honey left. (H181)
(S181) With just 5 ½ Jars of honey left. 5 ½ left.
　　　　　　　　　// Our honey. With just 6 ½ Jars left. (H180)
(S209) 4 ½. Only ours. Honey.
　　　　　　　　　　// Only for US. Honey. 7 ½. (H152)
(S238) 3 ½ left. Sweet / Honey.
　　　　　　// Honey. / 8 ½ left. / One Jar for two. Halfandhalf. (H123)
(S295) Even though he's my honey. My everything. My me.
　　　　　　　　　　// Sam spooning up honey. (H66)
(S318) and retrieves for US our last jar of honey. / (...) Just half.
　　　　　　　　　　　// Half a Jar goes. (H43)
(S319) savage separation. Our Jar over.
　　　　　　　　// Jars! One dozen Jars! / (...) Honey! (H42)

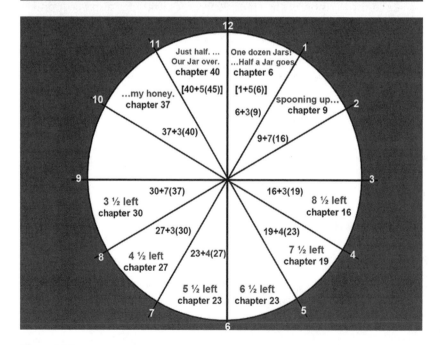

Figure 5.16
(a) "Honey Jars" as the passage of time. The duration of life and love (12 × ½) × 2. Symmetrical sequences: 42-1-23-57-29-28 | 28-29-57-23-1-42. (b) "Honey Jars" as the passage of time. Numbers from 1 to 12: ½ and 12, 3, 4, 5, 6, 7 and 8. Symmetrical sequences: 5-3-7-3-4 | 4-3-7-3-5. © Manuel Portela, 2009.

> her nose, compressing her heart. My breath
> rushing. Allone. Now. Here. Left only.
>
> (S328)

> Impossibly gone. Just still. Dead.
> To where I'm allready gonegoing.
> Yet over him still slobbering, kissing him,
> plugging his nose, pounding his heart. My breath
> pounding. Allone. Too left. Now. Here. Only.
>
> (H328)

One last reference is made on pages 353: "My hand falls. I'll eat no honey" (S353) and "My hand drops. I'll eat no honey" (H353). At the end of the novel, narrative symmetry implies that both characters die and that both survive. Up to this point, the story appeared to have a single chain of events told from two narrative perspectives. In the denouement, however, that single chain of events unfolds in two parallel sequences: in one of them, Sam dies and Hailey laments his death; in the other, Hailey dies and Sam laments her death. The myth of love occurs here in one of its more powerful *topoi:* the death of the beloved and the lamentation for that death:

Now what?
    Her death
clinging hard to Hailey's rigid lips. O! How?
Some course of course. If not at all obvious to me.
Only the saddest mystery cradled by her cold palms.
  My end denied by her end
almost ending me with all it won't harm.
    Because I can't end what I don't own.
Though there's got to be somehow I can join her?
    I freak. Shaking, streaming.
Tears unstopping globs of mess.
–O here. Let me go. Please.
So hacked and roped by this savage World.
    I'm too frightened.

(S335)

What's this?
    A Bee?
Still clinging to Sam's swollen wrist? My poison!
His poison? With nix of even paucities left over.
Still I scratch its sad sting over my skin.
  Across my gums. My demise denied by Sam's demise

denying me here what's my affliction.
    Because I can't start what I don't own.
Though there must be someway I can go too?
      I lose it. Skeeking, shaking.
On my back. Streaks unstopping slogs of goop.
–*O here. Release me. O please.*
Still harnessed to his toothy World.
      I'm so terrified.

(H335)

    This unfolding in the chain of events suggests the overlapping of alternative temporal states and alternative individual destinies. Linguistic and typographical symmetry has an equivalent in a narrative symmetry that forks paths in the chain of events. The cycle of separation-union-separation, an analog of the cycle life-death-life, is closed. But this closure is but one iteration of a recursive process that can continue in new iterations ad infinitum, since, whether as a circle or a Möbius strip, the book can always start over again. While it embodies death and separation, it also reaffirms the romantic myth of a union that desires to transcend death:

Hailey's my oblivion. For once. And allways.
Beyond even time's front. Because now
we are out of time. We are at once.
(S320)

Gold Eyes with flecks of Green.
(S330)

Sam's my oblivion. For once. And allways.
Beyond even time's front. Because now
we are out of time. We are at once.
(H320)

Green Eyes with flecks of Gold.
(H330)

    Representation of sexual relations has several instances, often metaphorically transfigured by reference to specific contexts, such as the flora and fauna or the automobile. Such metaphors make sexual allusions more or less explicit in language and page layout. Sex, which is omnipresent, is given many rich and inventive representations. Moreover, the copula is one of fundamental recurrences of the symbolic figure of the circle in the narrative. At a narrative level, the union of Hailey and Sam—typographically embodied in the circle around two vertical lines and also in the circle around the double numbers of the pages—enacts the geometric union of the two halves of the circle, which is graphically materialized in the layout of each page and the book as a whole. This deep link between narrative and bibliographic space is further stressed in the central chapter on pages 177–184. Here, a coital relationship coincides with the material center of the book. The copresence of both interior monologues is symbolized by their typographical and linguistic coincidence on pages 180–181. This coincidence is the only space-time of complete union and verbal identity between the two voices.

The relationship between the two characters manifests itself in the physicality of the book. The myth of a love fusion (also the topic of the conversation between Hailey and Sam during and after sexual intercourse) has a bibliographic embodiment through the momentary coincidence among the space of narrative, the space of language, and the space of the book. At this point *cunnus* and *phalus* are graphically depicted in the typographical composition of Hailey's and Sam's monologues. This process turns the typographical and phonic carnality of the letter into an erotic fetish. On pages S177//H184 and H177//S184, penis and vagina are visually marked by their layout as salience and recession (figure 5.17). These two half pages are, respectively, the beginning (177) and the end (184) of the coital relationship that occurs at the center of the book. Their iconic similarity to the objects of representation is a graphical symbol for the temporary fusion of love.

The symmetrical composition of the eighteen lines of each of the two half-pages allows the projection (by combining a rotation with a translation) of the half-page S177 onto the half-page H184, and vice versa. Moreover, both pages can be seen as part of a circular single text, since their linguistic structure and narrative implications lend themselves to a circular iteration. This is one of the most expressive uses of the tension between the stasis of autonomous page and the kinetics of the syntax of turning the pages over and around. This tension reflects the tension between the lyrical and the narrative dimensions of language in the work. It also evokes the tension between the fullness of time inhabited through sensations and the inexorable passage of time, which inscribes human experience in the biological and social process of history.

The phrases "That's too easy" (S177), "That's too easy" (H177), "That's too difficult" (H184), and "That's too difficult" (S184) contain co-occurrences of green and golden circles in the same word ('too') and in the same half-page. Golden circles and green circles, pictographic representations of the eyes of each character, are used on the same half pages in the central

Figure 5.17
Sex on the page. *Phallus* and *cunnus* in line layout (S177//H184 and H177//S184).
© 2006 by Mark Z. Danielewski. Used by permission of Pantheon Books, a division
of Random House, Inc.

chapter (S177–S184 and H177–H184). This co-occurrence captures in
graphic terms the dilemma of the union, which is also verbally marked by
the shift from first-person singular to first-person plural, emphasized in
the eighth narrative sequence (chapters 22 to 24). This temporary coincidence of Hailey and Sam is bibliographically marked by the coexistence of
the two characters on the same page opening and by the identity of their
thoughts and speeches (pages S180=H180 and H181=S181). Moreover,
separateness within union and union within separateness (whether between
two individuals or between individual and community) has a lexical
instance in two recurrent lexemes in the novel: "alone," which contains
"all one," "alone," and "a11one" (in Spectrum MT, the typeface used for
Sam and Hailey, "1" and "1" are similar); and "US," which contains "us,"
"United States," and the graphical symbols for reversal and recursion.

Within this vast set of symmetrical structures, symmetry breaking becomes another tool available for symbolic purposes. A break of symmetry in the networks of symbols established for Hailey and Sam occurs in one of the final pages: references to flora are placed in the speech of Sam (S357), and references to fauna appear in the speech of Hailey (H357). Each character is projecting the memory of the other onto the natural world. Both lists recapitulate eighteen references from the first chapter. Sam recapitulates the following plants, first mentioned on pages H1–H7: Aster, Yarrow, Buttercups, Clover, Tarragon, Tansy, Mustards, Daisies, Flax, Catnips, Mints, Bull Thistle, Lilacs, Wild Licorice, Birches, Tamarack Pine, Trembling Aspens, and Atlas Mountain Cedar. Hailey lists the following animals, first mentioned on pages S1–S7: Roughlegged Hawks, Mallards, Crows, Bighorn Sheep, Cottontails, Wasps, Milk Snakes, Toads, Brook Trout, Badgers, Ants, Cats, Deer, Crickets, Coyotes, Beavers, Golden Bears, and Bald Eagles. This final sequence of references to the natural world inverts the order of their first occurrence. If each item is identified by its respective page number, the following numerical sequence is obtained in both cases: 7–7–7–6-4–4-3–3-3–2-2–2-2–2-2–1-1–1. The sum of both lists equals 36, which suggests another overlapping circle: the circle of the natural world, with animals and plants forming each half of the circle. Symmetry, circularity, and reversion are lexically, graphically, and narratively reasserted. All of these patterns, or breaking of patterns, sustain various types of feedback loop between graphic and bibliographic levels (letter, line, page, and others), on the one hand, and language and narrative levels (words, sentences, sequence of actions), on the other.

On pages S180–S181 and H180–H181, the color mix highlights the following words: *you, Honey, Gold, Love, Horror, Gold, Honey, Everyone* (x2), eight words that are repeated in each half-page (figure 5.18). These words provide a key for the interpretation of the whole work. This key links the individual layer of story to the collective layer of history. The crossover of graphic properties between Sam's and Hailey's half pages signifies the temporary union that occurs at the center of the book. It is also there, in the eighth narrative sequence, that the center of the circle (and of the book as a circle) is reached. At that point, layout and typography emphasize symmetry according to the axes inside/outside, top/bottom, left-hand page/right-hand page. By using the opening to derive an internal axis of symmetry (4 + 4/4 + 4), "you" is symmetrical to "everyone," "honey" to "honey," "gold" to "gold," and "love" to "horror" on both Hailey and Sam's pages. The experience of duality between love and horror is embodied in the individual story and collective history. History, as mentioned above, is

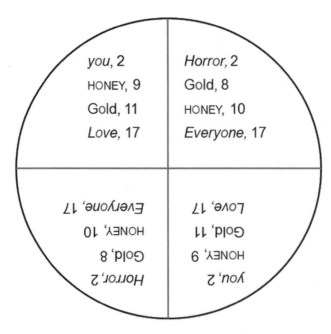

Figure 5.18
Six keywords linking Sam and Hailey, and both of them to the temporality of national and world historical events. Symmetrical sequences: 2-9-11-17 | 17-11-9-2; 2-8-10-17 | 17-10-8-2; 22 | 22; 98 | 89; 1110| 1011; 1717|1717. Sums: You (2) + Everyone (17) = 19; Honey (9) + Honey (10) = 19; Gold (11) + Gold (8) = 19; Love (17) + Horror (2) = 19. © Manuel Portela, 2009.

often represented in the inside column through political revolutions, social uprisings, battles and wars, human accidents, and natural catastrophes. The deaths of both characters and the violence of history equate, individually and collectively, the experience of horror in human life.

5.7 Writing Is Round

The written form of the central page numbers captures the conceptual tension between union and separation embodied in the book's structure. Numbers "180"/"181" and "181"/"180" can be read not only as markers of the half-sequence 1–360 and 360–1, but their actual shapes and relative positions can be read topographically, as happens with the flip-book animation of the double-numbered pages. In this case, the digit 8 standing in the middle of the other two digits, 1 and 0, functions as the axis of mirror symmetry, which combines either 1 and 0 or 1 and 1—the elementary units of machine language. Furthermore, it points to the infinite (∞) possibilities unleashed by the productivity of language when subject to the joint permutational powers of writing, codex, and reading. The double articulation that makes signification possible—by cutting out symbolic space through phonemic and graphemic differences—shows its similarity with digital representation and the principle of numerical difference of machine language. Verbal language and alphabetic writing operate on algorithmic principles that make them capable of automatic processing.

Only Revolutions presents us with the book as a programmable machine, a device with interdependent levels of coding that retroact on each other. The codifiability of the book takes place in the topography of the page, the syntax of pages and openings, the typographical properties of characters and visual layout, and the reading instructions contained in this set of performative markers. Typesetting and layout have recoded the bibliographic materiality of the informational structures of the codex in a self-reflexive form. Semiotic operations resignify the verbal and narrative elements by activating their specific relations to the bibliographic signifiers. This creates retroactions between semantic/narrative layers and bibliographic/graphic layers. Insofar as many operations rely on reading decisions taken on a constellated universe of signs, a substantial part of meaning in bibliographic, linguistic, and narrative spaces is the result of the multiple (anticipated and unanticipated) motions of reading.

The typesetting and layout in this work reinforce associative reading paths, with a significant degree of randomness, across the codex's signifying field. Readers experience the quantum distribution of fragments of meaning, perceiving them as a result of symmetries and broken symmetries, overlapping alternative states, uncertainty and incompleteness in the encounter between text and reader, and, above all, the vast set of (conscious and unconscious) mechanisms that bind the materiality of language to the materiality of writing and codex. The rhetoric of typographical styles reinforces the schematic nature of the oppositions. But their topography affirms the notational power of codex surfaces, multiplying the reading paths between signs. The paronomastic association of multiple lexemes and the radiant constellation of alternative reading paths have the effect of showing the potentiality of meaning. As a set of potential meanings, which overlap in undecidable ways, they point to the abstract nature of writing, language, and book and to their formal materialities. That abstractness determines both narrativity, as the effect of a particular reading path between signs, and semiosis as the general process of translating signs into other signs.

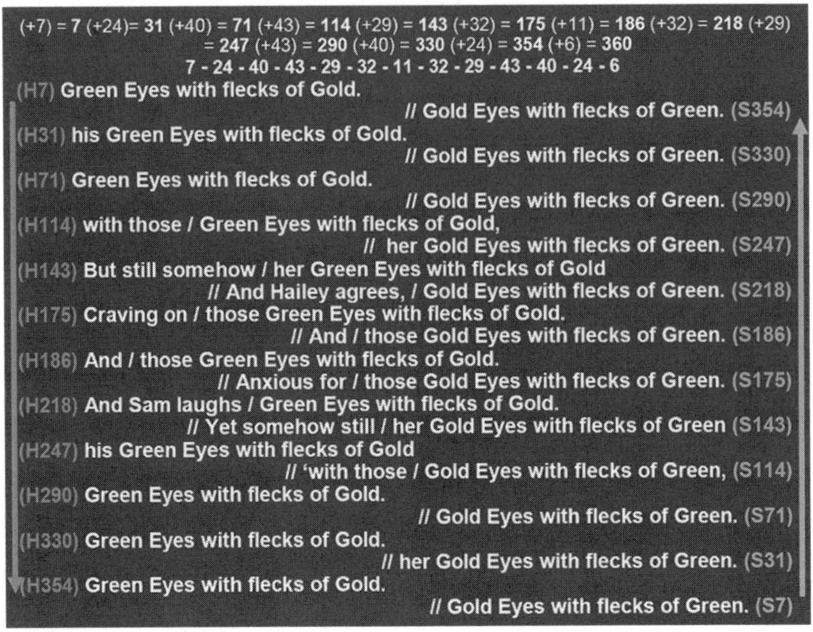

```
(+7) = 7 (+24)= 31 (+40) = 71 (+43) = 114 (+29) = 143 (+32) = 175 (+11) = 186 (+32) = 218 (+29)
               = 247 (+43) = 290 (+40) = 330 (+24) = 354 (+6) = 360
          7 - 24 - 40 - 43 - 29 - 32 - 11 - 32 - 29 - 43 - 40 - 24 - 6
```

(H7) **Green Eyes with flecks of Gold.**
                                              // Gold Eyes with flecks of Green. (S354)
(H31) **his Green Eyes with flecks of Gold.**
                                              // Gold Eyes with flecks of Green. (S330)
(H71) **Green Eyes with flecks of Gold.**
                                              // Gold Eyes with flecks of Green. (S290)
(H114) **with those / Green Eyes with flecks of Gold,**
                                         // her Gold Eyes with flecks of Green. (S247)
(H143) **But still somehow / her Green Eyes with flecks of Gold**
                              // And Hailey agrees, / Gold Eyes with flecks of Green. (S218)
(H175) **Craving on / those Green Eyes with flecks of Gold.**
                                 // And / those Gold Eyes with flecks of Green. (S186)
(H186) **And / those Green Eyes with flecks of Gold.**
                             // Anxious for / those Gold Eyes with flecks of Green. (S175)
(H218) **And Sam laughs / Green Eyes with flecks of Gold.**
                          // Yet somehow still / her Gold Eyes with flecks of Green (S143)
(H247) **his Green Eyes with flecks of Gold**
                           // 'with those / Gold Eyes with flecks of Green, (S114)
(H290) **Green Eyes with flecks of Gold.**
                                              // Gold Eyes with flecks of Green. (S71)
(H330) **Green Eyes with flecks of Gold.**
                                       // her Gold Eyes with flecks of Green. (S31)
(H354) **Green Eyes with flecks of Gold.**
                                              // Gold Eyes with flecks of Green. (S7)

Figure 5.19
"Green Eyes" //"Gold Eyes": reflections and symmetries, difference and repetition.
© Manuel Portela, 2009.

Retroaction between linguistic and bibliographic circularity is reinforced by a series of refrains that bind together the inverted half pages. These refrains are explicit markers for the connection between the verbi-narrative and the bibliotypographical layers. At those points, the work creates a loop that allows readers to cross fictional time and space (passing from the focalization of Sam to the focalization of Hailey, and vice versa, in divergent times) just by moving on the space of the page. This happens at least with six refrains: "the Wheel ESNW," "the Dream," "Honey Jars," "Green Eyes / Gold Eyes" (figure 5.19), "Flash / Wind / Chimes / Thunder" and "Leftwrist Twist." By rotating the page, readers find a variation of the refrain on the reverse page, as if that particular page opened a temporal corridor for a later or an earlier time in the narrative. This seemingly random connection, created by the page layout, has the paradoxical effect of reinforcing the idea of circularity. However, the possibility of moving at random between sectors of each page feeds the reconstellation of preconstituted narrative patterns, enabling readers to explore retroactions in the search for emerging patterns and meanings. Its bibliolinguistic cyclical and recursive structure implies not a mere repetition of a single course but an open exploration of those multicourses generated by various kinds of feedback between language and pagination.

Although they look back to the tradition of complex and dynamic print works, both novels by Danielewski should also be read as digital typographical novels. The visuality and bibliographicality of the print medium have been heightened by digital mediation in the production of the printed book. Digital mediation is reflected not only in the planning, preprinting, and final layout, but at the level of word processing in verbal composition as well. Duplication of Sam's and Hailey's monologues suggests that word processing tools also played a role in comparing, parsing, and sorting their respective texts. Syntactic and lexical parallelism of phrases and sentences, and their symmetrical segmentation in equivalent pages, open them up to a labyrinthine reading, that is, to a reading that intersperses the corresponding lines of Sam's and Hailey's pages.

Therefore, printness is also a product of the flexibility of the pixel and of the page as a bitmap. As N. Katherine Hayles (2002), Mark B. Hansen (2004), Jessica Pressman (2006), and Brian Chanen (2007) have argued in different ways about Danielewski's earlier novel, *House of Leaves* (2000), this is a case of remediation in which the print codex reappropriates new technologies and redefines its own materiality for the digital context. *Only Revolutions* strengthens self-referentiality and self-similarity using a bibliographic and mathematical trope that subsumes digitality in graphicality. Turning the book into a computational device, *Only Revolutions* links the digitality inherent in human language and alphabetic writing, as permutational devices based on recursive structures, to the system of differences that sustain the material and conceptual space of the codex. *Only Revolutions* shows the book as a semiotic machine in which the operations of typesetting, layout, and binding, on the one hand, and the operations of browsing and turning the pages, on the other, produce reading paths that codetermine textual possibilities at both semiotic and hermeneutic levels. The permutational function of the codex is performed through a typographical design (of letters, lines, and pages) that makes readers aware of the various layers of permutation as the basis for linguistic and bibliographic meaning. Instead of the common figure of the computer as a book, an extension of the informational structures of the codex, Danielewski's work gives us the book as a computer: a calculating machine that generates algorithms and geometrizes the plane and the space for writing and reading.

The Web site dedicated to the work is symptomatic of the new media ecology, which has extended into the electronic space all marketplace

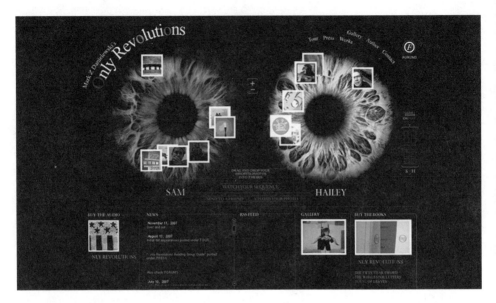

Figure 5.20
Only Revolutions: a Web site mirroring the book (screen capture). © 2006 by
Mark Z. Danielewski. Used by permission of Pantheon Books, a division of Random
House, Inc.

transactions, reconstituting in cyberspace the identity and modes of
circulation of commodities (figure 5.20).[17] But this Web site is not only a
place for merchandising or a meeting place for fans of a book-object
that has become a work of cult. In the design of the Web site, we find
algorithms that are identical to those that organize the book, emphasizing
the contiguity and symmetry between the two spaces. The spinning
of photos around both eyes—and the ability of each user to create his
or her particular sequence of images—is a virtual simulation of the
bibliographic orbits described by each reader as he or she moves around
between parts of the book. The computer's virtual space and the book's
virtual space are hypermediated by this self-consciousness of their specific
medium and the medium they are trying to emulate. An analysis of
the mediation processes involved in this work has to consider not only
the book-in-the-book and the computer-in-the-book, but the also the
book-in-the-computer. Self- and meta-referentiality in *Only Revolutions*
have transmedial implications. Codex and hypermedia are the two halves
in the intermediating circles between book-machine, computer-machine,
and reader-machine.

5.8   Reading Is Round

The 180-character strings in each of the columns suggest that the circle is completed only when one reads the second half, either following the axis of symmetry of the page or the axis of symmetry of the book. Accessing the equivalent halves in each narrative requires reading the symmetrical pages and the symmetrical chapters. The reader has to turn the book around 360 times, if she or he chooses to read page by page, or 45 times, if she or he reads chapter by chapter. These motions create a complex articulation between space and time, since any given time line in the story has been split into two symmetrical spaces that are apart in the book. To access the same chronological time, readers have to travel between opposite spaces of the book, describing circular motions. These circles intersect at the center of the book where the center of a three-dimensional space and the center of a two-dimensional plane coincide. It is as if time and space contracted or expanded as we move toward or away from the center. Both symmetrical sides of Hailey and Sam's narratives total 180-character strings: half of the circle. The other half consists of the 180-character strings formed by the two halves of the history column. This means that the circle symbolizes not only the desire for union of the two characters, but also the relationship between individual and collective destiny. The tension in the union between two individuals replicates the tension in the union between individual and society.

Disjunction between chronological time and bibliographic space is also a disjunction between the points of view of Sam and Hailey. Producing a coherent representation of the two characters and the events in which they participate involves joining the two corresponding halves (i.e., the symmetrical pages and chapters). The gradual construction of a global representation (the construction of a coherent narrative from the genre expectations associated with the novel form or narrative poem) is obtained through the presence of the experience of reading as a series of rotational and translational motions among sets of signs. In moving from one-half to its symmetric counterpart, whether at the page or chapter levels, readers have to negotiate the disjointed relationship between the sequential and the simultaneous. Simultaneous chronological times within the narrative (the times when Sam and Hailey coexist) are spatially dislocated within the book. This asymmetry between bibliographic space and narrative content foregrounds the process of mediation. Readers have an experience of the specific ergonomics of the work and the algorithms and rules that determine recursions and associations. Reading time is translated into narrative space, and narrative time is translated into bibliographic space. Narrative meaning becomes embodied in the linguistic and bibliographic signifiers themselves.

As seen in the previous sections, the calculus that Danielewski developed produces a set of numerical equivalences that translate combinations of linguistic and narrative syntax into geometric relations of the page's topography and the book's topology, and vice versa. The three- and bidimensional materiality of the book is foregrounded in a way that complicates the ergonomics of the physical relationship between reader and book. Self-awareness of reading paths within each page and across the book is obtained by making the act of rotating the pages or rotating the book an integral part of the novel's explicit meaning. The silent and automatic choreography of the hands in the act of reading the codex (opening the book and turning over the page) is made entirely audible by the motion of turning the book and pages around in both predetermined and random patterns. The sequence created by the organization that defines the codex form, and creates an expected reading direction, is multiplied by the book's symmetrical structure. Its circular symmetry offers readers multiple paths within and between pages.

Division of each page into four sections, corresponding to the 90 degrees of a quarter of a circle and the use of reversed reading directions, results in many circular readings. Such reading circles provide multisequential trajectories at the various levels of articulation (page, set of pages, entire codex). Since the fragments of each page are, in most instances, narrative and syntactic units with a significant degree of autonomy, circles of reading can be drawn almost anywhere in the book or the narrative. This means that the two preferred trajectories of reading (S1 to S360 and H1 to H360; or by symmetrical chapters—S1–S8/H1–H8, and so on) exist in a tension with a number of other possibilities inherent in the constellated and modularized page layout of the work. This tension can be played out at either the large-scale structures (page, group of pages and entire codex) or small-scale structures (sentence, line, word, alphanumerical strings), since readers can engage the textual connectivity at any of those scales.

Bibliographic space and narrative space become homologous because the physical motion of reading inscribes meaning in the material space of the book. Inscribing the circle and the Möbius strip as conceptual figures in the rectangular form of the page and in the prismatic form of the book, *Only Revolutions* creates symmetry between syntagm and line, between text and page, and between narrative and book. In other words, inscriptions in the imaginary space of the narrative maintain internal relationships that are homologous to the internal relationships created by printed inscriptions in the graphic plane of the pages and the topological space of the codex. Nothing seems to take place outside the book: the whole language and the whole story happen in its typography and in its topography, as if meaning could not dematerialize from its linguistic, graphic, and bibliographic signifiers.

This retroactive circuit between the verbi-narrative and the biblio-typographical levels is further reflected in sets of explicit and implicit markers, such as circular markers on page corners and leitmotif phrases or sentences. Danielewski's numerical and topological structuring of the relation between verbal and biblio-typographical forms works as an encoding that translates verbal and graphic correlations into numbers and strings of numbers. These numbers and strings of numbers may be said to simulate the formal manipulation of the verbal and graphic elements carried out by the codex's algorithm. They offer a numerical replica of recursivity, symmetry, and infinity as performed by the codex as a computing machine for talking about the endless possibilities of its own code.

The revolutions referred to in the title are the revolutions in the individual stories of Hailey and Sam—how their bodies orbit each other moved by the gravity of love and desire or how their car(s) travel(s) through the territory—and the revolutions in the history of the United States and the world, but also the revolutions of readers around the book—the way they describe circles and ellipses within its material and conceptual space as they turn the book around in their hands. This rotation becomes the figure for the act of reading itself and for the production of meaning as an infinitely recursive route between signs (figure 5.21).

Through a wide range of formal operations, *Only Revolutions* inscribes in its bibliographic dynamics the ergonomics of specific reading acts as paths from sign to sign and page to page. By transforming the book into an object that is both a game and a toy, it objectifies the motions of reading. It also shows the productivity of written language as a function of the potentiality of syntactic and typographical combinations: typographical syntax enhances the potentiality of linguistic syntax because it increases the number of potential permutations of verbal signs. Numerical restrictions governing the typographical, syntactic, and narrative combinations maximize the feedback loops among each of those three levels. The four sections of the page have been structured and mapped according to geometric and numerical coordinates, whose aim is to relate the topology of the page to the topology of language and narrative. The page is a map of its own bibliographic territory and a map of a fictional narrative space.

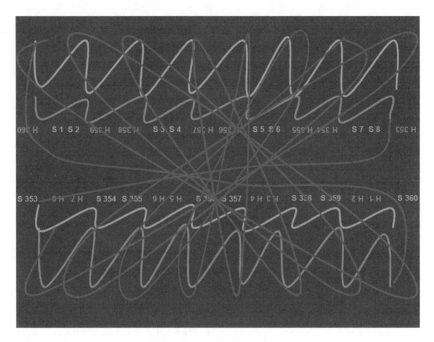

Figure 5.21
Orbits of reader and book: symmetry and recursion in the motions of reading. ©
Manuel Portela, 2009.

The U-turn required for reading each of the opposing surfaces on the
sheets of paper creates a choreographic analog of the Möbius strip, which
exists in the x- and y-axes of the page and in the z-axis of three-dimensional
handling of the book. The recursivity of reading motions from sign to sign
responds to the recursivity of linguistic and bibliographic structures. The
object becomes highly coconstructed by the act of reading as a coproducer
of the object that it interprets. The autopoietic property of bibliographic
space and the probabilistic nature of permutations of signifiers, which are
an essential part of the hallucinatory experience of reading, may be experienced through the multiple echoes between bibliographic and linguistic
spaces. This codetermination between object and subject draws attention
to the codex as a combinatorial textual machine, that is, as a device for
enhancing the digitality of language and of alphabetic writing.

Only Revolutions is an experiment with the codex as a tool for narrative
and poetic notation. Recursion inside language and inside narrative is
echoed and modeled on the recursions of typographical and bibliographic
structures. Meaning appears as a topological function of the spatial sym-

metries of the book, which feed back onto the linguistic and narrative planes. What the vast ensemble of algorithms in this work makes materially perceptible is the extent to which literature can be an exploration of meaning as an emergent and probabilistic phenomenon. A constellated and networked structure of signs, organized on the basis of numerical and topological constraints, results in a complex scripting of the chaotic motions of reading.

Ergodic textuality requires readers' semiotic intervention in realizing the potentialities contained in the textual algorithm. The text is a set of possibilities of meaning whose algorithms readers have to execute. The conversion of texton (stored text whose display depends on an algorithm) in scripton (text displayed as the result of an interaction between algorithm and reader) requires an additional level of intervention. Reading plays itself out not only as the interpretation of a code that preexists the work, but as a semiotic process that generates parts of the code that the reader uses for constructing and reading certain textual possibilities. Associations between signs depend on a calculation of probabilities determined by the algorithm of reading in response to the algorithm of writing. The more constellated the work is, the greater the number of combinations and paths. More than a bundle or cloud of interpretations of preexisting signs, reading is a bundle or cloud of motions between signs that are cogenerated by the reading motion itself. For the machine reader, the experience of reading becomes the experience of the particular algorithm that generates the code that makes it possible for him or her to read. Thanks to this code, the motion between signs that reproduces the textual surface becomes interpretable.

If alphabetic writing contains an analysis of the combinatorial principles of language (from a phonetic to a syntactical level and from a syntactic to a discursive level) and if the printed letter represents the mechanization of writing (from typeface design, font size, and font style to spacing, leading, alignment, and segmentation of words, lines, and sentences), the book has defined itself, from its ancient beginnings, as a simulator of the world that enhances language and writing with its own formal materiality. As producer of the world it simulates, *Only Revolutions* works by articulating the linguistic and typographic space with the poetic and narrative space through a bibliographic encoding that establishes relationships between the various conceptual and material spaces of letter, language, and codex.

The letters *S* and *H* symbolize not only the characters and the two halves of the story, but the specific productivity of the letter as a minimum unit of a narrative machine. This productivity of the letter is also a mirror image of the productivity of reading: shapes H and S describe the reading

Figure 5.22
(a) Symmetry in typeface design of the letters *S* and *H*: the symmetry of the letter
S over a point and the symmetry of the letter *H* over a point and two lines. (b) The
shapes of the letters *H* and *S* contain a representation of the recursions of reading
both within each page and between pages. (c) The topographies of the shapes H
and S describe the reading paths that generate line and page recombinations, either
according to symmetries created by horizontal, vertical, and diagonal axes (dependent on eye movements) or according to rotations and translations of the codex
(dependent on the motion of the hands). © Manuel Portela, 2009.

paths that generate line and page recombinations according to either symmetries created by horizontal, vertical, and diagonal axes (dependent on
the motion of the eyes) or according to rotations and translations of the
codex (dependent on the motion of the hands) (figure 5.22). Reflection
symmetries, rotation symmetries, and translation symmetries at the level
of letter shapes are similar to the symmetries that occur at the higher levels
of page layout, codex structure, and language structure. Thus, the geometric self-similarity of *H* and *S* is also a diagrammatic representation of a
whole series of reading motions triggered by print patterns. The narrative
machine is shown here as being constituted by the recursive dynamics
between the cascading levels of human language, alphabetic writing, and

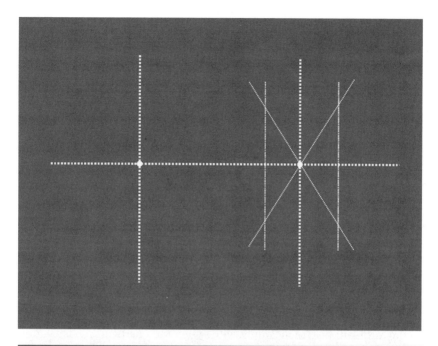

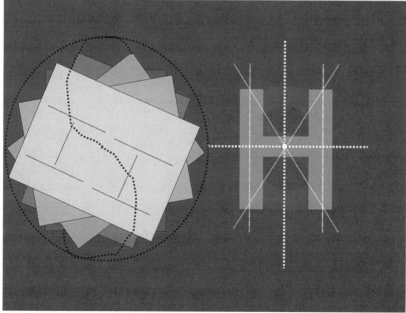

Figure 5.22
(continued)

printed codex. The particular form of codex patterning that Danielewski invented becomes a matrix for generating emergent meanings—unanticipated meanings produced by specific actualizations of potential reading motions. The bibliographic expression of endlessness and recursion may be formalized as $S + H = \infty$.

Only Revolutions is not only an attempt to represent the nature of human desire in the brief encounter with the other and the world, or an attempt to represent the nightmare of human history by a random and cumulative list of facts. *Only Revolutions* puts in the reader's hands a bibliographic emulation of the experience and the myth of love. The desire for embodied reference in verbal and erotic communication is transferred to the materials of codex and writing. The subtitle of the book, *The Democracy of Two Set Out and Chronologically Arranged*, suggests the political dimension of the union of love, and at the same time, it puts the body politic of the nation in the sphere of desire. And that sphere, or, rather, that Möbius strip, morphs into the democracy of the elliptical and circular orbits formed by reader and book in their particular rotations and translations.

Signs do not suffer me to merge with them. They just allow me to move in the turbulent field of meanings with which their particular constellation seduces my desire for interpretation. I go around and around, one more time I go around and around, and in that spiral vertigo, I experience the madness that there is in language. I go around and around, one more time I go around and around, and, caught in the infinitely recursive loop of reading, I am aware of the desire to read as one of the many forms of love. First an *S*, then an *H*; first an *H*, then an *S*; and in that SSSSSSSSSHHHHH-HHH HHHHHHHHSSSSSSSS I feel the chaos of the world reconstituting itself through the hallucinatory effect of the digit of the letter, the calculation of language, and the geometry of the codex as a recursive dispersal and proliferation of meaning in the strange looping of signs.

6 Mouse-Over Events: Meaning Emerges

6.1 Working Codes

Jim Andrews, a Canadian artist and programmer based in Vancouver, British Columbia, has been developing new digital Web-based forms and genres since 1995. His work investigates computer programming code as an expressive means for integrating image, sound, and word. He has also re-created works by Lionel Kearns, and, with Marko J. Niemi, he has recoded *First Screening: Computer Poems* (1984), a series of digital poems by bpNichol.[1] Andrews's intermedia, minimalist, and combinatorial approach is indebted to the objectivist and self-referential poetics of verbal and iconic signifiers of concrete poetry. In effect, he has described several of his early works as concrete digital poems. His electronic poetry contains a sustained reflection on the materiality of digital media and an exploration of the World Wide Web as a new writing and reading space. His digital poetics transforms interactive, kinetic, and multimedia features of digital literacy into powerful poetical toys. Feedback loops between a reader's interventions and textual displays highlight the codependence between the poem as algorithmic machine and the physical and cognitive operations of reading as part of the signifying field. The selected cybertexts are analyzed here as models for making algorithmic interactive processes materially present in the reader's perceptual and conceptual experience of the work.

Codework is a generic term used to describe works of electronic literature that make expressive use of computer code or pseudocode. This term is particularly apt for describing the creations of artists who write at the level of programming language code. Several articles, theses, and books have looked at the particularities of interactive animation in digital poetry (Lee 2002; Ikonen 2003; Simanowski 2002, 2004, 2011; Funkhouser 2005, 2008, 2012; Simanowski, Schäfer, and Gendolla 2010; Flores 2010; Memmott

2011; Johnston 2011), but the scripting, simulation, and modeling of reading through textual instruments has received less attention.[2] Noah Wardrip-Fruin's model of expressive processing (2007, 2008, 2009) contains a theory of playability that is useful for understanding interactions between internal and external processes in digital literature and for the multiple relations among surface, data, process, and interaction. Jim Andrews's texts have appropriated computer game functions and structures, such as iterations at increasing levels of difficulty, for creating reflexive interactions. Readers are made to perform operations on sets of objects and behaviors in ways that increase awareness of the work as an enfolding series of textual events resulting from program interactions. Aesthetic and mathematical investigations of digital playability as representation and performance of reading, his codeworks explore the intermedia convergence of visual and acoustic forms and genres through reflexive algorithms.

Minimalist and serialist approaches to poetic form define Andrews's works: each is composed of a relatively small number of constituent elements, which are then submitted to a large number of systematic permutations. In this way, the generative properties of natural language are mirrored in the generative properties of computer language. Digital textuality is investigated as an extension of the material space of phonological and grammatological difference, that is, as writing and reading space. His digital texts combine deterministic with randomized patterns: they are structured on the basis of programmed sequences of behaviors, each of which has to be activated by the reader or player, but the actual patterns displayed on the screen enact a random instantiation of a large number of potential occurrences. Serial permutations modified by readers' interventions open up the various sign fields to the variability and potentiality contained in the work's database. Letters, words, sounds, and animations can assume endless configurations in space and time.

Programmed interactions are used to make readers experience their own performance of the meaning of the text. As often happens in visual concrete texts, the operation of reading the text becomes part of the referential meaning of the text (see chapter 3). By creating a feedback loop between interpretation and embodied processing of the form, such works direct readers' attention to the perceptual and conceptual processing of the signifiers themselves. Reading is materialized on the surface of the text because the text makes readers perform what it says. Since textual reference points to the action of constructing meaning through the processing of visual and semantic forms, the very act of reading stands out as a major signifier in the works' field of signs. Readers see and feel themselves performing the act of reading, and that self-conscious performance becomes the meaning of the text. Their semiotic intervention at the textual level is also a simulation of the interpretative reproduction of the textual field. Meaning can be reproduced only as the effect of a specific reading motion and interpretative act. Programmed interaction in Andrews's computer poems enacts the cognitive and affective drama of reading as a turbulent field of motions from sign to sign, from sign to self, and from sign to world.

Arteroids (2001–2006), *Nio* (2001), *Stir/Fry Texts* (1999–2009), *On Lionel Kearns* (2004a), and *Enigma n* (1998) are works in which we can experience the performance of reading being enacted by the text as it responds to our playful actions. Readers' interventions codetermine aspects of the display, including readability, sequentiality, and spatiality of textual fragments. Andrews is particularly interested in exploring the programming features of digital media in order to make the playfulness of art and poetry into a structural element of his works. He uses conventions and tools of computer games as powerful rhetorical and poetical devices for interacting with multimedia objects. Digitality allows him to edit sound, image, motion, and alphabetic writing in both patterned and randomized permutations. Listening, seeing, and reading become a play with the ensemble of material and formal elements of a given work as a mode of sensory processing. Interactivity is programmed in ways that enhance self-consciousness of seeing and reading acts as part of the perceptual and signifying field: the reader/player becomes entangled in the sign field that she or he is trying to process, and the text can no longer be perceived as entirely preconstituted prior to a reading/playing act.

6.2 Playing Poems

Arteroids, a "visualkineticaudio text," is a formal parody of *Asteroids,* an early computer video game originally designed for the Atari computer in 1979.[3] Like software applications and computer games, *Arteroids* now exists in three major versions, developed over five years: version 1.0 (2001), version 2.6 (2004), and version 3.11 (2006). The first version is divided into two cantos: "Canto 1: Streaming (Texts)" and "Canto 2: Writing (Arteroids)." Later, this binary structure of the first version was redefined as "play mode" and "game mode," a distinction that Andrews elaborates in terms of the differences between art and game. Changes and additions to the original code have extended its interactive capabilities. One of the functionalities Andrews imagined (but remains unrealized in the work's

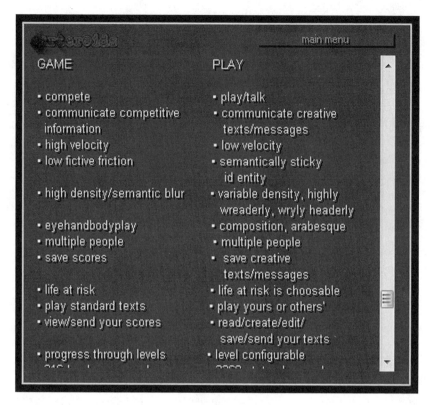

Figure 6.1
Jim Andrews, *Arteroids* (version 3.11, 2006): game mode versus play mode (screen capture). © Jim Andrews. Reproduced with permission.

latest version, 3.11) is the possibility of saving and e-mailing textual sequences generated by readers. Andrews has described this work as "a literary computer game for the web" (version 1.0, 2001) and "a literary shoot-em-up computer game—the battle of poetry against itself and the forces of dullness" (version 2.5, 2003).

In its third version, the poem is structured in two modes: the game mode and the play mode (figure 6.1). In game mode, the player/reader has no control over the four parameters (velocity, density, friction, and mortality) that define the behavior of his or her entity. In play mode, those four parameters, as well as the textual fragments that the player/reader has to shoot at, may be adjusted according to predefined controls. This distinction also comes from computer games: in play mode, players can configure the spatial architecture, characters, and so forth, customizing a number of display features of the graphical interface, while in game mode, they use predefined controls to interact with the programmed objects, trying to get to the end of each stage and move on to the next level. The number of permutations is also different in each mode: in game mode, the game-poem has 216 combinations (levels), while in play mode it has 3,360 levels ($12 \times 20 \times 14 = 3,360$). The role of the original shooting spaceship is played by the word *desire* in play mode (as well as by other words introduced by the player) and by the word *poetry* in game mode. Textual asteroids are organized into four sets of inner and outer lines of two different colors. In play mode, players can edit both textual asteroids and shooting word by overwriting the default elements (figure 6.2).

Andrews uses the instrumental semiotics of the computer game as a way of probing into the dynamics of language and signification in general: "*Arteroids* is about cracking language open" (2005). This description captures the dynamics of his work as both a self-reflexive engagement with the digital materiality and an exploration of the combinatorial properties

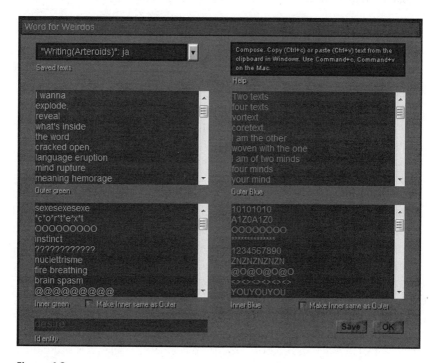

Figure 6.2

Jim Andrews, *Arteroids* (version 3.11, 2006): edit play mode (screen captures). © Jim Andrews. Reproduced with permission.

of verbal language. Digital code makes it possible for all sorts of objects to be treated as "material objects of information that have editable properties" (2005)—not just alphabetic writing but sound, image, motion, and any other spatial or temporal material component. The editability of digital entities is foregrounded in the lettristic explosions of words and phrases into visual constellations accompanied by sound explosions. The frequent modular articulation between sound units and visual units allows some of his textual instruments to be read also as visual music, as in the case of *Nio*. In Andrews's description of the sound layer in *Arteroids*, we have a good analog of how modularity works at the visual, sound, and linguistic levels:

> When the player executes a text, one of 21 sounds is selected. A random pitch-change is then made to the sound anywhere between ten semitones above the original pitch and 20 semitones below the original pitch. It is the pitch-change that gives Arteroids its sonic range into the animal and semi-human, the female, and the child, primarily. Pitch-change also provides greater variety with 21 petit death sounds, so that the sound is suitably rich in variety. (2005, online)

Language is decomposed into its graphemic and phonemic elements, down to its prearticulated visual and sound elements. As minimal constituent elements of a signifying process that translates their system of material differences into phonological, syntactic, and semantic layers, they also resemble the operations that translate electromagnetic pulses into machine code and machine code into human-readable and interpretable forms. Shootings and collisions point to the dynamics of creation and destruction of meaning as a function of semiosis, that is, the process of substituting signs for other signs and codes for other codes. While such dynamics is inherent in the way natural languages work, we are often unaware of such inner workings as the formal and material source for the possibility of meaning, and thus for the creation, definition, and redefinition of the human. Naturalization of pervasive discursive structures prevents us from being aware of the extraordinary fluidity and power of language as an infinitely renewable source for the generation and transformation of meaning. In its disarming simplicity, *Arteroids* offers a digital simulation of those deep furnaces of language.

"The battle of poetry against itself" is a suggestive image of our linguistic predicament as symbolic creatures who have to constantly struggle and fight with language in order to produce ourselves as social and individual subjects. By making words shoot at words on the computer monitor, Andrews has turned algorithmic features of computer games into literary and artistic tropes. Readers are made to perform retroactivity as part of the work's content and not just as a tool for achieving a set of goals or producing a series of effects. The tension between the immersive and the interactive is formally enacted at each level of the game by the tension between readability and the fragmentation of textual elements into their sound and graphic particles.

The player experiences the correlation between the inner motions of language in its formal workings and the outer motions of reading as yet another layer in the constitution of the textual field. Players can abandon themselves to the pleasures of the game and become aware of playfulness itself as the source for new forms and new perceptions. The text becomes a series of quantum states that respond to readers' interventions in its dynamic field. In Andrews's programmed poems, readers' interventions take place not just at the level of interpretation; they have been scripted as divergent possibilities in the code. Readers become coproducers of the text's semiotic texture whose particular formal and material instantiation is not entirely constituted before readers intervene. Meaning emerges as a function of the potentiality of semiotic structures in their response to actual haptic actions and eye movements by the reader/player. The ensemble of random fluctuations allows the emergence of new and unanticipated visual, sound, kinetic, and semantic patterns (figure 6.3).

6.3   Integrating Channels

According to Friedrich A. Kittler, the media ecology of the late nineteenth and early twentieth centuries disrupted any straightforward association between signifier and signified as function of the "inner self," the "soul," or the "individual." These "were only the effects of an illusion, neutralized through the hallucination of reading and widespread literacy" (1999, 151), which were maintained by the particular literary and educational practices of the nineteenth century. Kittler's hypothesis is that meaning as a "reading hallucination" depended on the particular performance required of print before the invention of optical and acoustic media: "As long as the book was responsible for all serial data flows, words quivered with sensuality and memory. It was the passion of all reading to hallucinate meaning between lines and letters: the visible and audible world of Romantic poetics" (10).

Kittler introduced the notion of reading as hallucination in *Discourse Networks 1800/1900* (1990) and later took it up in *Gramophone, Film, Typewriter* (1999) and *Optical Media* (2010). This notion is crucial in

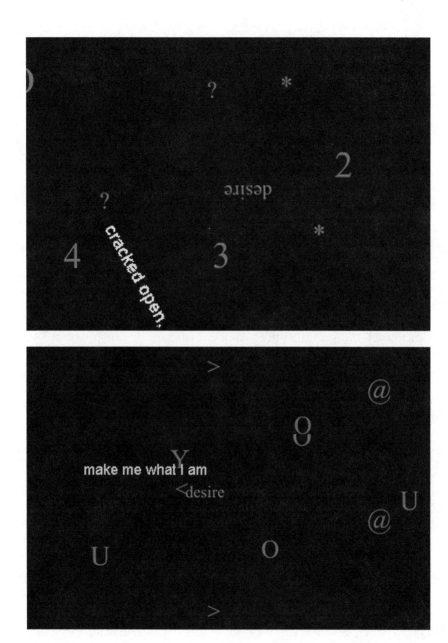

Figure 6.3
Jim Andrews, *Arteroids* (version 3.11, 2006): play mode (screen captures). © Jim Andrews. Reproduced with permission.

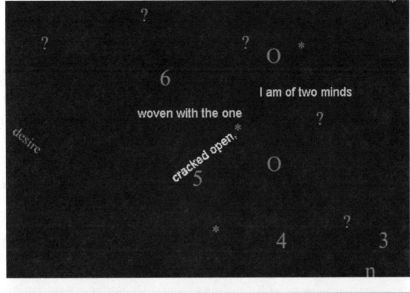

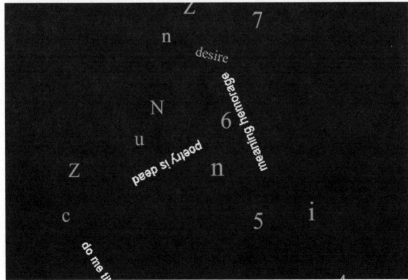

Figure 6.3
(continued)

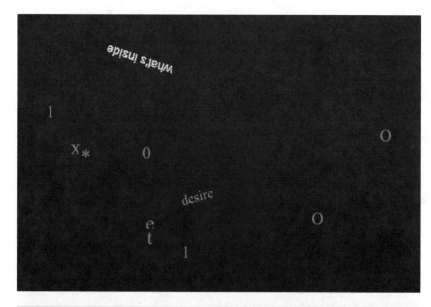

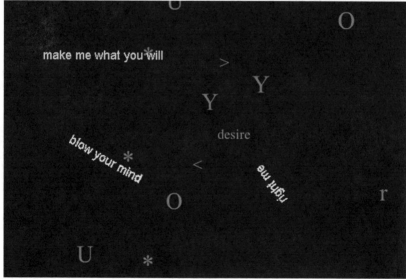

Figure 6.3
(continued)

Kittler's argument about the invention of photography and cinema as the expression of an optical desire that can be traced back to the camera obscura and the lanterna magica. The alphabet loses its hallucinatory power when technological media begin to take on the sound and visual channels of data and the typewriter keyboard replaces handwriting. The typewriter is the machine that fulfills this reembodiment of letters, which become mere material forms without a soul. The standardized letters of the typewriter severed the connection between paper and body, and typewriting became part of the technologizing of language and information. Once typewriters standardize and substitute handwriting and optical and acoustic media take over the audiovisual techniques that had become embodied in literary realism, sound and image are severed from the technology of reading. Cinema, phonography, and typewriting separated optical, acoustic, and written data flows.

Kittler's theory of optical and acoustic media is also based on the assumption that romantic literature and nineteenth-century reading practices strengthened the visuality and aurality of letter-based descriptions of the world. Romantic literary protocols prefigured the appearance of the new, automated techniques for recording visual and acoustic impressions. Audiovisual media are seen as historical descendants of the hallucinatory predisposition of nineteenth-century literacy techniques. But optic and acoustic media, being automatically inscribed, could capture the real beyond the symbolic grid imposed by the abstractness of language and writing: "From the beginning, the letters and their arrangement were standardized in the shapes of type and keyboard, while media were engulfed by the noise of the real—the fuzziness of cinematic pictures, the hissing of tape recordings" (Kittler 1999, 14). Phonography and film substituted the direct inscription of the real for the evocative effect (and affect) of writing and reading techniques.

Thus, in the context of nineteenth-century new media, writing becomes a separate channel, unable to contain either the full presence of the self or the full presence of the sounds and images of the world. Although writing remains entirely dependent on the symbolic for its ability to represent the world, the material experience of the combinatorial nature of language as embodied in the typewriter changes the relation between writing and self. Self becomes a function of the combinatorial processing of signs rather than the source and origin for the production of writing. Beginning in the late fifteenth century, typographical standardization of letter forms had contributed to increased legibility. This optimization of the channel, achieved through the patterning of character differences, had the long-term effect of favoring the semantic transparency of meaning over the semiotic visibility of the letter. The introduction of typewriters in the last quarter of the nineteenth century gave writers a mechanical experience of recursivity and permutation as linguistic properties, with significant consequences for modernist literary techniques.

In twentieth-century experimental literary practices, a new poetics of reading emerges. This is a poetics of reading that emulates the formal and psychological processing of letter shapes as a sequence of motions that associate letters in time and space. New writing and printing techniques and the conspicuous presence of visuality in the modern urban world of print and public lettering contributed to these changes. When the line as a basic unit of typographical composition is turned into a constellation of letters and words, the act of reading is foregrounded as material and physical processing of signs. Many visual typographical experiments in twentieth-century literature can be described as explorations of the dynamics of reading as a function of systematic differences created by traces, spaces, and reading motions. Concrete poetry, for example, is based on a thorough investigation of the minutiae of reading processes as both recognition of graphical forms and association of formal differences constrained by inscriptional spaces. Experimental practices developed intermedia forms of writing that associate audiovisual and writing media, thus exploring the integration of technoscientific media with the symbolic order of natural language.

Digital media, with their numerical and modular properties, created new conditions for the reintegration of optical, acoustic, and written data flows, thus challenging analog channel separation. The recombination of optical, acoustic, and written elements as modular collections of digital objects originates hybrid forms in which it is possible to recognize the simultaneous presence of cinematic techniques and literary techniques. New kinds of relations between letter-based forms and image-and-sound-based forms are emerging in our current technological context. As cinematic forms, digital kinetic works exhibit features that are similar to the abstract animation of the first decades of the twentieth century, as explored, for instance, in the visual music of experimental animators Oskar Fischinger, Mary Ellen Bute, Norman McLaren, and others. As literary forms, they update processes of visual and permutational literature of the second half of the twentieth century, particularly the 1960s and 1970s.

Andrews's spiraling and exploding constellations of letters externalize the symbolic grid of writing as a recursive stream of signs ready for human and machine processing. Their motion highlights the differential productivity of linguistic and written signs, while the dynamic functions of the interface involve human readers in the stochastic disorder of meaning production. But his written signs are also combined with digital processing of sound and image in ways that call attention to the integration of media forms and channels. The particular combination of optical, acoustic, and written media that we find in his works is an instance of the work of art as database in the age of digital reproduction.

The cinematic and sound layers associated with typographic and other graphical forms in digital intermedia forms imply an increasingly abstract perception of optical and acoustic data. Audiovisual modes of optic and acoustic presence and inscription of the real are transformed by the algorithmic modes of simulating and modeling the world. Mathematical modeling of inscriptional forms establishes new kinds of relations between capture and manipulation. Interface tools allow forms of manipulation that contribute to the textualization of media as particular modes of writing. The ongoing convergence fostered by digital media has produced a new mode of integrating writing with acoustic and optical channels that challenges the twentieth-century separation between audiovisual media and literature.

Nio stages the separation and integration of data channels through a multimedia database that synchronizes between sixteen sound loops and sixteen animation loops (figure 6.4).[4] Andrews has programmed this work so that for each sound phrase, there is a specific typographical animation, and vice versa. Sound and video loops can be sequenced at random, and up to six loops can run simultaneously. Because the order of synchronized sound-visual fragments as well as their combination is randomly determined, the result can be described as a stochastic work of visual music or as a cinematic notation for sound poetry.[5] The reader/player explores the combinatoric possibilities created by the algorithm's processing of the database of audiovisual digital objects, turning this work into a textual, sound, and video instrument. This stochastic feature is common to other of Andrews's letter-based works, in which letters are displayed as random constellations in response to readers' interactions. Trajectories and positions on the surface of the screen shift in response to specific actions. These actions in turn become part of the textual meaning of the work: a reader enacts the meaning of the text each time she or he gives an instruction that changes the behavior of the letters. In this case, visual and sound display is codependent on the reader's interventions:

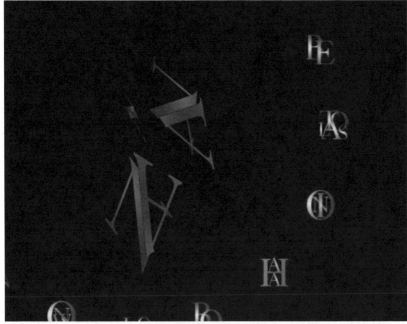

Figure 6.4
Jim Andrews, *Nio* (2001) (screen captures). © Jim Andrews. Reproduced with permission.

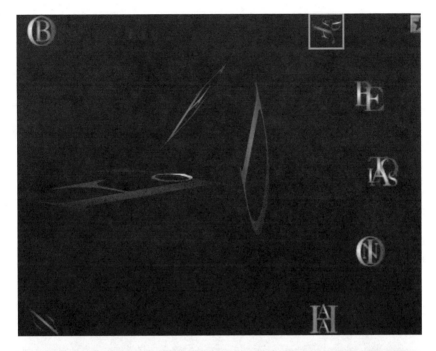

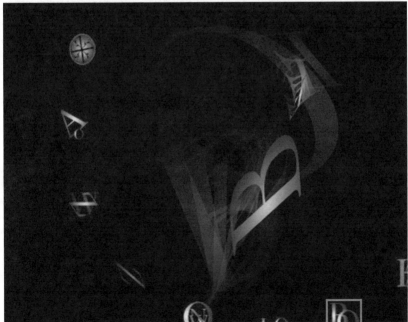

Figure 6.4
(continued)

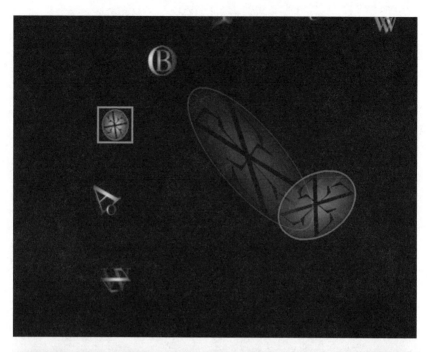

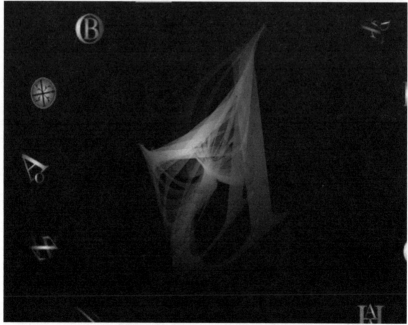

Figure 6.4
(continued)

The underlying program, which I wrote in Lingo, is a player, like the Real Player is a player, of synchronized, interactive layers and sequences of audio and animations for the Web. You interactively construct these layers and sequences of sound/animation. It synchronizes multiple layers of rhythmic sound and provides uninterrupted audio between sequenced sound files, and synchronizes the animations with the sound. (Andrews 2001a)

Jim Andrews's digital poems are based on kinetic and generative behaviors, and their algorithms manipulate their digital objects in terms of a multimedia syntax that relates cinematic, sound, and verbal layers. By integrating the processing of abstract (alphabetic letters) and concrete forms (icons, pictures, and sounds), his works challenge analog discontinuity between text, image, and sound, which are merged or recombined through the discreteness and modularity of digital materiality. Separation and integration of data streams (sound, visual, kinetic, and verbal) may be said to be at the core of his experiments, some of which originated in the tradition of intermedia works prior to the digital age.

6.4 Permutating Cut-Ups

In the series *Styr/Fry/Texts* (1999–2009), Andrews has programmed a cut-up technique to generate remixes of two or more source texts. Source texts have been fragmented into tight units or phrases that are interchangeable at given positions within the sentences. The cut-up texts are programmed to perform timed sequences of substitutions of their component units. Readers can stop this mouse-over motion of substitution at random, thus generating a particular occurrence of their permutational possibilities. The speed of automated permutations is usually too fast for readers to exercise complete control over the readable outcomes. However, Andrews stresses that he intended to produce meaningful associations, and not a mere realization of the algorithm's potential. Machinic behavior becomes a way of breaking up semantic coherence by forcing syntactic structures to generate new associations:

In fact the stir frys can be thought of as a certain sort of hyperlink structure or mapping from one text to another. Each individual text can be considered as a set of elements and the stir frys establish a one-to-one mapping between the elements of the various texts. But rather than the usual situation, where linking replaces the entire screen, mousing over stir fry text replaces only a part of the text and the body of the new text moves as an entity to adjust itself to the change, providing the pleasant illusion that it has some sort of unified character or personality even in its transformations. (Andrews 1999b)

"Log," by Jim Andrews and Brian Lennon (2000), is one of the spasmodic texts included under the general title *Stir/Fry/Texts* (figure 6.5). It begins with five entries, each containing five sentences. After each sentence, we have a digital record of five consecutive minutes, between 4:51:00 and 4:55:00. The twenty-five initial sentences contain the pronoun *I*. Once the reader moves the cursor over any of the segments of the initial text, they begin to change very quickly. The initial sentences appear in white, and the new ones appear in gray. This motion of substitution can render the words and sentences unreadable while in motion. This fast-forward and looping replacement of letters and words, and the resulting random permutations when the motion is stopped, define this work's reading experience:

04:51:00 - I split the full scale mark—I choked and drooled—I was memory bound—I muted analysis—I thought I'd start—
04:52:00 - I'd been aware—I'm dead I'm dead—I'm standing up—I'm what you want—I programmed it—
04:53:00 - I hit disconnect—I am not I—I caught your head—I changed my life—I was amazed—
04:54:00 - I had been feeling like a frond—I loved I died—I said I said—I went to a street—I waited—
04:55:00 - I was pressed down upon—I held it back—I went outside—I knew what it was—I altered— (Andrews and Lennon 2000)

Log refers to random processes in automatic and networked electronic text communication, which seem to work like cut-up poetry. Mutations caused by pointing to the text suggest, possibly, a dialogue with the registration of replies, hypertextual movement from link to link or even automatic spam messages—processes where the distinction between human-written and machine-generated text breaks down. After moving the cursor over the text several times, we become aware that each textual segment alternates with three other segments, programmed to permutate at that particular intersection. Spaces between the five initial entries are subsequently reconfigured until we get only one block of text without the times:

vox coriolis - it does not want to know - roaming whispered - set down that anguish - reversing tone - it was the end of all - it was the light - it was all night - speeding apart - what am I then - it rose - remotely sensing - electric vex - clocks chemistry - belonging beginning on that day - lips harboring seepage - nothing began - bright chills and chokes - parsed element 01 - it was my life - it turned - lovelens - ocean and avalanche - explain and cure - small exclamations - to blink, shortshort - to stall itself - strenuous read - return - at night - (Andrews and Lennon 2000)

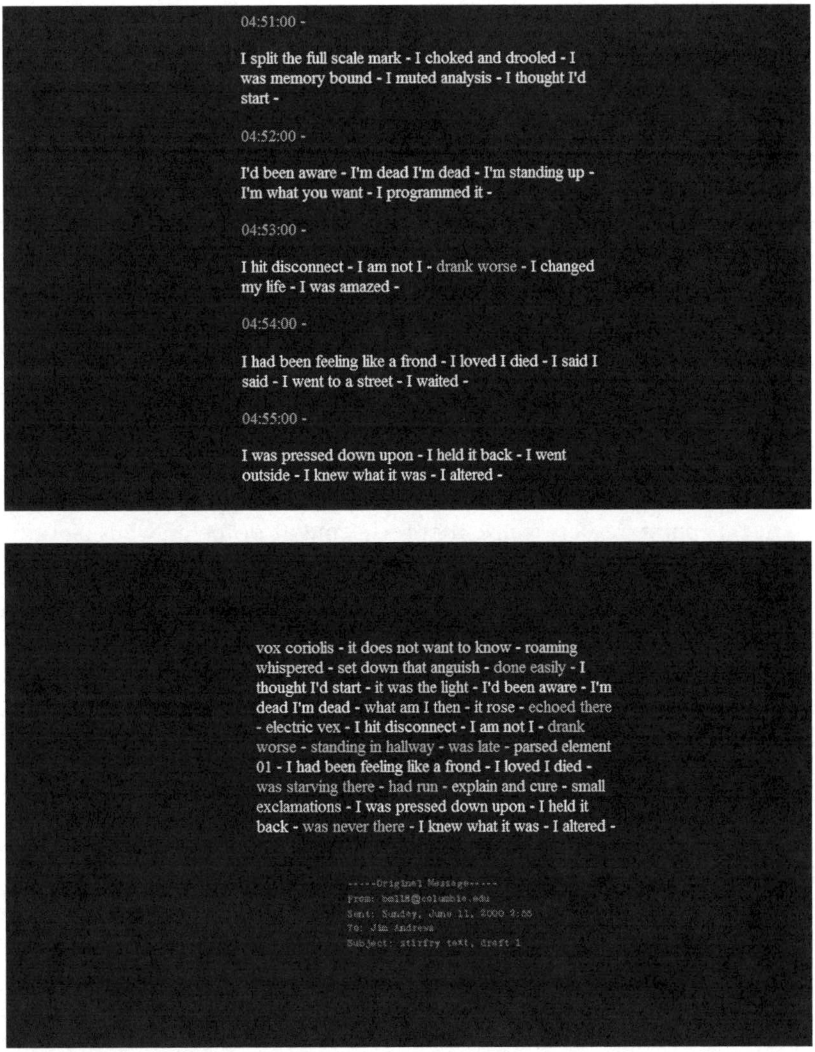

Figure 6.5
Jim Andrews and Brian Lennon, "Log" (2000), in *Stir/Fry/Texts* (screen captures).
© Jim Andrews. Reproduced with permission.

This frame of text contains thirty segments, exactly the same number of the first set if we add the five numerical entries. However, with a new click on the heading of the original e-mail that forms the bottom of "Log," a new sequence of five entries and twenty-five phrases appears, this time counting the time between 4:24:00 and 4:28:00. Again we have 25 + 5 sentence fragments:

04:24:00 - was intermittent—made contact—valued heights—done easily—milled out—
04:25:00 - loomed origin—breathed out—breathed in—had dreamed—echoed there—
04:26:00 - guessed again—drank suddenly—drank worse—standing in hallway—was late—
04:27:00 - protecting bones—made contact there—was starving there—had run—knew it was me—
04:28:00 - gave my name—had myself cut—was never there—was long ago—was ever— (Andrews and Lennon 2000)

At this point, readers realize that the elements of the previous block of text (the second sequence), and the elements of the new five entries of five sentence fragments each (the third sequence), both in gray, were those that permutated with the twenty-five sentences in white of the first sequence. Any motion of the cursor over the text recombines elements from these textual layers, producing a continuous textual mutation. Once the mouse stops, the text also stops, and the reader is faced with one instance of the collage resulting from using the mouse to stir and fry the text:

vox coriolis—it does not want to know—roaming whispered—valued heights—I muted analysis—it was the end of all—
04:25:00 - it was all night—speeding apart—I'm standing up—it rose—echoed there—
04:26:00 - clocks chemistry—drank suddenly—I caught your head—nothing began—was late—
04:27:00 - it was my life—it turned—was starving there—had run—explain and cure—
04:28:00 - to blink, shortshort—to stall itself—strenuous read—return—I altered—
(Andrews and Lennon 2000)

Randomness in the way these words, phrases, and sentence parts combine suggests an interweaving of voices in which textual fragments with the pronoun *I* are combined or replaced with more impersonal and abstract fragments. They suggest both machine-generated text and human-written text. The result is a fragmented narrative and the suggestion that machine-generated language has become part of the process of electronic composition. Parsing comes through as a property of both human and computer languages. The logging to which the text refers suggests a connection between the programmable machine as a generator of language and language itself as combinatorial machine. Both are involved in producing the self-as-constituted-by-language. The randomness of patterns reveals the stochastic nature of meaning and the open-ended nature of associations that allows the emergence of meaning from seemingly random collages. "Log" also simulates the flow of the signifiers in current digital synchronous and asynchronous communication: logging into the machine is also logging into the turbulent associations of language's generative and recursive mechanisms.

The series *Stir /Fry/Texts* contains a model of the patterning of language use as a set of self-generating discourses. Semantic coherence is obtained through repetition and variation of sentences and phrases that are automatically inserted into preformed syntactic structures. The fixity of text is raised to a heightened field dynamics by a form of writing that is temporal and temporary, whose traces change and reconfigure themselves as time passes. The intersection of different time sequences, which mixes and resequences the passage of time, suggests the intersection between structured forms and the representation of time. This reflection on the processing of natural language by machines has been the object of a more recent "stir fry text," *Kedrick James* (2009), in which Jim Andrews uses as his source text a doctoral dissertation that analyzes automated uses of e-mail and other forms of electronic written communication (figure 6.6).

In this case, the source text for Andrews's automated cut-ups is Kedrick James's poetics of spam and automated writing, from which he took four

Figure 6.6
Jim Andrews and Kedrick James, "Kedrick James" (2009), in *Stir/Fry/Texts* (screen capture). © Jim Andrews. Reproduced with permission.

samples of writing. These samples were cut up in ways that allow the random substitution of phrases and sentences within the textual matrix. The intersections between the sampled texts are programmed to exist in multiple states of superposition, mutual interruption, and cross-breeding. Since all samples talk about the disposable proliferation of discourse and the exposure to automated language artifacts, the resulting textual mash-up can be read as a series of self-describing sentences that comment on a process of which their own mode of production and display is a writing-and-reading instance.[6] Self-reflection on computer-mediated communication thus becomes an explicit element in both the algorithmic form and the discursive content of this work as a mirror image of automated discursive environments.

6.5   Programming Interactions

As we have seen, Jim Andrews has modeled the behavior of digital objects so that interfaces become a structural element in the semantics of the work. Readers/players are not only accessing the works' database through an algorithm that produces a given output. Mouse-over and mouse-clicking events are turned into an integral part of the textual field because they are experienced as constitutive of the field itself. Players/readers become aware of the contingent nature of a particular outcome, and hence of the singularity of a time-bound interaction that is both temporary and situated in time. The time of the machine executing the code meets the time of the player/reader activating the signifiers generated by the code.

This motion of signifiers, as a programmed and yet partially unanticipated kinetic interaction, becomes a way of visualizing the entanglement between linguistic signifiers and their digital code as expressed in material events on the screen. Writing and reading as codependent semiotic and cognitive operations have been scripted into the code in the form of loops and iterations that are responsive to actions that call attention to themselves. The self-referential linguistic and digital layer of the work is thus enacted through a scripted behavior that materializes an important part of the work's meaning in the relation between algorithmic processing and human haptic and visual processing of programmed signifiers. Andrews (1999a) has described this dynamic programming of Web writing as a particularly desirable human attribute in computer-mediated interactions:

The basic idea of DHTML (dynamic HTML) is to enable the writer to animate or change every part of the document from the background color to the text and font size and text and links to any other part of the document. Protean and responsive

[in] real time, interactive not just between the user and the text but most humanly interactive between people [in] real time and in the time of art and imagination. After all, part of the challenge and excitement of Web art is to locate/create the human dimensions of the technology. (Andrews 1999a)

Andrews's works may be said to simulate the making of meaning through an aesthetic engagement with the various dimensions of the digital writing and reading space. His works are perhaps better described as toys for probing the autopoietic features of textual fields through the use of the procedural and participatory affordances of the digital medium. They contain a simulation and a model for the play *of* signifiers and for the play *with* signifiers, digital and otherwise. They also explore the expressive virtualities of e-space and programmed forms for new textual experiments and for transcoding earlier sound and visual poetics.

In *On Lionel Kearns* (2004a), Andrews has produced a digital rewriting and transcoding of several texts by Kearns, including his remarkable minimalist concrete text "Birth of God/uniVerse" (1965), which was later turned into an animation film (1973). In the introduction to the work, Andrews describes *On Lionel Kearns* as a "binary meditation on the work of a pioneering Canadian poet contemplating digital poetics from the early sixties to the present" (Andrews 2004a). *On Lionel Kearns* uses a fractal attractor (the Sierpinkski gasket) to compose a complex intertextual meditation on Kearns's work and on his own interactive kinetic poetry. The fragments Andrews chose compose a meditation on poetry, life, language, identity, and death. Here are some of Kearns's writings that are fractalized on the screen:

They measure the distances and make their maps. The more detail they include, the longer the coastline grows. It is like writing a poem, or examining your life. Recollect each experience in infinite detail, and it will unfold endlessly. (Kearns, quoted in Andrews 2004a)

A person consents to a universe commissioned by his community, consigned by his culture, defined by his language. Take away the ability to make the word permanent, use a language that has never been constrained and confined by a thousand years of literacy, and you will have a strange and different instrument for dealing with life. You will have a different world. (Kearns, quoted in Andrews 2004a)

In theory, this old fellow is the same individual as the boy in the tub. How could that be, when every molecule of every cell in his body has been replaced several times during the last sixty-seven years? Is there any resemblance here? Not much, although he considers himself to be the same person: Lionel Kearns, a bit heavier and a lot worse for wear, but still breathing and thinking and talking. It is a matter of identity. DNA analyses will reveal a continuity of residual pattern and design, at least for now. But what will become of all this in a year? Ten years? One hundred years? Dust to dust, ashes to ashes. Entropy. Structural break down. Entropy. (Kearns, quoted in Andrews 2004a)

To consider one's life in the light of one's own impending death, that is a human experience, as opposed to the self awareness of a dog or a rat or a bacterium. The extended self-image in the context of time, that is what makes us human. But I cannot decide if it is an advantage or a disadvantage. (Kearns, quoted in Andrews 2004a)

And what has this to do with poetry and eating and crying in the silence of our lonely night and making love and dying much against our wills? If these words of mine become words in your head and so connect our lives for a moment, this will be meaning. Correspondence is what we seek, shreds of similarity, understanding, compassion. (Kearns, quoted in Andrews 2004a)

You are free to browse these pages, but I cannot answer your questions because I am too busy answering my own questions and posing new unanswerable questions. At this moment I know only that I am here and that others have been here before and have left something for me, as I leave something for you. Time is a ritual exchange, though the gifts move in a single direction. (Kearns, quoted in Andrews 2004a)

Andrews is anchoring his digital poetics in the exploratory poetics of Kearns and responding as reader and writer. The text becomes a site for the production of new meaning and for connecting his words and life with those of his predecessor. Subject to recursive fractal fragmentation, each sequence of text and images evolves from recognizable forms into black and white abstract patterns recursively nested in ever smaller geometric structures. Because dragging the mouse increases the rate of timed transformations happening on the screen, there is a continuing tension between legibility and dissolution of alphabetic letters and photographic images into fractal patterns (figure 6.7). Moused-over fractals work as a simulation of entropy and death at the level of signifiers. The act of mousing over the text or image increases its illegibility, thus destroying any possibility of arriving at a preconstituted disposable and stable text or image. Readers are physically reminded that they have to travel this space of signs at their own risk, as they realize that signs are responding dynamically to the ongoing interactions. The universal principle of nested binary differentiation and infinite regression, inherent in the zeros made of ones and in the ones made of zeros, suggests that recursivity and self-similarity sustain an infinite differential process at all levels of the code. Linguistic code, binary code, and DNA code are interactively and metaphorically scripted to give readers a perceptual experience of the threshold between meaning and entropy.

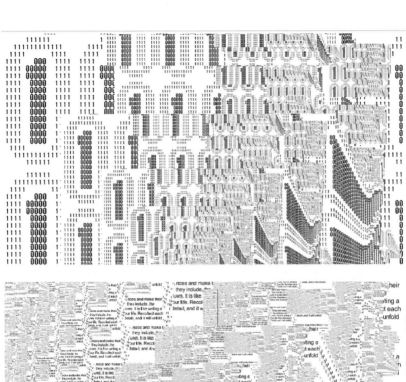

You can get a lot of information from this picture if you examine it closely. Notice the well-boiled baby boy. His name is Tenny, although he will eventually be known as Lionel Kearns. You will have to wait for a later screen to get the stories behind these names. Back to the photo. It was taken by Frank, also known as Charles Francis, CFK, or C.F. Kearns, and sometimes, in print, as Charley Brennan. He is the baby boy's father. If you look carefully at the photograph tacked on the wall above the tub, you will just make out the image of CFK leading a pack train of horses across a swollen river in the Rocky Mountains. That was the kind of thing he did. The mother is present here as well, although she offers support without intruding directly into the picture. Her strong and steady arm enters stage left. She is Dot, or Dorry, or Dorothy Welch, or Dorothy Kearns after she married CFK. The tub has a chipped pale green enamel exterior, and sits on stand in the kitchen of a house on the corner of Second and Anderson Streets, in Nelson, British Columbia, Canada. There is some evidence that this photograph was taken Feb.16, 1938, on the boy's first birthday.

You can get a lot of information from this picture if you examine it closely. Notice the well-boiled baby boy. His name is Tenny, although he will eventually be known as Lionel Kearns. You will have to wait for a later screen to get the stories behind these

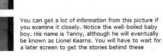

Figure 6.7

Jim Andrews, *On Lionel Kearns* (2004): fractal poetics (screen captures). © Jim Andrews. Reproduced with permission.

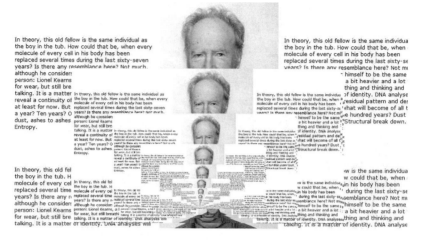

In theory, this old fellow is the same individual as the boy in the tub. How could that be, when every molecule of every cell in his body has been replaced several times during the last sixty-seven years? Is there any resemblance here? Not much. although he considers person: Lionel Kearns for wear, but still bre talking. It is a matter reveal a continuity of at least for now. But a year? Ten years? O dust, ashes to ashes Entropy.

In theory, this old fellow is the same individua the boy in the tub. How could that be, when molecule of every cell in his body has been replaced several times during the last sixty-se years? Is there any resemblance here? Not m himself to be the same a bit heavier and a lot thing and thinking and of identity. DNA analyse residual pattern and des what will become of all t e hundred years? Dust Structural break down.

In theory, this old fel the boy in the tub. H molecule of every cel replaced several time years? Is there any r although he consider person: Lionel Kearns for wear, but still bre talking. It is a matter of identity. DNA analyses will

w is the same individua w could that be, when in his body has been during the last sixty-se resemblance here? Not mi himself to be the same a bit heavier and a lot thing and thinking and talking. It is a matter of identity. DNA analyse

To consider one's life in the light of one's own impending death, that is a human experience, as opposed to the self awareness of a dog or a rat or a bacterium. The extended self-image in the context of time, that is what makes us human. But I cannot decide if it is an advantage or a disadvantage.

To consider one's life in the light of one's own impending death, that is a human experience, as opposed to the self awareness of a dog or a rat or a bacterium. The extended self-image in the context of time, that is what makes us human. But I cannot decide if it is an advantage or a disadvantage.

To consider one's life in the light of one's own impending death, that is a human experience, as opposed to the self awareness of a dog or a rat or a bacterium. The extended self-image in the context of time, that is what makes us human. But I cannot decide if it is an advantage or a disadvantage.

To consider one's life in the light of one's own impending death, that is a human experience, as opposed to the self awareness of a dog or a rat or a bacterium. The extended self-image in the context of time, that is what makes us human. But I cannot decide if it is an advantage or a disadvantage.

To consider one's life in the light of one's own impending death, that is a human experience, as opposed to the self awareness of a dog or a rat or a bacterium. The extended self-image in the context of time, that is what makes us human. But I cannot decide if it is an advantage or a disadvantage.

To consider one's life in the light of one's own impending death, that is a human experience, as opposed to the

Figure 6.7
(continued)

Andrews also includes in this work two poems published by Kearns in 1969: "Kinetic Poem" and "Participatory Poem." Both texts are appropriated for the programmatic statements they contain about a future poetics of the machine. Kearns is describing the machinic and cybernetic nature of the poem as a self-reflexive informational device, and he is also imagining the use of machines for making poems. Andrews has translated kineticism and participation into specific scripts that self-consciously display the virtualities of contemporary dynamic programming languages and the capabilities of the networked computer. "Kineticism" is materially enacted by applying a fractal attractor to the original poem in a way that turns its letters into the ones and zeros of binary code, exploding the legibility of alphanumeric signs into the multisensorial visuality and three-dimensionality of the computer screen. Participation, in turn, is scripted as field in a form that can be filled in and recorded by each user, a way of pursuing the original exhortation for readers to complete the poem (figure 6.8). In both instances, Andrews is giving us a digital poetics that stresses its specific modes of authorial programming, data processing, and reader interaction.

Participatory Poem

It has begun. Already the poets are working their cybernetic
    voodoo
Soon the thousand-foot television screens that have been set
    up in front of every house
Will light up automatically and display lifesize images of
    themselves
And God will be manifest as an enormous eye looking
    everywhere and in both directions
That is, from the inside out, and from the outside in,
    simultaneously
It is difficult to speculate as to the developments after this
    stage
But some of the more imaginative among us believe that

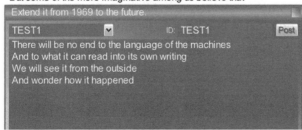

Figure 6.8
Jim Andrews, *On Lionel Kearns* (2004): "The reader is asked to complete the poem" (screen capture). © Jim Andrews. Reproduced with permission.

Kineticism and participation are already linked in Kearns's poetics as images of the possibilities inherent in poetry as a machine for interrogating language, self, and the world and for exploring the stochastic and combinatorial nature of meaning. Meaning emerges as the dynamic interaction between the verbal, sound, visual, and graphic materialities of writing, and the individual, subjective, historical, and imaginative interactions with those materialities. In Andrews's own work, kineticism and participation have been turned into digital instruments not just for adding his own personal questions to the world of meaning, but also for modeling the poem as a textual field that makes such interrogation possible through its endless signifying motions. Andrews's metareflexive digital poems script the motions of reading in the algorithms of the code in an attempt at making them perceptible in the visual and haptic surface interactions within an ensemble of coded objects. The hallucination of reading in his work comes not from the power of words to conjure up images and sounds as if they were perceptions of the real world, but from a kind of vertigo induced by making readers experience the pure potentiality of signifiers in their formal instantiation as products of writing, reading, and coding motions. Letters are hallucinogenic in displaying themselves as both products and producers of codes that become available for human perception and affect.

6.6 Visualizing Meanings

Enigma n is a magnificent simulation of the autopoietic features of the textual field and of the probabilistic nature of meaning. Instability of meaning arising from textual instability of signifiers is the specific theme of *Enigma n*. In this poem, readers can perform eight different iterations on seven letters ("Prod," "Stir," "Tame," "Spell," "0/1," "Colour," "Discombobulate," and "Speed"). The seven letters (which are the same in the poem title) move according to different trajectories and they can be stopped at any time, forming multiple and unpredictable patterns. When stopped, they form either the word *meaning*, in various configurations, or just a random constellation of its letters. The order of interactions is variable, changing both the sequence of kinetic events and the sequence of display screens resulting from readers' interventions. Variations affect a number of textual properties, including speed, trajectory, size, color, and position. In turn, the sequence of each of those changes can be recombined in multiple ways, raising the number of textual events and patterns (figure 6.9).

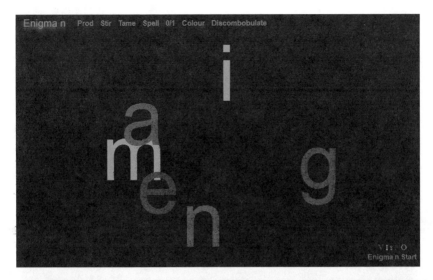

Figure 6.9
Jim Andrews, *Enigma n* (1998): "prod" + "color" + "discombobulate" + "spell" +
"0/1." (screen captures). © Jim Andrews. Reproduced with permission.

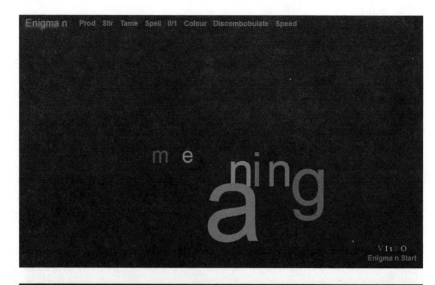

Figure 6.9
(continued)

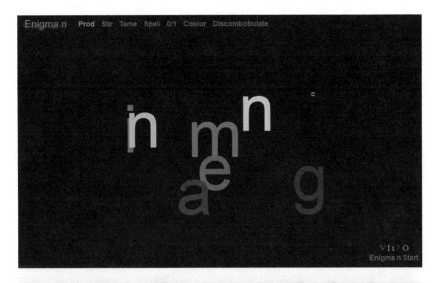

Figure 6.9
(continued)

To the extent that this text is also textual engine (i.e., an algorithm for generating semidetermined and random textual constellations), it can be described as cybertext and ergodic text, technotext, procedural work, and textual instrument. The outcome partly depends on a nontrivial extra-noematic textual intervention by readers that "focuses on the mechanical organization of text" (Aarseth 1997, 1). It works as a writing machine that reflects on its embodied form and "connects the technology that produces texts to the texts' verbal constructions" (Hayles 2002, 26). It contains a metapoetic procedural exploration of "the splitting of reading" (Bootz 2010, 22), and it is also a text "meant to be played" (Wardrip-Fruin 2009, 365–366). *Enigma n* engages several dimensions of programmed textuality, offering rich analytical possibilities to any of those four models for digital literature.

This type of textual device explicitly inscribes the hermeneutical function of sign interpretation in the work's semiotic dimension of sign manipulation. In effect, the act of reading as an active meaning-production process is the very process of engaging in the textual game as much as it is any particular textual state and interpretative conjecture produced by that game. What does it mean to play and read a work like this? It means that the reader, interacting with a programmed and temporized field of textual possibilities, generates part of the textual forms that he or she sees and reads. Interactive animation has been scripted in ways that inscribe the motion of reading back into the textual field. This repurposing of game scripts for literary play through the creation of ergodic textual instruments is at the core of cybertext poetics (Eskelinen 2012).

The reader actualizes a certain number of potential configurations and experiences in his or her own body the feedbacks between seeing and reading. The play of signifiers in the process of differentiation and association takes place at the material and interpretational levels, suggesting the correlative materiality of graphical and semantic form. In programmed animated texts, the display of writing is dependent on the lines of code that determine movement and textual changes. But without a specific interactive script, the motion of letters would enfold as a continuous movie, not as a responsive constellation open to player feedback. Textual motion in interactive dynamic works adds a perceptual visual or audiovisual awareness of material form that shows the operations of reading as semiotic recoding rather than just hermeneutical decoding. Meaning has to be produced by the act of performing the code, and this very performance becomes a referent of the work.

Enigma n is not fully produced without the reader's intervention in its field of signifiers. The text asks readers to produce certain instances of itself. Using the text's commands, readers generate a number of unique textual occurrences. Although these are ultimately performed by the underlying code, readers' interventions randomly select a variety of textual constellations. It is these constellations that constitute their textual event, a specific enactment of many potential formal instantiations. The code is generating the text for the reader, but at the same time, the reader is asked to generate certain textual occurrences by intervening in the stop-and-start motion procedure. The textual forms of *Enigma n* remain partially undetermined before readers' interventions. Once an intervention has occurred, textual properties reveal their dynamical codependence on that particular intervention.

The source code is the metatext that generates the display text, which is further subject to readers' textual interventions to realize the potential textual semiotic coding contained in its metatextual possibilities. Reading is scripted in the code as a set of instructions for displaying text in a way that makes readers aware of the dynamic nature of reading in its foregrounding, associating, recombining, and redisplaying of textual elements. Textual instantiations respond to mouse-over and mouse-clicking events by opening up the deterministic space of reactive feedback to the dialogical space of interactive feedback. Philippe Bootz has described this mode of reading in programmed digital poetry as cognitive reading, in which the reader assumes a position of metareader (see chapter 4). Readers see themselves reading as they experience both the textual mechanism and the effects of their intervention. Andrews uses the semiotic gap between texte-auteur (author-text) and texte-à-voir (text-to-be-seen) created by the machine processing of signs as a way of probing the formal and semantic productivity of language. Andrews's animated dynamic ideogram wants readers to perform the enigma of meaning.

An excerpt from the code with the author's comments reveals how the dynamic properties have been scripted (figure 6.10). Transformations in the material properties of the letters, in response to mouse-over and mouse-clicking interactions, are meant to create visual and haptic correlatives of the turbulence of meaning. It is as if changes in size, color, motion, distance, and relative position of letters to each other offered a visualization of the force fields of meaning. The particular shape of these force fields is experienced as a result of readers' interferences on linguistic and programming codes, thereby generating unique semiotic and interpretative events. Orbits of the seven letters suggest other lexical possibilities for their association, such as "image" and "game," at once a self-description of the visual process of this programmed work and a general model for the emergence of meaning out of graphonological permutations. Simulation of the

```
    function Follow(Mouse) {
            Mouse = window.event;
            MouseX= parseInt(Mouse.clientX);
            MouseY= parseInt(Mouse.clientY);
            if (jtimer < 200) {
                    e.style.cx= Math.round(0.9*e.style.cx+0.1*MousieX);
                    m.style.cx= Math.round(0.917*m.style.cx+0.083*MousieX);
                    aa.style.cx= Math.round(0.929*aa.style.cx+0.071*MousieX);
                    n.style.cx= Math.round(0.938*n.style.cx+0.063*MousieX);
                    ii.style.cy= Math.round(0.9*ii.style.cy+0.1*MousieY);
                    n2.style.cy= Math.round(0.917*n2.style.cy+0.083*MousieY);
                    g.style.cy= Math.round(0.929*g.style.cy+0.071*MousieY);
            } else if (jtimer < 400) {
                    e.style.cx= Math.round(0.9*e.style.cx+0.1*MousieX);
                    g.style.cx= Math.round(0.917*g.style.cx+0.083*MousieX);
                    aa.style.cx= Math.round(0.929*aa.style.cx+0.071*MousieX);
                    m.style.cx= Math.round(0.938*m.style.cx+0.063*MousieX);
                    ii.style.cx= Math.round(0.948*ii.style.cx+0.055*MousieX);
                    n2.style.cy= Math.round(0.9*n2.style.cy+0.1*MousieY);
                    n.style.cy= Math.round(0.929*n.style.cy+0.071*MousieY);
            } else {
                    e.style.cy= Math.round(0.9*e.style.cy+0.1*MousieY);
                    m.style.cy= Math.round(0.917*m.style.cy+0.083*MousieY);
                    aa.style.cy= Math.round(0.929*aa.style.cy+0.071*MousieY);
                    g.style.cy= Math.round(0.938*g.style.cy+0.063*MousieY);
                    n2.style.cx= Math.round(0.9*n2.style.cx+0.1*MousieX);
                    ii.style.cx= Math.round(0.917*ii.style.cx+0.083*MousieX);
                    n.style.cx= Math.round(0.929*n.style.cx+0.071*MousieX); }
            jtimer = (jtimer +1) % 601;} */
    function Homemouseover() {window.status="Enigma n home.";}
    function Prodmouseover() {window.status="Meaning prod. Prod meaning.";}
    function Stirmouseover() {window.status="Stir meaning. Meaning stir.";}
    function Tamemouseover() {window.status="Repeated tamings collapse meaning within itself.";}
    function Spellmouseover() {window.status="Spell meaning out. Spell for literalists.";}
    function StopStartmouseover() {window.status="Freeze/thaw meaning.";}
    function Colourmouseover() {window.status="Colour meaning.";}
    function Discombobulatemouseover() {window.status="Resize meaning.";}
    function Speedmouseover() {window.status="Adjust speed of meaning.";}
    function Aboutmouseover() {window.status="About meaning.";}
    function Runawaymouseover() {window.status="Dialog with Ted Warnell.";}
    function changespeed() {document.getElementById("spdfrm").style.visibility="visible";}
    function disappearform() {
            document.getElementById("spdfrm").style.visibility="hidden";
            document.getElementById("jmail").style.visibility="visible";
            document.getElementById("Run").style.visibility="visible";}
    function Imouseover() {
            //document.getElementById(id).style.color="#14c878";
            window.status="Meaning is yours to discover and create.";}
    function Iblur() {
            //document.getElementById(id).style.color='Gray';
            window.status="It is the world that you love, after all, is it not?";}
    function Iclick() {
            //document.getElementById(id).style.color="#31c6c6";
            window.status="What is fleeting? What endures?";}
    Comment: // Function Follow has been disabled. Detracted from focus. This function controls behavior
on mouse moves. When you move the mouse, notice that the letters seem to separate into two distinct groups.
When 0<=jtimer<200, the two groups are 'name' and 'gin'; when 200<=jtimer<400, the two groups are 'image'
and 'nn'; when 400<=jtimer<601, the two groups are 'game' and 'nin'. When the mouse moves, the x or y
component of the center of each letter (cx or cy) moves closer to the mouse. The basic formula (algebra added)
is cx=cx+(mouseX-cx)/s and for y, it's cy=cy+(mouseY-cy)/s where s is an integer. The bigger s is, the slower the
motion. This function is a late addition to Enigma n. I added it to increase interactivity and also introduce more
riddle./*
```

Figure 6.10

Jim Andrews, *Enigma n* (1998): code excerpt with author's comments. © Jim Andrews.
Reproduced with permission.

signifying dynamics of language is explicitly stated in Andrews's comments on the various functions, for instance, when the function "Spell" is described as "Spell meaning out. Spell for literalists," or when the function "Tame" is commented on as "Repeated tamings collapse meaning within itself." Although disabled, the scripting of the function "follow mouse" represents another layer of interaction in which the speed and trajectory of each letter would be correlated to mouse motions.

The dynamics of meaning production is experienced as a series of animated graphical metaphors that represent the fluctuations of meaning from stasis to controlled motion and chaotic motion. The orbital motions of letters seem to appropriate diagrammatic representations of the behaviors of atomic and subatomic particles and also the relative motions of planets, stars, and galaxies. Animation also suggests repeated and renewable cycles of appearance and disappearance, creation and destruction, emergence and immergence, looping back and forward in a process that can be endlessly iterated. The collapsing of the letters of the word *meaning* within themselves happens as readers/players repeatedly click on the function "Tame": the first clicks merely slow down the erratic orbits of the letters, but after nine or ten clicks, the letters seem to stop orbiting and just move slowly back and forth along a single axis that is only one letter wide (figure 6.11). This collapsing becomes a kinetic trope for a stabilized meaning, one in which the signifier's internal turbulence has been temporarily domesticated. In *Enigma n*, the play of signifiers in language has been materially enacted as a play with signifiers, giving readers/players a self-reflexive experience of the riddle and mystery of language through the flux and evanescence of meaning.

Twentieth-century linguistics and philosophy of language have unveiled some of the properties that make it possible for language to mean. Saussure has described languages as structured systems of differences. Signifiers cut up conceptual and referential space as a function of their phonological differences. Relations between signifier and signified, as well as relations between signifier and referent, are stabilized by the way social conventions and discourse formations enact the language contract within a community and across time. Culture and ideology, for example, operate by stabilizing certain modes of reference and meaning and by naturalizing certain kinds of privileged associations. However, such relations remain open to the turbulent generative processes that constitute language at the phonological, syntactic, semantic, and pragmatic levels and allow the continuing formation and transformation of subjectivity and social forms within language. Even for those who subscribe to universal evolutionary properties

Figure 6.11
Jim Andrews, *Enigma n* (1998): "function Tamemouseover" (screen captures). © Jim Andrews. Reproduced with permission.

Figure 6.11
(continued)

Figure 6.11
(continued)

of language and thought processes, such as mental categories and language structures, the possibilities for recombination and proliferation of meaning-producing differences seem endless. For poststructuralists, the instability of connections between signifiers and meanings came to be seen as inherent to signification, since meaning is a function of the very motion in the chain of signifiers, as each signified becomes a new signifier. The ability to reassociate and resignify is at the core of the way human beings use the engine of language, which constantly converts literal into metaphorical, and vice versa.

In the semiotic and hermeneutic exercise that Andrews proposed, "to make sense" is both to (re)stop and to (re)start the motion of letters. This dialectics produces "meaning," that is, the graphemic and phonological string we recognize as the word *meaning*. But it can also result in various sequences and random combinations of the letters themselves—not just in the visual constellations they form on the screen but in their individual graphic and cinematic properties (size, color, speed, trajectory, position). Paradoxically, to produce "meaning" seems be the very act of stopping the motion of meaning, which is the defining characteristic of meaning. Making sense, as a frozen material instantiation of form on computer screen, is suggested as both a redundancy and a tautology: "meaning" is played out as the coincidence of the word *meaning* with itself.

On the other hand, animation frames where letters take their proper orthographic order and phonological structure are challenged by those frames where their random arrangement suggests endless possibilities in their chaotic and turbulent motions. Thus, this may be the answer the poem offers to its own enigma "n": meaning may be defined by its exponential proliferation to the power of n. It is always materially enacted and cognitively embodied through the motion of an unstoppable signifying textual production and reception process. This process, while it subjects us to its own preconstituted relations of meaning production and consumption, also gives us the chance to step into the gap between signifier and signified in order to find and produce other meanings—in other words, multiple meanings rather than any singular meaning.

Arteroids, Nio, Stir/Fry/Texts, On Lionel Kearns, Enigma n, and other works by Jim Andrews have turned automated algorithms and other features of computer processing and display into new kinds of literary tropes. Poetry is enacted and embodied in his digital texts as the battle of language against itself and the battle of self against its language. Retroactions between self and language are emulated as retroactions between reader and machine. The loop in the code becomes a self-referential device for playing out the game of meaning. Readers/players experience the codependence between a given field of signs and their own interventions in that field. As readers respond to the programmed iterations, they also modify the textual and visual patterns available for seeing and reading or the sound patterns available for listening. From those unanticipated and semideter-mined patterns, meaning emerges.

As an emergent phenomenon, meaning is produced by the differential relations within the work's syntactic and semantic structures, the social space of available discourses, and the retroaction between human subject and computer code through the computerized algorithms. The simulation of these processes within the text itself instantiates what N. Katherine Hayles has described as the intermediating dynamics between human beings and machines. Andrews's interactive kinetic poems require readers to materially perform the patterns and motions of meaning. As techno-texts, they also make their readers experience the algorithmic character of digitality as an open system for exploring the chains of signification. Readers become aware of the ensemble made by signs and the human–machine processing of those signs.

6.7 Entangled Poetics

On the footsteps of a concrete poetics of sign reading, Jim Andrews's digital works script reading as an interactive choreography of signs. The motion of letters is both a re-presentation of inscriptional acts and a simulation of reading motions as prerequisites for semiotic processing. Thus the physi-ological and the hermeneutic become linked in the surface of the screen. What is specific about his algorithmic poetry is the way in which his pro-grammed poems make the interaction an explicit part of the semiotic field of the work. Simulation of this entanglement in textual fields is the main formal device in the works analyzed in the previous sections. The language game of the poem is turned into a digital game, in which the text has to be cogenerated and played by the reader. Interacting with signifiers, readers see their own reading motions being enacted on the screen. The reading of characters in motion, which already contain a simulation of reading, creates a loop between the actual motion on the screen and the embodied subjective motions required for triggering further motions on the screen.

As in a quantum optics experiment, motion is split between the timed motion of signs on the screen—whether in the form of abstract shapes, fragmented images, single letters, words, phrases, or sentences—and the motions generated by readers' interactions with those timed motions. The act of reading as a material processing of signs (an associative motion in the field of signs on the screen) becomes materially explicit as one dimension of the interpretative act: the text seems to contain a material inscription of the particular motion of reading that generates a given textual occurrence. It is as if interpretation could leave a semiotic trace in the actual textual surface. This loop highlights the codependence between a textual instance and a reading act, as if the reading motion itself, in its predictable and unpredictable associative paths, could be formally scripted by the program. In other words, reading responds to the program by feeding in its own motions as further executable data.

Andrews uses DHTML, ActionScript, JavaScript, and other languages to produce textual machines that engage readers with digital semiosis as a function of retroactive behaviors between readers' interventions and potential textual states. He has also developed a poetics of the Web as a specific reading and writing environment for human interactions. His permutational and time-based textual instruments contain scripts that may be said to visualize the dynamics of the textual field as a reading performance of a computer-mediated writing performance. In my speculative reading, they contain powerful meditations on the "productive character of the signifying field" (Drucker 2009a, 164) and advance a probabilistic approach to materiality (Drucker 2009b). To a certain extent, they visualize the multidimensionality of interpretation (McGann 2004) as an intervention that coproduces the text in the act of reading it. Readers are able to visualize the particular eventuality of the digital poem as a structured interaction between database and algorithm through a reflexive interface.

The text is materially coconstituted and codetermined by the act of reading/playing/visualizing the text, which exists as a series of discrete digital objects that have to be ordered and combined in response to actualizations of the potentiality codified in the algorithm. This rule-based, procedural, and ongoing construction of textual instances is reflected in Andrews's interface menus, which include instructions such as "Do the Text," "Stop the Text," and "Discipline the Text" (*Seattle Drift*), or "Prod meaning," "Stir meaning," and "Tame meaning" (*Enigma n*). In effect, his works can be read as visualizations of the Derridean redefinition of difference as the condition for the appearance of the sign. Andrews's animations provide a script for the motion of the signifying chains and the physical and mental action of processing those motions. They enable readers to visualize the formal nature of signifying processes and the historical and subjective determination of written signs by reading acts. His scripts are diagrammatic visualizations of writing and reading as entangled processes.

Writing cannot be separated from reading, and vice versa. Kineticism in his poetry is not only fulfilling a rhetorical function of iconic self-similarity between verbal form and visual reference. Textual kinetics engages with the very motion of signifiers at the fundamental level of semiological and hermeneutical possibilities. His code poetics is a poetics of writing and reading as a human game of signs that uses programmability to create a sensorial experience of digital, print, and verbal codes.

Randomized text is generated by the work's algorithms in response to haptic interactions. These semiotic reiterations of networks of signifiers, in turn, are available for reiterations of interpretive operations. Textual occurrences and interpretive moves become codependent and partially unpredictable. This particular textual structure exemplifies what Hayles has described as the recursive feedback dynamics of intermediation in human–computer interactions, a concept she developed to account for both the relations between paper and screen-based works and interaction between computer machines and readers in electronic literature (2005, 2008). It can also be seen as a model for subjectivity in textual fields as conceptualized by McGann (2001, 2004) and Johanna Drucker (2008, 2009a). Drucker (2008) has called our attention to the potentiality of e-space for showing the "dynamic nature of works as produced by interpretive acts":

The dynamic action encoded in a codex's program of text and paratext isn't merely a means of interconnecting static elements. That interpretive act, the creation of what I keep referring to as the phenomenal, virtual *e-space* of the codex, produces a work in each iteration. Making that fact evident requires vivid, graphic demonstration of what such a virtual *e-space* is as an emergent work, as the effect of interpretation. The capacity of electronic media to record and display reception histories, to produce them as an ongoing feature of a document, may prove to be the single most significant feature distinguishing e-books from their print precedent. An interface that creates a platform for interpretive acts to be noticed as such, called to our attention as performance. The idea is to mark the shift from the conception of books as artifacts, or documents as vehicles for delivery of content, and instead demonstrate the living, dynamic nature of works as produced by interpretive acts. (229–230)

Andrews's textual instruments create precisely a simulation of such dynamism by linking specific material instantiations of his digital multimedia texts to readers' moves in the textual game, and thus they attempt to make those interventions part of the work's material field. The production of the text through reading becomes the meaning of the text as the reader sees himself or herself producing the text through a playing or reading of the text.

7 Scripting the Act of Reading

7.1 Inside Out

The work of software artist John F. Simon Jr. is based on material operations that direct the viewer's attention to the incommensurability of hardware, software, and the instantiation of perceptual forms as processed by human senses.[1] His works are based on the display of code-generated images on wall-mounted screens. These LCD screens can also be enclosed into material structures, such as wall reliefs, Plexiglas, and Formica boxes. Screens embedded on frames or placed within mirrored boxes refer back to the tradition of painting and optical machines while highlighting the transience of time-based processes made possible by digital optical media. Time-based variations on a set of predefined parameters make images always display a bit different than they ever were. In response to time-based changes scripted in code, visual patterns develop in an endless series of combinations. The relationship between the digital and analog elements is continuously reworked through this correspondence between machine processing and machine display. In his programmed paintings, analytical and self-expressive uses of code stage the relation between machine and human processing in the production of emergent forms and emergent perceptions. Code is embodied as an ever-changing series of visual patterns that submit viewers to the open-ended unfolding of time.

In *CPU* (1999), the technical and aesthetic materiality of the computer is displayed as a system that links machine processing to human processing (figure 7.1). The double reference contained in its acronymic title—central processing unit or color processing unit—is echoed in the placement of screen display and computer circuits at the same level. The electromagnetic behaviors of processing chips are the origin of physical transformations that ultimately result in color-pattern variations. Electronic components responsible for sustaining the operation of the machine are

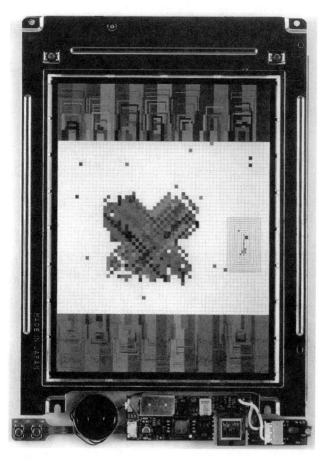

Figure 7.1
John F. Simon, Jr. *CPU* (*Central Processing Unit*) (1999). Custom software, Macintosh 280c, acrylic plastic. © John F. Simon Jr. Reproduced with permission.

made visible on the surface of the work. The actual processing in the circuits in response to coded instructions remains inaccessible in this exposure of the mechanism of the computer, which stresses the otherness of the machine's electromagnetic scale. Processing is the ensemble of cascading abstractions that define digital materiality from voltage differences to perceptible visual forms. Geometric color permutations generated by the programming code create a visual field that is open to perceptual categorization and patterning. Because permutations never repeat, the transience of the work is reenacted in the transience of perceiving the work: time of execution and time of perception are always only temporarily linked. Execution of the code by new processors and new screens exposes the material function of the hardware and software system in instantiating the work.

The changing nature of the work's formal materiality and the representational tension between immediacy and hypermediacy can be further illustrated with *Visions* (2009) (figure 7.2). *Visions* is made of a multicolor mirrored cabinet that houses an LCD screen display. The screen is concealed inside the cabinet where mirrors reflect the source images. Viewers see the reflections of the composite geometric images by looking through a pair of windows. One window allows the viewer to see the deconstruction of geometric patterns as they emerge from the background in a spiral motion that extends upward. The other window shows the reconstruction of the various patterns as they spiral downward. The symmetry in the pattern of motions and transformations is the result of a continuous process of repetition and difference programmed in the code. Images are being displayed at the same moment that they are being calculated. The living quality of this digital kaleidoscope derives from this moment-to-moment instantiation controlled by a code designed to introduce incremental changes upon iteration.

In *Visions*, generation and perception of images sustain a complex system of self-reflexive interactions. The act of seeing is both seeing an object through a medium and seeing the medium as that which enables the act of seeing an object. Reflected on mirrored surfaces, images are rendered as images of images. Viewers are asked to look through a window, only to see a mirror reflecting self-generated images. Because these images are generated by computer code, they seem to have no photographic referent outside the technical apparatus. Yet the mirrors give them an instantaneous optical existence that is already removed from their digital source in code and in screen display. Through this optical short circuit, digital and analog representations are placed in continuity. The optical referent

Figure 7.2
John F. Simon Jr., *Visions* (2009). Custom software, wood, plastic laminate, acrylic paint, mirrored plastic, LCD screen, Mac computer. © John F. Simon Jr. Reproduced with permission.

of *Visions* as the system made by computer display, mirror, window, and human vision can be extended to include the inner visions of the mind as abstract patterns of shapes and colors become a source for new ways of seeing the emerging patterns. Simon's optical digital works contain a meditation on the relation between code and display as conceptual and perceptual investigations on the nature and meaning of forms. In his working method, machine iteration is part of a creative feedback loop that enables the artist to discover emergent forms:

Software art aims at expanding and activating practices started by artists who have codified their artistic experience. In software writing I have learned that a set of well defined rules may result in unexpected effects. Usually I start a software project with an idea, which then I draw on paper, which helps me defining the rules which I encrypt in the software. The software numbers which control shapes and colors grow incrementally, while I add new rules which are inspired by what I see. In this way I explore the limits of the model; then a new mind model emerges from the process and a new feedback starts again. (Simon, quoted in Diacono 2009)

In Simon's programmed art, the relation between code and its visual instantiations is based on a feedback loop between the conceptual and the perceptual as modes of aesthetic experience and modes of poetic production. Visual concepts that may have originated in hand drawings are given coded form, and then changes at the level of code instantiate unforeseen visual patterns that in turn give rise to new drawings and new coding possibilities. This folding and unfolding of code-related forms that respond to viewers interventions on the formal display is the subject of the Internet-based work *Unfolding Object* (2002) (figure 7.3). Simon has described this work as "an endless book that rewrites itself and whose use dictates its

Figure 7.3
John F. Simon Jr., *Unfolding Object* (2002). Interactive networked code (Java applet with server database and servlets), dimensions variable. © John F. Simon, Jr. Reproduced with permission.

content" (quoted in Ippolito 2002). Simon is alluding to the programmed algorithmic procedures that generate the work's formal materiality and also to its construction as a perceived and collaborative object produced by the viewer/user.

Reading performs the space of writing each time a user perceives its forms. The field of performance becomes scripted in the evolving form of the object, denying its self-identity and autonomy. The object's unfolding is codependent on this coupling of code with use in time. The work's abstract shape is the record of the clicks and pings of users over a network. I have referred to this way of modeling an interaction through a script that attempts to capture an intervention in the material field of the work as *scripting reading*. The following section looks at digital writers who are explicitly using code to understand the material, conceptual, and affective dimension of reading in signifying processes.

7.2   Outside In

Philippe Bootz, John Cayley, Rui Torres, Eugenio Tisselli, Talan Memmott, David Jhave Johnston, and others have developed a poetics of programmability that addresses reading operations in digital works. Cayley uses the concept P=R=O=G=R=A=M=M=A=T=O=L=O=G=Y to refer to his approach, implying that he is looking at code as a particular mode of discourse and a particular mode of writing. His works often use transcoding between writing characters or systems and translation between natural languages as visual analogs for the workings of computer code and codes in general. By temporizing textual transformations, his digital poems reveal the inner workings of the layered and stratified processes of programming as a mode of writing that can be used to understand the materiality of speech and writing as signifying processes, while experimenting with the expressive use of programming codes as artificial languages.

Cayley's programmatic work has focused on natural language as the core of literary experience. He investigates the relations between natural languages and between natural languages and code through processes of translation and morphing that involve verbal texts and writing systems. In *Windsound* (1999), this mapping of signs between different sign systems is made present through a morphing between letter shapes that results in transient textual states read by a voice processor. The transient literal states give viewers and listeners a sense of the phonological and graphic space of recombination as both a potential semantic field and the pure materiality of the sounds of language and the traces of writing. Linguistic structure is but a temporary crystallization along the continuum of transliteral and transphonetic transformations. Having the machine perform the sound of the combinations shows the performance of code as a material correlative of the human performance of writing. Linguistic and alphabetic permutations are enhanced by numerical permutations of digital code.

Another occurrence of this manipulation of code to investigate language can be seen in *Overboard* (2004c, with Giles Perring) and in *Translation* (2004d, with Giles Perring), in which movements of surfacing, floating, or sinking are used for recombining letters and words in and out of legibility. In *Translation* (2004d), letter substitutions also suggest textual states that shift between German, French, and English, with excerpts from "On Language as Such and on the Language of Man" by Walter Benjamin alternating with excerpts from *In Search of Lost Time* and other texts by Marcel Proust (Cayley 2005) (figure 7.4). Letter permutations create a visualization of the interlinguistic gap between two natural language systems as texts are partially moved from one language into another. Because letters are "replaced by other letters that are in some way similar to those of the original text" (Cayley 2004c), word shapes are partially recognizable during the sinking and rising stages of replacement. Verbal phonographic coherence emerges as a transient moment in a continuous process of differentiation and substitution, and the text is only partially readable in any given language state.

This method creates a perception of the floating identity of signifiers as a consequence of differential relations and of the graphic and linguistic material constraints that afford and limit the differentiation. Meaningful and legible combinations emerge temporarily from within this interlinguistic and interwriting space, as if the very process of language codification could be formally and materially observed. Cayley is proposing a transcoding between languages that emphasizes the work's programming as an unfolding textual event and offers a series of transitional textual states capturing the signifying potentiality of interlinguistic and interwriting spaces. This timed restructuring of letter shapes and word signs is a material image of the general process of semiosis as a discrete process of sign substitution: substitutions within and between natural languages, within and between writing systems, within and between computer codes, and within and between all of those levels. This gestalt and probabilistic approach to legibility and translatability is a structural feature in other works by Cayley, including *RiverIsland* (2002b), *Imposition* (2007), and *Mirroring Tears: Visages* (2011, a collaboration with Penny Florence).

For more than a decade, Cayley's approach to algorithmic poetry has kept natural language processes at the center of digital poetics. One of his latest projects has moved further in the direction of metareading by

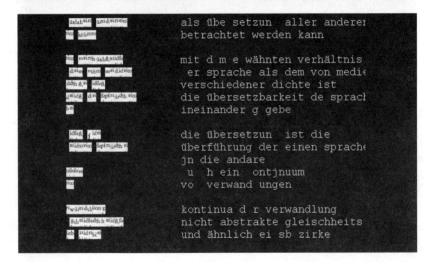

Figure 7.4
John Cayley, *Translation* (with Giles Perring, 2005), version 6 (screen captures). © John Cayley. Reproduced with permission.

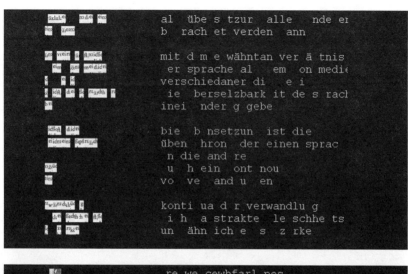

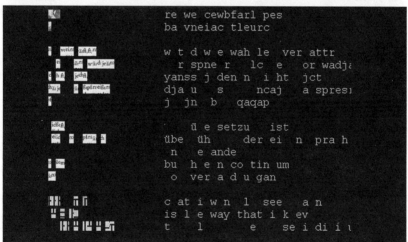

Figure 7.4
(continued)

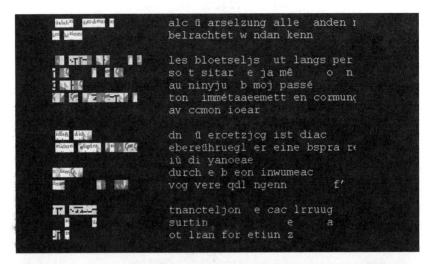

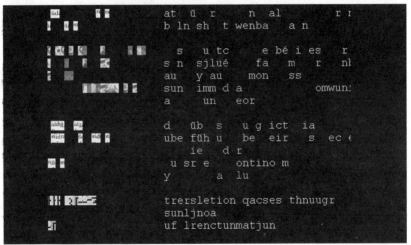

Figure 7.4
(continued)

attempting to mark specific modes and strategies of reading on the textual surface. The concept of metareader or cognitive reader is used here in the sense proposed by Bootz (2006) as "one who knows the 'texte-auteur' or its properties and who observes someone else in the process of reading." In *The Readers Project* (2009–2012, a work in progress by Cayley and Howe), algorithms visualize reading vectors as productive rewritings in a language field. A series of programmed readers highlights verbal elements in a given text's database of words and sentences according to specific protocols:

This project is an essay in language-driven digital art, in writing digital media. *The Readers Project* visualizes reading, although it does not do this in the sense of miming conventional human reading. Rather, the project explores and visualizes existing and alternative *vectors* of reading, vectors that are motivated by the properties and methods of language and language art. (Cayley 2010)

In early 2011, Cayley and Howe had already programmed six types of reading behaviors that they applied to different texts: a Simple Reader, a Perigram Reader, a Spawning Reader, a Mesostic Reader, an Unconstrained Perigram Reader, and a Grammatical Lookahead Reader (Cayley 2010) (figure 7.5). While the Simple Reader moves according to the standard Western left-to-write order of words, the Perigram Reader responds to adjacent words to the right of the read word (occurring in the same line and in the lines above and below). Whenever these words form a perigram, a sequence of statistically probable natural language occurrence, the conventional left-to-right sequence of reading gives place to perigrammatic constellations. The Spawning Reader spawns other readers in its neighborhood; the Mesostic Reader has a preset fragment of written language (word, phrase, or longer piece of text) and looks for words containing its sequence of letters (capitalizing one of them within each matched word) until the mesostic is completed. Words chosen to form mesostics are also selected on the basis of perigrams. The Unconstrained Perigram Reader searches for perigrams by looking at any adjacent word in its typographical neighborhood (without being constrained to words occurring to the right of the read word). The Grammatical Lookahead Reader learns from the grammatical structures already read and moves ahead highlighting similar syntactical patterns.

Cayley and Howe developed the concept of typographic neighborhood as a way of visualizing the various reading strategies. The definition of the pathways for the programmed readers is "based on linguistic properties and relationships between words that had been read and words in their neighborhood that might be read" (Cayley 2010). In their installations,

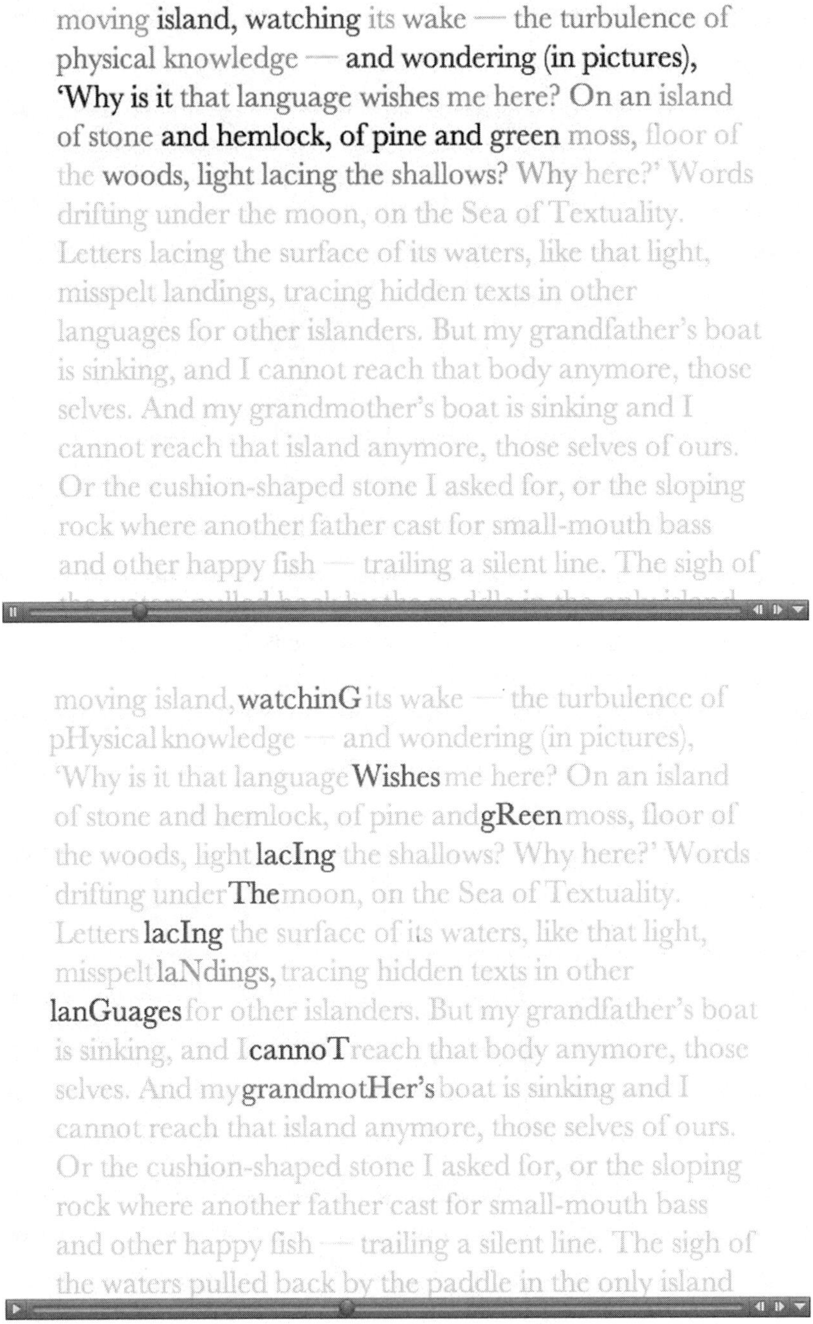

moving **island, watching** its wake — the turbulence of
physical knowledge — **and wondering (in pictures),**
'Why is it that language wishes me here? On an island
of stone **and hemlock, of pine and green** moss, floor of
the **woods, light lacing the shallows?** Why here?' Words
drifting under the moon, on the Sea of Textuality.
Letters lacing the surface of its waters, like that light,
misspelt landings, tracing hidden texts in other
languages for other islanders. But my grandfather's boat
is sinking, and I cannot reach that body anymore, those
selves. And my grandmother's boat is sinking and I
cannot reach that island anymore, those selves of ours.
Or the cushion-shaped stone I asked for, or the sloping
rock where another father cast for small-mouth bass
and other happy fish — trailing a silent line. The sigh of

moving island, **watchinG** its wake — the turbulence of
p**H**ysical knowledge — and wondering (in pictures),
'Why is it that language **Wishes** me here? On an island
of stone and hemlock, of pine and **gReen** moss, floor of
the woods, light **lacIng** the shallows? Why here?' Words
drifting under **The** moon, on the Sea of Textuality.
Letters **lacIng** the surface of its waters, like that light,
misspelt **laNdings,** tracing hidden texts in other
lanGuages for other islanders. But my grandfather's boat
is sinking, and I**cannoT** reach that body anymore, those
selves. And my **grandmotHer's** boat is sinking and I
cannot reach that island anymore, those selves of ours.
Or the cushion-shaped stone I asked for, or the sloping
rock where another father cast for small-mouth bass
and other happy fish — trailing a silent line. The sigh of
the waters pulled back by the paddle in the only island

Figure 7.5
John Cayley and Daniel Howe, *The Readers Project* (2009–2011): (a) Perigram Reader;
(b) Mesostic Reader; (c) Spawning Reader (screen captures). © John Cayley & Daniel
Howe. Reproduced with permission.

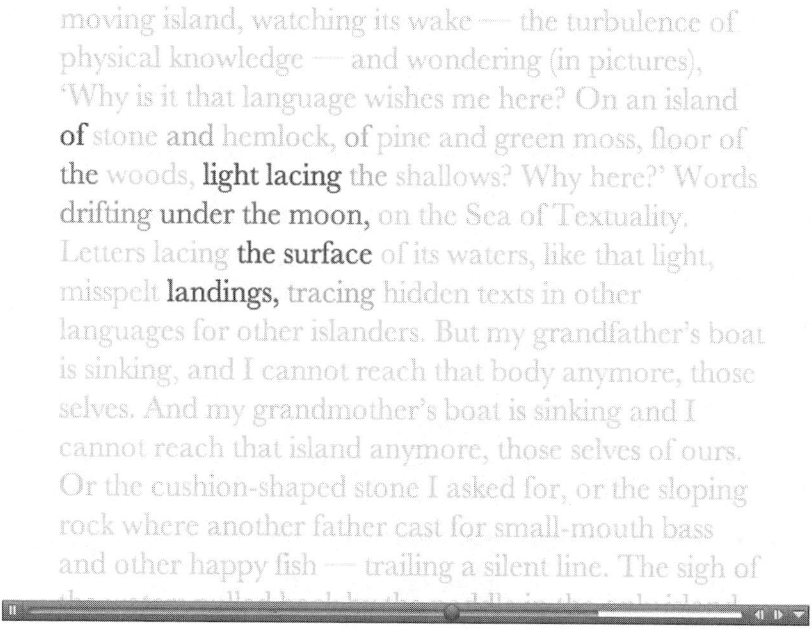

moving island, watching its wake — the turbulence of
physical knowledge — and wondering (in pictures),
'Why is it that language wishes me here? On an island
of stone and hemlock, of pine and green moss, floor of
the woods, **light lacing** the shallows? Why here?' Words
drifting **under the moon,** on the Sea of Textuality.
Letters lacing **the surface** of its waters, like that light,
misspelt **landings,** tracing hidden texts in other
languages for other islanders. But my grandfather's boat
is sinking, and I cannot reach that body anymore, those
selves. And my grandmother's boat is sinking and I
cannot reach that island anymore, those selves of ours.
Or the cushion-shaped stone I asked for, or the sloping
rock where another father cast for small-mouth bass
and other happy fish — trailing a silent line. The sigh of

Figure 7.5
(continued)

Cayley and Howe have applied those particular readers to Samuel Beckett's
"The Image" (1950) and Adam Smith's *An Inquiry into the Nature and Causes
of the Wealth of Nations* (1776). All readers are programmed to "perform
reading behaviors that are meaning-generative," and they have some char-
acteristics of cellular automata.

Paths and patterns that highlight words and phrases within a preexisting text give viewers a representation of acts of reading as performative or
deformative interventions that establish their cognitive and perceptual
associations and hierarchies within the textual field. Although *The Readers
Project* is not attempting to simulate a particular reading practice or the
actual ocular processing of text as the eyes move from point to point,
the various reading algorithms give the viewer a material perception of the
dynamic nature of reading. Reading traverses a field of signs, and this
traversing is creating its own particular linear and multilinear constellations. Each reading vector performs an iteration of a particular reading
behavior or strategy and thus becomes scripted in the textual surface. Each
of these inscriptions is the result of the machine's execution of the scripts
that constitute a given machinic reader's code.

Since these readings of the machine are offered as writing to human readers, the writing of reading and the reading as writing contained in *The Readers Project* turn readers into metareaders who are forced to read their own act of reading the program reading. The motion of reading, which is rhetorically enacted within the textual surface through textual animation, is also a perceptual reminder of the kineticism contained in the act of moving the eyes from letter to letter and from word to word. Because the programmed readers within the text are offering their particular mode of reading as yet another instance of writing to be read once again by a human reader, actual readings cannot be exactly mirrored or captured by the programmed readers, only reengaged as renewed encounters with signs. The particular mode of reading scripted in the reading machine and the human act of reading that particular mode reading create a metacognitive position. Automated generative writing is presented as an act of reading that rewrites the text and makes it available for literary reading. Cayley (2010) describes the resulting *mise-en-abîme* in this way:

The Readers Project is a visualization of reading but it is implicitly critical of conventional reading habits. Further, because the project's *readers* move within and are thus composed by the words within which they move, they also, effectively, write. They generate texts and the traces of their writings are offered to the project's human readers as such, as writing, as literary art; published as real-time streams of live-writing, available to anyone with internet access.

"Real-time streams of live-writing" is one manifestation of temporality in programmed signifiers. After clarifying the meanings of code and the ways in which code can be modulated by natural language, and vice versa, Cayley (2006) argues for the specificity of code as programming—as a program or set of methods that runs in time and produces writing. In the case of *The Readers Project*, this code-generated writing is the product of particular machinic readings that activate constellations of words in preexisting texts according to "specific reading strategies based upon linguistic feature analysis and real-time probability models harvested from search engines" (Cayley and Howe 2011). If "codework makes exterior the interior workings of the computer" (Raley, 2002), by programming readings of the text, Cayley and Howe exteriorize the inner workings of reading in the outer surface of writing. As programmed reading, the reading behaviors of the readers perform according to a script that highlights statistically frequent associations of words. The meaningfulness of reading behaviors depends on statistical constraints derived from analysis of the Internet itself as a natural language database. In this way, perigrammatic association of lexical items reflects human uses of linguistic repertoires, and it becomes an automated tool for an open exploration of other meaningful associations.

Cayley and Howe's algorithms for defining the various reading vectors manage to avoid the entropy of entirely random word selection while still making room for unexpected and improbable associations. The poetic effect is the product of this tension between the entire corpus of words in the chosen text as the work's database and the neighborhood rules that govern particular readings. Set up as an installation to be read by human readers, the strictly rule-based semiotic processing of word association executed by the machine enters the human processes of symbolic substitution and affective apprehension. The textual motion happening in the self-reading text conflicts with the actual reading motion of parsing the text at a human reader's pace. Because every machine reading is also a new instance of writing available for a human reader, the act of reading the machine reading becomes a model for the infinite iterability of writing as actualized by each reading act. The iterability of code is used for stressing the act of reading as a field of possibilities grounded on the iterability of writing.

7.3 Unwriting

Graphic, tactile, sound, and other hardware and software interfaces are important elements in the rhetoric of programmable media. Interfaces can be explored as constitutive spaces in the production of online-reading subjects. Consideration of the affordances of interfaces as constraints and possibilities is at the core of the digital poetics of authors such as Jason Nelson and Serge Bouchardon. The interface itself becomes the axis of their aesthetic investigations into human–computer interactions. Instead of taking for granted an instrumental separation between user's action and object's behavior, they formalize the work's spatial and temporal display in ways that show the constitutive nature of the interface as a reading, disciplining, conventional, and meaning-generating apparatus. Interface parody results in the defamiliarization of genres and forms as they are self-consciously emulated within a different semantic and pragmatic context. Self-reflexivity in these works takes the form of interface awareness and confronts users and players with the conventionality of the device used for interacting with multimodal textual objects generated by code.

Serge Bouchardon's digital texts may be described by the concepts of "playable media" and "textual instrument," in the sense defined by Noah Wardrip-Fruin (2007, 211). As playable textual experiences, they are framed as both games, with a preestablished set of elements and rules, and instruments that can be openly explored for new formal combinations and new insights. Bouchardon's reflexive poetics addresses human interfacing with digital devices. In his programmed works, he treats our experiences of computer-mediated communication, interactions with programs, and practices of online reading as a structural and thematic element. Programmability is used for showing the constraining and enabling functions of particular scripts in networked environments. Human–computer interfaces are experienced as representational conventions that induce certain kinds of expectation and particular modes of interaction. This second-degree enactment of interaction with programs and of networked communication is the subject, for example, of *Les 12 travaux de l'internaute* (Bouchardon, 2008).

The first work is structured as a game in twelve stages that confront users with difficulties in accessing sites and interacting with networked files and programs. The twelve labors of Hercules are ironically and parodically impersonated in the Internet user, who has to come to terms with multiple online frustrations in order to achieve "Web immortality." All the elements in the interface (graphic design, animations, interactivity, and soundtrack) are also parodies of game interfaces, while the actions of the player refer to common online experiences: "The Nemean Lyon" is the failure to connect; "The Lernaean Hydra" takes the form of intrusive pop-up windows; "The Ceryneian Hind" is translated into problems of interactivity motion through Web camera; "The Erymanthean Boar" re-creates the cognitive disorientation caused by the randomness of links; in "The Augean Stables," the player has to fight unwanted e-mail that accumulates in the inbox; "The Stymphalian Birds" are represented by banner ads that the user has to drive away; "The Cretan Bull" takes the shape of a virus that crashes the operating system; "The Mares of Diomedes" are cookies that store private information; "The Belt of Hippolyte" forces the user to search for information on the Net; "The Cattle of Geryon" requires the player to neutralize social networking harassment by someone who uses three different profiles; "The Apples of Hesperides" asks the user to contribute to universal knowledge by writing for Wikipedia; and, finally, in "Cerberus," a frequently visited Web site disappears and the user has to retrieve this page from the Internet's underworld.

The use of links to outside sources is a crucial element in the work's scripts for signifying the Internet, particularly in the stages "The Belt of Hippolyte" and "The Erymanthean Boar." The re-creation of online searches is the focus of "The Belt of Hippolyte." Like Hercules, readers are looking for the belt of the Amazon, but the available link will immediately lead them astray and away from their goal. Users find themselves immersed in a rain of falling numbers, with two bar codes at the bottom right of the screen, two white-on-black drawings of Amazons, and a link that leads to Amazon.com. The links to an online shopping site and a bar code for a particular book are reminders of the disconnection between string-based searches and contextually based referencing. They also suggest the continuous resignification of words operated by their association to technological changes and consumerist culture.

Links to external sites reinforce the interconnectedness that defines the Internet as a reading and social space. In "The Erymanthean Boar," for instance, the metaphor of the hypertext labyrinth as a new reading space is materialized through links to sites devoted to writing and reading experiments in digital media, including ongoing theoretical and archival work on hyperfiction and digital literature (figure 7.6). External links in this sequence take players to various sites: "Queneau" links to a site on Raymond Queneau's *Cent mille milliards de poems;* "Wiki" links to the Wikipedia entry for "Écriture"; "Alice" links to the hyperfiction *Inanimate Alice;* "ELO" links to the site of the Electronic Literature Organization; "Montfort" links to Nick Montfort's Web site; "Narrative" links to the *Interactive Narrative Data Basis;* and so on.[2] Playing the text in "The Erymanthean Boar" stage involves both the immersive motion within the three-dimensional space of the work's white and black labyrinth of words (arrow keys) and a motion across this particular visual space into external conceptual and material spaces (HTML links). The spatialized architectonic labyrinth of immersive presence within the work coexists with the spatialized conceptual labyrinth of endless networked information.

Multicursal, associative, and labyrinthine paths are instantiated formally as links that lead readers away from the work's frame across or into other frames of reference. Bouchardon's playable text addresses the material ergonomics and the social semiotics of online reading environments and offers links to ongoing experiments by digital writers as exemplary instances of its simulation of the Internet itself. It is a work that has made the networked programmability of online writing spaces an explicit element of its functionalities. In *The 12 Labours of the Internet User,* the mixed modalities and jump frames that Drucker (2011) describes and the reading for patterns that Hayles (2010) describes are staged within the technical and material affordances of hardware and software, but also within the social processes of information exchange and control. Cultural and social forms are embedded as conventions of the interface, which

Figure 7.6
Serge Bouchardon, Mathieu Brigolle, Aymeric Brisse, Christopher Espargeliere, Mikael Labrut, Jérémie Lequeux, and Adrien Pegaz-Blanc, *Les 12 travaux de l'internaute* (2008): "Le sanglier d'Erymanthe" (The Erymanthean Boar) (screen captures). © Serge Bouchardon, Jr. Reproduced with permission.

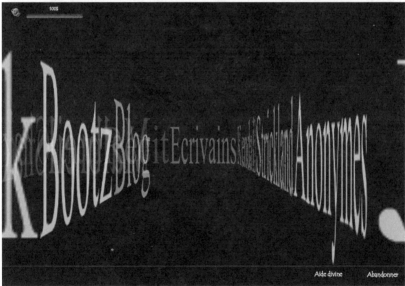

Figure 7.6
(continued)

constitute the user as a particular kind of human subject. Enabling cookies, searching for information, activating and stopping pop-ups and ads, losing connections, following links, and fighting viruses, for example, are perceived as markers of the social and economic mediations that constitute the electronic space as a particular kind of social text.

Similar simulations of the dynamics of codex reading fields have been made with playable texts in book form since the late 1990s. These computer-produced works have begun to remediate digital search for patterns of reading back into codex form. Data aggregation and data visualization are translated into book structure and page layout, sustaining new kinds of topological and conceptual spaces whose linguistic and physical form could be produced only with the help of computer tools and within the search and aggregation capabilities of networked databases. Relations between language and various levels of material and visual patterning in codex books by Mark Danielewski, Jonathan Safran Foer, Salvador Plascencia, Steve Tomasula, Kenneth Goldsmith, and others depend on the dynamics between distant, close, and machine reading created by computer-mediated multilayering of book elements. Such printed books assimilate the structures and patterns of software culture in their material and symbolic permutations.

One example of this computer-codex feedback is *Tree of Codes* (2010) by Jonathan Safran Foer, which uses the die-cut technique to produce a new work out of an earlier text. This work uses the x-, y-, and z-axes of codex space to recombine the text *of The Street of Crocodiles* by Bruno Schulz into a new story (figure 7.7). Syntactic articulation of narrative is achieved through the topographic articulation of inscriptions within and across pages: a different die-cut is applied to every page in ways that allow reading trajectories within the same page and over multiple pages at the same time. By cutting out a particular pattern on each page, which also opens a reading window onto subsequent pages, the two-dimensionality of page inscription is projected onto the three-dimensionality of codex space. The relative positions of printed text and cut-out holes are used to articulate a narrative. Organization of page and codex space makes readers experience the materiality of inscription as a narrative element in structuring verbal language. As a printed book, *Tree of Codes* has incorporated the mediation of digital tools in the mapping and prototyping of relations between text setting and paper cutting.

Tree of Codes is a reading of a prior text that cuts its way into a preconstituted syntactic and narrative order. By cutting itself into the inscriptions of a former text, a reading is converted into a new writing. This reading

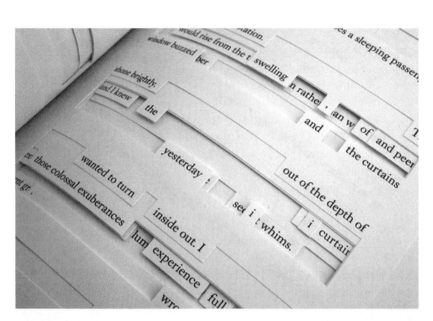

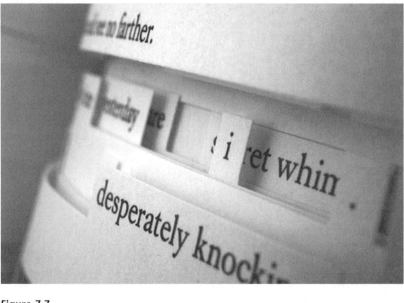

Figure 7.7
Jonathan Safran Foer, *Tree of Codes* (2010): details. © Jonathan Safran Foer. Reproduced with permission.

action on the field of signs becomes scripted in a new text, procedurally generated from a constrained textual database. This new text, in turn, has been page-set in ways that allow multiple trajectories across and within pages according to rearrangements of codex space materialized in cut-outs. Page holes function also as syntactic articulators of words, phrases, and sentences, enabling convergent and divergent reading paths. Language and narrative are interrupted by the materiality of paper articulations that destabilize the relative positions of verbal elements in each layer of reading. Through this device, the text is made simultaneously present to itself, conflating the conventional articulation of space and time in codex structures. Readers are made to experience the constitutive motion of reading in the material production of meaning.

The scripting of reading into writing is also a structural element in an interactive poem by Augusto de Campos in both its electronic screen and printed paper versions. "Sem saída" (no exit) (2000) is a material meditation on the labyrinthine processes of reading. In the electronic version, readers are called on to read seven sentences in seven successive stages (figure 7.8). Each sentence is gradually revealed as readers drag the mouse to the right. Sentences appear letter by letter, without word breaks, forming jagged lines in color across the black screen. Dragging the mouse to the left makes the revealed letters disappear. Once one full sentence is revealed, clicking the mouse launches the next textual stage, which is laid out according to the same principles, the only difference being the color and visual pattern of letters on the screen. Clicking the mouse after the last stage launches the seven sentences simultaneously, making their layers superimpose on the screen. This last stage also launches a sound file in which the seven sentences are read aloud simultaneously. Paths for individual sentences, which had been experienced as partial explorations of the labyrinth, are now combined to suggest the complete pattern of the textual labyrinth.

The motions of reading have been scripted in the temporal and spatial dimensions of the text. Called on by an interactive mouse-over script, the text offers its shapes to visual recognition and symbolic processing. This material transformation of visible form into readable form is rehearsed each time, as the reader gradually becomes familiar with its reading code (specific font faces, absence of word breaks, direction of reading, and overall spatial patterning of sentences). Passage of time is experienced as the actual passage of time in reading, while the sense of space becomes attached to the spatial navigation of signs on the screen. In other words, the experience of reading the text offers a semiotic analog for the

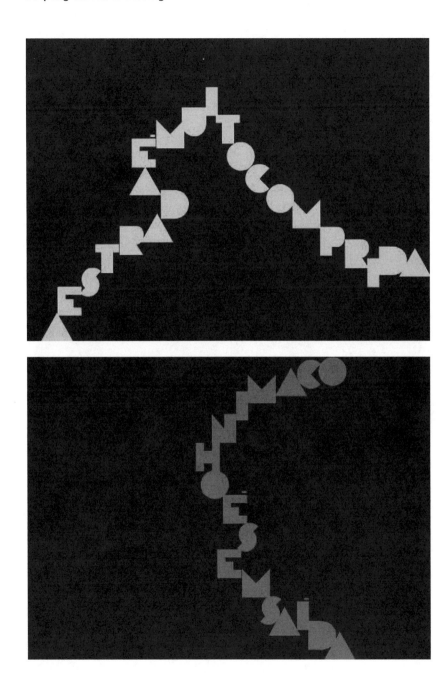

Figure 7.8
Augusto de Campos, "Sem saída" (No exit) (2000) (screen captures). © Augusto de Campos. Reproduced with permission.

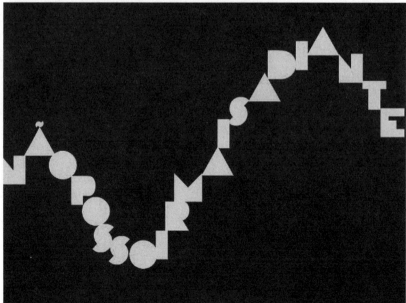

Figure 7.8
(continued)

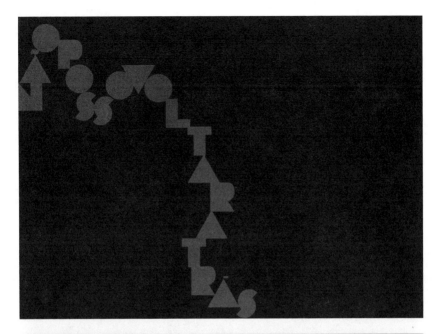

Figure 7.8
(continued)

Figure 7.8
(continued)

experiential meaning of the text. The equation between life and labyrinth, art and labyrinth, and meaning and labyrinth (three large-scale implicit references of the sentences) is literally materialized in the self-conscious perception of signs by the reader.

The progressive decipherment and recognition of forms further evokes the production of knowledge through reading as we move from local chains of association between letters, words, and sentences to global networks of relations at higher discursive levels. In this work, we find the three figures for reading explored in this book: the tree, the network, and the labyrinth. Textual syntax and its exploratory interface are hierarchically organized according to branching and nested structures that are timed and sequential. They are also linked as networks of associations between elements that are spatialized and simultaneously present. The figure of the labyrinth is created by movements of reading that traverse the textual field according to both arborescent structures, based on relations of dependence, and networked nodes, based on relations of association. Reading is scripted as a multicursal exploration of divergent and convergent paths through processes of recursion.

In the print version, the reader is asked to unravel the lines in different colors that cross and superimpose on the page (figure 7.9). Eye-mouse-screen-mind interaction is now substituted by eye-paper-print-mind interaction. Reading this version involves similar operations in recognizing and unscrambling as readable forms the ensemble of visual forms that compose the work. Through separation of color layers and decipherment of letters, words and sentences reenact the experience of translating the fuzziness of shapes into the abstract system of differences required for pattern recognition. While the sequencing of letter and word forms within each sentence will be similar to the temporized mediation of the mouse, the relative sequence of sentences will vary from reader to reader. Actualization of sequences in constellated texts is one instance of the performative production of text through reading interventions.

The performative nature of reading as producer of textual events can be summarized as follows: (1) the act of reading responds to bibliographic and electronic codes, the reading program contained in the spatialized, temporized and algorithmic materialization of writing; (2) the act of reading inscribes itself in the writing by priming, reordering, and reassociating elements according to specific modes of individual attention (cognitive, affective) and socialized protocols of reading; and (3) meaning becomes probabilistic and emergent as a result of the interaction between those two motions. Constellated, reticular, and permutative texts take advantage of

Figure 7.9
Augusto de Campos, "Sem saída" (No exit) (2000) (print version). © Augusto de Campos. Reproduced with permission.

the productivity of the act of reading by showing it as co-instantiator of its object (i.e., as an activator of dynamic relationships that constitute the textual field through reading interventions).

In "Sem saída" the act of reading with the eye and with the mind is the quintessential literary experience: "the road is very long," "the path has no exit," "curves deceive the eye," "i cannot go any further," "i cannot go back," "it took me all my life," "i never left the place." Echoing the myth of Theseus lost in the labyrinth, the self-descriptive text can also be read as an autobiography of the old artist who looks back on his life devoted to experiments with language and form. It works too as a general reflection on the production of self within the signifying chains of language. The labyrinth of reading enacts the literary condition of the self as a writing and reading subject. It is a self-reflexive ars poetica about the electronic reading space, in which eyes and hand attempt to find their way out within multiple trajectories of hyperlinks that lead from sign to sign to sign in a technotextual reiteration of writing as a network of cross-referenced inscriptions. In its joyful and self-ironic celebration of the achievements and shortcomings of concrete poetics, the rainbow colors of "Sem saída" seem to point to yet another tentative and provisional way out, this time offered by the digital medium as a way for extending and exploring poetic insights about the strange mediations that bring world to self in the labyrinth of language.

7.4 Unreading

Media reflexiveness is critically relevant for a deeper understanding of codex and computer as semiotic machines. Johanna Drucker, Gary Frost, Garrett Stewart, and others have shown how certain kinds of material interventions in books illuminate the particular nature of the medium as concept and object. Talan Memmott (2011) discusses the rhetorical and poetic features of electronic works in terms of signifying strategies embodied in particular uses of multimodality, procedurality, interaction, and interface design. His analysis of hypermedia contains a critical model that goes beyond the literary and looks into their "extreme reflexivity" (16) to investigate the nature of reading and writing in digital media. Writing about algorithmic criticism as a reading machine, Stephen Ramsay describes programming as an "enactment of a critical reading strategy" (2011, xi). N. Katherine Hayles's (2008, 2012) analyses of electronic literature for understanding general processes of intermediation, John Cayley's (2011, 2012) programmatological writing as linguistic and poetic investigation, and David Jhave Johnston's (2011) philosophical exploration of textual-audio-visual-interactive-animated forms are equally concerned with media reflexiveness as embodied critique.

Algorithms, scripts, animations, interfaces, visual texts, book structures, and other material forms simulate perceptual and reading acts in ways that are useful for a poetic and cognitive understanding of the performance of reading. Most of the works examined in this book can be described as aesthetic explorations of the medium through signifying strategies that give interactors a material awareness of the dynamic nature of the textual field. Specific formal operations induce self-reflexive reading acts that draw readers' attention to both the materiality of the communication process and the function of reading in the constitution of the signifying field. Self-reference to the work's program also works as a poetic device for activating the expressive presence of material codes as they interact with the semantic and discursive layers of the work. Aesthetic interventions on the reflexive layers of codex and electronic codes provide a critical opportunity for examining the signifying dynamics of both media and their relations. If material simulations of reading motions are embodied and enacted through expressive uses of formal devices in codices and computers, we can use those aesthetic simulations for a better understanding of reading in the production of meaning.

The selected works contain embodiments of reading in which literary objects are self-reflexively constituted by interactions between their material features and the physiological and interpretative processing of those features. Semantic and interpretative spaces are sustained by performative interventions in which language and discourse are experienced as material forms coinstantiated by the reading motions that make them readable. It is the formal enactment of those feedback loops that I have called *scripting reading motions*. Since readers experience their actions as constitutive of the field of meaning, I have suggested that the act of reading is written back into the works. A critical exploration of various kinds of mechanisms at play in those codex and computer loops opens them up to a new poetics of reading.

The rhetorical and poetical exploration of reading as a motion between signs has to be considered also in relation to conventions and practices associated with specific genres and forms. Large-scale technological changes—like those that introduced print textuality in a world of manuscript texts and digital textuality in a world of print texts—destabilize conventional forms and genres. The ensuing processes of remediation result in hybrid forms and genres that recombine features of old media with features of new media, transforming writing and reading practices. Because the production of forms in a new medium resignifies their constitutive elements, such differential functions are explicitly foregrounded and aesthetically investigated, particularly in transitional moments. Interactivity and reader participation have become dominant tropes for describing the writing and reading of electronic literature, but explicit appeals to readers' interventions in textual fields have had a continuing presence in print literature.

Literature can be defined as a mode of exploring and experiencing the potentiality of language and other nonlinguistic codes in the invention of the human. Computers have heightened our perception of literature as an exploration of the potentiality contained in signifiers. Considered as automaton, literature could be defined as a symbolic machine for describing and inventing the human through the processing of signifiers. Socially produced signifiers are permutated in a continuing attempt at renewing our sense of the world and our sense of self as historical and semiotic constructs. Algorithmic operativity has opened up natural language, and other visual and sound systems of signs, to a growing array of recursive, permutational, and stochastic processes. Through automatic processing, the proliferative nature of meaning becomes a material evidence of contemporary digital culture.

Computers have intensified the cyborg and prosthetic nature of both writing and reading. Semiotic possibilities become the unanticipated result of intermediations between humans and computing machines and between different media. The programming layer of contemporary software culture has established open-ended recombination of the modularities of digital media as a general method for artistic production. Used as critical and rhetorical tools, algorithms and databases have become a dominant symbolic form in artistic and cultural production. Hermeneutic possibilities are determined not only by historically situated interpretative communities, but also by computer-reader interactions designed to generate new kinds of unanticipated interpretative feedback loops and new social networks created and maintained by computer-mediated communication.

Reading is one of the technologies of the modern self, through which individuals improvise their subjectivity in symbolic exchanges. In the contemporary media environment, acts of reading involve the cognitive processing of both abstract writing systems and concrete audiovisual forms. Cognitive and affective responses to reading can be studied also in relation to retroactions among linguistic, bibliographic, electronic, and multimodal codes. Those retroactions create a performative cognitive system that links reading movements and semantic processing to the material, discursive, and cultural patterns encoded in the works. The motions of the reading self (eye, head, hands, fingers, voice, mind) in the processing of signs, codes, images, and sounds become a referential layer of the textual semantics.

Permutational, randomized, constellated, and multimodal forms were spaces for investigation in twentieth-century experimental practices long before the generalized use of digital computers. Electronic remediation of experimental intermedia works makes clear the presence of those structures of potentiality in nondigital works. There is an affinity between constellated visual texts as a field of possible paths, on the one hand, and the electronic versions of those print texts as an instantiation of choices that actualize some of those possibilities, on the other. The electronic version becomes a formal embodiment of a reading action on the printed constellation—a reading course or path. This remediation in turn creates a new sign field available for further interpretative acts.

Digital re-creations simulate the complex topologies of the reading spaces constituted by the interaction between graphicality and reading motions. Reading choreographs the motions of writing according to particular scripts and behaviors, calling attention to the performativity of signification. Digital recoding translates possibilities encoded in print layout while creating its own self-reflexive tropes. Added layers of self-reflexivity may extend self-reference from the visuality of the topographic print layout to the digitality of the new medium itself. The visual constellation shows itself not as a transparent sign but as a material form that has to be experienced as a reading code, that is, as a script or instruction for reading, before any meaning can be produced.

The foregrounding of reading codes in graphical surfaces becomes clear when they are treated as storyboards for digital animation. Multicursal visual constellations are translated into animation sequences as if they were scripts or sets of instructions for reading the work. Animation actualizes one or more of the potential trajectories and timed sequences contained within its spatialized field of signifiers. The text, which is semidetermined in the sense that its reading syntax admits of several possibilities, is partially coproduced by the way a given reading motion is enacted. This is one of the self-reflexive strategies for scripting reading in books and computers: formal operations are materially coded so as to make readers aware of the ongoing physical, physiological, and cultural processing of signs as a determining component in the production of meaning.

Certain kinds of operations require readers to engage with particular modes of bibliographic and computational inscription. Through such aesthetic engagements, readers experience how meaning is the effect of a particular embodiment or instantiation of form in a given material medium. This self-reflexive instantiation of form heightens the physical and conceptual experience of the mediated nature of meaning (the fact that meaning is produced by symbolic systems based on material differences that are open to reading performances). A complex system of differences—

linguistic, visual, aural, kinetic—allows the emergence of form. The self interacts with these material forms by means of self-conscious sensory and perceptual actions that translate into conceptual and discursive relations.

Writing and reading become codependent and intertwined as an entangled field maintained by the relations between the generative presence or absence of signs and their interpretative substitution. While self-reflexivity has often been analyzed in terms of the writing act, the rhetorical and poetical self-referential enactment and simulation of reading have received less critical attention. Self-reflexivity has been analyzed here as a conscious reading performance of the medium in which print and computer works inscribe or simulate the embodied performance of reading in their semiotic field. I have shown how those works use self-descriptive and metareading strategies to illuminate the physical and conceptual processing of inscriptional forms through reading motions.

Writing can be scripted as a print display of constellated signs—in visual texts—or as a computer program that performs iterative operations on a string of data—in algorithmic works whose display is structured on the basis of topographic patterns and generative syntactic permutations. In both scripts, it is the very motion of linking signs that is being enacted on the page or on the screen. This textual presence of reading interferes with the transparency of signifiers and denaturalizes the production of meaning and discourse. Thus *scripting* means writing as a specific representation and as a set of instructions for performing specific reading tasks. When translated into computer language, *scripting* also means writing the lines of code required for automating those representational and performative instructions.

Print and electronic works share a self-reflexive layer of meaning that is useful for understanding readers' interactions with a given sign field. Through analysis of this layer, we can point to feedback loops involved in scripting and reading acts in each of these media. These loops can be materially displayed in the work's surface and can be conceptually realized through semantic operations, but they are also bodily enacted through eye, hand, and body motions and through brain processing. The performance of reading is an embodied intervention in the sign field of the works, through which reading acts become materially and conceptually scripted in writing spaces. I have analyzed this entanglement between reading acts and material codes in two related domains: by looking at the instantiation of bookness and graphicality as materialized by a given codex dynamics and layout and by examining the foregrounding of digitality through specific uses of programming codes and user interfaces.

Legibility emerges from formal differences between signs executed by linguistic, bibliographic, and computational programs. Semiotic traces are reperformed by particular strategies of reading, which feed back onto the textual display and thus script themselves in the material field of the work. As a result, textual materiality and reading interventions become intertwined in the configured display and perceived form of these programmed and codex works. Reading motions activate the legible with the eventuality of their own performance, which has been scripted in bibliographic and digital codes in ways that point to the situated and emergent nature of meaning. It has been my purpose to show the critical relevance of self-reflexive and procedural functions in codex and computer codes, including their intermediations from paper to screen and from screen to paper, for understanding the complexities of reading as an embodied action that responds to material programs.

Notes

Chapter 1

1. Garrett Stewart (2006) has analyzed paintings of readers as a genre of its own, giving particular attention to the face of readers as sites where the affective, moral, and cognitive presence of reading is expressed.

2. This installation is part of the ongoing *The Readers Project* (2009–present) by John Cayley and Daniel Howe.

3. Eye-tracking techniques have been used to study interactions between modes of reading and viewing in nonlinear visual texts. The processing of textual syntax and visual pattern activates eye-movement patterns that mix reading eye movements with scene perception eye movements. New semantic relations result from these interactions. Reading patterns also confirm that constelled texts generate scanning motions across various trajectories and that fixations and saccades also target blank spaces. See, for instance, the research project directed by Andrew Michael Roberts (University of Dundee), "Poetry beyond Text: Vision, Text and Cognition" (2009–2011). Available at http://www.poetrybeyondtext.org.

4. Graphic experiments with textual surfaces have become a major narrative device in postmodernist novels, performing both mimetic and reflexive functions. See, for example, Glyn White's (2005) study of novels by Samuel Beckett, B. S. Johnson, Christine Brooke-Rose, and Alasdair Gray.

5. There are now several printed editions of this work: 1970 (Tetrad Press, limited edition), 1980 (Thames & Hudson, first edition), 1987 (first revised edition), 1997 (third edition), 2005 (fourth edition), and 2012 (fifth edition). Although many pages have been redesigned for each of the editions, I use facsimile reproductions from the earlier Tetrad Press edition. Each redesigned edition introduces many new references and extra layers of bibliographic self-reference by establishing its visual and verbal variations not just in relation to the source novel but also to Tom Phillips's earlier versions of the same treated pages. A version for iPad (*A Humument: A Treated Victorian Novel with Oracle Feature*) was published in 2010, with thirty-nine new previously unpublished pages. This version was updated in 2011, with further unpublished pages. In the fifth printed edition (*A Humument: A Treated Victorian*

Novel, London: Thames & Hudson, 2012), more than eighty pages have been redesigned.

6. See also figure 4.10 in chapter 4.

7. http://nickm.com/poems/ppg256.html. Version 'ppg256–1' (Nick Montfort, April 13, 2009) reads:

'perl -le 'sub b{@_=unpack"(A2)*,"pop;$_(rand@_)}sub w{"

".b("cococacamamadebapabohamolaburatamihopodito").b("estsnslldsckregspssted bsnelengkemsattewsntarshnknd")}{$_="\n\nthe."w."\n";$_=w." ".b("attoonnoof"). w if$l;s/(au)(ae)/a/;print;$l=0if$l++>rand 9;sleep 1;redo}#Rev2' .

8. For a chronological list of her works, see http://www.hotkey.net.au/~netwurker/free.htm.

THE CON.SOUL.E (2000),). "_(adDressed in a Skin C.ode_" (2003)

http://www.hotkey.net.au/~netwurker/xor/xor.html,   http://www.hotkey.net.au/~netwurker/bw. See also: http://knott404.blogspot.pt/ (2007–present) and http://netwurker.livejournal.com/ (2003–present).

9. Here is the author's full description of these works: "Elle est le 3° poème de la série des "petits poèmes à lecture inconfortable." Après le poème à raboter (le rabot poète, présenté à e-poetry 2007), le poème à brosser (brosse à dépoussiérer la fiction), voila le poème à touiller. *Les amis sur le seuil* sont ces rencontres que l'on fait et avec lesquelles on entretient des rapports qui ne sont pas vraiment familiers mais qui ne sont déjà plus anodins. *Les amis sur le seuil* sont donc dans cet entre-deux de la rencontre que constitue le seuil: lieu pas vraiment dehors mais pas non plus dedans, lieu d'échange sur lequel on ne reste pas, lieu de passage s'il en est, lieu indécis. Le lecteur est invité, par des procédés de touillage, à expérimenter cette indécision, ou plutôt cette tension entre le suggéré, le présent voilé et l'instant de communication dévoilée" (Bootz 2011).

Chapter 2

1. A digital facsimile (accompanied by the author's statement and detailed editorial description) is available at *Artists' Books Online*: http://www.artistsbooksonline.org/works/atoz.xml.

2. Cf. Drucker, "Critical Discussion" and "Detailed Analysis," in http://www.artistsbooksonline.org/works/wmfl/edition1.xml.

3. "The parameters of the codex form can be defined by stretching its basic elements to two extreme poles. At one extreme, the codex is a set of uniformly sized pages bound in a fixed and intentional sequence. At the other extreme it is an accumulation of non-uniform pages in an unintentional and unfixed sequence which is barely recognizable as a book. I suggest that both of these are book forms—that work equally with the idea of the codex as their point of reference—conceptually speaking" (Drucker 1995, 123).

Chapter 3

1. *Artéria,* volume 8, 2003–2004, http://www.arteria8.net. See, for instance, visual works by the following authors that were remade for computer screen: Aldo Fortes ("Cage" 1970s), Augusto de Campos ("Pérolas para Cummings," 1994–1995), Edgard Braga ("Cartoonpoem: poema da infância," 1974), Décio Pignatari ("Invenção 5: Cri\$to é a solução," 1967), Erthos Albino de Souza ("Volat irrevocabile tempus," 1988), Haroldo de Campos (Sapho, "Em torno a Selene esplêndida," 7-6th C B.C./1960s), José Lino Grünewald ("Forma," 1962), Julio Plaza ("TV," 1994), Lenora de Barros ("See Me," 1993), Paulo Miranda ("La vie en," 1977), Pedro Xisto ("Epitalâmio II," 1964), Ronaldo Azeredo ("Céu Mar," 1978), Villari Herrmann ("BR," 1974), and Zéluiz Valero ("." 1970s). Authors included in this issue are Alckmar Luiz dos Santos, Aldo Fortes, André Vallias, Arnaldo Antunes, Augusto de Campos, Avelino de Araújo, Brócolis VHS, Décio Pignatari, Diniz Júnior, Edgard Braga, Elson Fróes, Erthos Albino de Souza, Fábio Oliveira Nunes, Gilberto Prado, Glauco Mattoso, Haroldo de Campos, João Bandeira, Jorge Luiz Antônio, José Lino Grünewald, Josiel Vieira, Julio Mendonça, Julio Plaza, Lenora de Barros, Letícia Tonon, Lucio Agra, Omar Guedes, Omar Khouri, Paulo Miranda, Pedro Xisto, Peter de Brito, R2, Regina Célia Pinto, Regina Silveira, Roland de Azeredo Campos, Ronaldo Azeredo, Silvia Laurentiz, Sonia Fontanezi, Tadeu Jungle, Tiago Lafer, Vanderlei Lopes, Villari Herrmann, Walter Silveira, and Zéluiz Valero.

2. A research project at the University Fernando Pessoa in Portugal has been working to produce an archive of Portuguese experimental poetry. The first stage of this project (2005–2008), which digitized materials from the 1960s, is available online at http://www.po-ex.net. This site also includes digital re-creations of visual and concrete poems. The second stage of the project (PO-EX'70-80—A Digital Archive of Portuguese Experimental Literature: From Visual and Sound Poetry to Cybernetic Literature), scheduled for online publication in 2013, will expand this electronic archive to include the experimental literature of the 1970s and 1980s.

3. A special issue of the online journal *Errática* was published on the occasion of the eightieth birthday of Augusto de Campos (February 14, 2011): http://www.erratica.com.br/opus/104/index.html. This issue includes the following authors: Carlos Adriano, Ricardo Aleixo, Arnaldo Antunes, Lenora de Barros, Marcelo Brissac, Age de Carvalho, Adriana Calcanhotto, Cid Campos, Lica Cecato, Antonio Cicero, Nicole Cristofalo, André Dick, Eucanaã Ferraz, Jerusa Pires Ferreira, Francisco K, Omar Khouri, Fernando Laszlo, Guilherme Mansur, Tony de Marco, Charles A. Perrone, Neuza Pinheiro, Marcelo Tápia, André Vallias, and Caetano Veloso.

4. For an example of this complex layering of cultural and historical references in minimalist texts, see a postdeconstructionist reading of Gomringer's poem "Silencio" by McCaffery (2013).

5. On his visual and typographic translations, see Portela (2003).

6. *Signagens (Signages)* was produced between 1986 and 1989 with the technical collaboration of the Open University in Lisbon. It includes the following video

poems: "As fontes do texto" (The fountains of the text)—8'30"; "Sete setas" (Seven arrows)—1'29"; "Sede fuga" (Thirst escape)—1'23"; "Rede teia labirinto" (Net web labyrinth)—2'12"; "Vibrações" (Vibrations)—4'13"; "Um furo no universo" (A hole in the universe)—2'; "Come fome" (Eat hunger)—1'44"; "Hipnotismo" (Hypnosis)—33"; "Ponto sinal" (Period sign)—3'55"; "Polígono pessoal" (Personal polygon)—8'15"; "O soneto, oh!" (The sonnet, oh!)—5'34"; "Objectotem" (Objectotem)—5'37"; "Escrita da memória" (Memory's writing)—2'14"; "Concretas abstrações" (Concrete abstractions)—1'30"; "Dialuzando" (Daylighting)—5'; "Poética dos meios" (Poetics of the media)—9'50"; "Infografitos" (Infograffiti)—5'24"; "Ideovideo" (Ideovideo)—7'50"; "Metade de nada" (Half of nothing)—5'55"; "Do outro lado" (On the other side)—5'; and "Vibrações digitais dum protocubo" (Digital vibrations of a protocube)—5'20." Other video and computer poems by Melo e Castro: "Roda lume" (Wheel light) (1968–1969, 2' 43," remade in 1986); "Vogais, as cores radiantes" (Vowels, the radiant colors) (1986, 3' 10," original soundtrack by TELECTU); "Ian Palach" (Ian Palach)—5'40"; "Lixo super lixo" (Junk superjunk)—6'; and "Sonhos de geometria" (Dreams of geometry) (1993, 30', original soundtrack by TELECTU). All translations of original titles by E. M. de Melo e Castro. See E. M. de Melo e Castro (1996), http://www.ociocriativo.com.br/guests/meloecastro/texto5 .htm.

Chapter 4

1. For an extended study of L.A.I.R.E., see Reis (2005).

2. "La programmation est un nouveau matériau sculpté et modelé par les artistes. Dans la visée de Transitoire Observable, ce modelage passe par un travail sur la forme. Il s'agit d'une approche formaliste de cette dualité algorithmes/processus qui constitue la programmation. Ce qui est visé dans cette approche n'est ni le programme en tant qu'ensemble de lignes de textes ou de code bien formé, ni l'événement produit à l'exécution en tant que réalité audiovisuelle, mais le rapport qu'entretien cet événement avec, d'une part, la réalité algorithmique du code, et d'autre part la pragmatique de la lecture" (Bootz 2004).

3. For his defense of a "general art of programming," see Bootz (2005b). See also Glazier (2002, 2006), Baldwin (2003), Andrews (2004b), Cayley (2006), Peterson (2006), Bootz (2010), Memmott (2011), and Johnston (2011).

4. "L'œuvre est un système dont la lecture est une des fonctions internes," in "L'art des formes programmées," in *Alire 12*, February 2004, http://motsvoir.free.fr/ alire_12_edito.htm, section 4. Although this concept can be related to Aspen Aarseth's definiton of *cybertext* (1997), and N. Katherine Hayles's definition of *technotext* (2002), emphasis is placed on the enactment of reading performativity as an explicit function of textual encoding and execution in algorithmic procedural works.

5. For those interested in a selection of works in French, the best online sources are the archives of *Mots-Voir*, http://motsvoir.free.fr (2000–2004); *Transitoire Observable*, http://transitoireobs.free.fr/to (2003–2007); *Web Dock(s)*, an archive of digital

poetry published by the journal *Dock(s)* http://www.akenaton-docks.fr/DOCKS -datas_f/collect_f/generiqueanim.html (1999–2011); and *NT2 Nouvelles technologies nouvelles textualités*, a research lab and database of hypermedia works established in 2005 at the University of Quebec, Montreal, http://nt2.uqam.ca. One section of *Web Dock(s)*, "Poesie animé par ordinateur" (Computer poetry), online since 1999, collects works published between 1995 and 2011 (not all hyperlinks remain active). It includes many electronic works from Europe and America, and particularly a significant body of works by French artists or artists based in France: Julien d'Abrigeon, Roland Baladi, Ambroise Barras, Philippe Bootz, Patrick-Henri Burgaud, Gilles Boussois, Roland Caignard, Philippe Castellini, Alexandre Gherban, Roberto Gilli, Pascale Gustin, Roland Mannarini, Lorenzo Menoud, Jean Monod, Angel Rened, Gilles Richard, Wilfrid Rouff, Eric Sadin, Nicole Stenger, Eric Serandour, Julio Soto, Jean Torregrosa, Bernard Vanmalle, and Marc Veyrat. A French-language online journal, *BleuOrange: Revue de littérature hypermédiatique*, directed by Bertrand Gervais and published by the Université du Québec à Montréal since 2008, also contains recent work in French (http://revuebleuorange.org).

6. Half of the screen performs the commands "Listing Source Code + CR" (CRISP or CRACK), which reproduces and multiplies the source code on the screen, while the other is responding to the command "Split Code," which slices the source code. According to Antero de Alda, it is sufficient that the reader recognizes that what is being seen "on this side" of the screen is "a more or less faithful copy" of what the poem hides "on the other side" (e-mail message from the author, my translation).

7. Lluís Calvo and Pedro Valdeolmillos are the editors of *Epimone* (2004), an online anthology that includes works by authors working in Spanish, Catalan, Portuguese, and French, among other languages. The Web site Epimone includes thirty-four works by Spanish, French, Brazilian, Italian, Argentinian, German, Greek, North American, and Australian authors: Julien d'Abrigeon, Antoni Albalat, J. M. Calleja, Augusto de Campos, Paulo Carvajal, Steve Duffy, Domiziana Giordano, Carles Hac Mor, Dorothee Lang, Deena Larsen, Jason Nelson, Daniel Ruiz, Reiner Strasser, Ainize Txopitea, Ana María Uribe, André Vallias, Esther Xargay, and Komninos Zervos. *Epimone*, a flash Web site project (introduced in Catalan, Spanish, and English), describes itself as "a place where poetry and new media blend together" (http://www.epimone.net).

8. Raul Brandão published three versions of his novel: in 1917, 1921, and 1926.

9. *Poemário*, at http://telepoesis.net/poemario.

10. Tapor Tools and Web Frequency Indexer were used for lexical and statistical analysis. For word processing, Open Office was used. The lexicon was indexed in XML-tagged lists. Animations and hypermedia effects were obtained by using Flash. Languages used include ActionScript for text generation; XML for marking the lists of words and sounds; PHP for sending and recording text on the server; and Python for creating RSS feeds with the poem. The corpus contains 450 poems collected from ten Brazilian and Portuguese Web sites. Rui Torres (2006b) lists the following applications: "Macromedia Flash (Actionscript), OpenOffice Tools (for editing text,

creating lists and encoding XML), Web Frequency Indexer (for the determination of occurrences), Adobe Audition (for treatment of all audio) QuickTime VR, Vue and Cinema 4D (for 3D and panoramic views); Macromedia Authorware (for final integration of Flash and 3D)'. He also emphasizes the collaborative nature of the final work: 'Rui Torres (design, creation and development; programming in Actionscript, XML, animation, sound design), Nuno Filipe Ferreira, Filipe Valpereiro, and Jared Tarbel (Actionscript), Nuno M. Cardoso (voice); Luis Aly (sound), and Luis Carlos Petry (3D programming and topophilosophical environment)." A literary analysis of his works implies the consideration of programming languages and commercial applications as elements of their formal and generic description. It also requires a consideration of the division of work and collaboration that often goes into the creation of hypermedia works.

11. *Mar de Sophia* uses the Brazilian translation of *Alice's Adventures in Wonderland* by Clélia Regina Ramos, Editorial Arara Azul, published online at http://virtualbooks.terra.com.br/freebook/infantis/alice_no_pais_das_maravilhas.htm.

12. For a discussion of code as writing, see Glazier (2002). See also Glazier (2006), Hayles (2005), Bootz (2006, 2010), Cayley (2006), Tisselli (2010), Memmott (2011), and Johnston (2011). For critical approaches to the study of networked digital literature, see Schreibman and Siemens (2008), Kirschenbaum (2008), Hayles (2008), Gutierrez et al. (2009), and Simanowski, Schäfer, and Gendolla (2010). For an introduction to the software studies approach see Fuller (2008), Manovich (2008), and Wardrip-Fruin (2009).

13. Christine Hume's poem has been published in *The Other Voices International Project*, vol. 23 (2005): http://www.othervoicespoetry.org/vol23/hume/nocturnal.htm. The fragment beginning "Nine stitches and liquid morphine cannot keep it closed" appeared also, in a slightly different version, under the title "Lunar Halo" in *Typo Magazine*, no. 6 (2005). http://www.typomag.com/issue06/hume.html.

Chapter 5

1. Reviews published in the second half of 2006 highlighted those two features: "Mark Z. Danielewski is out to drag the novel kicking and screaming into the world of twenty-first century entertainment. *House of Leaves*, his first novel did an admirable job of starting the task, but *Only Revolutions* takes even bigger steps. Danielewski makes full use of the technology that has helped to create video games and surreal special effects in movies to create a complicated all-text reading experience. Thanks to the gift of layout programs such as the Adobe Creative Suite, with which this novel was created, the text is all over the page in a rainbow of colors. . . . Oh, it's a crazy-quilt mish-mash of several kitchen sinks and more than a few collages. But get down to the level of language, engage the novel as a reading experience, and there's no doubt that Danielewski is accomplishing precisely what he intends with a level of style that has literally never before been seen or even possible." Rick Kleffel, "*Only Revolutions,*" Bookotron.com, December 9, 2006, http://trashotron.

com/agony/reviews/2006-old/danielewski-only_re.htm. A similar assessment and hyperbolic tone can be found in reviews published in *Kirkus Reviews* (July 15, 2006), *Publishers Weekly* (August 28, 2006), *Los Angeles Times* (September 3, 2006), *Guardian* (September 30, 2006), *San Francisco Chronicle* (October 20, 2006), *Washington Post Book World* (October 22, 2006), *New York Times Book Review* (November 5, 2006), and *Bookmarks Magazine* (January–February 2007). See, for instance, Deborah Vankin, "Psychedelic Love," *Los Angeles Times*, September 3, 2006, R 9; Steven Poole, "O How Clever," *Guardian*, September 30, 2006, http://www.guardian.co.uk/books/2006/ sep/30/featuresreviews.guardianreview16; Mark S. Luce, "Journey through Time Turns Novel Upside Down. Literally," *San Francisco Chronicle,* October 20, 2006, http://www.sfgate.com/books/article/REVIEW-Journey-through-time-turns-novel -upside-2486175.php; Steven Moore, "Spin Cycle," *Washington Post Book World*, October 22, 2006, 13; and Troy Patterson, "Complete 360," *New York Times,* November 5, 2006. http://www.nytimes.com/2006/11/05/books/review/Patterson.t.html? _r=0. Since I finished this chapter in October 2009, several new studies have appeared: Assayag (2009), Leonard (2010), Aardse (2011), and Hayles (2012).

2. I use *ergodic* and *cybertextual* in the sense put forward by Espen Aarseth (1997), which implies both self-referential operations within the medium and readers' interventions in the construction of the semiotic field: "The concept of cybertext focuses on the mechanical organization of the text, by positing the intricacies of the medium as an integral part of the literary exchange. However, it also centers attention on the consumer, or user, of the text, as a more integrated figure than even reader-response theorists would claim. The performance of their reader takes place all in his head, while the user of cybertext also performs in an extranoematic sense" (1).

3. *House of Leaves* as both a thematization and performance of ancient and modern figures of the labyrinth has been analyzed by Cox (2006) and Hamilton (2008). Graulund (2006) examines its rhizomatic structure as a function of textual and paratextual relations.

4. For an analysis of this technotextual dimension in *House of Leaves*, see Hayles 2002, 2008). Mark B. N. Hansen (2004) reads *House Leaves* through the concept of digital topography, suggesting a retroactive effect of the computer on the printed page. These ideas are further developed by Pressman (2006) and Chanen (2007). Both read the typographical composition in *House of Leaves* as a print emulation of electronic text networks. We should bear in mind, however, that Danielewski has always stressed the freedoms of the paper-and-pencil medium and the three-dimensionality of the book as opposed to the two-dimensionality of the screen (see the interview by McCaffery and Gregory 2003). Although deeply dependent on digital tools, *House of Leaves* and *Only Revolutions* are ultimately concerned with the multidimensionality and the dynamics of the codex form as a complex inscriptional and topological space.

5. In mathematics, the symbol ∞ denotes an infinite limit beyond any particular assigned value. It was introduced by John Wallis in *De sectionibus conicis* (1655).

6. This pattern is broken only on the pages in which the history column has been left blank—for dates between "Jan 18 2006" and "Jan 19 2063" (pages H285–H360). In each of these seventy-six pages, there are only three character strings (those corresponding to date headings).

7. When quoting or referring to pages and columns, I use the following conventions: H or S followed by a page number—for example, H1 refers to page 1 by Hailey, and S1 refers to page 1 by Sam; two forward slashes (//) indicate reversed pages on the same surface—for example, S1//H360; one forward slash (/) indicates reversed symmetrical pages at opposite ends of the codex—for example, H1/S1; a sequence of pages is denoted as, for example, S1–S8; and the letter *h* before S or H refers to their respective history column—for example, hH1 or hS360.

8. Events for historical dates between "Jan 18 2006" and "Jan 19 2063" (pp. hH28 –hH360) were left blank, with the exception of date headers. Out of a possible total number of 90-character strings for the history column in each of those hH pages, only 3 strings—for date headers—have been filled in. In those 76 pages, there will be a total of 228 strings (= 76 × 3) instead of the expected 6,840 (= 76 × 90). Therefore this column has 6,612 fewer strings (= 6,840 – 228) than its equivalent in Sam's pages.

9. In this table, numbers correspond to chapters, dark gray cells represent Sam's chapters (reading in one direction), and light gray cells represent Hailey's (reading in reverse).

10. Here is one mathematical representation of its topology:
"One way to represent the Möbius strip as a subset of R^3 is using the parameterization:

$$x(u,v) = \left(1 + \tfrac{1}{2}v\cos\tfrac{1}{2}u\right)\cos u$$

$$y(u,v) = \left(1 + \tfrac{1}{2}v\cos\tfrac{1}{2}u\right)\sin u$$

$$z(u,v) = \tfrac{1}{2}v\sin\tfrac{1}{2}u$$

where $0 \le u < 2\pi$ and $-1 \le v \le 1$. This creates a Möbius strip of width 1 whose center circle has radius 1, lies in the *xy*-plane and is centered at (0, 0, 0). The parameter u runs around the strip while v moves from one edge to the other." http://en.wikipedia.org/wiki/Möbius_strip.

11. Cf. Danielewski (2007, reels 1–5, Circle Round a Stone).

12. Because four of the sixteen circular and elliptical disks spread across the gutter, it is very difficult to give an accurate number of the words (strings of characters beginning with capitalized words) in all sets. I believe that there is a geometric and numerical pattern at this level too. This pattern associates the disks in groups of two (one circular + one elliptical section), and the sum of each of these pairs generates numbers that repeat certain digits—for example, *Eye* lexicon (elliptical, 146) + *Color* lexicon (circular, 42) = 188, and *Architecture* lexicon (elliptical, 111) + *Into* lexicon (circular, 33) = 144. The total number of character strings is approximately eighteen hundred, which becomes another symbol for the circle (0) and the Möbius strip (8), for singleness (1) and union (0), for zero (0) and infinity (∞), for nothingness (0) and endlessness (0, ∞).

13. Numerical intervals between consecutive dates can be used as a matrix for generating palindromic and other symmetrical sequences of numbers—either digit by digit (e.g., 11, 33, 44, . . . ,1,221, 2,112, 2,332, 3,223 . . .), or in groups of two, three, or more digits. Symmetries are obtained by reading left to right and right to left; by reading groups of two, three, four, or more digits as recursive units within a larger sequence; and by taking the center of the sequence as the axis for recursion (e.g., 911,119/119,911, 12,101,012/10,121,210, 44,474,744/47,444,447 . . .). I took the opening (left + right pages) as the minimum unit of reading. Each opening has four calendar dates. This lets you generate four numbers (two in the numerical intervals of dates corresponding to Hailey's narrative and two in the numerical intervals corresponding to Sam's). By treating numbers in this way, we have four different reading positions (A + B/ C + D), an analog of the four parts of the circle that structures the arrangement of columns and character strings on each page. The only two exceptions are the first and last pages of each narrative (hH1//hS360 and hS1//hH360). In this case, only two positions were considered (A + B). The number of calendar days between consecutive dates grows larger as one moves from hH1 to hH360 and smaller as one moves from hS1 to hS360. When those co-occurring four numbers are taken together, they can be read in three different ways (horizontally, vertically, and diagonally) and in two directions each way. If combined according to symmetrical directions of reading, the iteration of these numbers can generate new numbers that have axes of symmetry and recursive sequences, many of which are palindromic. When grouped into units of two or three digits, all numbers generated by this iteration retain their identity when read from left to right or from right to left. The permutational principle implies changing the relative position of the digits (left + right / right + left). This suggests a homology with the double direction in the reading of the book. This homology is also present in the idea of union between two numerical units (as happens with the two individual characters in the novel). This basic permutation of elements also points to syntax (numerical, alphabetical, discursive, and bibliographic) as the fundamental mechanism for producing meaning, a mechanism that works by endless repetition and variation of its units. Being a matrix of four units, with a double orientation, these numbers also emulate the four bases of the genetic code (C, G, T, A).

14. Besides numerical palindromes, we find several anagrammatic, homophonic, and homographic relations, placed at equivalent relative positions on symmetrical pages. Some of the most frequent are *feer* and *free*; *chear* and *cheer*; *US* and *U.S.*; *allone*, *allways*, *allmost*, *allmighty*, and *allready*.

15. "Nov 22 1863," for instance, was chosen so that it was one hundred years before "Nov 22 1963" rather than for the first specific event listed in the column, which happened in Nov 23 1863—a message signed by North Carolina governor Zebulon Baird Vance (1830–1894), from which Danielewski has extracted the quote: "—*Abolition of slavery, confiscation of property, and territorial vassalage!*" (hH1).

16. Insofar as some of the events included in the history column were suggested by Danielewski's readers in an electronic forum, there is a level of integration of historical facts that assimilates different perspectives and different national histories under the general framework of military violence and political revolution. The collective import of the chronology reflects this process of consultation to a certain extent.

17. http://www.onlyrevolutions.com.

Chapter 6

1. In 2006, Andrews and Niemi produced an emulated version in the original code, as well as JavaScript, QuickTime, and HyperCard versions. Available at http://www.vispo.com/bp/index.htm.

2. "Textual Instrument" as defined by the *Electronic Literature Collection*, vol. 2 (2010): "A work written and coded in such a way that it is capable, by analogy with a musical instrument, of playing numerous compositions. The reader is invited to become an expert player of the piece, for skill at manipulating it, above and beyond familiarity with how its interface works, yields reading and viewing rewards. A closely related idea is that of the instrumental text, where an interface allows manipulations of a particular piece of writing in an interesting way." See http://collection.eliterature.org/2/extra/keywords.html.

3. http://vispo.com/arteroids/onarteroids.htm. From the *Wikipedia* entry: "*Asteroids* is a video arcade game released in 1979 by Atari Inc. It was one of the most popular and influential games of the Golden Age of Arcade Games. *Asteroids* uses vector graphics and a two-dimensional view that wraps around in both screen axes. The player controls a spaceship in an asteroid field which is periodically traversed by flying saucers. The object of the game is to shoot and destroy asteroids and saucers while not colliding with either, or being hit by the saucers' counter-fire." http://en.wikipedia.org/wiki/Asteroids_(video_game).

4. http://www.vispo.com/nio/index.htm. This work is also published in the *Electronic Literature Collection*, vol. 1 (2006): http://collection.eliterature.org/1/works/andrews__nio.html. "*Nio* is a collection of sound loops which can be combined at will by the user. Its 16 sound loops are represented with 16 letters or icons arranged in a circle. If you click them, you activate the sound belonging to it. An animation or composition of the icons involved is to be seen in the middle of the circle while music plays. The sounds, which all have the same length, have been recorded with Cakewalk and edited in Sound Forge. The animated images are made in Flash. The underlying program is written in Lingo and functions as an engine/player which synchronizes the various layers of sound sequences and animations" (Simanowski 2002, § 3, para. 2).

5. Jim Andrews: "One of the things about *Nio* is that it can deal with layers of rhythmic music. So you can take songs and chop them up into loops (even better if you have different recordings of the vocals, drums, etc) and then allow people to

rearrange the music arbitrarily or with constraints. And you can associate one or more animations (which themselves may be interactive) with each of the pieces of the song, so that you end up with a very different sort of music video for the Web than we have seen so far and perhaps a different song than you started out with. Very interactive and engagingly compositional both sonically and visually, hopefully" (Andrews 2001b).

6. See James (2009). This doctoral abstract addresses the accumulation of machine-generated language as a symptom of our increasingly computer-mediated and networked textual condition: "Turning originality in authorship upside down, writing post-person posits a vital new role of writer-teacher-researcher in promoting sustainable relationships between people and the automated information environments they inhabit. In particular, this study proposes a remedial approach to info-waste in networked systems of literate correspondence, using poetic inquiry to examine the contemporary problem of spam (unsolicited bulk and commercial email and net abuse), and to reframe this critical juridical-technical issue from a personal and literary perspective. Seen within the Western historical context of public postal systems and the rise of mass mail, the connection between modes of impersonal address in networked media and consumerist ideologies is theorized. Focusing on the troublesome immanence of disposability, informational excess is examined as a means of social inclusion and exclusion by tracing computer network spamming from the first bulk newsgroup postings to the current era of artificially intelligent robotic networks. Situated within an educational context of teaching and writing in the twenty-first century, an age post-personal discourse, this dissertation aims to enhance the critical pedagogical work of establishing diversity as fundamental to personal and social value systems with attention to how poetics can be applied to everyday digital literacies to increase language awareness, stimulate student creativity, and at the same time serve as a barometer of prevailing climate change in cyberspace." https://circle.ubc.ca/handle/2429/7449.

Chapter 7

1. See *Outside In: Ten Years of Software Art*, exhibition held at Collezione Maramotti, Reggio Emilia, March 8–May 3, 2009; and *Digital Paintings: John F. Simon, Jr.*, exhibition held at Louisiana Art and Science Museum, Baton Rouge, June 30–September 23, 2012. See also Ippolito (2002), Simon Jr. (2004), Caines (2009), Diacono (2009), and John F. Simon Jr.'s Web site: http://www.numeral.com.

2. Queneau: http://100000000000000poems.atspace.com. Wiki: http://fr.wikipedia.org/wiki/Écriture. Alice: http://www.inanimatealice.com. ELO: http://www.eliterature.org. Montfort: http://nickm.com. Narrative: http://www.utc.fr/~bouchard/recit/consultation/index.php.

References

Aardse, Kent Alexander. 2011. The Print Artifact in the Age of the Digital: The Writings of Mark Z. Danielewski and Steve Tomasula. Master's thesis, University of Lethbridge. http://hdl.handle.net/10133/3069.

Aarseth, Espen J. 1997. *Cybertext: Perspectives on Ergodic Literature*. Baltimore, MD: Johns Hopkins University Press.

Ablow, Rachel, ed. 2010. *The Feeling of Reading: Affective Experience and Victorian Literature*. Ann Arbor: University of Michigan Press.

Alda, Antero de. 2005. Poema em código. In *Scriptpoemas*. Script by Gerard Ferrandez (adapted). http://www.anterodealda.com/poema_codigo.htm.

Andrews, Jim. 1997. *Seattle Drift*. http://www.vispo.com/animisms/SeattleDrift.html.

Andrews, Jim. 1998. *Enigma n*. http://www.vispo.com/animisms/enigman/meaning.html.

Andrews, Jim. 1999–2009. *Stir/Fry/Texts*. http://vispo.com/StirFryTexts.

Andrews, Jim. 1999a. Architecture and the Literary. In *Stir/Fry/Texts*. http://vispo.com/StirFryTexts/architectureandtheliterary.html.

Andrews, Jim. 1999b. Stir Frys and Cut Ups. In *Stir/Fry/Texts*. http://www.vispo.com/StirFryTexts/text.html.

Andrews, Jim. 2001–2006. *Arteroids*: Version 1.0 (December 2001; "A Literary Computer Game for the Web"), Version 2.5 (June 23, 2003), Version 2.6 (February 15, 2004; "A Literary Computer Game for the Web—The Battle of Poetry Against Itself and the Forces of Dullness"), Version 3.11 (August 2006). http://vispo.com/arteroids/arteroids311.htm.

Andrews, Jim. 2001a. *Nio*. http://vispo.com/nio/index.htm.

Andrews, Jim. 2001b. Defib: Webartist Interview: Randy Adams with Jim Andrews about *Nio*. In *Turbulence: A Project of New Radio and Performing Arts, Inc.* http://www.turbulence.org/Works/Nio/interview.htm.

Andrews, Jim. 2001c. *Nio* and the Art of Interactive Audio for the Web. In *Turbulence: A Project of New Radio and Performing Arts, Inc.* http://www.turbulence.org/Works/Nio/The_Art_of_Interactive_Audio.htm.

Andrews, Jim. 2005. Games, Po, Art, Play, and Arteroids 2.03. http://vispo.com/arteroids/onarteroids.htm.

Andrews, Jim. 2004a. *On Lionel Kearns.* With text and film by Lionel Kearns. http://www.vispo.com/kearns/index.htm.

Andrews, Jim. 2004b. Language Explosion: Poetry and Entertainment in Arteroids 2.5. In *Gamers: Writers, Artists and Programmers on the Pleasures of Pixels*, edited by Shanna Compton, 213–224. Brooklyn, NY: Soft Skull Press.

Andrews, Jim, and Brian Lennon. 2000. Log. In *Stir/Fry/Texts.* http://www.vispo.com/StirFryTexts/BrianLennon.html.

Andrews, Jim, and Kedrick James. 2009. Kedrick James. In *Stir/Fry/Texts.* http://www.vispo.com/StirFryTexts/kedrick.htm.

Angel, Maria, and Anna Gibbs. 2009. On Moving and Being Moved: The Corporeality of Writing in Literary Fiction and New Media Art. In *Literature and Sensation*, edited by Anthony Uhlmann, Helen Groth, Paul Sheehan, and Stephen McLaren, 162–172. Cambridge: Cambridge Scholars Publishing.

Angel, Maria, and Anna Gibbs. 2010. Memory and Motion: The Body in Electronic Writing. In *Beyond the Screen: Transformations of Literary Structures, Interfaces and Genres*, edited by Jörgen Schäfer and Peter Gendolla, 123–136. Bielefeld: Transcript.

Aragão, António. 1964. Poemas Encontrados. Digital version by Rui Torres, Jared Tarbel, and Nuno Ferreira [2008]. http://po-ex.net/index.php?option=com_content&task=view&id=21&Itemid=35&.

Armstrong, Kate, and Michael Tippett. 2005. *Grafik Dynamo.* http://www.turbulence.org/Works/dynamo.

Assayag, Noam 2009. Mobilis in Mobile ou la poétique du livre à double-entrée: Only Revolutions de Mark Z. Danielewski à la lumière de l'oeuvre de Michel Butor. Master's thesis, Université de Paris III.

Baldwin, Sandy. 2003. Process Window: Code Work, Code Aesthetics, Code Poetics. In *Ergodic Poetry: A Special Section of the Cybertext Yearbook 2002: Publications of the Research Centre for Contemporary Culture*, edited by Loss Pequeño Glazier and John Cayley. Jyväskylä: University of Jyväskylä. http://cybertext.hum.jyu.fi/articles/109.pdf.

Baldwin, Sandy. 2009. Against Digital Poetics. *Electronic Book Review*, August 13. http://www.electronicbookreview.com/thread/electropoetics/absorbant.

Barbosa, Pedro 2001. O Computador como Máquina Semiótica. *Revista de Comunicação e Linguagens* 29: 303–327.

Barbosa, Pedro. 2006. Aspectos Quânticos do Cibertexto. *Cibertextualidades* 1: 11–42.

Bartscherer, Thomas, and Roderick Coover, eds. 2011. *Switching Codes: Thinking through Digital Technology in the Humanities and the Arts*. Chicago: University of Chicago Press.

Berry, David M., ed. 2012. *Understanding Digital Humanities*. Basingstoke, UK: Palgrave Macmillan.

Block, Friedrich W. 2010. How to Construct the Genre of Digital Poetry. In *Beyond the Screen: Transformations of Literary Structures, Interfaces and Genres*, edited by Jörgen Schäfer and Peter Gendolla, 391–402. Bielefeld: Transcript.

Block, Friedrich W., and Rui Torres. 2007. Poetic Transformations in(to) the Digital. In *Netzliteratur.net*. http://www.netzliteratur.net/block/poetic_transformations.html.

Blustein, James, David Rowe, and Ann-Barbara Graff. 2011. Making Sense in the Margins: A Field Study of Annotation? In *Research and Advanced Technology for Digital Libraries*, edited by Stefan Gradmann, Francesca Borri, Carlo Meghini, and Heiko Schuldt, 252–259. Heidelberg: Springer-Verlag.

Bolter, Jay David. 2001. *Writing Space: Computers, Hypertext, and the Remediation of Print*. Rev. ed. Mahwah, NJ: Erlbaum.

Bolter, Jay David, and Richard Grusin. 2000. *Remediation: Understanding New Media*. Cambridge, MA: MIT Press.

Bootz, Philippe. 2003. De Baudot à transitoire observable: Les approches sémiotiques en littérature numérique. http://transitoireobs.free.fr/to/html/novsemiotiq.htm.

Bootz, Philippe. 2004. L'art des formes programmées. In *Alire*, no. 12. http://motsvoir.free.fr/alire_12_edito.htm.

Bootz, Philippe. 2005a. Le rabot poète: Un petit poème à lecture inconfortable. http://epoetry.paragraphe.info/artists/oeuvres/bootz/rabot.htm.

Bootz, Philippe. 2005b. The Problematic of Form: Transitoire Observable: A Laboratory for Emergent Programmed Art. *Dichtung-digital*, no. 35. http://www.dichtung-digital.org/2005/1/Bootz/index.htm.

Bootz, Philippe. 2006. Digital Poetry: From Cybertext to Programmed Forms. *Leonardo Electronic Almanac* 14 (5–6). http://www.leoalmanac.org/journal/vol_14/lea_v14_n05-06/pbootz.html.

Bootz, Philippe. 2007. Petite brosse à dépoussiérer la fiction: Un petit poème à lecture inconfortable. http://www.bootz.fr/brosse/brosse.html.

Bootz, Philippe. 2010. The Unsatisfied Reading. In *Regards Croisés: Perspectives on Digital Literature*, edited by Philippe Bootz and Sandy Baldwin, 11–25. Morgantown: West Virginia University Press.

Bootz, Philippe, and Sandy Baldwin, eds. 2010. *Regards Croisés: Perspectives on Digital Literature*, Morgantown: West Virginia University Press.

Bootz, Philippe. 2011. Les amis sur le seuil: Un petit poème à lecture inconfortable. Musique de Marcel Frémiot. Laboratoire Musique et Informatique de Marseille. *BleuOrange: Revue de literature hypermédiatique*, no. 4. http://revuebleuorange.org/oeuvre/les-amis-sur-le-seuil.

Bootz, Philippe. 2012. Poésie numérique: Du cybertexte aux formes programées. *Revista de Estudos Literários* 2:186–202.

Bootz, Philippe, and Alexandra Saemmer. 2012. Semiotic Cross Analyses of Digital Poetry. Paper presented at "Electrifying Literature: Affordances and Constraints," Electronic Literature Organization Conference, June, 20–23, Morgantown, WV.

Borràs, Laura, Talan Memmott, Rita Raley, and Brian Stefans, eds. 2011. *Electronic Literature Collection*, Volume 2, Cambridge, MA: Electronic Literature Organization. http://collection.eliterature.org/2.

Bork, John. 2009. From Codework to Working Code: A Programmer's Approach to Digital Literacy. http://www.wcnet.org/~jrbork/ENC_6428_final/home.html.

Bouchardon, Serge, ed. 2007. *Un laboratoire de littératures: littérature numérique et internet*. Paris: Centre Georges Pompidou.

Bouchardon, Serge. 2008. *Les 12 travaux de l'internaute/ The 12 Labours of the Internet User*. http://www.les12travaux.com/, http://www.the12labors.com.

Bouchardon, Serge. 2009a. *Toucher* [Touch] http://www.to-touch.com.

Bouchardon, Serge. 2009b. *Littérature numérique: le récit interactif*. Paris: Lavoisier.

Buzzetti, Dino. 2002. Digital Representation and the Text Model. *New Literary History* 33:61–88.

Caines, Marcia. 2009. Outside In: Interview with John F. Simon Jr. *Cluster*, March 10. http://www.cluster.eu/2009/03/10/outside-in-interview-with-john-f-simon-jr.

Calvino, Italo. 1987. Cybernetics and Ghosts [Cibernetica e fantasmi, 1967]. In *The Uses of Literature*, 3–2. Translated by Patrick Creagh. New York: Mariner Books.

de Campos, Augusto. 1973. Código. http://www2.uol.com.br/augustodecampos/06_05.htm.

de Campos, Augusto. 1974. Tudo está dito. http://www2.uol.com.br/augustodecampos/06_08.htm.

de Campos, Augusto. 1994. coraçãocabeça. In *Despoesia*. São Paulo: Editora Perspectiva, 14–15. Digital version [2000] available at http://www2.uol.com.br/augustodecampos/coracaocabeca.htm.

de Campos, Augusto. 1994. SOS. In *Despoesia*. São Paulo: Editora Perspectiva, 27. Digital version [2000] available at http://www2.uol.com.br/augustodecampos/sos.htm.

de Campos, Augusto. 1988. Rã de basho. http://www2.uol.com.br/augustodecampos/08_03.htm.

de Campos, Augusto. 1994. *Despoesia*. São Paulo: Editora Perspectiva.

de Campos, Augusto. 2000. Sem saída. In *Clip-poemas* (1997–2003). http://www2.uol.com.br/augustodecampos/semsaida.htm.

de Campos, Augusto. 2003. *Não poemas*. São Paulo: Editora Perspectiva.

de Campos, Augusto, and Julio Plaza. 2010. *Poemobiles*. São Paulo: Annablume.

de Campos, Haroldo. 1992. O â mago do ô mega. In *Os melhores poemas de Haroldo de Campos*. Selected by Inês Oseki Dépré, 41–44. São Paulo: Global.

Carroll, Lewis. 1864. *Alice's Adventures Under Ground*. http://www.bl.uk/collections/treasures/alice/alice_broadband.htm?top.

Cavallo, Guglielmo, Roger Chartier, and Lydia G. Cochrane, eds. 2003. *A History of Reading in the West*. Amherst: University of Massachusetts Press.

Cayley, John. 1999. *Windsound*. http://programmatology.shadoof.net/index.php?p=works/wsqt/windsound.html.

Cayley, John. 2002a. The Code Is Not the Text (Unless It Is the Text). *Electronic Book Review*, October 9. http://www.electronicbookreview.com/thread/electropoetics/literal.

Cayley, John. 2002b. *RiverIsland*. http://programmatology.shadoof.net/index.php?p=works/riverisland/riverislandQT.html.

Cayley, John. 2003. Inner Workings: Code and Representations of Interiority in New Media Poetics. *Dichtung-Digital: Journal für Digitale Ästhetik*, no. 29. http://www.dichtung-digital.org/2003/issue/3/Cayley.htm.

Cayley, John. 2004a. Literal Art: Neither Lines nor Pixels But Letters. In *First Person: New Media as Story, Performance, and Game*, edited by Noah Wardrip-Fruin and Pat Harrigan, 208–217. Cambridge, MA: MIT Press.

Cayley, John. 2004b. O V E R B O A R D: An Example of Ambient Time-Based Poetics in Digital Art. *Dichtung-Digital: Journal für Digitale Ästhetik*, no. 32. www.dichtung-digital.org/2004/2-Cayley.htm.

Cayley, John, with Giles Perring. 2004c. *Overboard*. http://programmatology.shadoof
.net/index.php?p=works/overboard/overboard.html.

Cayley, John, with Giles Perring. 2004d. *Translation*. http://programmatology
.shadoof.net/index.php?p=works/translation/translation.html.

Cayley, John. 2005. Writing on Complex Surfaces. *Dichtung-Digital: Journal für Digitale Ästhetik*, no. 35. http://www.dichtung-digital.org/2005/2-Cayley.htm.

Cayley, John. 2006. Time Code Language: New Media Poetics and Programmed Signification. In *New Media Poetics: Contexts, Technotexts, and Theories*, edited by Adalaide Morris and Thomas Swiss, 307–334. Cambridge, MA: MIT Press.

Cayley, John. 2007. *Imposition*. http://programmatology.shadoof.net/index.php ?p=works/impose/imposition.html.

Cayley, John. 2010. The Gravity of the Leaf: Phenomenologies of Literary Inscription in Media-Constituted Diegetic Worlds. In *Beyond the Screen: Transformations of Literary Structures, Interfaces and Genres*, edited by Jörgen Schäfer and Peter Gendolla, 129–226. Bielefeld: Transcript.

Cayley, John. 2011. Writing to Be Found and Writing Readers. *Digital Humanities Quarterly* 5 (3). http://digitalhumanities.org/dhq/vol/5/3/000104/000104.html.

Cayley, John. 2012. Weapons of the Deconstructive Masses (WDM): Whatever Electronic Literature May or May Not Mean. *Revista de Estudos Literários* 2: 25–56.

Cayley, John, and Penny Florence. 2011. *Mirroring Tears: Visages*. http://programmatology.shadoof.net/applets/mirrortrans.

Cayley, John, and Daniel Howe. 2009–2012. *The Readers Project*. http://thereadersproject.org.

Chanen, Brian W. 2007. Surfing the Text: The Digital Environment in Mark Z. Danielewski's *House of Leaves*. *European Journal of English Studies* 11 (2): 163–176.

Chartier, Roger. 1995. *Forms and Meanings: Texts, Performances, and Audiences from Codex to Computer*. Philadelphia: University of Pennsylvania Press.

Chun, Wendy Hui Kyong. 2006. *Control and Freedom: Power and Paranoia in the Age of Fiber Optics*. Cambridge, MA: MIT Press.

Chun, Wendy Hui Kyong. 2011. *Programmed Visions: Software and Memory*. Cambridge, MA: MIT Press.

Cox, Geoff, Alex McLean, and Adrian Ward. 2004. Coding Praxis: Reconsidering the Aesthetics of Generative Code. *Read_Me: Software Art and Culture*, edited by Olga Goriunova and Alexei Shulgin, 161–174. Aarhus: Digital Aesthetics Research Centre, University of Aarhus. http://www.anti-thesis.net/contents/texts/praxis.pdf.

Cox, Katharine. 2006. What Has Made Me? Locating Mother in the Textual Labyrinth of Mark Z. Danielewski's *House of Leaves*. *Critical Survey* 18 (2): 4–15.

Cramer, Florian. 2005. *Words Made Flesh: Code, Culture, Imagination*. Rotterdam: Piet Zwart Institute. http://www.netzliteratur.net/cramer/wordsmadefleshpdf.pdf.

Cramer, Florian. 2007. *Exe.cut[up]able statements—Poetische kalküle und phantasmen*. München: Wilhelm Fink Verlag.

Danielewski, Mark Z. 2000. *House of Leaves*. New York: Pantheon Books.

Danielewski, Mark Z. 2006. *Only Revolutions: The Democracy of Two Set Out and Chronologically Arranged*. New York: Pantheon Books.

Darnton, Robert. 2007. "What Is the History of Books?" Revisited. *Modern Intellectual History* 4:495–508.

Darnton, Robert. 2010. *The Case for Books: Past, Present, and Future*. New York: Public Affairs.

Deegan, Marilyn, and Willard McCarty, eds. 2012. *Collaborative Research in the Digital Humanities*. Farnham: Ashgate.

Deegan, Marilyn, and Kathryn Sutherland, eds. 2009a. *Text Editing, Print and the Digital World*. Farnham: Ashgate.

Deegan, Marilyn, and Kathryn Sutherland. 2009b. *Transferred Illusions: Digital Technology and the Forms of Print*. Farnham: Ashgate.

Dehaene, Stanislas. 2009. *Reading in the Brain: The Science and Evolution of a Human Invention*. New York: Viking Press.

Diacono, Mario. 2009. *John F. Simon Jr.: Outside In: Ten Years of Software Art*. Pistoia: Gli Ori.

Douglas, Jane Yellowlees. 2000. *The End of Books—or Books without End? Reading Interactive Narratives*. Ann Arbor: University of Michigan Press.

Drucker, Johanna. 1977. *From A to Z: Our An (Collective Specifics) an im partial bibliography, Incidents in a Non-Relationship or: how I came to not know who is*. Oakland/ Berkeley, CA: Chased Press. http://www.artistsbooksonline.org/works/atoz.xml.

Drucker, Johanna. 1986. *Through Light and the Alphabet*. Berkeley: Druckwerk. http://www.artistsbooksonline.org/works/ligh.xml.

Drucker, Johanna. 1989. *The Word Made Flesh*. New York: Druckwerk. http://www.artistsbooksonline.org/works/wmfl.xml.

Drucker, Johanna. 1990. *The History of the/My Wor(l)d*, New York: Druckwerk. http://www.artistsbooksonline.org/works/hist.xml.

Drucker, Johanna. 1994. *A Chronology of Books from 1970 to 1994, Written on Occasion of the Show at Granary Books, New York City, June 1994.* http://epc.buffalo.edu/authors/drucker/chron.html.

Drucker, Johanna. 1995. *The Century of Artists' Books.* New York: Granary Books.

Drucker, Johanna. 1999. Experimental Narrative and Artists' Books. *Journal of Artists' Books,* no. 12: 3–25. http://www.journalofartistsbooks.org/past/pdfs//JAB12.pdf.

Drucker, Johanna. 2006a. Graphical Readings and the Visual Aesthetics of Textuality. *Text* 16:267–276.

Drucker, Johanna. 2006b. The Conceptual Framework of Artists' Books Online. In *Artists' Books Online: An Online Repository of Facsimiles, Metadata, and Criticism.* http://www.artistsbooksonline.org/mission.html.

Drucker, Johanna, ed. 2006c. *Artists' Books Online: An Online Repository of Facsimiles, Metadata, and Criticism.* http://www.artistsbooksonline.org.

Drucker, Johanna. 2007. Performative Metatexts in Metadata, and Mark-Up. *European Journal of English Studies* 11: 177–191.

Drucker, Johanna. 2008. The Virtual Codex from Page Space to E-space. In *A Companion to Digital Literary Studies,* edited by Susan Schreibman and Ray Siemens, 216–232. Oxford: Blackwell.

Drucker, Johanna. 2009a. *SpecLab: Digital Aesthetics and Projects in Speculative Computing.* Chicago: University of Chicago Press.

Drucker, Johanna. 2009b. Entity to Event: From Literal, Mechanistic Materiality to Probabilistic Materiality. *Parallax* 15 (4): 7–17.

Drucker, Johanna. 2010. Humanities Approaches to Graphical Display. *Digital Humanities Quarterly* 5 (1). http://digitalhumanities.org/dhq/vol/5/1/000091/000091.html.

Drucker, Johanna. 2011. Humanities Approaches to Interface Theory. *Culture Machine* 12. http://www.culturemachine.net/index.php/cm/article/view/434/462.

Drucker, Johanna, and Brad Freeman. 2001. *Emerging Sentience.* New York: JAB Books. http://www.artistsbooksonline.org/works/emrg.xml.

Eaves, Morris, Robert N. Essick, and Joseph Viscomi, eds. 1996-2012. *The William Blake Archive.* University of North Carolina at Chapel Hill. http://www.blakearchive.org.

Emerson, Lori. 2006. Numbered Space and Topographic Writing. *Leonardo Electronic Almanac,* 14 (5–6). http://www.leoalmanac.org/journal/vol_14/lea_v14_n05-06/lemerson.html.

Engberg, Maria. 2006. Morphing into New Modes of Writing: John Cayley's *RiverIsland. Leonardo Electronic Almanac New Media and Poetics* 14, (5–6). http://www.leoalmanac.org/journal/vol_14/lea_v14_n05-06/mengberg.html.

Engberg, Maria. 2010. Aesthetics of Visual Noise in Digital Literary Arts. In *Cybertext Yearbook 2010*, edited by Markku Eskelinen and Raine Koskimaa. Jyväskylä: University of Jyväskylä. http://cybertext.hum.jyu.fi/articles/138.pdf.

Eskelinen, Markku. 2012. *Cybertext Poetics: The Critical Landscape of New Media Literary Theory*. London: Continuum.

Febvre, Lucien, and Henri-Jean Martin. 1958. *L'apparition du livre*. Paris: Éditions Albin Michel.

Ferrando, Bartolomé. 2002. *Escrituras superpuestas*. Valencia: Universitat de Valencia.

Finkelstein, David, and Alistair McCleery, eds. 2002. *The Book History Reader*. London: Routledge.

Flores, Leonardo. 2010. Typing the Dancing Signifier: Jim Andrews' (Vis)Poetics. Ph.D. diss., University of Maryland. http://hdl.handle.net/1903/10799.

Foer, Jonathan Safran. 2010. *Tree of Codes*. London: Visual Editions.

Folsom, Ed, and Kenneth M. Price, eds. 1995–2012. *The Walt Whitman Archive*. Center for Digital Research in the Humanities at the University of Nebraska–Lincoln. http://www.whitmanarchive.org.

Freeman, Margaret H. 2008. Reading Readers Reading a Poem: From Conceptual to Cognitive Integration. *Cognitive Semiotics*, no. 2: 102–128.

Frost, Gary. 2004. Readers Guide to Book Action. In *Futureofthebook.com: Preservation and Persistence of the Changing Book*. http://futureofthebook.com/readers-guide-to-book-action.

Frost, Gary. 2005. Reading by Hand: Haptic Evaluation of Artists' Books. *Bonefolder: An e-Journal for the Bookbinder and Book Artist* 2 (1): 3–6. http://www.philobiblon.com/bonefolder/vol2no1contents.htm.

Frost, Gary. 2006. Formats of the Book: The Cursor, the Haptic and the Mirror: Three Formats of the Book. In *futureofthebook.com: Preservation and Persistence of the Changing Book*. http://futureofthebook.com/formats-of-the-book.

Frost, Gary. 2007. Mobility and Function in the Codex. In *futureofthebook.com: Preservation and Persistence of the Changing Book*. http://futureofthebook.com/mobility-and-function-in-the-codex.

Frost, Gary. 2008. The Changing Status of Physical Book Collections in Context with Their Mass Digitization. In *Futureofthebook.com: Preservation and Persistence of the*

Changing Book. http://futureofthebook.com/the-changing-status-of-physical-book
-collections-in-context-with-their-mass-digitization.

Fuller, Matthew. 2008. *Software Studies: A Lexicon.* Cambridge, MA: MIT Press.

Funkhouser, Chris. 2005. A Vanguard Projected in Motion: Early Kinetic Poetry in Portuguese. *Sirena: poesia, arte y critica,* 2: 152–164.

Funkhouser, C. T. 2007. *Prehistoric Digital Poetry: An Archaeology of Forms, 1959–1995.* Tuscaloosa: University of Alabama Press.

Funkhouser, Christopher. 2008. Digital Poetry: A Look at Generative, Visual, and Interconnected Possibilities in its First Four Decades. In *A Companion to Digital Literary Studies,* edited by Susan Schreibman and Ray Siemens, 318–335. Oxford: Blackwell.

Funkhouser, C. T. 2012. *New Directions in Digital Poetry.* London: Continuum.

Galloway, Alexander R. 2006. *Gaming: Essays on Algorithmic Culture.* Minneapolis: University of Minnesota Press.

Gendolla, Peter, and Jörgen Schäfer. 2007. Reading (in) the Net: Aesthetic Experience in Computer-Based Media. In *The Aesthetics of Net Literature: Writing, Reading and Playing in Programmable Media,* edited by Peter Gendolla and Jörgen Schäfer, 81–108. Bielefeld: Transcript.

Gherban, Alexandre. 2007a. *Essayeur sémantique.* http://www.akenaton-docks.fr/DOCKS-datas_f/collect_f/auteurs_f/G_f/GHERBAN_f/NATURE_F/garde.html.

Gherban, Alexandre. 2007b. *Robolettries.* http://www.akenaton-docks.fr/DOCKS
-datas_f/collect_f/auteurs_f/G_f/GHERBAN_f/ROBOTLET_F/roboltr1w.htm.

Glazier, Loss Pequeño. 2002. *Digital Poetics: The Making of E-Poetries.* Tuscaloosa: University of Alabama Press.

Glazier, Loss Pequeño. 2006. Code as Language. *Leonardo Electronic Almanac* 14 (5–6). http://www.leoalmanac.org/journal/vol_14/lea_v14_n05-06/lglazier.html.

Gold, Matthew K. 2012. *Debates in the Digital Humanities.* Minneapolis: University of Minnesota Press.

Gomringer, Eugen. 1953. *Konstellationen constellations constellaciones.* Berne, Switzerland: Spiral Press.

Graulund, Rune. 2006. Text and Paratext in Mark Z. *Danielewski's House of Leaves. Word and Image* 22 (4): 379–389.

Gutierrez, Juan B., Mark C. Marino, Pablo Gervás, and Laura Borràs Castanyer. 2009. Electronic Literature as an Information System. *Hyperrhiz: New Media Cultures,* no. 6. http://www.hyperrhiz.net/hyperrhiz06/19-essays/74-electronic-literature-as
-an-information-system.

Hamilton, Natalie. 2008. The A-Mazing House: The Labyrinth as Theme and Form in Mark Z. Danielewski's *House of Leaves*. *Critique* 50 (1): 3–15.

Hansen, Mark B. N. 2004. The Digital Topography of Mark Z. Danielewski's *House of Leaves*. *Contemporary Literature* 45 (4):597–636.

Harm, Michael W., and Mark S. Seidenberg. 2004. Computing the Meanings of Words in Reading: Cooperative Division of Labor between Visual and Phonological Processes. *Psychological Review* 111 (3): 662–720.

Hatherly, Ana. 1975. *A Reinvenção da Leitura: Breve Ensaio Crítico seguido de 19 Textos Visuais*. Lisboa: Futura.

Hayles, N. Katherine. 2002. *Writing Machines*. Cambridge, MA: MIT Press.

Hayles, N. Katherine. 2005. *My Mother Was a Computer: Digital Subjects and Literary Texts*. Chicago: University of Chicago Press.

Hayles, N. Katherine. 2006. The Time of Digital Poetry: From Object to Event. In *New Media Poetics: Contexts, Technotexts, and Theories*, edited by Adalaide Morris and Thomas Swiss, 143–164. Cambridge, MA: MIT Press.

Hayles, N. Katherine. 2008. *Electronic Literature: New Horizons for the Literary*. Notre Dame, IN: University of Notre Dame.

Hayles, N. Katherine. 2010. How We Read: Close, Hyper, Machine. *ADE Bulletin* 150: 62–79. http://www.mla.org/adefl_bulletin_c_ade_150_62.

Hayles, N. Katherine. 2012. *How We Think: Digital Media and Contemporary Technogenesis*. Chicago: University Chicago Press.

Hayles, N. Katherine, Nick Montfort, Scott Rettberg, and Stephanie Strickland, eds. 2006. *Electronic Literature Collection*, vol. 1, College Park, MD: Electronic Literature Organization. http://collection.eliterature.org/1.

Helder, Herberto. 1964a. A Máquina de Emaranhar Paisagens. Digital version in Sintext, a textual engine by Pedro Barbosa, based on code by Abílio Cavalheiro [2008]. http://po-ex.net/index.php?option=com_content&task=view&id=18&Itemid=35&limit=1&limitstart=1.

Helder, Herberto. 1964b. *Electronicolírica*. Lisboa: Guimarães Editores.

Helder, Herberto. 1964c. Hipopótamos. Digital version by Rodrigo Melo [2008]. http://po-ex.net/index.php?option=com_content&task=view&id=90&Itemid=35.

Hillesund, Terje. 2010. Digital Reading Spaces: How Expert Readers Handle Books, the Web and Electronic Paper. *First Monday* 15 (10). http://firstmonday.org/htbin/cgiwrap/bin/ojs/index.php/fm/article/view/2762/2504.

Howe, Daniel C., and John Cayley. 2011. *The Readers Project*: Procedural Agents and Literary Vectors. *Leonardo* 44 (4): 317–324.

Hume, Christine. 2005. Nocturnal Dimensions of the Future. *The Other Voices International Project* 23. http://www.othervoicespoetry.org/vol23/hume/nocturnal .htm.

Ikonen, Teemu. 2003. Moving Text in Avant-Garde Poetry: Towards a Poetics of Textual Motion. *Dichtung-Digital: Journal für Digitale Ästhetik,* no. 30. http://www .dichtung-digital.org/2003/issue/4/ikonen/index.htm.

Ippolito, Jon. 2002. Unfolding Object in *Guggenheim Collection Online* [object 2002.16]. http://www.guggenheim.org/new-york/collections/collection-online.

Iuli, Cristina. 2010. Playing with Codes: Steve Tomasula's *Vas, an Opera in Flatland. Writing Technologies* 3:64–85. http://www.ntu.ac.uk/writing_technologies/current _journal/107436.pdf.

James, Kedrick Platon. 2009. Writing Post-Person: Literacy, Poetics, and Sustainability in the Age of Disposable Information. Ph.D. diss., University of British Columbia. https://circle.ubc.ca/handle/2429/7449.

Johns, Adrian. 1998. *The Nature of the Book: Print and Knowledge in the Making.* Chicago: University of Chicago Press.

Johnston, David Jhave. 2010. *Zero Whack.* http://glia.ca/2010/ZERO-WHACK.

Johnston, David Jhave. 2011. Aesthetic Animism: Digital Poetry as Ontological Probe. Montreal: Concordia University. http://glia.ca/conu/THESIS/public/David _Johnston_THESIS_FINAL_JAN_2012.pdf.

Khouri, Omar, and Fábio Oliveira Nunes, eds. 2003–2004. *Artéria,* no. 8. http://www .arteria8.net.

Kirschenbaum, Matthew G. 1997. "Through Light and the Alphabet": An Interview with Johanna Drucker. *Postmodern Culture* 7:3. http://pmc.iath.virginia.edu/ text-only/issue.597/kirschenbaum.597.

Kirschenbaum, Matthew G. 2008. *Mechanisms: New Media and the Forensic Imagination.* Cambridge, MA: MIT Press.

Kirschenbaum, Matthew G. 2010. What Is Digital Humanities and What's It Doing in English Departments? *ADE Bulletin,* no. 150: 55–61. http://www.ade.org/cgi-shl/ docstudio/docs.pl?adefl_bulletin_d_ade_150_55.pdf.

Kittler, Friedrich A. 1990. *Discourse Networks 1800/1900.* Translated by Michael Metteer, with Chris Cullens. Stanford, CA: Stanford University Press.

Kittler, Friedrich A. 1999. *Gramophone, Film, Typewriter.* Translated by Geoffrey Winthrop-Young and Michael Wutz. Stanford, CA: Stanford University Press.

Kittler, Friedrich A. 2010. *Optical Media: Berlin Lectures 1999.* Translated by Anthony Enns. Cambridge: Polity Press.

Knowles, Kim, Anna Katharina Schaffner, Ulrich Weger, and Andrew Michael Roberts. 2012. Reading Space in Visual Poetry: New Cognitive Perspectives. *Writing Technologies* 4:75–106.

Koolen, Corina, Alex Garnett, and Ray Siemens, and the INKE, ETCL and PKP Research Groups. 2011. Electronic Environments for Reading: An Annotated Bibliography of Pertinent Hardware and Software. http://web.uvic.ca/~siemens/pub/2011%20E-ReadingEnvironments.pdf.

Koskimaa, Raine. 2000. Digital Literature: From Text to Hypertext and Beyond. Ph.D. diss., University of Jyväskylä. http://www.cc.jyu.fi/~koskimaa/thesis.

Kress, Günter. 2003. *Literacy in the New Media Age*. London: Routledge.

Kress, Günter, and Theo Van Leeuwen. 2001. *Multimodal Discourse: The Modes and Media of Contemporary Communication*. London: Arnold.

Lee, Shuen-shing. 2002. Explorations of Ergodic Literature: The Interlaced Poetics of Representation and Simulation. *Dichtung-Digital: Journal für Digitale Ästhetik*, no. 25. http://www.dichtung-digital.org/2002/05/26-Lee/index.htm.

Leonard, Philip. 2010. "Without return. without place": Rewriting the Book and the Nation in *Only Revolutions*. *Writing Technologies* 3:42–63. http://www.ntu.ac.uk/writing_technologies/current_journal/107435.pdf.

Liu, Alan. 2009. The End of the End of the Book: Dead Books, Lively Margins, and Social Computing. *Michigan Quarterly Review* 48 (4): 499–520.

Liu, Yanping, and Erik Reichle. 2010. The Emergence of Adaptive Eye Movements in Reading. In *Proceedings of the 32nd Annual Conference of the Cognitive Science Society*, edited by S. Ohlsson and R. Catrambone, 1136–1141. Austin, TX: Cognitive Science Society. http://csjarchive.cogsci.rpi.edu/proceedings/2010/papers/0336/index.html.

Longtin, Catherine-Marie, and Fanny Meunier. 2005. Morphological Decomposition in Early Visual Word Processing. *Journal of Memory and Language* 53 (1): 26–41. http://www.sciencedirect.com/science/article/pii/S0749596X05000288.

Loyer, Erik. 2002. *Hollowbound Book*. http://erikloyer.com/index.php/projects/detail/hollowbound_book.

Lyons, Joan. 2004. *Abecê: Mexico City Book 2*. http://www.artistsbooksonline.org/works/abec.xml.

Mangen, Anne. 2008. Hypertext Fiction Reading: Haptics and Immersion. *Journal of Research in Reading* 31 (4): 404–419.

Manovich, Lev. 2001. *The Language of New Media*. Cambridge, MA: MIT Press.

Manovich, Lev. 2007. Database as Symbolic Form. In *Database Aesthetics: Art in the Age of Information Overflow*, edited by Victoria Vesna, 39–60. Minneapolis: University of Minnesota Press.

Manovich, Lev. 2008. *Software Takes Command.* http://lab.softwarestudies.com/2008/11/softbook.html.

Manovich, Lev. 2010. What Is Visualization? http://manovich.net/2010/10/25/new-article-what-is-visualization/

Manovich, Lev, Jeremy Douglass, and William Huber. 2011. Understanding Scanlation: How to Read One Million Fan-Translated Manga Pages. *Image and Narrative* 12:190–227. http://www.imageandnarrative.be/index.php/imagenarrative/article/viewFile/133/104.

Marino, Mark C. 2006. Critical Code Studies. *Electronic Book Review*, April 12. http://www.electronicbookreview.com/thread/electropoetics/codology.

Marques, José-Alberto. 1966. Dois fragmentos de uma experiância. Digital version by Rodrigo Melo [2008]. http://po-ex.net/index.php?option=com_content&task=view&id=93&Itemid=35.

Marques, José-Alberto. 1967. Homeóstato 1. Digital version in processing by Eugenio Tisselli [2008]. http://po-ex.net/index.php?option=com_content&task=view&id=108&Itemid=35.

Mateas, Michael, and Nick Montfort. 2005. A Box, Darkly: Obfuscation, Weird Languages, and Code Aesthetics. In *Proceedings of the 6th Digital Arts and Culture Conference*, 144–153. University of Copenhagen. http://nickm.com/cis/a_box_darkly.pdf.

McCaffery, Larry, and Sinda Gregory. 2003. Haunted House: An Interview with Mark Z. Danielewski. *Critique* 44 (2): 99–135.

McCaffery, Steve. 2013. Politics, Context and the Constellation: A Case Study of Eugen Gomringer's "Silencio." *European Journal of English Studies* 17 (1): 10–22.

McCaffery, Steve, and bp Nichol. 2000. The Book as Machine [1972]. In *A Book of the Book: Some Works and Projections about the Book and Writing*, edited by Jerome Rothenberg and Steven Clay, 17–24. New York: Granary Books.

McCarty, Willard. 2003. Humanities Computing. In *Encyclopedia of Library and Information Science*, 1224–1235. New York: Marcel Dekker.

McCarty, Willard. 2005. *Humanities Computing.* Basingstoke: Palgrave Macmillan.

McCarty, Willard. 2010. *Text and Genre in Reconstruction: Effects of Digitalization on Ideas, Behaviours, Products and Institutions.* Cambridge: Open Book Publishers.

McGann, Jerome. 1991. *The Textual Condition.* Princeton, NJ: Princeton University Press.

McGann, Jerome. 1993. *Black Riders: The Visible Language of Modernism.* Princeton, NJ: Princeton University Press.

McGann, Jerome. 1996. The Rationale of Hypertext. *Text* 9:11–32.

McGann, Jerome. 2001. *Radiant Textuality: Literature after the World Wide Web*. New York: Palgrave.

McGann, Jerome. 2002. Textonics: Literary and Cultural Studies in a Quantum World. http://www.ciberscopio.net/artigos/tema2/clit_01.html.

McGann, Jerome. 2003. Texts in N-Dimensions and Interpretation in a New Key [Discourse and Interpretation in N-Dimensions]. *Text Technology* 12 (2). http://texttechnology.mcmaster.ca/pdf/vol12_2_02.pdf.

McGann, Jerome. 2004. Marking Texts of Many Dimensions. In *A Companion to Digital Humanities*, edited by Susan Schreibman, Ray Siemens, and John Unsworth, 198–217. Oxford: Blackwell.

McGann, Jerome, ed. 1993–2008. *The Rossetti Archive*. Institute for Advanced Technology in the Humanities at the University of Virginia. http://www.rossettiarchive.org.

McGann, Jerome, with Andrew Stauffer, Dana Wheeles, and Michael Pickard, eds. 2010. *Online Humanities Scholarship: The Shape of Things to Come*. Houston, TX: Rice University Press.

McKenzie, D. F. 2004. *Bibliography and the Sociology of Texts*. Cambridge: Cambridge University Press.

McLeod, Randall. 2004. Gerard Hopkins and the Shapes of His Sonnets. In *VoiceTextHypertext: Emerging Practices in Textual Studies*, edited by Raimonda Modiano, Leroy F. Searle, and Peter Shillingsburg, 177–297. Seattle: University of Washington Press.

Melo e Castro, E. M. de. 1962a. Ideogramas. Readings by Américo Rodrigues [2006] of eleven Ideograms by E. M. de Melo e Castro. http://po-ex.net/index.php?option=com_content&task=view&id=20&Itemid=35&.

Melo e Castro, E. M. de. 1962b. Edifício. Digital version by Rui Torres and Jared Tarbel [2008]. http://po-ex.net/index.php?option=com_content&task=view&id=39&Itemid=35&.

Melo e Castro, E. M. de. 1964. Transparência/Oblivion. Digital version by Rodrigo Melo and Pedro Reis [2008]. http://po-ex.net/index.php?option=com_content&task=view&id=91&Itemid=35&.

Melo e Castro, E. M. de. 1966. Mapa do deserto. Digital version by Rui Torres and Jared Tarbel [2008]. http://po-ex.net/index.php?option=com_content&task=view&id=23&Itemid=35&.

Melo e Castro, E. M. de. 1986–1989. *Signagens*. Lisboa: Universidade Aberta [VHS video].

Melo e Castro, E. M. de. 1996–1999. Videopoetry. In E. M. de Melo e Castro, *Infopoesia, Produções Brasileiras*. http://www.ociocriativo.com.br/guests/meloecastro/texto5.htm.

Memmott, Talan. 2003. *Self Portrait(s) [as Other(s)]*. http://collection.eliterature. org/1/works/memmott__self_portraits_as_others.html.

Memmott, Talan. 2011. Digital Rhetoric and Poetics: Signifying Strategies in Electronic Literature. Ph.D. diss., Malmö University. http://dspace.mah.se/handle/2043/12547.

Miller, Callie. 2007. LAist Interview: Mark Z. Danielewski. *LAist*, October 23, 2007. http://mobile.laist.com/2007/10/23/laist_interview_55.php.

Montfort, Nick. 2003. *Twisty Little Passages: An Approach to Interactive Fiction*. Cambridge, MA: MIT Press.

Montfort, Nick. 2007. *Ppg256 Poetry Generator Series*. http://nickm.com/poems/ppg256.html.

Montfort, Nick, and Stephanie Strickland. 2011. *Sea and Spar between. Dear Navigator*, no. 2. http://blogs.saic.edu/dearnavigator/winter2010/nick-montfort-stephanie-strickland-sea-and-spar-between.

Moretti, Franco. 2007. *Graphs, Maps, Trees: Abstract Models for Literary History*. London: Verso.

Morgan, Edwin. 1980. *The Second Life*. Edinburgh: Edinburgh University Press.

Morris, Adalaide, and Thomas Swiss, eds. 2006. *New Media Poetics: Contexts, Technotexts, and Theories*. Cambridge, MA: MIT Press.

Murray, Janet H. 1998. *Hamlet on the Holodeck: The Future of Narrative in Cyberspace*. Cambridge, MA: MIT Press.

Murray, Janet H. 2012. *Inventing the Medium: Principles of Interaction Design as Cultural Practice*. Cambridge, MA: MIT Press.

Nazir, Tatjana A., Nadia Ben-Boutayab, Nathalie Decoppet, Avital Deutsch, and Ram Frost. 2004. Reading Habits, Perceptual Learning, and Recognition of Printed Words. *Brain and Language* 88 (3): 294–311. http://www.sciencedirect.com/science/article/pii/S0093934X03001688.

Nelson, Jason. 2004. *Hymns of the Drowning Swimmer*. http://secrettechnology.com/hymns/navigate.html.

Nelson, Jason, with Christine Hume. 2007. *Dimension Is Night Is Night*. http://www.secrettechnology.com/night/xtine.html.

Nichol, bp. 1984. *First Screening: Computer Poems*. Reconstructed by Jim Andrews and Marko J. Niemi [2007]. http://www.vispo.com/bp/index.htm.

Perloff, Marjorie. 2006. Screening the Page/ Paging the Screen: Digital Poetics and the Differential Text. In *New Media Poetics: Contexts, Technotexts, and Theories*, edited by Adalaide Morris and Thomas Swiss, 143–164. Cambridge, MA: MIT Press.

Peterson, Tim. 2006. New Media Poetry and Poetics. From Concrete to Codework: Praxis in Networked and Programmable Media. *Leonardo Electronic Almanac* 14 (5–6). http://www.leoalmanac.org/journal/vol_14/lea_v14_n05-06/tpeterson.html.

Phillips, Tom. 1971–1975. *A Humument.* Vols. I-VIII. London: Tetrad Press Edition. http://humument.com/gallery/tetrad/0/001010/index.html.

Phillips, Tom. 1987. *A Humument: A Treated Victorian Novel.* Rev. ed. London: Thames and Hudson.

Phillips, Tom. 2005. *A Humument: A Treated Victorian Novel* 4th ed. London: Thames and Hudson.

Phillips, Tom. 2008. *A Humument: The Complete 4th Edition: A Slideshow.* http://humument.com/gallery/slideshow.html.

Phillips, Tom. 2012. *A Humument Gallery.* http://gallery.humument.com.

Portela, Manuel. 2000. Typographic Translation: The Portuguese Edition of *Tristram Shandy.* In *Ma(r)king the Text: The Presentation of Meaning on the Literary Page*, edited by Joe Bray, Miriam Handley, and Anne Henry, 291–308. Aldershot: Ashgate.

Portela, Manuel. 2003. Untranslations and Transcreations. *Text* 15:305–320.

Portela, Manuel. 2006. Concrete and Digital Poetics. *Leonardo Electronic Almanac* 14 (5–6). http://www.leoalmanac.org/journal/vol_14/lea_v14_n05-06/mportela.html.

Portela, Manuel. 2009. Flash Script Poex: A Recodificação Digital do Poema Experimental. *Cibertextualidades* 3:43–57.

Portela, Manuel. 2012. Autoauthor, Autotext, Autoreader: The Poem as Self-assembled Database. *Writing Technologies* 4:43–74. http://www.ntu.ac.uk/writing_technologies/current_journal/124936.pdf.

Pressman, Jessica. 2006. *House of Leaves:* Reading the Networked Novel. *Studies in American Fiction* 34 (1): 108–128.

Pressman, Jessica. 2007. Reading the Code between the Words: The Role of Translation in Young-hae Chang Heavy Industries's *Nippon. Dichtung-Digital: Journal für Digitale Ästhetik*, no. 37. http://www.dichtung-digital.org/2007/Pressman/Pressman.htm.

Pressman, Jessica. 2009. The Aesthetic of Bookishness in Twenty-First-Century Literature. *Michigan Quarterly Review* 48 (4): 465–482. http://hdl.handle.net/2027/spo.act2080.0048.402.

Price, Leah. 2009. From the History of a Book to a "History of the Book." *Representations* 108:120–138.

Price, Leah. 2012. *How to Do Things with Books in Victorian Britain.* Princeton, NJ: Princeton University Press.

Pynte, Joël, and Alan Kennedy. 2006. An Influence over Eye Movements in Reading Exerted from beyond the Level of the Word: Evidence from Reading English and French. *Vision Research* 46 (22): 3786–3801. http://www.sciencedirect.com/science/article/pii/S0042698906003087.

Raley, Rita. 2002. Interferences: [Net.Writing] and the Practice of Codework. *Electronic Book Review*, September 9. http://www.electronicbookreview.com/thread/electropoetics/net.writing.

Raley, Rita. 2006. Code.surface || Code.depth. *Dichtung-Digital: Journal für Digitale Ästhetik*, no. 36. http://www.dichtung-digital.org/2006/01/Raley/index.htm.

Ramsay, Stephen. 2011. *Reading Machines: Toward an Algorithmic Criticism*. Champaign: University of Illinois Press.

Rayner, Keith. 2009. Eye Movements and Attention in Reading, Visual Search, and Scene Perception. *Quarterly Journal of Experimental Psychology* 62 (8): 1457–1506.

Reis, Pedro. 2005. Repercussões do uso criativo das tecnologias digitais da comunicação no sistema literário: O caso da poesia intermediática electrónica. [Repercussions of the creative use of digital communication technology on the literary system: The case of intermedia electronic poetry] Ph.D. diss., University of Lisbon.

Rey, Arnaud, Johannes C. Ziegler, and Arthur M. Jacobs. 2000. Graphemes are Perceptual Reading Units. *Cognition* 75 (1): B1–B12.

Roberts, Andrew Michael, Jane Stabler, Martin H. Fischer, and Lisa Otty. 2013. Space and Pattern in Linear and Postlinear Poetry: Empirical and Theoretical Approaches. *European Journal of English Studies* 17 (1): 23–40.

Rodrigues, Tiago Gomez. 2002. *Concretus: um concretismo animado*. Porto: Marquês Produções. [CD-ROM; includes digital versions of the following ideograms "Tontura," by E. M. de Melo e Castro; "Arranhisso," by Salette Tavares; "Cascata," "Cubo," and "Esfera," by Tiago Gomez Rodrigues.]

di Rosario, Giovanna. 2011. Electronic Poetry: Understanding Poetry in the Digital Environment. Ph.D. diss., University of Jyväskylä. http://dissertations.jyu.fi/studhum/9789513943356.pdf.

Ryan, Marie-Laure. 2008. What Has the Computer Done for the Word? *Genre* 41 (3–4): 33–58.

Ryan, Marie-Laure. 2010. Between Play and Politics: Dysfunctionality in Digital Art. *Electronic Book Review*, March 3. http://www.electronicbookreview.com/thread/imagenarrative/diegetic.

Saemmer, Alexandra. 2007. *Matières textuelles sur support informatique*. Saint-Étienne: Publications de l'Université de Saint-Étienne.

Saenger, Paul. 1997. *Space between Words: The Origins of Silent Reading*. Stanford, CA: Stanford University Press.

Schäfer, Jörgen, and Peter Gendolla, eds. 2010. *Beyond the Screen: Transformations of Literary Structures, Interfaces and Genres*. Bielefeld: Transcript Verlag.

Schaffner, Anna Katharina. 2010. From Concrete to Digital: The Reconceptualization of Poetic Space. In *Beyond the Screen: Transformations of Literary Structures, Interfaces and Genres*, edited by Jörgen Schäfer and Peter Gendolla, 179–198. Bielefeld: Transcript.

Schreibman, Susan, and Ray Siemens eds. 2008. *A Companion to Digital Literary Studies*. Oxford: Blackwell. http://www.digitalhumanities.org/companionDLS.

Schreibman, Susan, Ray Siemens, and John Unsworth, eds. 2004. *A Companion to Digital Humanities*. Oxford: Blackwell. http://www.digitalhumanities.org/companion.

Seaman, Bill. 2007. Recombinant Poetics and Related Database Aesthetics. In *Database Aesthetics: Art in the Age of Information Overflow*, edited by Victoria Vesna, 121–141. Minneapolis: University of Minnesota Press.

Shillingsburg, Peter L. 2006. *From Gutenberg to Google: Electronic Representations of Literary Texts*. Cambridge: Cambridge University Press.

Shklovsky, Viktor. 1965 [1917]. Art as Technique. In *Russian Formalist Criticism: Four Essays*, edited by Lee T. Lemon and Marion J. Reis, 3–24. Lincoln: University of Nebraska Press.

Simanowski, Roberto. 2002. Fighting/Dancing Words: Jim Andrews' Kinetic, Concrete Audiovisual Poetry. *Dichtung-Digital: Journal für Digitale Ästhetik*, no. 21. http://www.dichtung-digital.org/2002/01/10-Simanowski/cramer.htm.

Simanowski, Roberto. 2004. Concrete Poetry in Digital Media. Its Predecessors, Its Presence and Its Future. *Dichtung-Digital: Journal für Digitale Ästhetik*, no. 33. http://www.dichtung-digital.org/2004/3/simanowski/index.htm.

Simanowski, Roberto. 2011. *Digital Art and Meaning: Reading Kinetic Poetry, Text Machines, Mapping Art, and Interactive Installations*. Minneapolis: University of Minnesota Press.

Simanowski, Roberto, Jörgen Schäfer, and Peter Gendolla, eds. 2010. *Reading Moving Letters: Digital Literature in Research and Teaching—A Handbook*. Bielefeld: Transcript.

Simon, John F. Jr. 1999. *CPU*. Custom software, Macintosh 280c, acrylic plastic.

Simon, John F. Jr. 2002. *Unfolding Object*. http://unfoldingobject.guggenheim.org.

Simon, John F. Jr. 2004. *Seeing Double*. New York: Solomon R. Guggenheim Museum. http://variablemedia.net/e/seeingdouble/index.html.

Simon, John F. Jr. 2009. *Visions*. Custom software, wood, plastic laminate, acrylic paint, mirrored plastic, LCD screen, Mac computer.

Smith, Keith A. 1995. *Structure of the Visual Book*. Rochester, NY: Keith Smith Books.

Smith, Keith A. 2000. The Book as Physical Object. In *A Book of the Book: Some Works and Projections about the Book & Writing*, edited by Jerome Rothenberg and Steven Clay, 54–70. New York: Granary Books.

Smith, Martha Nell, ed. 1994–2012. *Dickinson Electronic Archives*. Institute for Advanced Technology in the Humanities at the University of Virginia. http://www.emilydickinson.org.

Snowling, Margaret J., and Charles Hulme, eds. 2007. *The Science of Reading: A Handbook*. Malden, MA: Wiley-Blackwell.

Stefans, Brian Kim. 2011. Comedies of Separation: Toward a Theory of the Ludic Book. *Journal of Electronic Publishing*, 14 (2). http://dx.doi.org/10.3998/3336451.0014.207.

Sterne, Laurence. 1759–1767. *The Life and Opinions of Tristram Shandy, Gentleman*. London. http://www.tristramshandyweb.it.

Sterne, Laurence. 1984 [1759–1767]. *The Life and Opinions of Tristram Shandy, Gentleman*, edited by Melvyn and Joan New. Gainesville: University Presses of Florida.

Stewart, Garrett. 2006. *The Look of Reading: Book, Painting, Text*. Chicago: University of Chicago Press.

Stewart, Garrett. 2010. Bookwork as Demediation. *Critical Inquiry* 36:410–457.

Stewart, Garrett. 2011. *Bookwork: Medium to Object to Concept to Art*. Chicago: University of Chicago Press.

Strickland, Stephanie. 2006. Writing the Virtual: Eleven Dimensions of E-Poetry. *Leonardo Electronic Almanac* 1 (5–6). http://www.leoalmanac.org/journal/vol_14/lea_v14_n05-06/sstrickland.html.

Tabbi, Joseph. 2010. *Graphic Sublime: On the Art and Designwriting of Kate Armstrong and Michael Tippett*. Grande Prairie, Alberta: Prairie Art Gallery.

Tavares, Salette. 1964. Poemas em efe. Digital version by Rodrigo Melo [2008]. http://po-ex.net/index.php?option=com_content&task=view&id=92&Itemid=35&.

Tavares, Salette. 1966. Al gar ismos Alfinete. Digital version by Rui Torres and Jared Tarbel [2008]. http://po-ex.net/index.php?option=com_content&task=view&id=24&Itemid=35&.

Tisselli, Eugenio. 2010. Narrative Motors. In *Regards Croisés: Perspectives on Digital Literature*, edited by Philippe Bootz and Sandy Baldwin, 1–10. Morgantown: West Virginia University Press.

Tomasula, Steve. 2002. *VAS: An Opera in Flatland*. Art and design by Stephen Farrell. Chicago: University of Chicago Press.

Torres, Rui. 2005a. *Amor de Clarice*. http://telepoesis.net/amorclarice/amor.html.

Torres, Rui. 2005b. *Mar de Sophia*. http://telepoesis.net/mardesophia/.

Torres, Rui. 2006a. Ler Clarice Lispector, re-escrevendo *Amor*. In *Portal da ciberliteratura: Arqueologia da ciberliteratura Luso-brasileira*. http://po-ex.net/ciberliteratura/index.php?option=com_content&task=view&id=95&Itemid=32.

Torres, Rui. 2006b. *Mar de Sophia: Um poema não se programa*. Porto: CETIC. http://po-ex.net/ciberliteratura/index.php?option=com_content&task=view&id=47&Itemid=39.

Torres, Rui. 2008. *Húmus poema contínuo*. http://telepoesis.net/humus/humus.html.

Torres, Rui. 2008. *Poemas no meio do caminho*. http://telepoesis.net/caminho/caminho1.html.

Torres, Rui. 2010. *Herberto Helder Leitor de Raul Brandão: Uma Leitura de Húmus, Poema-Montagem*. Porto: Edições Universidade Fernando Pessoa.

Torres, Rui, ed. 2013. *PO.EX: Arquivo Digital da Literatura Experimental Portuguesa*. Porto, Portugal: Universidade Fernando Pessoa. http://www.po-ex.net.

Turkeltaulb, Peter E., Lynn Gareau, D. Lynn Flowers, Thomas A. Zeffiro, and Guinevere F. Eden. 2003. Development of Neural Mechanisms for Reading. *Nature Neuroscience* 6 (7): 767–773.

Uribe, Ana Maria. 1997–2003. *Anipoemas*. http://www.vispo.com/uribe/anipoemas.html.

Uribe, Ana Maria. 1997–2003. *Tipoemas*. http://www.vispo.com/uribe/tipoemas.html.

Valdeolmillos, Pedro. 2004. Caosflor/Chaosflower. In *Epimone*. http://www.epimone.net/pieces/caosflor/index.html.

Valdeolmillos, Pedro, and Lluís Calvo, eds. 2004. *Epímone*. http://www.epimone.net.

Vallias, André. 1991. *Nous n'avons pas compris Descartes*. http://www.andrevallias.com/poemas/nous.htm.

Vallias, André. 2003. *De verso*. http://www.andrevallias.com/deverso/deverso.htm.

Vallias, André, and Eucanaã Ferraz, eds. 2011. Homenagem: Augusto, 80. *Errática*, no. 104. http://www.erratica.com.br/opus/104/index.html.

Vesna, Victoria. 2007. Seeing the World in a Grain of Sand: The Database Aesthetics of Everything. In *Database Aesthetics: Art in the Age of Information Overflow*, edited by Victoria Vesna. Minneapolis: University of Minnesota Press.

Wardrip-Fruin, Noah. 2007. Playable Media and Textual Instruments. In *The Aesthetics of Net Literature: Writing, Reading and Playing in Programmable Media*, edited by Peter Gendolla and Jörgen Schäfer, 211–253. Bielefeld: Transcript.

Wardrip-Fruin, Noah. 2008. Reading Digital Literature: Surface, Data, Interaction, and Expressive Processing. In *A Companion to Digital Literary Studies*, edited by Susan Schreibman and Ray Siemens, 163–182. Oxford: Blackwell.

Wardrip-Fruin, Noah. 2009. *Expressive Processing: Digital Fictions, Computer Games, and Software Studies*. Cambridge, MA: MIT Press.

Ware, Colin. 2008. *Visual Thinking for Design*. Burlington, MA: Morgan Kaufmann.

White, Glyn. 2005. *Reading the Graphic Surface: The Presence of the Book in Prose Fiction*. Manchester: Manchester University Press.

Wiese, Maíra Borges. 2012. *A Poesia Digital de André Vallias*. Master's thesis. University of Coimbra.

Wolf, Maryanne. 2007. *Proust and the Squid: The Story and Science of the Reading Brain*. New York: HarperCollins.

Wurth, Kiene Brillenburg. 2006. Multimediality, Intermediality, and Medially Complex Digital Poetry. *Révue des Littératures de l'Union Européene*, no. 5: 1–18. http://www.rilune.org/mono5/3_brillenburg.pdf.

Wurth, Kiene Brillenburg, Sara Rosa Espi, and Inge van de Ven. 2013. Visual Text and Media Divergence: Analogue Literary Writing in a Digital Age. *European Journal of English Studies* 17 (1): 92–108.

Index